Economic Archaeology

Towards an Integration of Ecological and Social Approaches

edited by

Alison Sheridan and Geoff Bailey

BAR International Series 96
1981

B.A.R.

B.A.R., 122 Banbury Road, Oxford OX2 7BP, England

B. A. R. -S96, 1981: "Economic Archaeology"

ISBN 9780860541134 paperback
ISBN 9781407353203 e-book
DOI https://doi.org/10.30861/9780860541134
A catalogue record for this book is available from the British Library
This book is available at www.barpublishing.com

CONTENTS

SECTION III

ARCHAEOLOGICAL CASE STUDIES

THE CONTRIBUTORS

Geoff Bailey,
Department of Archaeology, Cambridge University.

Barbara Bender,
Department of Anthropology, University College, London.

John Bintliff,
Undergraduate School of Studies in Archaeological Sciences, University of Bradford.

Richard Bradley,
Department of Archaeology, University of Reading.

Iain Davidson,
Department of Prehistory and Archaeology, University of New England, Armidale, New South Wales, Australia.

Robert Foley,
Department of Anthropology, University of Durham.

Clive Gamble,
Department of Archaeology, University of Southampton.

Bernd-Rüdiger Götze,
Institut für Ur- und Frühgeschichte, Universität zu Freiburg-im-Breisgau, W. Germany.

Paul Halstead,
King's College, Cambridge.

Tim Ingold,
Department of Social Anthropology, University of Manchester.

Kristian Kristiansen,
Miljøministeriet, Fredningsstyrelsen, København, Denmark.

James Lewthwaite,
Gonville and Caius College, Cambridge.

Carol MacCormack,
Ross Institute, London School of Hygiene and Tropical Medicine, University of London.

Henrietta Moore,
Newnham College, Cambridge.

John O'Shea,
Department of Anthropology, University of Iowa, Iowa, U.S.A.

Peter Rowley-Conwy,
Magdalene College, Cambridge.

Alison Sheridan,
New Hall, Cambridge.

Volker von Thienen,
Wissenschaftszentrum Berlin (IIUG), Berlin, W. Germany.

Christopher Tilley,
Peterhouse, Cambridge.

PREFACE

This volume is the result of a conference called "Economic Archaeology — Towards an Integrated Approach", which was organized by one of us (A. S.) and which took place at New Hall, Cambridge, in January 1979. Thanks are due to all those who contributed to the success of the conference. In particular we would like to express our appreciation to the following: Mark Burkill, for masterminding the finances; Mark Gregson, Paul Lane, Deirdre Lee, David Reese, Jim Lewthwaite, Donald Shimmin, Jan Auton and Jane Grenville, for organizing projectors, food and other necessities; and to those who chaired the discussion sessions, especially Wilf Shawcross, Ian Hodder and Kristian Kristiansen. The conference could not have taken place without the generous financial assistance of Christ's College and the kind support of the staff of New Hall.

Many of the conference papers are included here, some in revised form. Other papers have been written specially for the present volume. Our thanks go to all who have contributed, whether their pieces have been included here or not. Finally, we are grateful to the General Editors of B. A. R. for their unfailing patience and advice in bringing the project to fruition.

1. INTRODUCTION: ECOLOGICAL AND SOCIAL PERSPECTIVES IN ECONOMIC ARCHAEOLOGY

Geoff Bailey and Alison Sheridan

In recent decades archaeological interest in economic behaviour has oscillated along a continuum of attitudes ranging from emphasis on biological and ecological factors at one extreme to stress on social, cultural and ideological ones at the other. A wide, and sometimes confusing, array of definitions of 'economy' and 'economic behaviour' has thus developed, and although the phrase 'economic archaeology' implies the existence of a fixed domain of study — distinct from that of, say, 'social archaeology' — there are many who would doubt the legitimacy of such a distinction. This variety of opinion arises in part from the difficulty and diversity of a subject matter which ranges from the living floors of Plio-Pleistocene hominids to the temples and palaces of urban societies. It also reflects deeply divided theories and philosophies about the motivations of human behaviour and about the nature and causes of social evolution, divisions related to the unresolved struggle of Western thought to transcend the traditional dichotomy between mind and matter. It is the purpose of this volume to bring together the various current approaches to economic archaeology, to identify the reasons for their apparent lack of integration and to indicate the possible ways in which a more integrated approach might be developed. By way of an introduction, this paper will briefly characterise these different perspectives, sketch the structure of the volume and discuss some of the issues raised by specific papers within it.

The ecological perspective

The polarity of views mentioned above has been especially prominent in British archaeology, where the principal stimulus has been the elaboration of a school of thought which has come to dominate archaeological approaches to prehistoric economy over the past decade. Palaeoeconomy, developed by Eric Higgs and his students in Cambridge in the late 1960s and early 1970s, offers a framework which draws on concepts from biology, ethology and ecology as a basis for analysing long-term relationships between the key variables of human population, food resources and technology. Attention is focused on the exploitation strategies used to obtain food supplies, and the developments of later Pleistocene and post-Pleistocene times are, to a large extent, regarded as the record of attempts to feed a growing population within the limits imposed by the natural environment, with the aid of technology. All other aspects of human behaviour, such as settlement location, modes of social organisation or belief systems, are seen as determined by, or peripheral to, this central process.

Palaeoeconomic ideas were developed in response to a number of factors, including the cultural idealism that prevailed in much archaeological interpretation of the time, and the more specific challenges raised by the problem of the origins of agriculture (see Davidson and Bailey, this volume, for historical background). Despite its multifarious origins and course of early development, it nevertheless marked a clear shift towards an extreme pole of thinking, reaching its apogee in the Palaeoeconomy volume of 1975. Assertions that

> "human culture is a part, but certainly not the pre-eminent part, of the behaviour of the species" (Higgs 1975: vii),

and that the interest of palaeoeconomy is in

> "the major factors which direct and determine human behaviour and development .... in the constraints, rather than in the noise of choice which tends in any case to operate upon the short-term trivia" (Higgs and Jarman: 4-5),

have done much to alienate the approach for many people, and have attracted much justifiable, and some unjustifiable criticism. If such statements have resulted in a considerable sense of dissatisfaction, nevertheless the palaeoeconomic approach represents one of the few systematic attempts in recent years — in British archaeology at least — to develop a theory and methodology of economic archaeology. For this reason alone, as well as for the polemic which some of its more outspoken assertions has stimulated, it forms an important starting point for discussion.

The social perspective

At the opposite pole there has emerged a variety of models inspired by concepts drawn from social anthropology and sociology. These include Marxist, neo-Marxist and structuralist examples, which are united in stressing the impossibility of defining 'economy' without reference to the context of social relations and ideological or cognitive schemata (e.g. Clammer 1978). Those who adopt such a perspective usually stress the uniqueness of human behaviour — a uniqueness manifested, for example, in man's capacity for symbolic communication — and argue for its partial or total independence from the ecological forces which appear to dominate the natural world. The 'natural' environment and ecosystem are regarded as being generally of secondary or intermittent importance in determining human behaviour: although they may dictate the range of available subsistence resources, they do not determine the exact subsistence strategies pursued by a group, or its form of social organisation, or the attitudes and beliefs of its members. In the definition of 'economy', attention does not focus exclusively on subsistence food production, but ranges to the manufacture or extraction of edible and non-edible consumer goods for exchange. Some (e.g. Bourdieu 1977) would even include the production of children and of 'symbolic capital' as activities which can properly be called 'economic'. Clearly, such a definition implies that the reproduction of the social group, and the management of social relationships, is at least as important as the reproduction of the species as a whole. Although human ecologists and palaeoeconomists often criticise this perspective as being short-sighted, many of its supporters would argue that equally plausible, or indeed more plausible, 'social' explanations could be constructed for many variations in patterns of subsistence.

Wider aspects of the debate

This polarity of thought is not confined to British archaeology, but is characteristic of a more general debate in archaeology and social anthropology elsewhere. In America, where the 'ecological perspective' manifested itself in the form of cultural ecology much earlier and more clearly than in Britain, the confrontation of viewpoints can be extreme. The long-standing and acrimonious debate between Harris (1974) and Chagnon (1968), over the question of whether warfare in 'primitive' societies is a response to protein deficiency or to specific social causes (or even to a 'warlike mentality'), is a classic example. Similarly, Sahlins' Culture and Practical Reason (1976a) stands out as a systematic attack on the characterisation of non-Industrial man as Homo economicus, whose actions conform to a universal rational model of behaviour as dictated by ecological necessity. More recently the debate has been sharpened by the introduction of sociobiological theories, the most extreme versions of which claim that all human behaviour is genetically determined. Some of the reactions to such assertions can appear to produce equally extreme arguments, including the suggestion that behaviour is determined by an autonomous force of social logic (Sahlins 1976a, 1976b).

In Europe the conflict between 'ecological' and 'social' models has been relatively subdued. A more prominent focus of debate — in social anthropology and sociology at least — has been the classical historical-materialist model of society as comprising an economic base and an ideological, legal and political superstructure (cf. Clammer 1978, Giddens 1979). This model falls within the category designated above as 'social', in that the economic base is defined in terms of a combination of resources, technical forces and social relations. However, the crux of the debate between classical Marxist and neo-Marxist or structuralist interpretations of social evolution is essentially analogous to that between opposed ecological and social theories of human development. Although the 'economic base' has a different definition in classical Marxist models from the one suggested in ecological models, both versions are involved in debates about the extent to which this economic base determines, or is determined by, social relationships and belief systems.

It would be misleading to over-exaggerate differences of viewpoint and to characterise the study of economic behaviour solely in terms of opposed extremes, or to overlook existing attempts at compromise or integration. As long ago as 1952 Grahame Clark emphasised in Prehistoric Europe: the Economic Basis, that people adapt to a social as well as a natural environment, and included a consideration of exchange as well as subsistence production in his survey. Similarly Childe observed that

> "the environment of a prehistoric society is not just that reconstructed by geologists or palaeobotanists, but that known or knowable by the society with its existing material and conceptual equipment."
> (1958: 73)

More recent attempts to pursue integrated interpretations are exemplified by Flannery (1972) and Rappaport (1979), with archaeological and contemporary data respectively.

Within much existing archaeological work, however, there remains a fairly marked lack of integration, both at the theoretical and methodological level, between broadly ecological and broadly sociological approaches to similar problems. This is manifest in several ways: as a contrast between an emphasis on earlier prehistory, seen as the record of hunter-gatherers tied quite closely to the possibilities and limitations of the natural environment, and later prehistory with a focus on urban settlement and stratified societies; between a definition of economy in ecological terms as a set of relationships between populations and food resources, and a sociological definition in terms of a set of relationships between individuals and social groups; between long-term and short-term processes; and between subsistence and exchange studies. It is this disjunction between ecological and social perspectives which forms the main point of frefeference for the present collection of papers and to which we refer in the title of the volume.

Towards an integrated approach

The original aim of the conference which gave rise to the present volume was to promote the development of a theoretical and methodological approach which combined ecological and social perspectives and resolved their former points of opposition. However, as might be expected from the disparity between existing points of view, and as will be apparent from the varied contributions to the present volume, there are widely differing opinions about how such an integration might be achieved, and whether it is possible or even desirable. It might therefore be asked how economic archaeology is to be defined, and whether it can or should exist at all as a unified field of study. Before we describe the individual contributions to this volume, then, we will present our own opinion on the topic.

We take the term 'economy' to refer to the extraction, distribution and use of resources (in the broadest sense of that term) for socially as well as biologically determined purposes. 'Economic archaeology', then, is a general term designed to cover studies of human economy in the above sense. We use the term descriptively to define a general field of study, rather than polemically to characterise a particular school of thought or a particular group of techniques. We also use the term inclusively to cover any contribution to this area of interest, whether or not it is archaeological in the strict sense, rather than exclusively to demarcate a particular type of archaeology distinct from, and to some extent in competition with, other "archaeologies". In this sense economic archaeology clearly has a different focus from palaeoeconomy, as it subsumes the specific problems and relationships of importance to the palaeoeconomic perspective in a broader definition, one which emphasises more explicitly social and cultural influences as well.

To name a single field of study in this way is not of course sufficient to ensure that its subject matter will be pursued in a unified or integrated fashion. Nevertheless the characterisation of economic archaeology in the above terms may help to place in perspective the barriers that exist between the study of ecological and social processes, and to encourage the investigation of problems which seek to surmount those barriers. Such problems might include an examination of the way in which "social" activities such as exchange or storage act as responses to ecological constraints, or the way in which natural (and human) resources are manipulated in the establishment, reproduction and transformation of patterns of social order (Kus 1979, Earle and Ericson 1977). What is perhaps most urgently needed is a willingness to explore alternative models and hypotheses of long-term development, and above all a commitment to empirical testing in the archaeological record. This is especially needed in the crucial transitional periods of the late Pleistocene and early Holocene, where hypotheses of demographic and ecological causality still hold sway.

Obviously, this ideal state of affairs is far from becoming reality, even in this volume — not least because the very definition of 'ecological' and 'cultural' or 'social' currently rests on epistemologically insecure premises (cf. Kus 1979, Sahlins 1976b). We are also aware of the dangers involved in any act of definition, let alone the definition of 'economic archaeology', since these tend to reify abstract concepts, and to perpetrate traditional distinctions between 'economic', 'social' and 'ritual', which reflect not the archaeological reality we seek to discover, but our own intellectual preconceptions. At the same time, however, there are equal dangers of being so vague about the boundaries of discussion as to convey the impression of an amorphous muddle of unrelated concepts and studies. One of the first tasks of economic archaeology should be, then, the re-appraisal of the intellectual preconceptions which have led us to distinguish between 'ecological' and 'social' processes in the first place. It is hoped that the papers in Sections One and Two will help to achieve this goal.

Outline of the book

The papers in Section One of the volume set the scene for discussion by outlining some of the problems and possibilities of current approaches to economic archaeology, and demonstrating some of the ways in which their current lack of integration is manifested. Particular emphasis is placed on a re-assessment of palaeoeconomic principles and methods. Thus Davidson discusses the history of palaeoeconomy and the questions which it set out to answer, examines some of the criticism to which it has been subjected, and reasserts the positive values of the approach. Bintliff makes the important contribution of demonstrating the achievements of the field applications of palaeoeconomy, and showing how their results relate to the assumptions and hypotheses of theoretical palaeoeconomy. In particular, he offers a re-appraisal of the controversial techniques of site catchment and site territorial analysis — techniques closely associated with the development of the approach — and emphasises their virtues in producting new information about subsistence patterns and determinants of site location. Rowley-Conwy and Lewthwaite offer a critical examination of the concept of seasonal mobility and its application to hunter-gatherer and pastoralist economies respectively. Both discuss the problems connected with applying simplistic ecological models of economic behaviour to evidence of actual prehistoric activities, and both question the validity of attempts to relate palaeoeconomic theories about long-term trends to archaeological data representing static (and often fuzzy) snapshots along the course of time.

The remaining papers in this section examine the advantages and limitations of looking at economic archaeology from radically different viewpoints. Foley highlights one aspect of the non-integration of approaches in his discussion of the current basis of ecological theory and its divergence from the ecological thinking implicit in palaeoeconomic interpretations. He demonstrates this by reference to the debate about human evolution as an adaptive process, pointing out inconsistencies between ecological and palaeoeconomic models. He concludes that the range of behavioural variability that is consistent with ecological principles is wider than is implied by palaeoeconomic expectations, and thus requires new criteria to distinguish between ecological and cultural aspects of behaviour.

From a radically different perspective, Götze and von Thienen examine Habermas' theory of social evolution and the difficulties of testing it and relating it to the archaeological record. Their contribution illustrates the deep rift which exists between palaeoeconomic and sociological approaches to human behaviour, and suggests that this is not entirely a function of the differing time perspectives of the two approaches. Pointing to "vague sketches of man's early progress", and to the overtones of determinism in Habermas' arguments about the primacy of "structures of consciousness", they accurately identify one of the main sources of friction between the different schools of thought.

Finally, at the methodological level, Moore discusses ethno-archaeological approaches to the study of bone refuse, and the role of cultural and cognitive factors in the formation of the archaeological record. Criticising existing palaeoeconomic studies for interpreting faunal assemblages only in functional, subsistence terms, she demonstrates how the arrangement of bone refuse in a settlement can reflect the system of cultural classification belonging to its occupants. Most importantly, her paper suggests the possibility of identifying the nature of prehistoric belief and symbol systems and their transformation through time.

Section Two offers a variety of theoretical approaches to the problem of integration: of how one might seek to integrate studies of the long-term and the short-term, ecology and social organisation, belief and action, subsistence and exchange. Bailey discusses the effect that varying time-scales may have on the processes and problems amenable to study, with particular reference to the development of palaeoeconomic ideas. He suggests that the type of theory preferred, whether more or less ecological, will depend on the scale of analysis adopted. In effect, there can be no completely integrated interpretation of particular patterns and trends, only interpretations that are more or less appropriate in relation to the time perspective of the observer.

Ingold brings an understanding of ecological theory to bear on problems of Marxist analysis and elaborates a theory of reciprocal interaction between social and ecological factors. He sees the pattern of social evolution as the product of a conjunction of social and ecological systems in which qualitative transformations in the social relations of production set the dominant pattern, and ecological factors operate as negative constraints. It is, he suggests, determinate without being unilinear: its determinacy arises from the fact that "each conjunction of social and ecological systems contains within itself the conditions of its future development" (p. 126).

Tilley goes one step further by adopting a perspective on social and economic change which draws on ideas of action theory and dialectical structuralism. He argues that economic action and its transformation can only be adequately analysed in terms of its ideological basis — i.e. in terms of underlying "structures of meaning", such as notions of purity and pollution, which give behaviour its meaning and convert it into social action. The social formation can, he suggests, be visualised as being in a constant state of change; rapid or radical change may result from the opposition between conflicting structures, when the principles which order behaviour into socially rational action become confused.

The implicit challenge by palaeoeconomists to sociologically- and anthropologically-oriented archaeologists to produce alternative theories about long-term social and economic change is taken up by Bender. She claims to present a Marxist perspective on long-term processes, and argues that the dynamics of alliance systems — systems which cannot be explained merely as a response to ecological imperatives — can be responsible for the intensification of production and productivity which characterises the gatherer-hunter to farmer transition. A similar conclusion is reached in MacCormack's paper. She compares an historical-materialist view and a social/cognitive view of the relationship between exchange and hierarchy, and emphasises the primacy of the process of social reproduction over that of biological reproduction, showing how this influences demographic structure and the production of subsistence and luxury goods.

Finally O'Shea elaborates the concept of 'social storage' as one of a range of responses for coping with seasonal and inter-annual fluctuations in available food resources. This paper attempts to integrate 'the social' with 'the ecological' in a different way from the previous two contributions. Whereas Bender and MacCormack stress the influence of social or cultural imperatives on subsistence and material production, O'Shea demonstrates how a social institution can fulfil an important ecological function.

The papers in Section Three present archaeological case studies which explore different aspects of the inter-relationship between social and ecological parameters of behaviour. Halstead takes up the theme of social storage and examines how insurance against fluctuating crop yields in marginal environments may help to account for social and political developments in the Aegean Bronze Age. His paper, like O'Shea's, attempts to demonstrate the ways in which social relations form an integral — and sometimes predictable — component of ecology.

Gamble's paper offers an interesting contrast in looking at the same material from a different point of view. He discusses the phenomenon of surplus production and its political manipulation in the process of establishing centralised power. He argues that the fact of production above subsistence level is not sufficient, by itself, to promote changes in social organisation. Instead, he takes as his initial condition the existence of élites wishing to broaden their effective power by making inroads into the productive and reproductive autonomy of small communities.

Bradley shifts the focus of attention to bronze age Europe and the 'Urnfield phenomenon'. Seeking an explanation that avoids the determinism of existing versions, he suggests that the key to the observed pattern of population growth and agricultural intensification is the need of an existing élite to maintain its non-egalitarian social system. Just as in Gamble's Aegean model, the effective basis of the élite's power is seen as control over surplus production. Bradley suggests that the clear geographical shift in the distribution of prestige artifacts towards areas of high agricultural potential reflects the degree of security of the élite's control. In times when their power was threatened, by land exhaustion or some other factor, the élite were forced to assume a more direct control over the production of non-luxury items.

Another re-interpretation of Bronze Age data, this time from Scandinavia, is offered in the final chapter by Kristian Kristiansen. Adopting a structural-Marxist perspective, he argues that strategies of production, exchange and consumption can only be understood as parts of a wider system of social reproduction. The operation of the latter, he claims, can be detected archaeologically by a detailed examination of evidence for social ranking, circulation and consumption of exchange items and subsistence production on an inter-regional scale. Echoing Bradley's suggestions, he concludes that " if we want to explain the economic dynamics of the Nordic Bronze Age, it is necessary to focus attention on the functioning of the political systems, that is the mode of exchange and the possible ways it was imbedded in and correlated with systems of rank and political control" (p. 254).

Discussion

It was perhaps predictable that in a volume dedicated to integrating the approaches to economic archaeology, many of the contributors still work from perspectives which emphasise either ecological or social/cultural constraints on human behaviour. Contrast, for example, Bender's and Tilley's treatment of environmental factors as boundary conditions affecting largely autonomous processes of social and conceptual development, with Halstead's and O'Shea's characterisation of environmental fluctuations as a primary problem of survival, to which social storage is an adaptive response. Both may constitute valid representations of real-life conditions in featured case studies, but they apply to such different levels of generality that it is difficult to appreciate their relevance to each other. Nevertheless, the varied papers in this volume do contribute — albeit indirectly, in some cases — to the development of new lines of inquiry in the study of past economic behaviour, by pointing out the shortcomings of existing approaches and the problems and possibilities of constructing alternatives. Some aspects of this contribution are worth considering here, as a focus for further discussion and investigation.

An important finding apparent from the various discussions of ecological approaches is that there is no agreement about a unified ecological theory applicable to human hehaviour, any more than there is agreement about a unified theory of social development. A major focus of controversy in ecological theory, which must temper the confidence with which it can be lifted out of its original context in the natural world and applied without modification to human behaviour, is the level at which selection processes operate. One aspect of this debate, emphasised by Foley, is the conflict between theories of individual selection and group selection. According to the current consensus among biologists, selection processes operate on individuals (or individuals and their closely related kin) rather than on groups. This conclusion follows from the theory of natural selection, which rests on the assumption that all behavioural traits are transmitted genetically from generation to generation through the process of reproduction. Whether this applies to human behaviour is a matter of great controversy, and involves assumptions against which Ingold raises serious objections. On the other hand, as Foley demonstrates, a high level of variability in behaviour, which many might regard as the distinctive feature of human culture, is precisely what would be predicted by modern ecological theory. This contrasts with the implicit view of ecological constraints as imposing uniformity and restricting the choice of alternatives. The current distinction between "ecological" and "cultural" determinants of economic behaviour may then be quite misleading, so that future debates about their articulation are likely to take on a different character.

Another aspect of the ecological debate, referred to by Bailey, is the effect of time-scale on long-term evolutionary processes, and the question of whether these are simply the summation of small-scale selection processes visible in "ecological time", or whether they depend on additional processes not visible in the short term.

Regardless of whether ecological theory developed for animal behaviour can be applied to human social evolution, current ecological controversies raise an issue which re-emerges in one form or another in a number of the papers in Section Two. This issue is the scale at which influencing factors and causal processes are thought to operate, and the choice of an appropriate frame of reference for studying economic behaviour and its development. There is considerable uncertainty about whether the processes under study equally affect individuals, social groups or larger population entities, whether they operate consciously or unconsciously, over longer or shorter time spans, continuously or intermittently. Bailey, for example, stresses the time-dependence of causal processes and suggests that the articulation between the different constraints on behaviour takes the form of a dichotomy between long-term ecological processes and short-term social ones. Ingold, in contrast, rejects such a chronological distinction, proposing instead a dialectical relationship between social relations of production and ecological conditions of reproduction. A third view is expressed by Tilley and Bender, who suggest that social constraints on behaviour are always both dominant and determinant, and that ecological constraints have — since the late Pleistocene, at any rate — occupied a subordinate role. The frames of reference selected by these various contributors show a similar divergence. Whereas Bailey concentrates part of his attention on the behaviour patterns created by large population aggregates over long time periods, Ingold and Tilley focus on the behavioural dynamics of smaller groups, regarding (relatively) short-term developments as being of the greatest evolutionary significance. Bender, similarly, focuses on the processes which occupy decades and centuries rather than millenia, but concentrates on the articulation between individual social groups and larger aggregates. The question arises: how is one to decide between these alternative models?

The simple, if disappointing, answer to this question which emerges from Section Two is that the conceptual equipment currently employed in archaeology may be inadequate to deal with such matters. In considering Tilley's contribution, for instance, we see that the gulf between palaeoeconomic/ecological and Marxist/structuralist approaches involves not only differing conceptions of the uniqueness (or otherwise) of the human race, but also wholly different epistemologies. Tilley contrasts the current ecological and palaeoeconomic uses of positivism, in which laws are tested in quantitative and empirical terms against allegedly 'objective' facts, and Marxist and structuralist approaches which evaluate theories in terms of their rigour and logical coherence (cf. Hindess and Hirst 1975: 1-3). It is clear that, before a universally acceptable model of economic behaviour and its constraints is achieved, some epistemological common ground between the extreme empiricism of palaeoeconomy and the extreme abstraction of certain Marxist or structuralist approaches must be reached. Goody's Production and Reproduction (1976), which combines logical and empirical tests in the study of the relationship between modes of subsistence and modes of inheritance, offers an example of the way in which such an approach might be developed.

Turning to the empirical level of investigation, how do the papers in Section Three and elsewhere contribute to the development of an integrated methodological approach to economic archaeology?

A simple, but important, contribution is the re-assertion of a neglected fact: that the type of data studied, and the type of analytical technique used, do not necessarily limit one to a particular type of explanation. The study of animal bones, for example, yields not only information about diet and husbandry, but also clues about cultural classificatory systems, as Moore and Tilley emphasise. Similarly the reconstruction of palaeoenvironments does not necessarily commit one to some form of environmental determinism. On the contrary, the analysis of environmental data, by showing where patterns of land use deviate from expectation, may highlight quite subtle changes in social and economic organisation. Although floral, faunal and environmental data may be the most tangible and accessible raw material for establishing patterns and trends in subsistence production, that is no reason why the patterns and trends so established should be explained exclusively in ecological or environmental terms. MacCormack and Bender identify a number of social processes which may affect the nature and level of subsistence production, and these need to be considered as plausible alternatives alongside the more familiar hypotheses of environmental change and demographic pressure.

The second point — that the use of a particular analytical technique does not necessarily commit one to a particular theoretical stance — is highlighted in the debate about the value and uses of site catchment analysis (Bintliff, Davidson, Bailey). At one level the reconstruction of potentially available food resources within specified distance thresholds of an archaeological site — more strictly territorial analysis as many of its practitioners would prefer to call it (Higgs and Vita-Finzi 1972) — is an operational procedure designed to provide more and better information about subsistence patterns and site location. At another level, the assumptions which make such an operation possible embody a theory about the determinants of subsistence and settlement strategies. Many of the charges of environmental determinism levelled against this approach have confused the two levels: such criticism ought to be restricted to the second level, rather than directed at the technique itself. The latter is essentially a flexible tool, which can be adapted to test a completely different set of theories, if required. Gamble's use of 'polity catchment analysis' demonstrates one way in which the basic idea might be further developed. As Davidson emphasises, and as was foreshadowed by Sturdy (1975) and Flannery (1976), what is required for the full development of the technique is not a test of its basic assumptions in some "ideal" and probably non-existent ethnographic context; what is required is greater imagination in archaeological research design.

Perhaps the most important contribution of the papers in Section Three is their demonstration that short-term processes, such as the development of social hierarchies, can indeed be reconstructed from archaeological data. This is due not so much to developments in dating techniques, but to an increasing awareness of the archaeological correlates of social change, and to the re-examination of existing data from new perspectives.

The conclusions reached by Halstead, Gamble and Bradley underline the important effects that the natural environment exercises in imposing constraints on human hehaviour, although it is acknowledged that these effects can be realised through man's mismanagement, as in over-exploitation of soils, as well as through the natural agency of climatic fluctuations and the like. At the same time, all these contributors stress the crucial role played by human strategies for extracting and allocating resources in determining the effect of environmental limitations, and thereby guiding the course of subsequent economic developments. None is willing to concede that the overall patterns of activity observed in his case study represent a unidirectional response to a single complex of long-term ecological pressures. In this sense all these case studies bear witness to the practicability of the integrative models presented in Section Two.

Matters of uncertainty and debate remain, as in the different views of Halstead and Gamble over whether strategies of resource use are to be seen simply as mechanisms for adapting to powerful environmental limitations, or as the response to largely independent social pressures, such as the desire of an emergent élite to expand and consolidate its power. The papers of Section Three also deal mainly with bronze age societies, and thus with relatively short time spans and a varied and prolific supply of archaeological data. If they tend, for this reason, to favour the exploration of social models, they nevertheless present a challenge to the ecological and palaeoeconomic theories that have tended to prevail amongst students of earlier periods, and provide fresh perspectives in the search for integration.

It may seem from what we have said above that much of the present volume is rather abstract and theoretical in tone, and that it simply rehashes old debates which have mouldered without productive outcome in archaeology and anthropology for many a decade. Although this may be partly true, at least a an attempt has been made to bring together and to resolve some of the polarities which have resulted in the past from too strict an adherence to "cultural" or "natural" models of human hehaviour. Many will feel that this volume fails to achieve the ideal of an "integrated approach", or that such an ideal is unattainable. Nevertheless we believe that such a goal is worth pursuing, whatever the stimulus to be derived from more narrowly focused polemic, and that the first steps towards this goal have been made. If the present volume helps to promote communication across existing boundaries, if it highlights the positive contributions that strictly archaeological data can make to theoretical issues of general interest in the human sciences, and if, above all, it encourages the production of new archaeological case studies, without which many of the problems at issue are likely to remain unresolved, then the effort will have been worthwhile.

References

Bourdieu, P., 1977. Outline of a Theory of Practice. Cambridge: Cambridge University Press.

Chagnon, N., 1968. "Yanomamö social organization and warfare" in War: The Anthropology of Armed Conflict and Aggression, eds. M. Fried, R. Murphy and M. Harris. New York: Natural History Press.

Childe, V. G., 1958. "Retrospect". Antiquity 32: 69-74.

Clammer, J. (ed.), 1978. The New Economic Anthropology. London: Macmillan.

Earle, T. K. and Ericson, J. E. (eds.), 1977. Exchange Systems in Prehistory. New York: Academic Press.

Flannery, K. V., 1972. "The cultural evolution of civilizations". Ann. Rev. Ecology and Systematics 3: 399-426.

Flannery, K. V. (ed.), 1976. The Early Mesoamerican Village. New York: Academic Press.

Giddens, A., 1979. Central Problems in Social Theory. London: Macmillan.

Goody, J., 1976. Production and Reproduction. Cambridge: Cambridge University Press.

Harris, M., 1974. Cows, Pigs, Wars and Witches: The Riddle of Culture. New York: Random House.

Higgs, E. S., 1975. "Introduction" in Palaeoeconomy, ed., E. S. Higgs. London: Cambridge University Press; vii-viii.

Higgs, E. S. and Jarman, M. R., 1975. "Palaeoeconomy" in Palaeoeconomy, ed. E. S. Higgs. London: Cambridge University Press; 1-7.

Higgs, E. S. and Vita-Finzi, C., 1972. "Prehistoric economies: a territorial approach" in Papers in Economic Prehistory, ed. E. S. Higgs. London: Cambridge University Press; 27-36.

Hindess, B. and Hirst, P. Q., 1975. Pre-Capitalist Modes of Production. London: Routledge and Kegan Paul.

Kus, S. M., 1979. Archaeology and Ideology: the Symbolic Organization of Space. Unpublished Ph.D. thesis, University of Michigan.

Rappaport, R., 1979. Ecology, Meaning and Religion. Richmond: North Atlantic Books.

Sahlins, M. D., 1976a. Culture and Practical Reason. Chicago: Chicago University Press.

Sahlins, M. D., 1976b. The Use and Abuse of Biology. London: Tavistock.

Sturdy, D. A., 1975. "Some reindeer economies in prehistoric Europe" in Palaeoeconomy, ed. E. S. Higgs. London: Cambridge University Press; 55-95.

SECTION 1

PROBLEMS IN ECONOMIC ARCHAEOLOGY

2. CAN WE STUDY PREHISTORIC ECONOMY FOR FISHER-GATHERER-HUNTERS? AN HISTORICAL APPROACH TO CAMBRIDGE 'PALAEOECONOMY'

Iain Davidson

Introduction

The study of prehistoric economy is concerned with the choices which were made in the production and consumption of resources during prehistory. For later periods of prehistory there are many materials which are perceived as resources, and which survive archaeologically, but for earlier prehistory, most of the evidence from archaeology for the management of resources is evidence about diet or subsistence. If we are to integrate the study of earlier and later prehistory, and understand the sources of the wealth which created the distribution and consumption of exotic items, then we must formulate the problem of the nature of the economy in earlier prehistory in terms of choices which are economic.

One approach to this problem was made by E. S. Higgs and his students and colleagues in the decade and a half before his death in 1976. During this time Higgs started and directed the Major Research Project on the Early History of Agriculture for the British Academy. One of the publications arising from this project was a book called Palaeoeconomy (Higgs 1975), and I will refer to the ideas which were developed during this period, and to the group of researchers, under the title 'Palaeoeconomy'. This group never adequately defined what they meant by economy but in this paper I will show how an analysis of their work and ideas allows the development of concepts which may be applied to any period of prehistory to show the changing nature of economies.

The problems of central concern for the 'Palaeoeconomy' group were the nature of economies before the introduction of agriculture, and the processes of transformation of those economies into agriculture. I believe that these are mostly still unsolved, but that the problems can now be seen more clearly.

There are two ways of getting at the problem: the age-old practice of using surviving FGHs[1] as sources of analogy, and the direct investigation of the archaeological record. The first way is well trodden, but like the primrose path, it is littered with pious phrases explaining the difficulty of the use of analogy, most of which are ignored when the final reckoning is made. Some have used the ethnographic record as a mine for explicating curious objects,

---

1. I use the abbreviation FGH as noun and adjective to mean Fisher-Gatherer-Hunter. The order is based for simplicity on the alphabet!

or for fleshing out the interpretation of artefacts with the practices which created them. Others have sought principles which relate the form of the residues of activities to the activities, although the latter, and the materials on which they were practised may have changed. Sahlins' (1974) characterisation of FGH as the "original affluent society" is an attractive soubriquet of the latter type, which aptly illustrates the pitfalls.

The phrase was an important corrective to the dismal view which preceded it, but the emphasis on the content of the original FGHs masked the contradictions in their economy which made it possible or necessary for original FGHs to change that economy. An alternative to this characterisation would be that only by being affluent, in Sahlins' sense, could any FGH group have survived into the twentieth century as FGHs. Their affluence was not therefore a characteristic of the FGH way of life but of the fact of their survival. Of course, Sahlins had no evidence that this affluence was original except the belief that there must be something in common between the surviving FGHs and the original FGHs, and that that something is most likely to be the economy.

But archaeologists have not been notably more careful in their discussion of the economy of prehistoric FGHs, and since the 'Man the Hunter' conference (Lee and De Vore 1968) they have tended to believe in that affluence, and that plant foods constitute important parts of the diet of most FGHs. Although there has been an increase in the numbers of studies of animal bones from presumably FGH sites, and especially an increase in reports which do not just regard the fauna as an indicator of climate, there has been far too little discussion of their economic implications. Here is one of the central conceptual problems in the study of FGH economies: what is the difference between economy and diet, and how can the difference be studied, when most of the evidence is evidence for diet and probably only for part of the diet? Let us consider how the analysis and interpretation of sites and their faunal assemblages can be considered in terms of economy.

We have now an enormous number of sites for which we can say, 'The pre-Bongo-Bongoans were eating the flesh of the Boojum', but this can only be a statement about economy if we can tell the importance of the Boojum in the diet, the nutrition, the hunting practices and the beliefs of this prehistoric group of Bongo-Bongo. Most obviously we may ask if there were likely to be any Boojums in that environment. There is clearly a difference in quality between the statements "The economy was based on the Boojum" and "The inhabitants travelled five hundred miles to catch the Boojum". On the whole of course nobody travelled so far, nor based their economy on a beast so rare, but the example illustrates the point that it may be possible to describe the relationship between FGH groups and the animals they killed in more interesting detail than that provided by the convenient labels which are usually used.

The use of faunal remains for this purpose has a long history as a glance at Prehistoric Times (Lubbock 1865) will show, but the practice was not developed, as attention on palaeolithic fauna swung in the direction of dating, and attention on the economy of FGHs turned to ethnography. The faunal analysis and interpretation of Star Carr (Clark 1954) were not, in that sense original, but they were a rare restatement of the belief that the best way to find out about what happened in the past was to look at archaeological remains.

History

The beginnings of 'Palaeoeconomy'

It is curious then to consider the history of the development of ideas by Higgs. His first faunal report considered the remains from Haua Fteah primarily in terms of the information that they gave about climate (Higgs 1961) and only later did he consider the evidence about human behaviour that could be gleaned from more penetrating analysis. Indeed, the first of his papers to do so (Higgs and White 1963; cf. Ewbank et al., 1964) presents a curious contrast to the later work of the Higgsians. Here Higgs was trying to show that the evidence did not support the common guess that iron age farmers had slaughtered their animals in the autumn, because of the costs of overwintering. In most of the later Higgsian work the attempt was to show the seasonal use of sites, partly through the study of faunal remains.

The recognition that transhumant Vlach shepherds walked their sheep past Asprochaliko and Kastritsa (Higgs and Vita-Finzi 1966) led to a whole series of undergraduates learning language laboratory phrases to ask shepherds where they take their sheep in winter in order to qualify for the renowned rigours of Long Vacation field work in Greece, Israel, Turkey and most of the other countries which border on the Mediterranean. Those clever enough to do research as post-graduates had to add summer to their vocabulary, as they suffered the rigours of a mediterranean winter.

But there was little follow-up from faunal studies.

The Greek interpretation from observation of modern shepherds suggested that two palaeolithic, and hence FGH sites might be linked by seasonal movement following game. There was no test of this hypothesis from the fauna. Indeed it could be argued that the relative abundance of *Equus hydruntinus* in the remains from Kastritsa as opposed to their relative scarcity at Asprochaliko (Higgs and Webley 1971) suggests the presence of a resource which the occupants of Kastritsa could have used in winter when the deer had migrated past Asprochaliko to the coast. Nevertheless the Greek experience led to the important recognition that there were many sorts of relationships between Man and animals, and to the development of this theme in the "Origins of Agriculture: a reconsideration" paper (Higgs and Jarman 1969), in *Antiquity*.

Antiquity and beyond

The *Antiquity* paper has been widely quoted, but often misunderstood. It discussed the criteria which had been used to identify domestication of animals. If these criteria were used selectively with other animals, those animals *should* be said to be domesticated. Indeed this first part of the paper is often taken to be saying that the Rhino of Ehringsdorf, for example, were domesticated. The much more important part of the paper is the one which stresses the relationships between Man and animals—what Shawcross called *zoocresis* (1975)—and that these can be studied directly through the analysis of faunal remains. Not until 1976 did a Higgsian define the sorts of relationship which might be recognised (Jarman 1976) and then only after a similar attempt by Brothwell (1975). This lack of nomenclature made the discussion of alternative relationships more difficult, but it was the obstinate contradiction in the work of Higgs and his students which was the major obstacle to the acceptance that the important part of the Antiquity paper was its second half. Vita-Finzi and Higgs (1970) discussed the possibility of domestic gazelle in the Natufian of Mt. Carmel; Jarman (1971) turned to various deer in Northern Italy at the beginning of the Neolithic there, suggesting they were exploited 'in much the same way' as later animals regarded as domesticated; Jarman (1972) implied as much for the relationships with Red Deer throughout the Upper Palaeolithic in southern Europe; Legge (1972) considered the relevance of Egyptian taming of a range of animals in his discussion of gazelle in the Natufian and other Middle Eastern mesolithic sites. It is significant, too, that the cover of Papers in Economic Prehistory (Higgs 1972) illustrated a plant formerly domesticated, but with which there was now no such relationship. I referred to the possibility of herding of Ibex (Davidson 1972a and b) with distressing lack of precision, but Sturdy did not claim domestication of his Reindeer. He defined a relationship of loose herding with corralling in his suggestive attempt to be precise about the relationships which sustained late Glacial groups in the North European Plain (Sturdy 1975). Finally, the choice of one-hour catchments for agricultural sites, and two-hour catchments for FGH sites (Vita-Finzi and Higgs 1970), preserved the dichotomy which the Antiquity paper had queried.

Just as the really important part of the Antiquity paper is usually ignored so the important point of the Site Catchment Analysis (SCA) paper (Vita-Finzi and Higgs 1970) has been submerged by the number of indifferent uses to which SCA has been put. The original paper defined a problem—what was the relative importance of plants and animals in the relationships between Natufians and their environment? The quality of archaeological evidence for the plants is not as good as the evidence for the animals, whatever the improvements to recovery techniques (see Jarman, Legge and Charles 1972). This is because the animal remains result from being eaten, while, as Dennell (e.g. 1972) has pointed out so clearly, on the whole the plant remains result from not being eaten. It is therefore necessary to obtain some evidence for their relative importance by considering the choice in the location of sites in relation to areas of availability of particular sorts of resource. And, despite Flannery's (1976) important comments on the resource potential calculations and his developments of the methodology, I believe that the problem of Natufian cereal use was illuminated by SCA. Cereals were little represented in the Natufian cave sites because they were of relatively little importance, compared with the importance of animals. They later gained in importance, and sites were then chosen with site-catchments which allowed a greater amount of cereal resources to be exploited. It matters relatively little whether the cereals or the animals were domesticated, since the change of site, and change of site environment which was preferred demonstrates a choice in the use of resources which is the fundamental choice in the steps towards modern agricultural systems.

One final note of criticism before I concentrate on the positive aspects which this phase in Cambridge 'Palaeoeconomy' brought to the study of prehistoric economy, and how these positive aspects differ from and improve upon the attempts of some other scholars to cope with the same problems.

In what is perhaps the most detailed faunal report by Higgsians, Jarman and Jarman (1968) showed the wide range of patterns of exploitation of the faunal community at Knossos. Here, we may be fairly confident that all of the animals were domesticated, since all were introduced at the first colonisation by Man more than nine millennia ago (see e.g. Evans 1964). The Jarmans concluded that the range of relationships from the Neolithic to the Roman period is as great as the range of relationships represented by the time span across the introduction of agriculture. This is sleight of hand, of course, because there was no such span in Crete, and because nothing had been shown anywhere relevant to the discussion about the relationships before the introduction of agriculture. Others were doing the same sort of thing at the time. Hole, Flannery and Neely (1969) assumed that the patterning of faunal remains at Yafteh Cave was the result of slaughtering wild animals. They then argued for the presence of early domesticated animals at other Deh Luran sites by comparing the patterning of faunal remains there with Yafteh Cave. That argument is very nearly circular.

It is a disappointing tale, with an ending of melodramatic proportions. Eric Higgs has died, and the developing study sadly misses his inspiration. The two Jarmans, Sturdy and Vita-Finzi are no longer involved in archaeology and several others whose names are not recorded here but who contributed inspiration and perspiration in the cause of developing these themes are also not directly concerned with archaeology. Here truly is a lost generation in the study of prehistory.

The positive contributions

It is easy to criticise, or to blame, and to mourn, but essential also to recognise what the important contributions were, and how we can build on them. One of the weaknesses, claimed as a strength by some, was a lack of explicit theory. A review of British developments in archaeological theory shows no contribution in the study of prehistoric economy (Chapman 1980). Yet the conceptual developments were there, and could be developed, and were capable of expression in terms of the operational study of the archaeological record.

At one level, the emphasis on faunal and environmental studies in British archaeology by Higgs and students such as Higham (1967; 1968; 1969), showed the way to the enhanced sophistication of zooarchaeological studies in the 1970s. Too much should not be made of this, however, as other stimuli also contributed, and Dutch (e.g. Clason 1972; Degerbøl 1963), Americans (e.g. Reed 1960; Perkins 1964) and others (e.g. Bouchud 1966; Ducos 1968) were already moving in this direction, as were others in Britain. But there were other levels, which make a unique contribution in combination.

Four Principles

The four major contributions to a theory of the study of prehistoric economies were: 1) the emphasis on the study of relationships; 2) a return to empiricism; 3) recognition that this can be combined with the extraction from ethnography of principles about the requirements of particular environments for their exploitation; and 4) that choice must be shown by defining a field from which choices were made. Combination of these four principles can lead to the study of economic prehistory for any period, any economy and any level of integration of the elements of the economy. I will deal with each in order, and discuss its relationship to the contributions made by other scholars in the field, and show how the combination of these principles leads to solution of some of the problems left unsolved by other scholars.

1) The study of relationships

One of the purposes of the Antiquity paper was to free the study of early economies from the rigid dichotomous classification of domesticated/wild, in its several forms. Only by recognising the existence of other categories of relationship could progress be made in studying the transition from one to the other. Ingold (1980) has recently given us a very complete discussion of the steps in the transition between hunting, pastoralism and ranching as these may be deduced from the study of modern Reindeer and economies based on them. But he recognises that because of the entirely different quality of the relationships of hunting and of pastoralism it is impossible to achieve the transition from one to the other by intensification of existing relationships. Ingold therefore opposes the view that pastoralism can result directly from the appropriation of wild herds. The problem is then put back into the archaeological record, of recognising the steps which led to any such transition. It seems likely that the concentration by archaeologists on the study of particular intensification of exploitation of species which provided major amounts of food (staples?) obscures the study of the development of relationships with animals which later became important with a different kind of relationship. Saxon (1978) suggested that the collapse of gazelle and ammotragus economies in Palestine and in Algeria respectively, opened the way for the introduction of herded animals from elsewhere. But the problem still remains of recognizing the source of those new herds. The search for origins in this way tends to put back and further back the search, and into more remote and less researched geographical areas. The buck must start somewhere too.

I suspect that as we gain a greater insight into the exploitation not of single species, but of communities of species, more light will be thrown on this problem. In particular, the Natufian gazelle economies may have been dominated by gazelle, but they were also exploiting some goats and some cereals. The switch from gazelle to goats may appear to be dramatic, but it should be seen in the context of the growth of importance of one species over another, rather than the introduction of an entirely unfamiliar species. In this case the economy contained the seeds of its own transformation. Flannery (1969) suggested that 'domestication' arose in generalized rather than specialized economies.

The study of relationships led naturally to systems theory (Flannery 1968; Harris 1977), which by its very nature tends to emphasise continuous processes (pace Catastrophe Theory: see e.g. Renfrew 1978). Unfortunately, systems theory approaches have tended to introduce many variables which are not susceptible to study archaeologically, and avoid the formulation of the problems in terms which can be studied through archaeology. Clarke (1978:116; cf. Clarke 1968) stressed that "the economic subsystem must keep the whole system in a stable relationship with the environment", so that the 'Palaeoeconomists' ' belief in the primacy of the economy had some support from those more open-minded. But there was a real weakness in the failure by 'Palaeoeconomists' to take adequate account of a wider range of variables. The failure to consider artifacts led to the easy jibes about the adequacy of their methods for recognizing the types of relationships between Man and animals which was one of the last gasps of the Agriculture project (Jarman 1976; Clark 1976).

2) Return to empiricism

The characteristic lack of explicit theory in the development of the ideas of Palaeoeconomy until the brief and simple statements of the introduction to the Palaeoeconomy volume (Higgs and Jarman 1975), was deliberately contrasted with the need to consider archaeological data. Thus Payne (1968), and Jarman (1969) considered the existing evidence for particular species of animal which were candidates for consideration as early domesticates, while Heather Jarman (1972) considered the evidence for the early cultivation of cereals. The Jarman and Jarman paper (1968) was the most complete expression by 'Palaeoeconomists' of the belief in the potential of the archaeological record to provide detailed information about the patterns of exploitation of different species at different time periods. Here was the range of relationships which were foreshadowed in the Antiquity paper.

Against this it will be argued that all archaeologists have published data. Indeed I would suggest that it is the ease with which archaeological data can be described that has led to the slow development of theory in this branch of anthropology relative to others. A social relationship can only be recognised after a theoretical statement, a pyramid or a gold mask can be described by any archaeologist unaware of the importance of tombs for the living, or of ritual symbolism for reinforcing hierarchies. The pre-Bongo-Bongo ate their Boojums, but the archaeologist did not need to bother about the activities which led to the Boojum bones being left at the site.

The need to make conceptual changes within the context of the data to which they may be applied is reflected in the history of the New Archaeology. As a recent editorial in American Antiquity (Hole 1978) pointed out, the early stages of this development were rather unrelated to dirt archaeology, but recently Americans have reaped the benefits of the real conceptual advances made earlier. Binford's work was mostly supported by data (e.g. Binford and Binford 1966), but the "Post-Pleistocene Adaptations" paper (Binford 1968) did not question the archaeologist's ability to recognize the adaptations which did take place. In providing approaches to precisely this problem, Higgs was concerned implicitly with middle range (Binford 1977) or Interpretive (Clarke 1973) theory: SCA in particular showed how archaeological data might be interpreted in terms of human economic activities.

The other aspect of the return to empiricism which must be emphasised was the need to show the nature of the economy without the guess work which had been common before. This is the importance of the 'Autumn killing' paper (Higgs and White 1963), it replaced the guess with data—it tested the hypothesis—without making a noise about the theoretical desirability of conducting science in this way. The need for this was particularly acute in Europe where the lessons of Star Carr (Clark 1954) had hardly been followed up. Fauna were primarily a clue to climate for most palaeolithic sites, and the nature of archaeological economies could be inferred by some simple ethnographic analogies, from societies at a similar level of development—an attitude hardly more sophisticated than that of Sollas (1911). Such naive attitudes to ethnography had, incidentally, encouraged the belief that there was little to be learned from the archaeological study of the prehistory of the Australian Aboriginals. Radiocarbon dating released fauna from the role it had in dating, so that faunal remains could be interpreted as a sample created by human activity rather than as a sample created by climatic change. Radiocarbon dating also allowed the investigation of problems in Australian archaeology which could not be solved by study of the living aborigines—age. This investigation showed that all was not static in Australian prehistory (Mulvaney and Joyce 1965), so that the easy application of parallels from recent Australian Aborigines could not be done. Yet Higgs also turned to the ethnographic record of Europe.

3) Ethnographic principles

Graham Clark has championed the use of information from the ethnographies to illuminate archaeology (e.g. 1952; 1967) but there has been relatively less explicit concern with the uses of ethnography in archaeology among British archaeologists than among American or Australian archaeologists, and little discussion in Britain of their inherent difficulties (although cf. Moore this volume). The 'Palaeoeconomists' were no exception. There are two primary uses, both without discussion; one is the transhumant Vlach shepherds which I have already mentioned, and the other is the use of the 10 kilometre radius in SCA derived from the distance within which Lee (1965) recorded that the !Kung limit their activities. In both of these instances the analogy is based on the principle which is illustrated, rather than the specifics. Sturdy (1972a) also extracted a principle from his study of a modern Reindeer ranching situation in terms of the behaviour which is permitted by the behavioural characteristics of Reindeer.

In the first example it was not the actual route which was important, but the direction of the route between upland pasture in the mountains, and lowland pasture near the coast. Investigation of this principle showed that the constraint would have been greater during the cold periods when there was permanent snow on the mountains; this did not prove that therefore the response to the constraint was seasonal movement by humans as well as animals. In the second example, a simple point is made that there is a limit to the distance which may be covered in a day. In the limiting case, it would not be possible to cover twelve hours travel and return; the limit of habitual activities must be less. Lee's example simply provided a scale for this limit. The data from the !Kung provide adequate indication that the range of activities from a base camp may cover a wider radius, but an overnight 'site' may be necessary (see Lee 1979: 226). All that SCA did was to extract the energetic principle that there is a limit to the radius of activities, suggest that this limit is determined by time, and not distance, and define an arbitrary limit.

Sturdy (1972b) extracted a principle about Reindeer behaviour, and applied it on the assumption that that characteristic of Reindeer was less likely to have changed than the human behaviour associated with Reindeer. One must of course question this assumption in the light of the differences in behaviour between wild and domesticated Reindeer. Two points follow from this. First, some assumption of constancy of this sort is necessary, even if it is only to assume that the physical properties of flint have remained constant, so that conchoidal fractures always result from similar forces. Secondly, it is just this problem which makes the study of the processes of domestication so difficult (see discusssion in Ingold 1980:95-112), because it is difficult to decide on the appropriate analogue.

As usual, though, the abuse of analogy reared its ugly head again. In my own work, it was tempting to follow the cañadas or stock routes which are marked on the 1:50 000 maps in the hope of finding that archaeological sites lay along them. Such a strategy would ignore the fact that most of these routes also fall along municipal boundaries because local and regional political considerations control the movement of stock, in addition to the ecological imperatives of seasonal resource availability, and the economic ones of availability of markets and towns for the shepherds to return to (cf. Lewthwaite this volume).

I can, however, extract the principles of the patterns of resource scarcity which any economic adaptation to the Iberian environment had to cope with, and see the sequences of changing behaviour revealed by archaeology as a set of adjustments to these patterns. Each of these adjustments is influenced in turn by the history of adjustments which preceded it, as well as by the ecology. In this way a study of prehistoric economy can escape the charge of determinism which is so often laid by those who see only the abuse, but not the potential of the approach. Jochim's (1976) stimulating approach could be made more generally applicable by considering a wider range of goals and strategies as these may change through time.

Binford is the most consistent practitioner of this use of principles rather than particular parallels (e.g. Binford and Bertram 1977; Binford 1978). The study of the effect of attritional processes on bone is important for all taphonomic studies, and quite independent of the fact that these original studies were done on Reindeer bones and sheep bones, with dogs as the agents of attrition. This principle can or could (with suitable modifications to the methodology) be applied to most archaeological situations because the mechanism of attrition is isolated in the analysis. Binford's work with the Nunamiut and the economic anatomy of Reindeer shows that enormous amounts of information about past activities could be obtained from the analysis of the detailed composition of faunal assemblages from single period occupations, and that the variability of assemblages can be explained without positing cultural changes, and without suggesting specialized economies because particular sites had specialised assemblages. But little can be learned from these synchronic studies about the nature of the changes through time in the relationships among the variables which are analysed in this way.

The understanding of general system states of a particular modern group may not reveal the way in which a society will change in response to particular pressures. But provided this is understood, any greater understanding of how FGH systems articulate must enhance our interpretations. By the same token, Binford's recent work (1980) described ideal types of FGH system organization as either collectors or foragers. If this makes the recognition of the transition from one form of FGH economy to another more difficult to recognize, then Binford's analysis will have done an unintended disservice by creating another dichotomy on the basis of modern observations, which hinders understanding of change. Awareness of this danger should allow the full importance of the analysis to be realized.

4) Choice from a field of choice

The distinctive contribution of SCA, whatever its detractors find to criticise, was the recognition that it is possible by describing the environment of the site to assess the POTENTIAL resources made available by the choice of that site. It is impossible to stress too strongly that that is all SCA allows. It says, and can say, nothing about the resources which were chosen once that field of potential resources was itself chosen. Clearly, however, the economic situation of the pre-Bongians was much worse if they chose to exploit Boojums from a site where the Boojum would not live, than if they camped near the fields that the Boojums loved.

Of course even this much inference is not easy. The original SCA paper attempted to go beyond the assessment of modern resource potential by some analysis of the local geomorphology, but the relationship between the assessment of potential resources and this geomorphological study was not successfully made, and is very difficult in practice. Other indicators of the precise content of the environment in terms of available resources are rarely more precise. We may claim to reconstruct vegetation by sophisticated use of pollen analyses or other environmental indicators but it would be difficult to tell how many Boojums hid beneath those fronds. And if we cannot tell how many Boojums there were, how can we assess the economy in terms of the relation between the resources which were chosen and the resources which were available?

As usual with these problems, the germs of the answer were there in the original work, but they were not explicitly stated, so that the importance of the point has been missed. The original SCA paper did not show that the Natufians were not exploiting cereals because there were not enough grasses in the immediate environment of the sites. Flannery (1976) showed that was a weak argument. The case could only be made by showing the nature of the resources available at different periods, and comparing the archaeological evidence with that. The movement away from rocky environments with their caves and grazing and some cereals to plains with their grasses and the need to protect goats, was accompanied by a rise in the importance of remains of cereal exploitation and the selective exploitation of goats. Undoubtedly the diversity of different sorts of site in the Natufian suggests a more complex system of economic relations than the simple opposition which was demonstrated by the SCA paper, but the start had been made. Individual sites could give an altogether misleading understanding of the nature of prehistoric economy. The SCA paper concentrated on one category of Natufian sites and tended to underestimate the amount of variability between them, and their roles relative to each other, but it did concentrate attention onto groups of sites and compared them with groups of sites of different periods.

The importance of considering variability between sites of similar periods is shown by my own analyses of the late Palaeolithic in eastern Spain (Davidson 1972a and b; 1976a and b). Les Mallaetes (Davidson 1976a) could only be considered in the context on an understanding of its relations with Parpalló only three kilometres away. Over a period of 20,000 years the function of the site of Les Mallaetes changed to allow greater exploitation of caprines. Over the same period (Bofinger and Davidson 1977) Parpalló was used fairly consistently for the exploitation of both caprines and Red Deer. Indeed my recently completed analyses suggest that there was even a slight reduction in the ratio of caprines to deer at Parpalló. The site catchments of Les Mallaetes and Parpalló showed a very strong degree of overlap. At Volcán some twenty kilometres away caprines were almost absent (Davidson 1972a and b), although much of the reason for the difference between Volcán and the other two sites must be attributed to environmental differences between the site catchments. These three sites, and others in the area of Gandía were all used at similar times during the millennia leading up to the introduction of <u>Capra hircus</u> and sheep (Davidson 1976a) and of wheat (Hopf 1966). By considering any one of these sites in isolation one might conclude that the resources which were exploited from the site were in proportion to the abundance of those resources in the environment. Changes in the relative abundance of resources through time might then be explained in terms of changes in the environment. But these contemporary sites show different patterns of change through time, which are not just responses to the different effects of climatic changes on different local environments. By looking at all the sites together we can appreciate that their roles in an economy were shifting through time in response to choices which the human groups were making. Response to the introduction of sheep, goats and wheat was just one choice of many which were continually being made. Les Mallaetes and Parpalló were able to adjust their roles for a short while, but the disruption of the overall exploitation system is indicated by the occupation of new sites in the Neolithic (Martí 1977), and the beginnings of entirely new settlement systems in the Bronze Age. Binford (1978:496-497) cited Vierra as showing that there may be sites which did not change their function even though the economic system itself was changing. This result seems to be indicated partly by Parpalló but also by some of the Epipalaeolithic sites studied by Fortea (1973) in eastern Spain.

In all of these examples the synchronic economic situation is only revealed by thorough understanding of the diachronic economic changes. We can tell that the Boojum was a choice prey because when the system state changed (e.g. through environmental change) the Bongo-Bongo still chose the Boojum.

<u>Conclusions</u>

I believe that the essential elements for the study of prehistoric economy were outlined by the various developing studies of 'Palaeoeconomy' up to the death of Eric Higgs. I have attempted to draw these threads together and show that they provide a conceptual framework for studying prehistoric economy which goes beyond earlier work, and which is echoed by later, independent studies by many other authorities.

It is also possible to isolate four principles for the study of prehistoric economy, which distinguish the study of prehistoric economy from the study of an ecological or environmental approach, and which enable an understanding of the continuities between early and later prehistory. There is a danger evident in the other papers of this volume (cf. Foley and Gamble) that the discipline will polarize again, as Rowley-Conwy has characterized it. We must recognize that for most of the Palaeolithic most of the data are diet oriented, and that the challenge is therefore to explain diet in terms of economic choice. When we have done that we can begin to show the emergence of choices which ended up in the acquisition of wealth and prestige and the social differentiation which enables students of later prehistory to seek their comfortable ease in the background provided by selective use of studies of modern social organization. Such a framework would enable us to consider the role of the information exchange indicated by Palaeolithic 'art' (Gamble 1980) in regional economic integration.

I believe that the four essential elements are:

i) study of individual sites, especially their diachronic patterning

ii) study of those individual sites in comparison with other sites studied in the same way

iii) study of individual sites diachronically with respect to diachronic studies of the environment

iv) study of site systems with respect to diachronic environmental studies.

Because of uncertainty about the nature of environments from which choices were being made it is only through the successful combination of these four elements that we can begin to study the economy, when the economy must be revealed primarily through changes in dietary remains. By showing that dietary choices were economic we might begin to integrate earlier and later prehistory.

Acknowledgements

I would like to thank Bob Chapman for providing an academic environment within which to let these ideas develop, and Jan Chapman for typing my mosaic draft into a readable form. I am extremely thankful to Alison Sheridan for her thoughtful editorial comments on an earlier draft of this paper. It will be obvious that my experience of the development of ideas outlined here was an intensely personal one. I learnt much directly from all of the 'Palaeoeconomists' whose publications I have criticised here, and my gratitude to them is undiminished by my opinions about their work. I have written this critique in order to re-emphasise the positive virtues of the 'Palaeo-economy' approach at a time when so many people seem intent on moving in the directions which Eric Higgs tried to provide an alternative to. I would like to think that he would have recognized his inspiration in this paper. He would no doubt have pointed out where I am mistaken, and for this I alone am responsible.

Reading 28 April 1980

References

Binford, L. R., 1968. "Post-Pleistocene adaptations" in New Perspectives in Archaeology, eds. L. R. and S. R. Binford. Chicago: Aldine; 313-341.

Binford, L. R., 1977. "General introduction" in For Theory Building in Archaeology, ed. L. R. Binford. London: Academic Press; 1-10.

Binford, L. R., 1978. Nunamiut Ethnoarchaeology. London: Academic Press.

Binford, L. R., 1980. "Willow smoke and dogs' tails: hunter-gatherer settlement systems and archaeological site formation." Amer. Ant. 45:4-20.

Binford, L. R. and Bertram, J. B., 1977. "Bone frequencies—and attritional processes" in For Theory Building in Archaeology, ed. L. R. Binford. London: Academic Press; 77-153.

Binford, L. R. and S. R., 1966. "A preliminary analysis of functional variability, in the Mousterian of Levallois facies." Amer. Anth. 68:238-295.

Bofinger, E. and Davidson, I., 1977. "Radiocarbon age and depth: a statistical treatment of two sequences of dates from Spain." J. Arch. Sci. 4:231-243.

Bouchud, J., 1966. Essai sur le Renne et la Climatologie du Paléolithique Moyen et Supérieur. Périgueux: Imprimerie Magne.

Brothwell, D., 1975. "Salvaging the term 'domestication' for certain types of man-animal relationship: the possible value of an eight-point scoring system." J. Arch. Sci. 2:397-400.

Chapman, R. W., 1980. 'Evolution récente de l'Archéologie théorique en Grande Bretagne.' Nouvelles de l'Archéologie 3:16-28.

Clark, J. G. D., 1952. Prehistoric Europe: the Economic Basis. Cambridge: Cambridge University Press.

Clark, J. G. D., 1954. Excavations at Star Carr. Cambridge: Cambridge University Press.

Clark, J. G. D., 1967. Stone Age Hunters. London: Thames and Hudson.

Clark, J. G. D., 1976. Discussion. Philosophical Transactions of the Royal Society of London B 275:95.

Clarke, D. L., 1968. Analytical Archaeology. London: Methuen.

Clarke, D. L., 1973. "Archaeology: the loss of innocence." Antiquity 47:6-18.

Clarke, D. L., 1978. Analytical Archaeology. London: Methuen (2nd. edn., revised by R. W. Chapman).

Clason, A. T., 1972. "Some remarks on the use and presentation of archaeozoological data." Helinium 12, 139-153.

Davidson, I., 1972a. "The animal economy of La Cueva del Volcán del Faro, Cullera, Valencia, Spain." Transactions of the Cave Research Group of Great Britain 14:23-32.

Davidson, I., 1973b. "The fauna from La Cueva del Volcán del Faro (Cullera, Valencia)." Archivo de Prehistoria Levantina 13:7-15.

Davidson, I., 1976a. "Les Mallaetes and Mondúver: the economy of a human group in prehistoric Spain" in Problems in Economic and Social Archaeology, eds. G. De. G. Sieveking, I. Longworth and K. Wilson. London: Duckworth; 483-499.

Davidson, I., 1976b. "Seasonality in Spain." Zephyrus 26-27:167-173.

Degerbøl, M., 1963. "Prehistoric cattle in Denmark and adjacent areas" in Man and Cattle, eds. A. E. Mourant and F. E. Zeuner. London: Occasional Papers of the Royal Anthropological Institute 18:68-79.

Dennell, R. W., 1972. "The interpretation of plant remains: Bulgaria" in Papers in Economic Prehistory, ed. E. S. Higgs. London: Cambridge University Press; 149-160.

Ducos, P., 1968. L'Origine des Animaux Domestiques en Palestine. Bordeaux: Publications d'Institut Préhistorique, Université de Bordeaux 6.

Evans, J. D., 1964. "Excavations in the neolithic settlement of Knossos, 1957-60, Part I." Ann. Brit. Sch. Athens 59:132-240.

Ewbank, J. M., Phillipson, D. W. and Whitehouse, R. D. with Higgs, E. S., 1964. "Sheep in the Iron Age: a method of study." P.P.S. 30:423-426.

Flannery, K. V., 1968. "Archaeological systems theory and early Meso-america" in Anthropological Archaeology in the Americas, ed. B. J. Meggers. Washington D.C.: Anthropological Society of Washington; 67-87.

Flannery, K. V., 1969. "Origins and ecological effects of early domestication in Iran and the Near East" in The Domestication and Exploitation of Plants and Animals, eds. P. J. Ucko and G. W. Dimbleby. London: Duckworth; 73-100.

Flannery, K. V., 1976. "The village and its catchment area: Introduction" in The Early Mesoamerican Village, ed. K. V. Flannery. New York: Academic press; 91-95.

Fortea Pérez, J., 1973. Los Complejos Microlaminares y Geométricos del Epipaleolítico Mediterraneo Español. Salamanca: Facultad de Filosofia y Letras, Universidad de Salamanca.

Gamble, C., 1980. "Information exchange in the Palaeolithic". Nature 283: 522-523.

Harris, D. R., 1977. "Alternative pathways to agriculture" in The Origins of Agriculture, ed. C. A. Reed. The Hague: Mouton; 179-243.

Higgs. E. S., 1961. "Some Pleistocene faunas of the Mediterranean coastal areas." P.P.S. 27:144-154.

Higgs, E. S. (ed.), 1972. Papers in Economic Prehistory. London: Cambridge University Press.

Higgs, E. S. and Jarman, M. R., 1969. "The origins of agriculture: a reconsideration." Antiquity 43:31-44.

Higgs, E. S. and Jarman, M. R., 1975. "Palaeoeconomy" in Palaeoeconomy, ed. E. S. Higgs. London: Cambridge University Press; 1-8.

Higgs, E.S. and Vita-Finzi, C., 1966. "The climate, environment and industries of stone age Greece: Part II." P. P. S. 32:1-29.

Higgs, E. S. and Webley, D., 1971. "Further information concerning the environment of palaeolithic man in Epirus." P.P.S. 37:367-380.

Higgs, E. S. and White, J. P., 1963. "Autumn killing." Antiquity 37:282-289.

Higham, C. F. W., 1967. "Stock rearing as a cultural factor in prehistoric Europe." P.P.S. 33:84-106.

Higham, C. F. W., 1968. "Trends in prehistoric European caprovine husbandry." Man 3:64-75.

Higham, C. F. W., 1969. "Towards an economic prehistory of Europe." Curr. Anth. 10:139-150.

Hole, F., 1978. Editorial. Amer. Ant. 43:151-152.

Hole, F., Flannery, K. V. and Neely, J. A., 1969. "Prehistory and human ecology of the Deh Luran plain". Mem. Museum of Anthropology, University of Michigan 1.

Hopf, M., 1966. "Triticum monococcum L. y Triticum dicoccum Schübl, en el neolítico antiguo español." Archivo de Prehistoria Levantina 11: 53-74.

Ingold, T., 1980. Hunters, Pastoralists and Ranchers: Reindeer Economies and their Transformations. Cambridge: Cambridge University Press.

Jarman, H. N., 1972. "The origins of wheat and barley cultivation" in Papers in Economic Prehistory, ed. E. S. Higgs. London: Cambridge University Press; 15-26.

Jarman, H. N. and M. R., 1968. "The fauna and economy of early neolithic Knossos." Ann. Brit. Sch. Athens 63:241-264.

Jarman, H. N., Legge, A. J. and Charles, J. A., 1972. "Retrieval of plant remains from archaeological sites by froth flotation" in Papers in Economic Prehistory, ed. E. S. Higgs. London: Cambridge University Press; 39-48.

Jarman, M. R., 1969. "The prehistory of Upper Pleistocene and Recent cattle. Part I: east Mediterranean with references to North West Europe." P.P.S.35:236-266.

Jarman, M. R., 1971. "Culture and economy in the north Italian Neolithic". World Archaeology 2:255-265.

Jarman, M. R., 1972. "European red deer economies and the advent of the Neolithic" in Papers in Economic Prehistory, ed. E. S. Higgs. London: Cambridge University Press; 125-147.

Jarman, M. R., 1976. "Early animal hubandry." Philosophical Transactions of the Royal Society of London B 275:85-94.

Jochim, M. A., 1976. Hunter-gatherer Subsistence and Settlement. London: Academic Press.

Lee, R. B., 1965. Subsistence Ecology of !Kung Bushmen. Unpublished Ph.D. thesis, University of California, Berkeley.

Lee, R. B., 1979. The !Kung San. Cambridge: Cambridge University Press.

Lee, R. B. and DeVore, I. (eds.), 1968. Man the Hunter. Chicago: Aldine.

Legge, A. J., 1972. "Prehistoric exploitation of the gazelle in Palestine" in Papers in Economic Prehistory, ed. E. S. Higgs. London: Cambridge University Press; 119-124.

Lubbock, J., 1865. Prehistoric Times as Illustrated by Ancient Remains, and the Manners and Customs of Modern Savages. London: Williams and Norgate.

Martí Oliver, B., 1977. La Cova de L'Or (Beniarrés). Valencia: Trabajo vario del Servicio de Investigación Prehistórica.

Mulvaney, D. J. and Joyce, E. B., 1965. "Archaeological and geomorphological investigations on Mt. Moffat Station, Queensland, Australia." P.P.S. 31:147-212.

Payne, S., 1968. "The origins of domestic sheep and goats: a reconsideration in the light of the fossil evidence." P.P.S. 34:368-384.

Perkins, D., 1964. "Prehistoric fauna from Shanidar, Iraq." Science 144: 1565-1566.

Reed, C. A., 1960. "A review of the archaeological evidence on animal domestication in the prehistoric Near East" in Prehistoric Investigations in Iraqi Kurdistan, eds. R. J. Braidwood and B. Howe. Chicago: Oriental Institute, University of Chicago; 119-145.

Renfrew, A.C., 1978. "Trajectory discontinuity and morphogenesis: the implications of Catastrophe Theory for archaeology." Amer. Ant. 43:203-222.

Sahlins, M. D., 1974. Stone Age Economics. London: Tavistock.

Saxon, E. C., 1978. "Mesolithic coastal economies in the Levant and North Africa" in Views of the Past, ed. L. G. Freeman. The Hague: Mouton; 357-361.

Shawcross, W., 1975. "Some studies of the influences of prehistoric human predation on marine animal population dynamics" in Maritime Adaptions of the Pacific, eds. R. W. Casteel and E.J. Quimby. The Hague: Mouton; 39-66.

Sollas, W. J., 1911. Ancient Hunters and their Modern Representatives. London: Macmillan.

Sturdy, D. A., 1972a. "The exploitation patterns of a modern reindeer economy in West Greenland" in Papers in Economic Prehistory, ed. E. S. Higgs. London: Cambridge University Press; 161-168.

Sturdy, D. A., 1972b. Reindeer Economies in Late Ice Age Europe. Unpublished Ph.D. thesis, University of Cambridge.

Sturdy, D. A., 1975. "Some reindeer economies in prehistoric Europe" in Palaeoeconomy, ed. E. S. Higgs. London: Cambridge University Press; 55-95.

Vita-Finzi, C. and Higgs, E.S., 1970. "Prehistoric economy in the Mount Carmel area of Palestine: site catchment analysis." P.P.S. 36:1-37.

3. THEORY AND REALITY IN PALAEOECONOMY: SOME WORDS OF ENCOURAGMENT TO THE ARCHAEOLOGIST

John Bintliff

Preface

When I came to the conference on 'Economic Archaeology' I was more than a little taken aback by the desire of most of those present to want to talk about 'Social Archaeology' instead. I suppose I really should not have been so surprised, for British Theoretical Archaeology (or more accurately in this context, Cambridge-centred Theoretical Archaeology!) is at the moment passing from an early (Archaic?/Classic?) mini-paradigm of Renfrewsian 'Social Archaeology' (Renfrew 1973), to a mature (Classic?/Decadent?) mini-paradigm still based on social anthropology but on more recent research concerns — as, 'Structuralist Archaeology'. The idea of holding a conference on the 'Economic Subsystem' was perhaps something of a 'Retrospective' for the once dominant Cambridge Palaeoeconomy School (Higgs 1972, 1975), which represented the key mini-paradigm (at Cambridge!) in the early '70s. Personally, I have begun to feel a little 'jet-lagged' from the rapidity of these shifts of emphasis, since they tend to leave a trail of shivering and only half-washed babies behind them. It was surely the greatest promise held out, again at Cambridge, by our much-lamented David Clarke, in his later writings, that he was showing us the way to reconcile hitherto competing research orientations into a coherent but pluralistic research universe, in which the main advantages of each research group were stressed and acknowledged by practioners within groups belonging to different spheres of interest. We are clearly as far away as ever from recognising in ourselves the lessons of 'Critical Self-Consciousness' (Clarke 1973).

* * * *

Optimism

All too often archaeology students' essays end as follows: "In conclusion, we really know almost nothing about this subject, and must wait for the results of future, more careful, research"; many of those who teach archaeology, and quite a few of those attending this conference will also wish to decry our feeble state of knowledge concerning Economic Archaeology. Yet it seems to me that we deserve to be thoroughly optimistic about just how much we do know, and about the way modern archaeology is leaping forward in its skill of recovering and interpreting data relevant to this topic. Arguably the subject is in a healthy and rapidly advancing state, not the confused hag some would portray.

In offering these words of encouragement I would like to examine some current approaches to economic prehistory, moving up the pyramid of economic activity: starting at the broad base, the production, consumption and utilisation of local foodstuffs and raw materials in a subsistence context; then up to the level of regional internal exchange and redistribution; finally to the level of inter-regional exchange and professional marketing. My main emphasis however will be on subsistence and the all-important interaction between that and exchange systems.

The Subsistence Economy

Landscape Reconstruction:

With subsistence activity, a satisfactory analysis of palaeoeconomy demands a reasonable fit between the body of current theory, a set of controls of an analogue nature, and the recoverable archaeological data i.e. the 'palaeoreality'. Fundamental also, and seriously neglected by the Cambridge Palaeoeconomy School in the post-Godwin and early Higgs years, is a proper awareness of the need to reconstruct the landscape contemporary to the sites being analysed. We have in fact come a long way from Cyril Fox with his simple plotting of distributions against an assumed landscape (*cf.* Figure 59 and pp. 135-137, in Evans 1975), and this first hurdle to palaeoeconomy is well on the way to being universally conquered with a battery of techniques from Quaternary Science, including a blanket of pollen analyses (*cf.* for example Spratt and Simmons 1976), landsnail and insect studies (*cf.* for example Figure 22.2 in Bowen 1978), and areal geomorphology (*cf.* for example Bintliff 1976).

Land Potential:

Given the contemporary landscape, can we evaluate its potential for palaeoeconomy? Allowing for changing crop and herd yields and suspected technological competence, it is possible to map potential land utilisation for various types of economy: this has generally been done for mixed farming economies (*cf.* the soil map and land potential map for the Ayiofarango Valley, Crete in Blackman, Branigan *et al.*, 1977). Such a map could be converted for basically pastoral or hunter/gatherer economies, and for the latter we might consider in this respect the stimulating studies of Grahame Clark (1972), Paul Mellars (1975), David Clarke (1977), and Jochim (1976). Besides foodstuffs the same mapping can be done, for example, for chert, building stone, copper resources (*cf.* Sherratt 1977, Figures 9, 10 and 15).

Maximal and Empirical Extraction Rates:

Valid criticisms have been levelled at the equation of potential economy with a practised palaeoeconomy, with its assumption of a maximising approach, or the lesser sin of using selected empirical ethnohistoric analogues without any underlying general theory of Carrying versus Carried Capacity (*cf.* for example Clarke 1972, Thomas 1972, with the discussion by Hassan and Glassow in Schiffer 1978). But such models are invaluable heuristic devices to demonstrate the range of possible exploitative strategies and extractive potential within which the actual economic strategy was selected. Nonetheless the significance of selection amongst alternatives, and the realisation that it is exceedingly rare to find practised economies from ethnohistory that regularly approach anything near their regional carrying capacity, have created a demand for more sophisticated treatment of the data.

Approximate Extraction Rate and Strategies Actually Selected:

What can be done is all very well in theory, the economic potential, but how can we investigate the economic behaviour of subsistence communities actually in operation in a landscape for a given period? (i) Direct information can be obtained from studying the distribution of settlement and activity areas. We find for example suggestions of contrasted locations for early hominid strains in the different micro-environments around Lake Rudolf, or the distinct locational emphases shown by our neolithic and early bronze age sites as opposed to our later bronze age sites in Southern England (cf. Barrett 1976: 297-299) — reflecting a major shift in the economic importance of certain soils. However, such plausible spatial interpretations, even where reinforced by the application of techniques such as Catchment Analysis and other locational devices (see below), must receive adequate backup from (ii) Excavation to confirm the nature of foodstuff and raw material extraction from the landscape. Thanks to the probing and illuminating papers of Payne (1972 a, b) and Dennell (1972, 1974 a, b, 1976), however, we are now all very much aware of the severe problems in trying to reconstruct a site economy via floral and faunal samples from its partial excavation. The relevance of recent advances in archaeological sampling theory to combat these difficulties is underlined in important contributions by Cherry and Gamble to the Sampling in British Archaeology volume (Cherry et al., 1978). (iii) Increasingly the two former approaches can be supplemented by landscape sampling analysis — indications from the site catchment area of distinct Man/landscape interactions (cf. the mosaic of arable and pasture indicators for earlier bronze age Wiltshire in Bradley, 1978, Figures 6-7, or the excellent land use analyses spanning many periods on the island of Sylt in Kossack et al., 1974). Closely associated with such evidence, for much of later prehistory, is that obtained from the mapping and dating of field systems; the results of which have revolutionised landscape archaeology over much of Northwest Europe. An excellent example of the fruitful matching of settlement and monument distributions to changing field systems is provided by the Rams Hill publication (Bradley et al., 1975), and the wider implications are seen in the recent CBA Lowland Zone volume (Limbrey and Evans 1978) and, for the Continent, the work of Brongers (1976) and a number of Scandinavian scholars (cf. Kristiansen et al., 1978).

Catchment analysis:

But in particular, especially where hitherto land use behaviour has not been detected, fossilised, as in 'iii', we must also consistently apply what I still believe to be the most useful locational tool derived by archaeology from human geography: Site Catchment Analysis. Let me comment that after accomplishing around 300 studies using a variant of the technique, many of which offered modern settlement and land use control, I find its main principles virtually faultless. Namely that something like 99% of sites, by virtue of the Least Effort principle, dominate resources of radially decreasing value to their inferred or known chief exploitative activities; that within almost all cases, resources that offer primary life support for a community lie within limited radius of it; that the catchment diagram for a site, with practical allowance for landscape change, provides a highly reliable mirror for its former occupants' subsistence and surplus production priorities, that can also prove highly consistent examined together with a series from sites of the same cultural background. The repetitiveness of site catchment results is one of the most striking features of regional applications of the method (cf. for example the Romanellian in Southern Italy in Jarman 1972, Figure 18.5; or the Mt. Carmel coastal plain series in Vita-Finzi et al., 1970). Or to take a more chronologically dynamic view, note the highly informative contrast between early Neolithic land choosiness and the push into marginal lands by the later neolithic in Central Europe (Figures 3-4 in Jarman et al., 1977). Consider the stimulating achievement of Ellison and Harriss (1972) in being able to generalise typical catchments for sites in Southern England from bronze age to Saxon times. Then turn to that admirable analysis of the Tell Gezer catchment in Israel, where Webley (1972) modified the land potential over time to mirror the effect of changes inferred in agricultural technology, successfully matching implied food support (on empirical extraction rating) to indications of population density for the late prehistoric town.

In my own ongoing research, the difficulty in using the 'classic' one and two hour thresholds, designed as maxima for single sites, when the district settlement pattern of arguably contemporary sites suggests more variable, and usually smaller, territories, has been met by applying Thiessen polygon analysis in tandem with a catchment study of the resultant implied territorial cells (cf. Bintliff 1977a, Appx. A and work in preparation). This recent work allows one to recognise a class of asymmetric catchments where the site territory is well within any threshold to intensive exploitative activity out from the home base. The interplay of Thiessen and Catchment analyses offers invaluable insights, such as the possible recognition of common land modules for mixed farming settlements of comparable size. I should like to leave the discussion of the relationship between these cells of theoretical land use, and the dynamic picture of changing intensity of use of each cell (raised challengingly by Flannery 1976, Ch. 4), for a lengthy treatment I am preparing for publication in the near future, but it does not affect our growing appreciation of conceptual 'modules' of territory that seem to form a framework within which extractive variety occurs over time.[1]

We are, then, now approaching a position where we can produce period by period mapping of land exploitation, district by district, on a qualitative, pie-chart priority list basis, for fruitful comparison with historical data (such as, for example, the Kent abbey records reproduced in Derby 1976, Figure 36). In summary, the techniques discussed hitherto offer a guide to priorities and dominant strategies for local extractive economies in a subsistence context. With the site faunal and floral data we are regrettably still in the sphere of qualitative measurements (and the same is true for raw material), whilst in the wider landscape around the site it is only with field evidence of type 'iii' that we can begin to suggest in a semi-quantitative form the degree of 'cropping' of the land potential.

Intensity of Exploitation:

So we are still some distance from a definitive mode of analysis to tackle the relationship between theoretical carrying capacity for a district, the actual population cover at period X, and its extraction rate and selection strategy for resources. How do we progress from here? Firstly, we can calculate as indicated earlier, the theoretical carrying capacities with varied economic strategies, allowing a range for factors such as length of fallow, etc.; hopefully we might be able to narrow down the actual strategies and priorities from excavation data and locational studies. Secondly we can use the best available estimates of settlement numbers and size to suggest the order of population who might actually have been locally maintained.

A simple comparison of both indices could be an adequate guide to intensity of foodstuff exploitation, if we were convinced of (and hence allowed for) but a minority of foodstuffs being imported into the district or exported for raw materials etc. Thus, for example, for a well-surveyed valley in Crete, my estimates of bronze age population on a mixed farming strategy, a sensible fallow, and a due respect for the tolerance of the poorer soils, produced 70-140 people, allowing surplus olive oil for obtaining metal and 'taxes'. In terms of carrying capacity maxima, this would be perhaps 50-75% of total valley capacity under a maximisation strategy. This figure compared well to the bronze age settlement evidence, the later historical population totals, and with predicted population from a series of dated communal tombs lining the valley (Blackman, Branigan et al., 1977). To take another example: in the Plain of Troy, in the absence of detailed site survey, only prominent tell mounds are recorded, possibly local centres such as Troy itself. Theoretical carrying capacity for the region, allowing for landscape and technological change, is strikingly similar to recent population cover, but the limited area of the tell sites suggests either a prehistoric population living remarkably below capacity, or else the existence of a dense pattern of lowly farmstead sites awaiting survey discovery. Considering the partial field walking undertaken over the last 100 years, and despite the élite nature of the Troy community for much of its life, I suspect the truth to lie more towards the former explanation. But the importance of such competing views is that they are testable in the Troy region via a short-term survey programme with strong geomorphogical expertise (Bintliffe, forthcoming). I would also cite again, for a final illustration, the fine Tell Gezer study and its population/resources analysis. In Britain the current emphasis on sites in their landscape and as integral parts of patterned site distributions is already encouraging similar calculations; reflect for example on the wealth of data emerging for the iron age and Romano-British landscape in regional projects such as that in the Nene Valley. On a much vaster scale, the whole of Pharaonic Egypt has been the object of Karl Butzer's estimates of population cover, combining land use data, landscape change research, technological innovation and plentiful historical sources (Butzer 1976).

The use of real-world analogues as in the study of Jochim (1976) and examples of my own work noted above, allows an essential corrective to any simple assumptions of maximisation to carrying capacity limits. Apparent 'under-exploitation' may be the result of a sensible recognition of the need for adequate long-term safety margins, rather than 'stagnation' or 'incompetence'. The feedback from carrying capacity estimates, to actual estimates of population density from archaeological survey, offers a suggestive rating of the cultures concerned in terms of the degree of such a 'safety-margin', and hence by implication the degree of 'stress' on the land potential. Our next goal in this area of research, is then to construct some general theoretical models on as wide a range as possible of ethnohistoric examples, for generalising on the links between settlement density/land potential/extraction rate and strategy, especially as regards the long and short term effects of varying these elements in respect to each other. To give an example of the future potential of such an approach, I offer some preliminary analyses from my current research on the development of population on the Greek Mainland. Recent ethnographic studies have suggested that a frequent rate of actual to potential carrying capacity for farming populations lies somewhere around 30-40% of potential. Given the recurrent difficulties with the climate in the Mediterranean, allied to fluctuations in crop/herd health and cultural factors, let us take the lower figure as a securely viable long term population/land extraction ratio to total capacity. I am at present studying data for rural densities in Classical Greece, that would in these terms suggest a dangerously high population, placing the landscape and contemporary communities under considerable 'stress'.[2] A similar, but less dramatic push of population well beyond our level of a 'safety-margin' extraction/population ratio, may be demonstrable for Mycenaean rural densities. In neither case, and this is highly significant, do I consider a major part of supportive foodstuffs to have been imported, so as to relieve such densities. The virtual depopulation of the rural landscape in the periods following Mycenaean and Classical times, indicated hitherto on available data, might now be suggested, controversially, as a predictable consequence of the observed pressures; were these marginal situations merely precipitated by internal or external conflict? A complementary line of research to test such an hypothesis might be to subject associated burial populations to the kind of dietary analysis so stimulatingly discussed for the Maya civilisation by Rathje (1969).

The Non-Subsistence Sector

In the studies cited and suggestions offered hitherto, it must be admitted that calculations assume a reasonable match of available resources, technology, local population density and local extraction rate — even if the extraction rate is estimated via analogue controls and internal feedback from the sources noted (settlement evidence, etc.). Our next crucial difficulty is to balance any calculations thus far obtained for the relationship between local resources and local population, against the estimates for additional extractive activity undertaken for inter/intraregional exchange and the support of regional specialists and administrators.

One conceivably effective approach to this problem is to try and trace surplus production to its goal. In the case of food, it is quite possible to estimate the population at central places such as bronze age palaces; rather more difficult but feasible to estimate the approximate proportion not significantly food-producing (here a careful comparison of activity and residence data from excavations with historical analogues would be instructive); we are then left with a figure for required regional foodstuff support. A study of the storage capacity of the Minoan palace of Mallia, by French scholars (Van Effenterre et al., 1963), has already been able to suggest the necessary regional catchment required to fill these presumably hierarchically redistributed stocks. But this approach is limited to smallscale, highly regionally introverted systems where we have reason to 'delimit' the flow of food and raw material chains to geographical 'boxes' amenable to the techniques discussed earlier.

Secondly, we can attempt to quantify the circulation within a region of internally and/or externally exchanged raw materials, probably as a generalisation from a parameterised sample of finds at a spectrum of sites across the settlement hierarchy; then the corresponding surplus implied for local foodstuffs or local raw material will provide two obvious theoretical equivalences to investigate. The documentation of raw material distribution is now highly advanced and one of the most significant breakthroughs in economic archaeology (and particularly flourishing at my own department of Archaeological Sciences at Bradford!). Vital to the isolation of raw material and finished artefact exchange are techniques of physical analysis such as neutron activation, X-ray fluorescence, ceramic petrology. Archaeological landscapes, once dotted with exchange networks defined on intuitive typological similarities, can now be reanalysed and checked with the sophistication of archaeological science (strikingly successful examples being the obsidian 'trade', cf. Hallam et al., 1976, or the tracing of Late Saxon pottery products from individual kilns, cf. Ipson in prep.). The matching of artefact distribution patterns to distinct modes of exchange and servicing have been fruitfully explored by Ian Hodder (Hodder and Orton 1976). Especially interesting in his British work is the suggestion of continuities of 'servicing catchments' (cf. op.cit., Figure 4.20).

The reciprocal movement of foodstuffs in exchange for raw material is an exceedingly difficult task to trace in average conditions of archaeological preservation, but such activity should have been commonplace in most developed societies. If we turn to mutual exchange of foodstuffs, between subregions or whole regions, survival and recovery limitations in most archaeological environments cause formidable problems of detection. We may hope to identify for a chosen region of study the final result of intra and inter-regional movement of foodstuffs and raw material, from an analysis of the settlement data, from the study of the proportions of semi- or non-food-producing strata in the population, and via estimates of the level of supply and consumption of local and foreign raw materials. For identifying the relative weighting to be assigned to possible imported foodstuffs, locational analysis cannot normally offer sufficient quantitative information for the local contribution, as we have seen, unless we are fortunate enough to possess detailed land use evidence within the local catchments concerned. We might look forward (optimistically) to a time when site faunal and floral study will be refined enough to offer realistic weightings for food sources, sufficient to pinpoint a significant consumption of certain species considered to be imported (on grounds such as environmental constraints, or catchment/land use indications); or for the same reasons, the reverse, the export from a site of locally produced foodstuffs or herd by-products. It is exceedingly rare that we can spot the products conveyed in such transactions, and usually this is from surrogate evidence, for example closed pot shapes in Mycenaean pottery exported to the Levant that may have contained olive oil. Again then we stand at one of the major research barriers in palaeoeconomy, — but surely this is, for future ranks of research students, a stimulant rather than a depressant!

However, as I shall demonstrate at length in a forthcoming publication, any tendency amongst contemporary archaeologists to stress inter-regional exchange of foodstuffs (or indeed other raw materials) as a dominant and central factor in the dynamics of the typical prehistoric economy, is entirely anachronistic, and a misconception of the nature and functioning of prehistoric communities. I shall be presenting detailed arguments to support the following crucial propositions regarding prehistoric food production:

(i) In the vast majority of such societies, exchangeable or 'marketable' or redistributable foodstuffs constitute no more than a small proportion of total food extracted from the environment, which is predominantly consumed by the primary producers.

(ii) In the vast majority of such societies, this non-subsistence foodstuff element is predominantly consumed regionally, not inter-regionally, and almost entirely within the confines of smallscale sociopolitical systems and geographical regions, analysable with the techniques discussed earlier.

(iii) The demand for, and consumption of, raw materials necessarily imported into such societies is, in the vast majority of cases, never crucial enough to create a shift in the balance of local food production from a predominant orientation towards subsistence followed by a support role for regional specialists (cf. propositions 'i' and 'ii').

These key propositions allow, as you will note, for a significant minority of exceptions, represented by ports of trade, copper and salt-mining communities, etc. But allowing for this minority, we reach some far-reaching corallaries:

(A) The average prehistoric settlement can be expected to be primarily extracting foodstuffs and other raw material from its local environment for its own support. It is therefore decidedly liable to conform to the constraints of Least Effort and the Land Rent, in other words will be highly amenable to inferences drawn from its study by Catchment and other means of Locational Analysis.

(B) For prehistoric societies, the regional settlement system, is, with rare exceptions, the most significant unit for analysis regarding the production and consumption of exchangeable foodstuffs and most other raw materials. Such a smallscale system is very suitable for analysis of the subsistence/non-subsistence balance with the approaches outlined earlier.

(C) If we consider food production in a regional population, it is highly plausible that striking alterations in the balance of primary productive sector versus semi- or non-productive strata — such as are associated frequently with the growth and decline of higher cultures and primary civilisations, stem most often from internal re-organisation of basically introverted regional systems of production and consumption. My current working hypothesis is that this is to be related to fluctuations in the local extraction rate, and the ratio of actual to potential carrying-capacity. Similarly, the running-down or collapse of complex regional systems of this type, can I suggest most often be explained by investigating the negative consequences of this local re-organisation process.

Such an argument also has implications, with naturally rather less force, for much larger-scale cultural systems of historic times. My own field experience suggests that where there is a castle, an abbey, a palace, a market centre, — in other words a nucleus for exploitation, control and servicing of lower levels in a settlement hierarchy, there will also be, with rare exceptions, the human raw material — i.e. a local concentration of people who are primary producers of foodstuffs (and still to a major extent for their own subsistence). And as previously argued, it is from the careful study of this hierarchy of settlements and their catchments, their accompanying imports, that the overall balance of subsistence against exchange and redistribution may be analysed.

Thus, we are always aware that Roman villas were an intricate part of an economy with a strong market sector, and could sometimes arise as a 'rural retreat' for the wealthier urban population. Yet a balance had usually to be sought between production for the regional and even inter-regional market, a pleasing view and good access to the road network, and the constraints and opportunities imposed by the physical landscape, coupled to the desirability of providing the immediate subsistence support of staff and villa owners for a cross-section of foodstuffs and raw materials. The network of Late Roman villas in the Chilterns (Bintliff, in preparation) is surely then suitable for an analysis of this subsistence/exchange interface which would involve Catchment Analysis and other locational approaches, carrying capacity study, the evaluation of excavated environmental data, estimates of villa population and of imported raw material requirements. On our Corollary 'B', most of the non-subsistence sector of production should be amenable to study and identification in terms of the immediate regional archaeology (and in this instance attention would naturally concentrate on the supportive requirements of the regional service centre of Verulamium). The calculations involved may fruitfully be compared to tangible investment in villa furnishings, and at least in some cases suspected territorial fertility seems to correspond to the degree of impressiveness of the villa complex. With greater documentary support available, one could begin to investigate the same interface for medieval peasant communities. There are even some instances where the medieval parish network seems to mirror that of villas in the same district (cf. Fowler 1976, Fig. 1.9), almost a laboratory situation for isolating the nature and degree of change between the ancient and medieval rural economy. Would you be surprised to learn that Bradford archaeology students have been practising Catchment Analysis on medieval villages all over Britain with highly successful results?

The Hodder/Frere controversy (cf. their contributions in Rodwell and Rowley 1975) as to whether the lesser walled towns of Roman Britain were patterned according to military or marketing considerations, — indeed the whole debate about regional centres and their locational priorities, — obscures the underlying rationale to both regional control and servicing: in most such cases there must exist a local concentration of population to be controlled or serviced, and a priori the subsistence wherewithal on which that population and indeed the regional centre are founded and maintained. An illustration of the same principle can be seen with the Saxon network of fortified townships or 'burhs' (cf. Biddle 1976, Fig. 3.3). Almost every farm of Alfred's kingdom was within a day's walk (30 km) of two such refuges from the Danes, in which sense they are strategic foundations. But at the same time, if we exclude the poorer and marginal lands of the kingdom with their arguably low population, the rural communities of the remaining, high population density lands of that kingdom lay within a day return of a burh (15 km), as a possible local centre for marketing and general servicing. Hence the later development (and sometimes prior existence) of many burhs as typical market towns.

Even specialist trading centres can generally be shown to hinge upon an adjacent hinterland of dense local population, and the latter in turn upon concentrations of local agricultural resources (far less frequently on local raw materials). Hengistbury Head, for example (cf. Cunliffe 1977, Fig. 7) a suspected iron age community of this class, is axial to the territories of two densely-farmed and settled tribal hinterlands.

I have tried in this paper to present what I see to be the current state of play in field applications of palaeoeconomy, with the emphasis on prehistory, but with some comments on historic archaeology. Difficulties and barriers to analysis and interpretation do indeed abound, but I hope I have suggested some promising approaches for scaling these obstacles. Provocatively I have proposed that some of the most prominent fences can be admired from a distance, then merely circumvented on well-made tracks, without loss of insight.

Footnotes

1. Objections are commonly raised to the use of Catchment Analysis (CA). The more vociferous critics tend to be scholars with little or no experience of fieldwork and the interaction of modern and ancient settlements with their environmental setting. Their objections are therefore theoretical, and are of the nature of "Surely it is too deterministic", or "How can we ever know that the land was used exactly as you suggest?". More substantive comments might have been expected from that supposed compendium of Man-Landscape research techniques for archaeologists: Hodder and Orton's 'Spatial Analysis in Archaeology' (1976). However, whilst I admire the battery of techniques eclectically assembled from modern Human Geography, and find the modelling of artefact exchange (see p. 41) illuminating and relevant, I find the tome as a whole conjuring up a vision of the archetypical armchair scholar, — this time with very smallscale maps, a collection of symbols and a calculator. The landscape seems to be featureless, isotropic, and the societies from the first assumed to be best approached via models and techniques developed from 20th century industrial landscapes. We search almost in vain for any inkling of understanding of the nature of pre-Industrial economies and their characteristic settlement patterns, tied so closely as they were

to the production of foodstuffs. The massive literature that geographers have assembled relating to the links between human geography and physical relief, geomorphology and pedology, vegetational zones, etc.—all is ignored in favour of maps in which at the most the sea and major rivers are allowed some effect on distributions of sites and finds.

The brief discussion of Catchment Analysis appears near the end of the book, appropriately as a kind of afterthought, and the technique is rather superficially dismissed; largely on theoretical grounds, but there is some concession to empirical evidence questioning its validity. We read, rather cryptically, that African societies exist where the villages are surrounded by very poor land, thereby disproving the idea of a decline in human agricultural input with distance from home base. Are you content with this argument? I must confess that for a long while I noted this fact as a cautionary tale, suspending my critical faculties. But really we should ask how this contradictory state of affairs arose. Even if we accept that these villages lie amid the poorest land, I would like to know the reason, be it merely caprice, or due to some compulsion emanating from the pressing demands of native structuralist principles, — thus reversing what would seem to us to be economic common sense. So I went, not only to the short paper raising these issues (Jackson 1972), but to the most important of the primary sources for such situations, Pelissier's Les Paysans de Senegal (1966). It is from the latter that we discover the following: these villages were originally located in good agricultural situations, in woodland with reasonable soils. Cultivation took place on an Infield/Outfield basis. The Infield was cultivated on a short fallow, and was naturally the land innermost to the village. The Outfield was in the woodland and scrub beyond, and consisted of temporary clearance plots for shifting cultivation, with prolonged fallow intervals, together with grazing zones. The more concentrated effort on the Infield led to its deterioration, lacking the woodland recovery episodes. However the underlying potential of the soil, and a low but significant degree of manuring due to the passage of stock into the Outfield, allows the Infield to continue in short fallow cultivation for many of these communities. Where the soil is unable to cope, and permanent loss of fertility arises due to processes that are irreversible such as laterisation, the community will regularly shift its base to begin the cycle all over again.

Given all the facts, it seems to me that these communities should be considered as offering supporting, rather than conflicting, evidence for the principles of Catchment Analysis. The land nearest the home base is more intensively used than that further out; permanent decline in the Infield, despite a great and continuing land potential in the Outfield, prompts relocation of the community to a more fertile position for the Infield.

Much more serious criticism can be found in a reasonably balanced review of Catchment Analysis by Donna Roper (1979). The key difficulties that arise from that discussion seem to be as follows:

(a) With so few empirical values for the limit of the catchment, from ethnography and history, the size of a site territory is an initial stumbling-block before territorial content can be evaluated accurately.

Roper indicates that many recent applications of CA advocate preliminary definition of territory from the analysis of the contemporary settlement pattern surrounding the site under study, using Thiessen polygons or similar approaches. This is a development I have also, and independently arrived at (see p. 38). One might now proceed to modify, if desirable, the 'equality principle' underpinning Thiessen analysis, using some variant of weighting (e.g. gravity models) based on relative site size or inferred/known site function.

(b) If sites are assumed to have been located in order to control key resources, then there should be a correlation between resource potential and the importance of a site in the regional settlement hierarchy.

This postulate is not part of the original theory of CA, and it is not surprising that its success in testable situations is rather variable. It is most important to recall that the primary papers on CA by Higgs *et al.*, argued that *most* sites in *less complex* societies should be rewardingly investigated by CA. It is expected that sites will be found where the predicted fit between catchment and site type is clearly unsatisfactory, and this should stimulate specific research into the particular nature of site occupation, the possible relationships with other sites and so on. CA does however assume that *most* sites are in fact sufficiently dependent on local foodstuff availability to reflect the disposition of notable quantities of such resources in their reconstructed catchments. As far as I am aware, this postulate has not been refuted, and indeed my data and that of most active field palaeoeconomists consistently supports it. The flexibility of this approach is appropriate to the empirical patterns that seem to be emerging, as we can see e.g. from Peebles' application of CA to settlement patterns of the Moundville phase in the southern States (1978). Small and very large sites show a good correlation with land potential, but middle range sites fit less satisfactorily. One might suggest here that the basic unit of settlement, the village, is located according to local support availability in primary foodstuffs, i.e. its status is reflected in its chosen catchment. The largest sites, district centres, may owe part of their original impetus to unusually rich localised resources, and even when dependent on outside support at a mature stage of development, such immediately accessible resources should act as a buffer against minor shortfalls in outside contributions to the economy. Middle range sites, minor centres, possibly act as foci for groups of villages, and their rise may be due less to their own catchment potential than to the demand for service-centres at an intermediate level in range of functions and in terms of accessibility.

In conclusion, it is often necessary to remind those who do not practise Catchment Analysis, that deviations from expectation are both included in the general theory underlying the technique, and are indeed a fruitful source of contrast to the more common experience of expectation fulfilment. Sites where the population seems to outstrip local resources, encourages us to investigate the role of extra-catchment interactions, or the possibility of short-lived hyper-exploitation. On the other hand, we might find the reverse, rich catchment resources but a 'misfit' minor site; here we are being stimulated to investigate models such as a 'pioneer' situation, implying an early and perhaps truncated development of exploitation.

With such examples, the role of micro-environmental studies in recovering actual land use palimpsests, and of artefact analysis for exchange studies, will be of crucial assistance.

2. Apart from my own earlier research, some of this data stems from the collected endeavours of the Boeotia Survey, under the joint directorship of myself and Anthony Snodgrass of Cambridge University.

References

Barrett, J., 1976. "Deverel-Rimbury: problems of chronology and interpretation" in Settlement and Economy in the Third and Second Millenia B.C., eds. C. Burgess and R. Miket. Oxford: B.A.R. 33: 289-307.

Biddle, M., 1976. "Towns" in The Archaeology of Anglo-Saxon England, ed. D. M. Wilson. London: Methuen: 99-150.

Bintliff, J. L., 1976. "The Plain of Macedon and the neolithic site of Nea Nikomedeia". P.P.S. 42: 241-262.

Bintliff, J. L., 1977a. Natural Environment and Human Settlement in Prehistoric Greece. Oxford: B.A.R. Suppl. Ser. 28 (1-2).

Bintliff, J. L., 1977b. "New approaches to human geography. Prehistoric Greece: a case study" in An Historical Geography of the Balkans, ed. F. W. Carter. London: Academic Press: 59-114.

Blackman, D. and Branigan, K. (eds.), 1977. "An archaeological survey of the lower catchment of the Ayiofarango valley." Ann. Brit. Sch. Athens 72: 13-84.

Bowen, H. C. and Fowler, P. J., 1978. "An investigation of the Wessex Linear Ditch system" in Early Land Allotment, eds. H. C. Bowen and P. J. Fowler. Oxford: B.A.R. 48; 149-153.

Bradley, R., 1978. "Colonisation and land use in the Late Neolithic and Early Bronze Age" in The Effect of Man on the Landscape: the Lowland Zone, eds. S. Limbrey and J. G. Evans. C.B.A. Research report 21. London: Council for British Archaeology; 95-103.

Bradley, R. and Ellison, A., 1975. Rams Hill. Oxford: B.A.R. 19.

Brongers, J. A., 1976. Air Photography and Celtic Field Research in the Netherlands. Amersfoort: Nederlandse Oudheden 6.

Butzer, K. W., 1976. Early Hydraulic Civilisation in Egypt. Chicago: Aldine.

Cherry, J. F., Gamble, C. and Shennan, S. (eds.), 1978. Sampling in Contemporary British Archaeology. Oxford: B.A.R. 50.

Clark, J. G. D., 1972. Star Carr: a case study in Bioarchaeology. Cambridge, Mass: Addison-Wesley Modular Publications in Anthropology 10.

Clarke, D. L., 1972. "A provisional model of an iron age society and its settlement system" in Models in Archaeology, ed. D. L. Clarke. London: Methuen; 801-869.

Clarke, D. L., 1973. "Archaeology: the loss of innocence." Antiquity 47: 6-18.

Clarke, D. L., 1977. "Mesolithic Europe: the economic basis" in Problems in Economic and Social Archaeology, eds. G. de G. Sieveking, I. Longworth and K. Wilson. London: Duckworth; 449-481.

Cunliffe, B., 1977. "Hill-forts and oppida in Britain" in Problems in Economic and Social Archaeology, eds. G. de G. Sieveking, I. Longworth and K. Wilson. London: Duckworth; 343-358.

Dennell, R. W., 1972. "The interpretation of plant remains: Bulgaria" in Papers in Economic Prehistory, ed. E. S. Higgs. London: Cambridge University Press; 149-159.

Dennell, R. W., 1974a. "The purity of prehistoric crops." P.P.S. 40: 132-135.

Dennell, R. W., 1974b. "Botanical evidence for crop processing activities". J. Arch. Sci. 1: 275-284.

Dennell, R. W., 1976. "The economic importance of plant resources represented on archaeological sites". J. Arch. Sci. 3: 229-247.

Derby, H. C., 1976. A New Historical Geography of England before 1600. Cambridge: Cambridge University Press.

Effenterre, H. van, Pareyn, C., Dewolf, Y. and Postel, F., 1963. Mallia: Etude du Site. Etudes Crétoises 13. Paris: Paul Geuthner.

Ellison, A. and Harriss, J., 1972. "Settlement and land use in the prehistory and early history of southern England: a study based on locational models" in Models in Archaeology, ed. D. L. Clarke. London: Methuen; 911-962.

Evans, J. G., 1975. The Environment of Early Man in the British Isles. London: Elek.

Flannery, K. V. (ed.), 1976. The Early Mesoamerican Village. New York: Academic Press.

Fowler, P. J., 1976. "Agriculture and rural settlement" in The Archaeology of Anglo-Saxon England, ed. D. M. Wilson. London: Methuen; 23-48.

Hallam, B. R., Warren, S. and Renfrew, C., 1976. "Obsidian in the West Mediterranean". P.P.S. 42: 85-110.

Higgs, E. S. (ed.), 1972. Papers in Economic Prehistory. London: Cambridge University Press.

Higgs, E. S. (ed.), 1975. Palaeoeconomy. London: Cambridge University Press.

Hodder, I. and Orton, C., 1976. Spatial Analysis in Archaeology. Cambridge: Cambridge University Press.

Jackson, R., 1972. "A vicious circle? — The consequences of von Thünen in tropical Africa". Area 4: 258-261.

Jarman, M. R., 1972. "A territorial model for archaeology: behavioural and geographical approach" in Models in Archaeology, ed. D. L. Clarke. London: Methuen; 705-733.

Jarman, H. N. and Bay-Petersen, J. L., 1977. "Agriculture in prehistoric Europe — the lowlands" in The Early History of Agriculture, ed. J. Hutchinson. Oxford: Oxford University Press.

Jochim, M. A., 1976. Hunter-gatherer Subsistence and Settlement: a Predictive Model. London: Academic Press.

Kossack, G., Harck, O. and Reichstein, J., 1974. "Zehn Jahre Siedlungsforschung in Archsum auf Sylt". Ber. der Römisch-Germanischen Kommission 55: 261-427.

Kristiansen, K. and Paludan-Müller, C., 1978. New Directions in Scandinavian Archaeology. Copenhagen: National Museum of Denmark.

Limbrey, S. and Evans, J. G. (eds.), 1978. The Effect of Man on the Landscape: the Lowland Zone. C.B.A. Research report 21. London: Council for British Archaeology.

Mellars, P., 1975. "Ungulate populations, economic patterns, and the mesolithic landscape" in The Effect of Man on the Landscape: the Highland Zone, eds. J. G. Evans, S. Limbrey and H. Cleere. C.B.A. Research report 11. London: Council for British Archaeology; 49-56.

Payne, S., 1972a. "Partial recovery and sample bias: the results of some sieving experiments" in Papers in Economic Prehistory, ed. E. S. Higgs. London: Cambridge University Press; 49-64.

Payne, S., 1972b. "On the interpretation of bone samples from archaeological deposits" in Papers in Economic Prehistory, ed. E. S. Higgs. London: Cambridge University Press; 65-82.

Peebles, C. S., 1978. "Determinants of settlement size and location in the Moundville phase" in Mississippian Settlement Patterns, ed. B. D. Smith. New York: Academic Press; 369-416.

Pelissier, P., 1966. Les Paysans du Senegal. St. Yrieix.

Rathje, W. L., 1969. "Socio-political implications of lowland Maya burials: methodology and tentative hypotheses". World Arch. 1: 359-374.

Renfrew, A. C., 1973. Social Archaeology. Inaugural Lecture, Southampton University, March 20th., 1973. Southampton: Southampton University Press.

Rodwell, W. and Rowley, T. (eds.), 1975. The 'Small Towns' of Roman Britain. Oxford: B.A.R. 15.

Roper, D. C., 1979. "The method and theory of site catchment analysis: a review" in Advances in Archaeological Method and Theory, Vol. 2, ed. M. B. Schiffer. New York: Academic Press; 120-140.

Schiffer, M. B., (ed.), 1978. Advances in Archaeological Method and Theory, Vol. 1. New York: Academic Press.

Sherratt, A., 1977. "Resources, technology and trade: an essay in early European metallurgy" in Problems in Economic and Social Archaeology, eds. G. de G. Sieveking, I. Longworth and K. Wilson. London: Duckworth; 557-581.

Spratt, D. A. and Simmons, I. G., 1976. "Prehistoric activity and environment in the North York Moors". J. Arch. Sci. 3: 193-210.

Thomas, D. H., 1972. "A computer simulation model of Great Basin Shoshonean subsistence and settlement patterns" in Models in Archaeology, ed. D. L. Clarke. London: Methuen; 671-704.

Vita-Finzi, C. and Higgs, E. S., 1970. "Prehistoric economy in the Mt. Carmel area of Palestine: site catchment analysis". P.P.S. 36: 1-37.

Webley, D., 1972. "Soils and site location in prehistoric Palestine" in Papers in Economic Prehistory, ed. E. S. Higgs. London: Cambridge University Press; 169-180.

4. MESOLITHIC DANISH BACON: PERMANENT AND TEMPORARY SITES IN THE DANISH MESOLITHIC

Peter Rowley-Conwy

The dichotomy of "subsistence" versus "social" is partly one that has arisen as a result of differences in the interests of different archaeologists. This has led to something of a chronological difference arising to match: the subsistence-orientated archaeologist has concentrated on simpler economic systems, hunters and subsistence farmers, i.e. usually mesolithic and neolithic, whereas the social-orientated archaeologist has more often gone for the complex socio-economic systems of the later prehistoric and early historic periods. The unfortunate result is the emergence of a "never-the-twain-shall-meet" state of affairs, as it is rather rare for the two types of archaeologist to be working on material directly relevant to each other. As a result serious discussion is rare, a more common occurrence being verbal sniping when the other party is not present.

This brief contribution will examine an assumption often made by the subsistence school—namely that hunters' sites are generally for primary subsistence purposes, i.e. that food resources procured from a particular site are for more or less immediate consumption. The aim is frequently to establish a seasonal rota, with hunters moving from one site to the next, performing subsistence activities at each one. It is my experience of archaeological discussions that the view that this is what hunters always do is the result of the misapplication of certain recent anthropological source works to the prehistoric situation.

The works most often used by archaeologists are perhaps those by Sahlins (1974), Service (1966) and in particular Lee and DeVore (1968). In all these works the equation simplest economy = mobile economy is emphasised. Archaeologists have gone one further and assumed that because all simplest-cum-mobile economies discussed are hunters, therefore all hunters have simplest-cum-mobile economies. What the archaeologist often seeks to demonstrate (the seasonal rota) has often in fact been assumed in advance. This is despite the fact that all the authors mentioned above are at pains to emphasise that by no means all hunters fulfil this model. That all hunters in the past fulfilled this model seems even less likely—in Sahlins' words, present hunters are "displaced persons," they are "the paleolithic disenfranchised, occupying marginal haunts ... sanctuaries of an era, places so beyond the range of the main centres of cultural advance as to be allowed some respite from the planetary advance of cultural evolution" (1974:8). In other words, an area in which hunters live today is only an area nobody has ever bothered to plough. To use such marginal situations as the basis for generalizations about prehistoric hunters seems less than justifiable.

As an example of prehistoric hunters unlikely to fulfil the mobility model we may take the Ertebølle culture of Jutland, characterized by its well-known shell-middens. Some attempts have been made to apply the standard hunter model to this culture, involving movement to and from the coast on a seasonal basis. Examination of this is worthwhile.

There is a shortage of inland sites. If we leave aside the mixed surface scatters formerly known as the Gudenå culture (see Andersen and Sterum 1971), on which, in the absence of organic remains, no work relevant to this problem has been done, only one major site is available.

Ringkloster lies 14 km inland, on the edge of a former lake (Andersen 1973-4). Indulging in seasonal determination, we find a number of winter and spring indicators:

1. Many pine marten bones—the furs are of much better quality in winter.
2. Pig tooth eruption suggests that virtually all animals were killed between November and May.
3. Many of the red and roe deer (about one quarter) were newborn—not juvenile, but so young that they may have been foetal. Probably born in spring.
4. Some migratory birds present only in winter and spring.

It must be emphasised that these results are provisional.

Some coastal sites contain large numbers of fish bones, most probably indicating a summer occupation. Thus one might be tempted to say that the seasonal rota has been established—coastal in summer, inland in winter. However, there is evidence that things are by no means this simple.

Other coastal sites in the same area show winter occupation, not summer as we should expect. Sites are known concentrating on such specific winter visitors as small whales and migratory swans.

Some Ertebølle middens thus present evidence of seasonal occupation, albeit not the same season in each case. Others are less amenable and refuse to give such a clear picture. One could argue that factors of deposition or preservation are working to confuse us and that the seasonal picture is just no longer visible. However, there is some evidence that some sites were occupied all year round. At the type site of Ertebølle itself, for example, bones of both summer and winter visiting birds were found (Winge 1900), and the pig tooth eruption shows no seasonal concentration of killing was taking place.

The implications of permanent settlements in a hunting economy are large. Firstly it is likely that none of the sites are pure subsistence sites: the pattern is more likely to be one of permanently occupied base camps being maintained only in part by subsistence activities carried out from these sites, and in part by supplies brought back from special purpose, seasonal sites visited by small groups from the parent settlement.

Ringkloster falls into place as a special purpose seasonal site: pig (the predominant animal) is represented by many teeth, scapuli and humeri (i.e. front ends) but fewer pelves, femora etc. (back ends). These back ends are an easy load for one man to carry on his shoulders, and the less productive front ends would be left behind—Eskimo do the same thing with caribou today. Danish bacon has evidently been exported for a long time. The numbers of newborn deer (with soft spotted skins suitable for making clothing) and pine martens suggest that procurement of clothing was another purpose of the site. The coastal sites could have seen the exporting of fish, whale and swan meat back to the parent settlement.

Seasonal variation of food supply is the usual factor preventing hunters from living in one place all year round. That such settlement was possible in the Ertebølle is because migratory food resources arrived in the same general area all the year round, thus rendering feasible their exploitation through the combination of permanent sites and briefly occupied special purpose camps. Such migratory resources were available not least in what would otherwise have been the worst time of the year—winter. The most difficult time of the year would therefore probably have been the spring, after the departure of the winter visitors and before the benefits of the new growing season could be felt. It is here that oysters might have been vital—these animals breed in May and June, and are at their most tasty and nutritious in the last couple of months leading up to this, just when they would have been needed. Permanent settlement was thus permitted by fortunate environmental circumstances.

The social implications are major. Lee and DeVore (1968) list the following characteristics of their "nomadic style":-

1. Mobility limits personal property to what can be carried.

2. Group size is small, usually under 50.

3. Local groups do not usually own particular resources.

4. Food surpluses are rare; from this it follows that work effort is continual throughout the year.

5. Particular groups do not identify with particular areas due to too much intergroup visiting and mobility.

Sedentary hunters (e.g. those around the northern Pacific such as the N.W. Coast Indians, the Alaskan and Bering Strait Eskimo and the Ainu) usually contradict each of these:-

1. There is much personal property. Items that cannot be carried can be stored on the settlement.

2. Groups may sometimes be up to 1000 or more in size.

3. Local groups, families or chiefs usually do own particular resource points, often at some distance from the main site and exploited from special purpose seasonal camps.

4. Food surplus and storage is vital, and work occurs in concentrated bursts during e.g. the salmon catching and drying period, followed by periods of inactivity.

5. Sedentism is by definition the identification of a group with an area. Intergroup mobility and visiting however goes on as before.

One more aspect may be added: there is generally a much more complex social structure among sedentary hunters. Among the Bushmen, there is no internal dispute-solving mechanism, so disputing parties fission and move elsewhere (Lee 1972). Among sedentary hunters social stratification and control is sufficiently developed to allow disputes to be solved internally, so fissioning does not occur.

The degree to which sedentary hunters "mimic" farmers is thus rather striking. The major difference appears to be between "sedentary" and "mobile", rather than between "hunter" and "farmer". In the case of the Jutland Ertebølle (assuming that prehistoric sedentary hunters displayed the same characteristics as their modern-day counterparts) this leads to some interesting possibilities.

Recent C14 dates, and recent re-evaluations of older C14 dates, have suggested that there was probably well over 1000 years between the arrival of farming in continental northern Germany and its subsequent spread to Denmark. After a quick spread across Europe, the process stops for over a millennium. We are drawn to the conclusion that "social" factors are unlikely to have inhibited the spread of farming in Jutland—the sedentary hunters were probably at a broadly similar level of social complexity to the farmers further south, and could have made the transition to farming more easily than most groups. Arguably, the rich environment may have made farming unnecessary. Other factors must be invoked to explain the appearance of farming when it did finally arrive—possibly the disappearance of the important oyster (which disappears at the same time as the start of farming) may have been the spur needed to bring the old economy into imbalance.

I started this paper by criticizing one assumption I claimed was made by some "subsistence-orientated" archaeologists. However, it must by now be clear that a change as major as that from hunting to farming can scarcely be studied usefully without a detailed examination of the organic remains. This leads me to wonder whether studies of other important changes visible in the archaeological record which ignore the economic base might not be making a serious mistake in so doing.

References

Andersen, S. H., 1973-4. "Ringkloster: en jysk inlandsboplads med Ertebøllekultur." Kuml 1973-4:11-108.

Andersen, S. H., and Sterum, N., 1971. "Gudenåkulturen." Holstebro Museum Årsskrift (1970-1):14-32.

Lee, R. B., 1972. "Work effort, group structure and land-use in contemporary hunter-gatherers" in Man, Settlement and Urbanism, eds. P. J. Ucko, R. Tringham and G. W. Dimbleby. London: Duckworth; 177-186.

Lee, R. B. and DeVore, I., 1968. Man the Hunter. Chicago: Aldine.

Sahlins, M. D., 1974. Stone Age Economics. London: Tavistock.

Service, E. R., 1966. The Hunters. Englewood Cliffs, N.J.: Prentice-Hall.

Winge, H., 1900. Sections on faunal remains, in Affaldsdynger fra stenalderen i Danmark, eds. A. P. Madsen, S. Müller, C. Neergaard, E. Rostrup, K. J. V. Steenstrup and H. Winge. Copenhagen: C. A. Reitzel.

5. PLAINS TAILS FROM THE HILLS: TRANSHUMANCE IN MEDITERRANEAN ARCHAEOLOGY

James Lewthwaite

Introduction

In this essay I hope to question the degree to which extensive pastoralism in general and transhumant systems in particular can be regarded as stable, efficient long-term strategies in the Mediterranean, primarily using data from the Tyrrhenian Islands (Sardinia and Corsica). A justification for this exercise in historical reinterpretation on the part of a student of prehistory seems appropriate; mine is that anglo-celtic archaeologists from non-subsistence backgrounds in the temperate zone approach the Mediterranean with preconceptions based on an over-familiarity with classical and historical sources; these gravely predetermine the hypotheses which they are prepared to offer in prehistoric contexts. Had transhumance entered archaeological discussion from the data-base, my approach would be different; but, in fact, transhumant economies were expected of the data as a matter of course and only sufficient observations collated (high altitude sites, alignments along transhumant routes) to "prove" this (Barker 1975; Soutou 1959; contra, Lorblanchet 1965). Therefore, it seems more logical to return to the roots of the controlling model—historical situations—to demonstrate the objective inefficiency and impermanence of transhumant systems except as "tactical" adaptations to the anomalous conditions of the medieval and early modern Mediterranean. Besides the purely "idiographic" aspect there is a more general concern with the abstraction of "mobile economies" as a categorically efficient adaptation to areas with "complementary resources", a simplification which I believe invalid in terms of the variables selected and the evaluation of costs in comparison with alternatives.

The Classic Derivation of Transhumance from Ecological Premises

The "Collective Unconscious" model of the functioning of transhumance, drawing particularly on inter-war sources (e.g. Carrier 1932) may be represented as follows:

Premise (1): "Areas of potentially productive arable being limited in extent and scattered in distribution in the Mediterranean, large zones are suitable for human settlement only under a pastoral regime; population pressure will inevitably bring this about."

Premise (2): "The limiting factor on pastoral systems is the existence of seasonal bottlenecks in both upland and lowland ecological zones, forcing stock numbers to be kept far below the mean, let alone the maximum, productivity of grazing resources".

Premise (3): "The existence of areas of steep relief all along the margins of the Mediterranean brings zones of contrasting and complementary ecology into proximity, minimizing the cost of distance".

Solution: "A mobile pastoral economy, exploiting each zone at the time of maximum productivity in turn, i.e. summering in the uplands and wintering in the lowlands."

Proof: "Mobile pastoral ways of life, as predicted, can be shown to have existed throughout the medieval and early modern periods, with roots in Classical Antiquity. Only the steep demographic increase in the nineteenth century disturbed this equilibrium, leading to the agricultural colonization of the areas of winter pasture and the collapse of the system".

Testing the model against historical data

The Tyrrhenian Islands offer a particularly suitable test area for the ecologically-reductionist model, in view of the limited extent of commercial pressures and the variety of landscapes. The islands form a narrow longitudinal transect of the ecological zones of the W. Mediterranean, complicated by differences in relief, geological composition and vegetational history.

Premise (1): Potentially productive arable is limited in Corsica to the very small areas of recent alluvium; the older, Pleistocene, alluvium is poor in texture and useful minerals, while the greatest extent of the island possesses only a thin cover of acid sands on steep slopes (Carlotti 1936). On the other hand, much of W. and S. Sardinia is fertile: the extensive pediments of Pleistocene alluvium, being derived from better parent materials, are highly productive under cereals, as are the soft sediments of the piedmont zone (Mori 1975). Therefore, most of Corsica would appear "relegated to pastoralism", but only the eastern plateaux of its larger neighbour.

Premise (2): Sardinia lies further south and at a lower altitude (mean altitude 344 m, Corsica 568 m) so that precipitation is limited, seasonal and markedly fluctuating. A minimum of three months drought is experienced at all altitudes, increasing to six in the lowlands, but balanced by winter cold in the uplands (Le Lannou 1941): this is critical for the growing season and for the direct effect on animals, above c. 700 m (Bergeron 1967). Corsica, however, presents a classic picture of concentric, sharply differentiated ecological belts girdling the two main massifs, extending from mediterranean evergreens through deciduous and coniferous forest to alpine pastures; the climatic and vegetational regimes of uplands and lowlands are distinct and contrasting (Plesnik 1976).

Premise (3): The tabular relief, great extent and absence of ecological variety of Sardinia result in a lack of "complementarity" over long distances, while at the local level relief is sufficient to make movement laborious and time-consuming over much of the island (Le Lannou 1941). On the other hand, in Corsica, only 25 km (as the crow flies) separate the beach at Porto from 2,710 m Monte Cinto (Renucci 1974:24). Ecological variety effected by aspect and other local factors characterize the numerous small cells which compose the Corsican landscape (Blanchard 1914).

Predicted Solutions: Logically, Sardinia is less fitted for pastoralism than Corsica: the West and South appear particularly suitable for agriculture. Transhumance would be neither necessary nor desirable in the former, indispensable in the latter.

Historical solutions: The classic model of populations of humans and animals migrating seasonally between pastures, the diet of the former consisting purely of the products of the latter, is hardly ever found. In fact, large-scale sheep movements and large-scale sheep raising were more prevalent in Sardinia (Le Lannou 1941); transhumance, as understood in W. Corsica in particular, was often an agricultural rather than a pastoral practice (Blanchard 1914).

First, it must be noted that the massive fluctuations in population, changes in settlement, concentration and distribution and the external impositions on the islanders were all the more profound for being negative: the archaism and self-sufficiency of much traditional culture being a form of involution characteristic of pauperised communities (Bodemann and Allahar 1980). The effect of the historical vicissitudes was to reinforce the natural constraints by bringing about the wholesale abandonment of the fertile coastal lowlands: settlements became concentrated in the plateaux and basins at c. 500-600 m, and population concentrated in a relatively small number of large settlements surrounded by extensive wastes. Therefore, precisely the poorer environment of the uplands bore a disproportionate burden of effective population pressure, while the richer alluvium, the lagoons and the coastal fishing niches could be exploited only temporarily or at the cost of constant journeying from a distant village (Mori 1975:24ff; Day 1975; Blanchard 1914; Renucci 1974).

Yet the medieval Tyrrhenians, despite the poverty of their effective environment, were essentially cultivators and consumers of cereals! Insofar as substitution occurred, chestnuts replaced cereals where the requisite warm, humid, slightly acid environment existed (Blanchard 1914:220-224). The ager lying so far from the main settlement, migrations of labourers and the transport either of consumers to produce or vice versa were required: naturally the cost of distance led to distinct zones with characteristic periodicities and intensities of the working of the lowland grain-growing areas, which, especially in Corsica, remained the source of the subsistence of absentee peasants (Pieretti 1947). In the case of the communes of Cape Corse, there was not enough local land even after the construction of terraces, so that navigation across the Gulf of St. Florent to the Desert of the Agriates was undertaken seasonally. Thus the compilers of the 1789 Plan Terrier regarded only 2% of the communes of Corsica as pastoral in economy, even these not necessarily being pastoral in diet, but acquiring cereals in exchange for dairy products.

Shepherds did exist, but the ratio of sheep to people rules out a sheep economy (see note one; e.g. in 1770 there were only slightly more ovicaprines in Corsica than people—c. 160,000 of the former and c. 130,000 of the latter—Pomponi 1978): even after the massive expansion in sheep numbers in the 1890s, especially in Sardinia, there were only about ten sheep per person in "pastoral" Fonni or Gavoi recently (Bergeron 1967). True pastoralism often preceded permanent emigration, while the relative disadvantage of the shepherd compared with the cultivator is revealed by the dependence of the former on merchants, unless, like the Niolinchi, they were prepared to sell their own products all over Corsica.

The pastoralisation of Tyrrhenian landscapes has taken place very recently, in Corsica opportunistically profiting from the decline of agriculture, in Sardinia as a function of the agricultural renaissance, in both as a result of the vacant niche in the world economy for ovicaprine cheeses (Pernet and Lenclud 1977; Le Lannou 1941).

Interpretation

The myth of archaic pastoralism dies hard. Pastoralism is not a substitute for agriculture in unfavourable circumstances! Both forms of economy depend on herbaceous growth, which dairy pastoralism channels through the extra trophic level of the flock, leading to a minimum 90% loss of efficiency. The additional costs of grazing poor pasture and of transhumant movements have never actually been calculated other than schematically (Osuji 1974).

At the archaeological level, neither of the classic variables is truly independent; both sheep and grass are present as the result of human actions, although it seems unlikely that the propagation of either was achieved with pastoralism in mind, as it were. Sheep begin to appear in the West Mediterranean in the 6th millennium b.c. from their Anatolian—W. Iranian centre of domestication (Poplin 1977; Ducos 1977). The Tyrrhenian mouflon is now known to be a feral, whose diet and limited scale of annual movement are nonetheless interesting (Pfeffer 1967).

Grassland, apart from certain very limited stretches of alpine pasture, occurs only as a microenvironmental phenomenon in the undisturbed W. Mediterranean landscape, the early Holocene forest being far more dominated by deciduous species than is realised, (Pons et al. 1979). Since deciduous forest does not burn well clearance must have been carried out mechanically, a laborious procedure.

The term, "complementarity", is also deceptive; the uplands are disadvantaged absolutely in most respects (see note 4 and Le Houerou, 1977). In fact, grazing lasted 6-9 months in the lowlands in transhumant regimes, whether "inverse" or "normal"; these terms refer to the location of sheep-ownership far more than that of sheep! The latter is in fact very abnormal in this area, while the former clearly rests on the distribution of piracy and malaria as much as that of grass.

The subordinate role of the pastoral sector

The real question is therefore; why keep sheep at all? Not for meat—the pig is a more efficient converter of plant matter into protein, which in S. W. Iberia or the mountains of Corsica was managed extensively through the "acorn-hog economy" (Parsons 1962; Silbert 1978). Not for wool, until the appearance of fine-woolled breeds, partly in the Roman, but more especially in the Early Medieval periods. Dairying is unlikely to have supported whole communities till the time of the market economy, in view of the extensive space required.

The large numbers of W. Mediterranean sheep maintained until the modern period seem rather to have functioned as producers of manure; the sheep is a relatively good converter of plant matter into dung, without which agriculture, even on the richer soils, would not have been possible. So far from replacing agriculture in areas of poor soils, the keeping of flocks of ovicaprines became even more involved in its survival (see note 2). Such a case was the Niolo, where Blanchard observed that the supposedly pastoral inhabitants kept as many ovicaprines as were necessary to fertilise their cereal plots (Blanchard 1914:235), though this imposed the removal of the flocks to the lowlands during the period of winter cold, since the alternative of stabling and fodder-production would have led to a vicious circle of means and ends. At a wider level, the traditional fallow rotations of much of the W. Mediterranean, including S. Sardinia, have been re-interpreted by Silbert (Silbert 1978). Where Le Lannou saw atavistic conflict between peasant and pastoralist, Silbert has suggested a long term adjustment of lowland regimes to the opportunity of acquiring the manure of upland flocks during their enforced sojourn, a practice effectively to the disadvantage of the latter. Similarly, the integration of the transhumant flocks of the Cevenol-Garrigue drailles into the farming systems of the villagers at either end of the transhumance, through nocturnal folding on fallow-fields, is suggestive of a similar concern (Brisebarre 1978; Sorre 1912). (I am indebted to J. Kolars' article (Kolars 1966) for this train of thought).

Where the northerner has assumed moisture to have been the key variable, and fallow patterns principally moisture-retention devices, the native Mediterranean tradition has emphasised the need for a supply of organic nutrients (e.g. in Bolens 1972).

If this was the case, then the variables relevant to sheep numbers were more numerous and complex than those traditionally assumed. A series of linked equilibria were involved: on the one hand, the maintenance of the cereal infield (the replacement of the nutrients extracted in the crop cycle); on the other, the ability of the grazed outfield to regenerate after depletion. The maintenance of an equilibrium between grassland (the crop of the outfield) and tree growth (the fallow, recovery phase) involves sheep densities of a narrow band of tolerance; too many and too few being equally disastrous (Baticle 1974; Metailie 1978) (See note 3).

The maintenance of flocks, even as a sub-system of an agricultural economy, is not necessarily a succession of identical annual cycles, nor are bottlenecks only found at the seasonal level. Grazing fluctuations exist at least over 4-yearly cycles, through which the flock would have to be adjusted by a number of tactics, of which transhumance would not necessarily be the most effective (Pernet and Lenclud 1977). Common sense dictates that a rigid adaptation to a permanent condition of variability would be inappropriate.

I therefore propose that transhumance be regarded as a tactical adaptation deployed in the peculiarly difficult circumstances of the medieval Mediterranean, rather than a long term strategy which prehistorians should anticipate finding in earlier contexts.

Palaeoeconomists have been guilty of the Panglossist belief that all is for the best in the best of all possible worlds; what exists, even persists, is not always "successful" beyond its own confines. There are two complementary remedies; awareness of alternatives (a greater familiarity with historical rural ethnography) and evaluation of effectiveness (a greater familiarity with the ecology of sheep and grass and the ergology of agriculture and pastoralism). To attempt to interrogate the limited sample of material culture available with the hazy notions of folk culture widespread at present is unlikely to be successful; the search for the oldest transhumance trail as unrewarding as that for the oldest matrilineal potsherd.

NOTES

(1) Flock size, product and the shepherd
The ratio of sheep to shepherd has been confused with that of sheep to consumer, which is the only figure relevant to an estimation of the importance of the pastoral sector.

Subsistence requirements: Dahl and Hjort calculate (Dahl and Hjort 1976: 220) that a nuclear family of six require over 200 goats or over 100 sheep to provide calories of 75 and 60, respectively, for proteins alone.

Dairy shepherding: Baticle observes (Baticle 1974) that a shepherd can cope with a maximum of 150 ewes milked twice daily during the lactation cycle— this is precisely the figure most commonly encountered in the historical literature.

Clearly, the problem is not one of manpower at the subsistence level; as in 19th century Bastelica, one family member could cope with the family sheep (Bigot, 1889); but at a stocking rate of 2-3 sheep per hectare, a lot of land would have to be maintained in grass, which through the same extensive means, could have supported cereals proper.

Wool, droving and the Mesta system
The key to understanding the Mesta or contemporary Dogana della Mena delle Pecore is the fact that far larger groups of sheep could be managed by fewer men since they were not milked. Large, homogenous areas of grazing were, therefore, required, but were easily acquired in the conditions of low population density and strong political backing, while the demand for wool from the developing textile industries of Italy and Flanders was constant. To interpret this economic specialisation which occurred simultaneously in many parts of Europe as the result of Mediterranean conditions seems unjustified; rather a sort of macro-von Thünen zoning was emerging (Bautier 1969). Baticle gives an average of 3,000 sheep for a flock involved in a wool producing system, managed by 3 men and their dogs.

Dogs and walls
Two under-researched dimensions of shepherding are the history of the sheep dog (De Planhol 1969) and the dry-stone wall, in view of the perceptive remark that "shepherds ..... replace what in other countries would be represented by some form of fence" (Roe, in Christodoulou, 1959:187).

The Corsican solution

Ravis-Giordani's work in the Niolo (Ravis-Giordani 1975) questions the assumption that the physical presence of the shepherd is required in mid-summer. The lactation cycle of the sheep ceases at this time and in any case can be manipulated through the timing of lambing: shepherding is therefore not immediately profitable. The Corsican shepherd maintains a high level of rusticity and territorial familiarity (imbestita) in his flock, so that he can abandon them for the summer and retrieve them, unscattered, in the autumn (see also Pernet and Lenclud, 1978 and Cristofini *et al.* 1978).

(2) Manure

A sheep can produce 500 kg, or ten times its own weight, per annum (Baticle 1974).

(3) Grassland maintenance

Older authors emphasise the role of the incendiary shepherd in degrading the forest heritage, producing entirely hypothetical but widely and uncritically reproduced schemes of degradation of forest into macchia, garrigue and grass. J. P. Metailie's observations in the Pyrenees (Metailie 1978) corrects this: (1) The best way to maintain high-quality pasture is to graze land with the correct density of sheep. (2) Fire does not reduce mature forest to grass but maintain an equilibrium between the herbaceous and ligneous species within the saltus; burning at a periodicity of seven years is adequate, and does not lead to any measurable degradation; in fact the location and timing of burning is very sophisticated. The effect is to maintain the necessary diversity at the floristic level within a small catchment, so that species with different maturation times are always present. This confirms Naveh's argument that prescribed burning is a valuable way of maintaining diversity and raising productivity (Naveh 1974). (3) The problem of grazing is created by the following dilemma; 85% of vegetative growth takes place in spring, the rest in the autumn, practically none in the other seasons. Therefore there are two, equally awkward solutions to stocking rates: (a) if the maximum number of sheep which can be kept alive in the worst periods is kept, by resorting to the consumption of leaves, twigs, acorns, dried grass, etc., then the pasture will be undergrazed, reverting to unpalatable and eventually inedible ligneous species. Fire can be employed to keep this in check, but the sheep tend to select the most palatable of the resultant species and gradually impoverish the floristic quality. (b) If, on the other hand, the grazing available in spring is consumed fully, then alternative sources of grazing beyond the spring catchment must be created, by transhumance or the raising of fodder crops (see also Long 1960).

Fallow, stubble and waste are nearly complementary, the crises of such an outfield-infield system arising in late spring and early autumn (Le Houerou 1977:258). It is at these times that the sheep-raising peasants of the Campidano ascend the Giara di Gesturi plateau (Le Lannou 1941; Bergeron 1967).

The Inra-Sei team in the Castagniccia have produced a typology and seriation of pastoral practices which should aid archaeologists in modelling the forms of early husbandry (Cristofini *et al.* 1978). This suggests that fodder crops need not necessarily be thought of as a recent and intensive development, especially in view of the cyclic crises in natural grazing availability.

(4) Altitude

Complementarity is a qualitative concept; quantitively there is no doubt of the overall disadvantages of high altitude settlement, as revealed in the decline of plant production. A mean temperature gradient of 0.5C/100 m (Le Houerou 1974:234) reduces the growing season by, on average, one week every 200 m (Baticle 1974:83). At 1,000 m the growing season is some 170 days; at 2,000 m only 95. Pasture yield decreases by a half between the "plain" and 1,200 m, and to only a fifth of the former at 2,000 m (Baticle 1974:84). There is, however, a qualitative improvement, and sanitary advantages.

References

Barker, G. W., 1975. "Prehistoric territories and economies in central Italy" in Palaeoeconomy, ed. E. S. Higgs. London: Cambridge University Press; 111-176.

Baticle, Y., 1974. L'Elevage Ovin dans les Pays Européens de la Méditerranée Occidentale. Dijon: Université de Dijon, Publication 47.

Bautier, R. H., 1969. "Les mutations agricoles des XIV et XV siècles." Bull. Philologique et Historique 1967:1-28.

Bergeron, R., 1967. "Problèmes de la vie pastorale en Sardaigne". Revue de Géographie de Lyon 42:311-328.

Bigot, M., 1889 (reprinted 1971). "Paysans Corses en communauté". Les Ouvriers des Deux Mondes (2nd series):18. (Bastia: U Muntese)

Blanchard, R., 1914. "Les genres de vie en Corse et leur évolution". Recueil des Travaux de l'Institut Alpin de Grenoble 2:187-238.

Bodemann, Y. M. and Allahar, A., 1980. "The micro-organisation of backwardness in central Sardinia". J. Peasant Studies 7:458-476.

Bolens, L., 1972. "Engrais et protection de la fertilité dans l'agronomie hispano-arabe, XI-XII siècles". Etudes Rurales 46:35-59

Brisebarre, A. M., 1978. Bergers des Cévennes. Paris: Berger-Levrault.

Carlotti, J., 1936. Monographie Agricole de la Corse. Ajaccio:D.D.A.

Carrier, E., 1932. Water and Grass. London: Christophers.

Christodoulou, D., 1959. The Evaluation of the Rural Land Use Pattern in Cyprus. Bude: Geographical Publications.

Cristofini, B., Deffontaines, J-P., Raichon, C. and de Verneuil, B., 1978. "Pratiques d'élevage en Castagniccia". Etudes Rurales 71-72:89-109.

Dahl, G. and Hjort, A., 1976. Having Herds. Stockholm: University of Stockholm Press.

Day, J., 1975. "Malthus dementi?" Annales-Economies, Sociétés, Civilisations 30:684-702.

De Planhol, X., 1969. "Le chien de berger". Bull. Ass. Géog. Français 370.

Ducos, P., 1977. "Les débuts de l'élevage du mouton au proche-orient". Ethnozootechnie 21:33-37

Jarman, M. and Webley, D., 1975. "Settlement and land-use in Capitanata, Italy" in Palaeoeconomy, ed. E.S. Higgs. London: Cambridge University Press; 177-221.

Kolars, J., 1966. "Locational aspects of cultural ecology: in the case of the goat in non-western agriculture". Geographical Review 56:577-584.

Le Houerou, H. N., 1974. "Fire and vegetation in the Mediterranean basin". Procs. 13th Annual Tall Timbers Fire Ecology Conference: 237-277.

Le Lannou, M., 1941 (reprinted 1971). Patres et Paysans de la Sardaigne. Tours: Arrault (Cagliari: La Zattera).

Long, G., 1960. "Les terrains de parcours de plaine, de plateau et de basse montagne dans la région méditerranéenne". Fourrages 4:99-127.

Lorblanchet, M., 1965. "Contribution à l'étude du peuplement des grands Causses". Bull. Soc. Préh. Franc. 43:667-712.

Metailie, J. P., 1976. "Les incendies pastoraux dans les Pyrenées centrales". Revue Géographique des Pyrénées et du Sud-Ouest 49:517-526.

Mori, A., 1975. Sardegna, Le Regioni d'Italia. Turin: U.T.E.T.

Naveh, Z., 1974. "The effects of fire in the Mediterranean region" in Fire and Ecosystems, eds. T. T. Kozlowski and C. E. Ahlgren. New York: Academic Press; 401-434.

Osuji, P., 1974. "The physiology of eating and the energy expenditure of the ruminant at pasture". J. Range Management 27:437-443.

Parsons, J. J., 1962. "The acorn-hog economy of the oak woodlands of southwestern Spain." Geographical Review 52:211-235.

Pernet, F. and Lenclud, G., 1977. Berger en Corse. Grenoble: Presses Universitaires de Grenoble.

Pernet, F. and Lenclud, G., 1978. "Resources du milieu, gestion du troupeau et évolution sociale: le cas de Corse". Etudes Rurales 71-72: 49-87.

Pfeffer, P., 1967. "Le mouflon de Corse." Mammalia 31 (supplement).

Pieretti, A., 1947. "Les formes d'exploitation et de peuplement d'une plaine méditerrannéenne". Bull. Soc. Géographique et Economique Coloniale 63:7-20.

Plesnik, P., 1971. "Différentiation verticale et horizontale des formations des Pyrénées". Revue Géographique des Pyrénées et du Sud-Ouest 42:31-47.

Plesnik, P., 1976. "The vegetation relations in Corsica". Univ. Comneniana Acta Fac. Rer. Nat., Ser. Geog-Phys. 2:3-38.

Pomponi, F., 1978. "Population, structures agraires et production en Corse (1770-1914)" in Pieve e Paesi, ed. G. Ravis-Giordani. Paris: C.N.R.S.; 271-364.

Pons, A., et al., 1979. Compte-Rendu de l'Activité Scientifique du Laboratoire Botanique et Pollen-analytique, Faculté de la Science et Technologie, St.-Jérôme. Aix-Marseille: E.R.A. 404 (1977-8)

Poplin, F., 1977. "Paléontologie du mouton". Ethnozootechnie 21:9-10.

Ravis-Giordani, G., 1975. "Le troupeau errant" in Ethnologie et Histoire, eds. A. Casanova and C. Jest. Paris: P.U.F.: 285-302.

Renucci, J., 1974. Corse Traditionelle et Corse Nouvelle. Lyon: Audin.

Silbert, A., 1978. Le Portugal Mediterranéen à la Fin de l'Ancien Régime. Lisbon: Instituto Nacional de Investigação Cientifica.

Sorre, M., 1912. "Etude sur la transhumance". Bull. Soc. Languedocienne Géographique 35:1-40

Soutou, A., 1959. "La draille d'Aubrac". Cahiers Ligures de Préhistoire et d'Archéologie 8:37-51.

6. ASPECTS OF VARIABILITY IN PALAEOECOLOGICAL STUDIES

Robert Foley

Introduction

This paper will examine the extent to which evolutionary and ecological theory may be usefully employed in the study of prehistoric human adaptation. Two main points will be made. Firstly, that many of the principles underlying various ideas in palaeoeconomy and cultural ecology are inconsistent with the ecological and evolutionary theory employed in other branches of the biological sciences. And secondly, that the way in which biological theory predicts and accounts for variability provides a powerful analytical device in the study of human palaeoecology.

The context of this paper is the general field of human palaeoecology — the study of the principles governing human adaptation in the past. More specifically, the comments made here are concerned with the validity of the theories that have been put forward to account for the development of prehistoric economy. First, variability in the biological sciences will be discussed. Second, palaeoeconomic and cultural ecological theory will be examined in terms of the way they articulate with biological notions of variability. In the light of the inadequacies of this articulation some alternative approaches to the explanation of variability in palaeoecological data will be suggested, and finally the implications for archaeology will be discussed.

The nature of variation

Variability may be defined as the tendency of phenomena within a class to differ one from another. The problem of variability underlies all science. Observed variation generates scientific problems, and the ability of a theory to account for observed variation is an important criterion for its acceptance. This is as true for prehistory as for any other scientific discipline. Early archaeologists were concerned with explaining the technological and stylistic variation in material culture items in terms of chronology. It is this, after all, that underlies the Three Age System. Alternative approaches to the problem of systematic variation in archaeological data have generated competing explanations. A classic example of explicit discussion of the problem of archaeological variability is the debate on the Mousterian. In this case the observed variation in lithic form and frequency were alternatively explained in terms of time (Mellars 1970), ethnicity (Bordes 1973) and function (Binford and Binford 1966).

If it is accepted that the function of a scientific theory is to account for variability in a set of data, then it follows that in the construction of any theory it is necessary to formulate explicitly the nature of the variation to which the data will conform. Only then will it be possible to evaluate the extent to which the theory successfully accounts for the data. Equally, criticism of a theory may then take the form either of showing that the data does not conform to predicted levels and structure of variation, or that the expectations were unrealistic.

Placing these principles in the context of prehistoric adaptation it may be suggested that: 1) we may treat palaeoecological theories in terms of (a) the way they predict variability in archaeological data, and (b) then account for the variation in observed archaeological data; and 2) we may consider the criticisms that have been levelled at palaeoecological explanations in the same light. These are important questions. In broad terms, palaeoecological and palaeoeconomic theorists have attempted to show that environments and resource availability significantly constrain human behaviour. Equally, critics have attempted to show that this is not the case. In simple terms much of the debate on causality of behaviour has been based on the assumption that a high level of intra-population variability reflects a large element of cultural choice, and is therefore incompatible with the operation of environmental and biological processes. There has thus been a tendency to accept high variability in behaviour as a sufficient refutation of environmental and biological determinism.

Within biology, variation in form underpins the theory of natural selection. In <u>Origin of Species</u> Darwin set out to account for observed variability of organic form within and between species. Darwin could do little to explain the origins or cause of that variability, lacking as he did knowledge of Mendelian genetics, but he showed the <u>maintenance</u> of biological variation to be integrally related with natural selection and the evolution of adaptive forms. Thus the occurrence of variation in the biological world is a central component of adaptive and evolutionary processes. From this we may perhaps develop three points that are relevant to the study of human palaeoecology. Firstly, some degree of variation is an expected phenomenon in biologically-based data. Thus it is not the presence of variation in data on prehistoric adaptation that requires explanation, but its structure and form. The variants that occur form the basis for evolution, change, and development in adaptation. Secondly, variability in adaptive form <u>within</u> a population is not only to be expected, but may itself be adaptive. And thirdly, it is important and necessary to recognise and distinguish between different levels of variation — i.e. within and between classes. For example, palaeoeconomists have tended to concentrate on inter-group variability and disregard or minimise the importance of intra-group variation. Conversely, the critics of ecologically-oriented approaches have stressed the importance of this intra-population variability. Any theory must account for both levels.

<u>Variability in palaeoecological studies</u>

In further examining this problem it is necessary to make explicit a distinction between the general field of human palaeoecology — i.e. the study of prehistoric human adaptation — and the specific theories developed by the late Eric Higgs and members of the British Academy Major Research Project into the Early History of Agriculture, and which are generally referred to as "palaeoeconomics". As this paper is concerned with the problems of articulating this set of theories to a larger body of theory, it is necessary to identify the main elements of the Higgs-Jarman model (Higgs and Jarman 1969; Higgs 1972; Higgs 1975).

1) that there is an underlying rationality to human behaviour.
2) that human economic behaviour is distance-dependent (based on least effort), as illustrated by the assumptions and methodology of site-catchment analysis.
3) that economic behaviour must be adaptive for it to be visible in the archaeological record; maladaptive strategies will not persist long enough to be recorded.
4) that the resources available in relation to population levels determine the strategy operated, and that under normal circumstances only one strategy will be appropriate in the long term.
5) that over time a close level of symbiotic inter-action and inter-dependence based on mutual advantage will develop between a human population and its resources.
6) that this inter-dependence is the basis of domestication, placing the problems of the origins of agriculture into a broader spatial and temporal context than was previously considered necessary.

As the Higgs-Jarman model was developed in a biological context it is reasonable to examine the extent to which the assumptions underlying it conform to biological theory. In particular, does the Higgs-Jarman model predict the same structure of variability as the evolutionary and ecological theory from which it is ultimately derived?

Firstly, there is an assumption that groups as a whole exist in a relationship with their resources, from which it would appear that groups adapt, rather than individuals. It is this assumption that leads to statements in cultural ecology as "the Hadza rely mainly on wild vegetable matter for their food" (Woodburn 1968: 51), and similar comments with regard to archaeological units. The usefulness of such summary statements is not disputed, but their simplifying element is not wholly beneficial. The behaviour of a population is the sum of the behaviour of the individuals within that population, and that behaviour will be variable. Thus the methodological propensity to reduce composite subsistence strategies to a modal form disguises the underlying variability. In the analysis of adaptive strategy it is necessary to break down the population-resource relationship into its component parts. These component parts are the individuals or groups of individuals that actually carry out the subsistence activities; their strategies will inevitably vary because of the inherently non-uniform distribution of resources and the inequality of settlement locations in relation to those resources. Non-uniform spatial patterning of resource availability results in intra-population variability in subsistence strategy. This variability cannot simply be subsumed within the modal strategy for the group as a whole. In summary, the different starting points of individuals — spatial, social and physiological — leads them to adopt variable strategies for survival. The interaction of these will determine rates of success and rates of change. More importantly, though, in the context of this paper, it cannot be assumed that ecologically or environmentally determined behaviour will be uniform. Intra-population variability in subsistence strategy is as consistent with ecological theory as it is with cultural idiosyncracy.

A second underlying assumption that is often held in work on man-environment relationships is that where ecological processes are operating a stable relationship will be the outcome. Certainly much work in theoretical ecology has been devoted to an understanding of ecological stability. However, while ecological theory may predict in some cases (such as mature or complex ecosystems and even-numbered predator-prey systems) a tendency towards stability, this cannot be extended to an asumption that ecological systems are stable. Two important factors are involved here. Firstly, simple environmental, and hence resource, stability cannot be assumed given the increasing amount of evidence showing climatic change on scales of 10^1 to 10^6 years (Goudie 1977). Thus diachronic variability may be expected even if the human population is attempting to achieve stability. And secondly if, as was argued above, a group's subsistence strategy is the composite sum of individual and sub-group strategies, then there is no single strategy in relation to a single set of resources, but a cluster of separate although related strategies. It may reasonably be inferred that stability is less likely to occur in this context. Recent work by theoretical ecologists is relevant here. For example, the development of the concept of the Evolutionarily Stable Strategy by Maynard-Smith (1976) indicates that the potential of an animal's adaptive strategy must be assessed in the context of alternative, contiguous and competing strategies, and that under some conditions stability may never occur. This explanation has recently been put forward by Krebs et al.(1978), to account for the high oscillations in some small mammal populations in northern Europe and Canada. Such a principle may be extended to human behavioural ecology, and oscillating and conflicting subsistence strategies may be the outcome of inherent instability. Thus a population under the control of ecological processes need not necessarily attain stability; higher rates of diachronic variability in subsistence strategy may perhaps have occurred than has previously been expected.

The third theme that is frequently to be found in analyses of the relationship between man and his resources may be derived from the above discussion of stability. Stability implies a balance between resource use and resource availability in such a way that the resource base is not impaired. Much of the work in both palaeoecology and cultural ecology has been devoted to showing that human populations conserve the resources on which they depend (e.g. Lee 1968; Rappaport 1968). The results of various ethnographic works have been extended to a commonly held assumption that prehistoric man employed subsistence strategies that conserved the resource base. The theoretical principles for this assumption are derived from Wynne-Edwards' (1962) theory of group selection and population regulation by social behaviour. It is pertinent to note, however, that in the considerable literature on the question of population control in animals (see Sinclair 1973 for a review of this subject) that Wynne-Edwards' views represent one extreme, and that the general consensus among most ecologists is that density-dependent mechanisms, based on individual levels of selection, are a more appropriate model. This has been further enhanced by recent work in evolutionary theory (Wilson 1975; Dawkins 1976), and in a recent paper (1978:19) Wynne-Edwards himself admits that he cannot devise a biological mechanism to account for group selection. Thus the principles of population regulation employed by human ecologists are now markedly divergent from those used in other branches of ecology. It is far from clear the extent to which this is justified for prehistoric man, and it would seem reasonable to suggest that, lacking evidence to the contrary, human ecologists should not expect resource conservation as a product of a successful adaptation. The consequences of this would be the prediction of increased variability in resource exploitation patterns by prehistoric man.

The main points of the arguments presented here may be summarised as follows: palaeoecological studies in general, and palaeoeconomic work in particular, have been based on assumptions that minimise expectations of intra-population variability; it has been shown here that these assumptions are at variance with basic ecological principles. As a result palaeoecological analyses have been unable to account for high levels of intra-population variability, leaving the validity of hypotheses of ecological causality in question. However, it is suggested that ecological principles are in accord with higher levels of variability. It is worthwhile remembering that it is the continued occurrence of variation in living organisms that forms the basis for the theory that must underlie all ecology- Darwinian natural selection.

Alternative models for behavioural ecology

How can these considerations be used to set up alternative expectations for prehistoric human adaptation, based on sound ecological and evolutionary principles? The goal towards which we should be moving is the development of a theory of behavioural ecology. Hominids, under selective pressures, will adapt to local conditions through a variety of means. These may be physiological or behavioural, although it is increasingly clear that such a distinction is far from precise. However, with regard to the differences in adaptation within the hominid population it is obvious that the primary mode of adaptation is behavioural. Consequently, behavioural ecology is the correct framework for the analysis of human adaptation. This means that we are investigating both the way in which behavioural flexibility is employed as a means of ecological adaptation and also the way in which ecological factors affect human behaviour.

It has been argued here that unrealistic expectations of variability in biological systems employed in palaeoecological analysis has led to considerable criticism. The same concept of variability may also be used to erect an alternative framework. Several biological uses of the principle of variability may be suggested:

1) Polytypic species: the human species is generally described as polytypic — i.e. it is highly variable in morphology and behaviour. This reflects the enormous geographical range of the species, the diversity of habitats occupied, and adaptive strategies pursued. Thus high variability is to be expected. What is needed, however, are models describing expected levels of inter-population variability for complex, wide-ranging species against which we can measure observed variation.

2) Selective pressure: species exhibiting little variation are usually assumed to be under stringent selective pressure — i.e. variants on the normal morphs are highly disadvantageous. Conversely high variability may be interpreted as being a reflection of relaxed selective pressures. Thus in pursuing the problem of ecological causality in human behaviour degrees of intra-population variability may be employed as a measure of the constraints operating on them.

3) Variability and geographical range: Mayr (1963) has argued that populations in the centre of a species range will be more variable than those on the periphery, where selective pressures will by definition be more rigourous. Thorne (in press) has persuasively argued that this principle applied to hominid evolution during the Pleistocene. Such a model may also be applied to the degrees of variation in behavioural and adaptive aspects of human palaeoecology.

4) Spatial uniformity: few environments are uniform, and most resources tend to be unevenly distributed across a landscape. In many ways it is this non-uniformity that provides the ecological basis for adaptive variability. The point to stress is that the variability that ensues from the non-uniform destribution of resources will be reflected in the structure of the adaptive strategy. Consequently palaeoecological data must be scanned for the extent to which they reflect degrees of clustering, dispersal and uneven availability (both temporally and spatially) of resources. In this context it would be inappropriate to reduce the variability in human behaviour to a central mode, for it represents sub-partitioning of the niche occupied by a human population, and competition for the optimal points within a complex niche.

5) Competition: it should be remembered that underlying all discussions of variability and natural selection in adaptation the mechanism involved must be competition. Competition occurs at many levels (inter-specific, intra-specific, etc.), but virtually no attention has been paid in studies of human adaptation to the role of competition between individuals and sub-populations. It is this competition, its intensity and structure, that must form the basis of any variability that occurs. Thus it is necessary to develop models of the way in which intra-group competition will inhibit or encourage variation in subsistence strategy.

6) Strategy: the term is a useful concept in the analysis of adaptive activities. A strategy is a programme of moves selected from a pool of possible moves, under certain circumstances (see Diamond 1977 for a full discussion). If, as has been suggested here, a population does not have a single strategy in relation to its resources, but rather that individuals or sub-populations have available to them a series of possible relationships circumscribed by availability and competitive ability, then the resulting variation may best be studied as a set of competing and interacting strategies. This leads into the field of game theory — i.e. defining the alternatives available to the player, ascribing pay-offs for particular moves, and calculating the risks, returns, and penalties of the available strategies in the context of the strategies pursued by other players. In ecological terms this would require defining the resources available, the potential strategies of exploitation, and analysing them in the context of non-uniform resource distribution, competition, and interaction between strategies. Following this procedure human palaeoecologists could begin to use the Evolutionarily Stable Strategy (ESS) based on a game-theoretical methodology (Maynard-Smith 1976).

7) Balanced Polyethism: another suitable model for analysing intra-population variability is that of balanced polyethism. Derived from the principle of polymorphism — the occurrence of two or more genotypes within a population — polyethism refers to the occurrence of two or more behavioural strategies within a population (Wilson 1975). As with polymorphism, these may or may not be balanced — i.e. at a stable frequency. The point is that neither one nor other of the behaviours gives an overall advantage — its advantage is dependent upon its frequency. For example, growing millet may only be advantageous in the context of the majority of the farmers growing maize; the advantage given to the minority of farmers growing millet will gradually cause their numbers to increase, but as they increase the advantages of growing millet will decrease. Eventually either a balance will be achieved, or alternatively the two behavioural strategies may oscillate between the extremes. The point is that there is no single Evolutionarily Stable Strategy; success is dependent upon frequency. This model would seem to have considerable potential for the study of human palaeoecology where levels of intra-population variability may be high.

Archaeological and Methodological Implications

Having examined the theoretical constructs that may be derived from the ecological and evolutionary principles of biological variation, it emerges that variability is a normal expectation of organic systems at several levels, and that variability is itself adaptive. Such a proposition will necessarily have implications for archaeological methodology.

1) Ecological theory does not predict uniformity; ecological explanations of prehistoric patterns have often been criticised because such patterns exhibit high variability. It has been suggested here that there is no a priori reason why this should not be the case. At the simplest, even where an environment gives an advantage to one strategy, it is unlikely that such a strategy would account for the full range of resources. Consequently subsidiary strategies may occur. Archaeologists must explore the possibilities of sympatric and inter-related resource exploitation strategies.

2) Following from this, it is unlikely that a single adaptive strategy is the only one appropriate in an area, particularly where productivity is high. This implies that palaeoeconomists have been too rigidly deterministic in their models.

3) Equally, considerable temporal and spatial variability may be expected in any set of regional archaeological data. To interpret it archaeologists must make use of more formal predictive models to distinguish between variability that is the product of "noise" such as sampling or preservation factors, and ecological variability.

4) On theoretical grounds it is clear that small scale, repetitive mechanisms are the primary factors in adaptation. Broad, long-term trends may be perceived, but no ecological mechanism of an equivalent scale may be invoked as an explanatory device. From an archaeological point of view this is unfortunate, as the nature of archaeological data inhibits the investigation of the small scale. In particular, it has been suggested that

contemporaneous variants of adaptive strategies may well have been pursued by prehistoric man; archaeologists may not be able to define or identify contemporanity on a fine enough scale to test this proposition.

Conclusions

In this paper I have tried to show that any development in the study of human palaeoecology will depend upon the construction of models describing the way in which archaeological data may be expected to vary if ecological processes are operating. The main purpose has been to argue for a closer and more systematic investigation of the levels and structures of variability in prehistoric data. A further point that has been established, and is of more direct application in the study of human behaviour in prehistory, is that adaptive strategies will seldom be optimal, either because external conditions are not stable, or else because no single adaptive strategy provides an overall selective advantage. Adaptation will necessarily often involve a compromise between conflicting selective pressures.

References

Binford, L. R. and S. R., 1966. " A preliminary analysis of functional variability in the Mousterian of Levallois facies". Amer. Anth. 68: 238-295.

Bordes, F., 1973. "On the chronology and contemporaneity of different palaeolithic cultures in France" in The Explanation of Culture Change, ed. A. C. Renfrew. London: Duckworth; 217-226.

Dawkins, R., 1976. The Selfish Gene. London: Oxford University Press.

Diamond, J. M., 1977. "Distributional strategies" in Sunda and Sahul, eds. H. Allen, J. Golson and R. Jones. London: Academic Press; 295-315.

Goudie, A., 1977. Environmental Change. Oxford: Clarendon Press.

Higgs, E. S. (ed.), 1972. Papers in Economic Prehistory. London: Cambridge University Press.

Higgs, E. S. (ed.), 1975. Palaeoeconomy. London: Cambridge University Press.

Higgs, E. S. and Jarman, M. R., 1969. "The origins of agriculture: a reconsideration". Antiquity 43: 31-41.

Krebs, C. J., Redfield, J. A. and Taitt, M. J., 1978. "A pulsed-removal experiment on the vole Microtus townsendi". Can. J. Zool. 56: 2253-2262.

Lee, R. B., 1968. "What hunters do for a living, or how to make out on scarce resources" in Man the Hunter, eds. R. B. Lee and I. DeVore. Chicago: Aldine; 30-48.

Maynard-Smith, J., 1976. "Evolution and the Theory of Games". Amer. Scient. 64: 41-45.

Mayr, E., 1963. Animal Species and Evolution. Cambridge, Mass.: Harvard University Press.

Mellars, P., 1970. "Some comments on the notion of functional variability in stone tool assemblages". World Arch. 2: 74-89.

Rappaport, R., 1968. Pigs for the Ancestors. New Haven: Yale University Press.

Sinclair, A. R. E., 1973. "Regulation and population models for a tropical ruminant". E. Afr. Wildl. J. 11: 306-316.

Thorne, A. G., (in press). "The centre and the edge: the significance of Australasian hominids to African palaeoanthropology". Proceedings of the VIII Pan-African Congress of Prehistory and Quaternary Studies (Nairobi 1977).

Wilson, E. O., 1975. Sociobiology: a New Synthesis. Cambridge, Mass.: Harvard University Press.

Woodburn, J., 1968. "An introduction to Hadza ecology" in Man the Hunter, eds. R. B. Lee and I. DeVore. Chicago: Aldine; 49-55.

Wynne-Edwards, V. C., 1962. Animal Dispersion in Relation to Social Behaviour. Edinburgh: Oliver and Boyd.

Wynne-Edwards, V. C., 1978. "Intrinsic population control: an introduction" in Population Control by Social Behaviour, eds. F. J. Ebling and D. M. Stoddart. Symposia of the Institute of Biology 23. London: Institute of Biology; 1-22.

7. ARCHAEOLOGICAL REMARKS ON A REVISED THEORY OF SOCIAL EVOLUTION

Bernd-Rüdiger Goetzee and Volker von Thienen

Preface

The papers so far presented have focused on palaeoeconomic and palaeoecological approaches to the study of economic behaviour and human evolution. By way of contrast, we will deal here with a sociological model of economy and evolution. A consideration of Habermas' 'revised' theory of social evolution is useful in two respects: firstly, it indicates the extent of the rift between ecological and social perspectives on the same basic problems; secondly, it illustrates the fundamental disagreement, running through sociological theory, about the role of material and ideological aspects of behaviour in social evolution. This paper will examine the problems of relating Habermas' evolutionary model to archaeological data, and of verifying or falsifying it as a theory. The value of such a theory to economic archaeology will be considered.

Introduction

The history of science has taught us that sociology, archaeology and anthropology formerly undertook their researches independently of each other. Each subject was assigned to its own limited area in the wide field of cultural problems. For example, archaeologists had to answer the question: "What kind of funny find is this and how old is it?", while sociologists had to concentrate on the problems of our present societies. However, recognising that this approach would lead to a dead end, people turned to an explicitly interdisciplinary approach several years ago. Examples include the experiments of the New Archaeology (Bayard 1978). But now it is not only archaeologists who are examining related, and even unrelated, disciplines for possible new insights.

The attempt to relate prehistory to a universal historical context is as old as the research in these areas itself. The popularity of such attitudes is due to a certain extent, to a bourgeois wish to prove its own progess. The concept of prehistoric archaeology has not been untouched by the different uses made of it by diverse philosophies of history and ideologies. In Germany, at least, this science is primarily committed to gathering empirical data—not only because research policy demands it. This situation was created by the shock of having results prescribed administratively by all-encompassing ideologies, as is the case today in the GDR, where prehistoric research is submitted to a certain kind of orthodox historical materialism. Another example is the racist research conducted under the Nazi regime. There are, however, dangers in pursuing primarily analytical research. While the bare collection of facts and figures can degenerate into a kind of "l'art pour l'art", ignored by the public, the neglect of theories developed in related social sciences can rob the field of useful inputs.

In the following pages, discussion will focus on a new theory of social evolution. This theory aspires to describing a logic of development inherent in all human history.

Habermas and "Towards a reconstruction of historical materialism"

The key proponent of this new theory of evolution is Jürgen Habermas, author of "Towards a reconstruction of historical materialism" (1975; cf. 1976 and Ignatow 1977). He develops a new approach with respect to scientific intention and causal connection, which differs from that expounded in the theses of classical historical materialism (cf. Jäggi and Honneth 1977).

A significant aspect of Habermas' deliberations is his renunciation of the teleological perspective. He recognises that any postulated logical progress within institutional systems, world-views and moral beliefs admits no combinations about possible social development in the future. He does not even presuppose the existence of an historical subject which, like Marx' working class, enacts history (cf. Fleischer 1970).

Habermas suggests that the human race discovers itself, and thereby liberates itself from the inner and outer compulsion of tradition, when it becomes aware of its own history. In this sense, society can begin to affect its own evolution. He rejects the idea of classical historical materialism that evolution is based "in the final analysis" — as Engels says — on the development of productive facilities, i.e. technology and technological know-how. Habermas makes a distinction between skilfulness and social organisation of work, which Marx saw as a dialectical unit called "praxis". In contrast to Marx and Engels, he argues that social systems of belief and morality enter social orgnaisation and rule the extent and direction of the development of innovative productive facilities. The consequences for a social-scientific reconstruction of history are obvious. If productive facilities do not remain the only driving force behind human evolution, this evolution cannot be described satisfactorily by the parameters of classical historical materialism (cf. Marcuse and Habermas 1978).

Habermas' evolutionary sequence, based on three postulated steps of progress in social systems of communication, morality and law, bears some resemblance to the model of ontogenesis as constructed by genetic structuralists. These three evolutionary steps are supposed to characterise certain societies and to establish the scope within which evolution is possible.

While pre-neolithic folk had a "symbolic interaction system" with a "preconventional differentiation of level between action and norm", Habermas postulates that neolithic societies were directed by "conventional interaction systems" with a "conventional differentiation of level between action and norm', a "mythical world-view still enmeshed in the system of action" and a preconventional "resolution of conflicts". Early civilisation should differ from neolithic societies by "a differentiated mythical world-view which can assume functions for political authorities" and a resolution of conflicts, which is "dependent on the ruler" (1975: 295).

Obviously this theory of evolution, with its abstract level of arguing, is difficult to translate even into macrosociological relations, the more so since those relations are not clear at all. The hypothetical character of this theory becomes particularly evident when Habermas discusses archaeological phenomena. Key elements of his model are derived primarily from the models of prehistory and early history developed by K. Eder (Eder 1973, 1976, 1977).

Eder assumes the existence of "archaic social structures, characterised by equality of 'rights'" (1973: 8ff., 18, unauthorized translation), behind which modestly hides an early form of communism. Considering the likely nature of prehistoric social organisation, economy and trade, Eder idealises ancient times by proposing the fiction that people aimed at a strategy of "minimising work efforts". It is not important for our discussion to examine the extent to which this self-defined Marxist hypothesis relates to the original theoretical framework developed by Marx. Habermas, in any case, accepts Eder's historical model, which results in a critical comparison of "successful" steps of evolution (— in Eder's terms —) and "evolutionary dead ends" (cf. Eder 1976). The only type of development he considers successful is that which leads to a bourgeois capitalist society. Other types of society — e.g. matriarchal systems, chiefdoms, or asiatic variants — are disqualified as faults of progress.

While Eder takes a relatively uncomplicated and generous attitude towards interpreting rather ambivalent empirical data, Habermas refers to this interpretation but suspends his periodical systems of communication and social interaction somewhere above history without defining its relationship. Nevertheless he states that with the origin of homo sapiens a so-called "organic-cultural mixture of evolution" had been replaced by a "social evolution". After this, exogamy, "on which the socialisation of man is based", is supposed to have resulted in "a broad .... dispersion and mingling of genetic substance" (Habermas 1976: 147, unauthorized translation). The intention of this strange construction is clear. The strength of his argument for a social evolution ordered according to structures of consciousness would be seriously impaired by the admission of a further biological evolution in prehistory and early history. In fact, however, such an interpretation of genesis presumes the existence of a "First Man".

Already the Australanthropos of 2.6 million years ago is qualified as a "human being" by recognising the Pebble Cultures and the Osteodontoceratic culture as evidence of a 'noosphere' (cf. Gerhardt 1975: 123ff.; Leakey and Isaac 1978, esp. 84ff.). This argument is based on the fact that "man as he is known today disappears from the strata somewhere between 10,000 and 50,000 years ago". One is therefore able to detect the biological alterations of HUMAN beings ever further in the past. There is no indication that the biological alteration of man had stopped anywhere — and certainly not in arguments of a biologically relatively tiny span of 50,000 years. The mechanism of natural evolution cannot be plausibly considered as terminated simply because no cause is recognisable at the time. On the other hand, with respect to the socialisation processes of early men based on exogamy, all that can be said today is that his mating behaviour has escaped the archaeologist's spade till now.

Evidently such vague sketches of early man's progess reflect a certain lack of explanatory power with respect to prehistoric phenomena. Habermas indicates his awareness of this gap when he confesses to have no way of arranging the thoughts and actions of prehistoric people according to evolutionary steps of consciousness. This happens mainly because Habermas confidently relies on the products of a scientific strategy born of certain ideas about evolution itself — a strategy also shared by archaeology. Symptomatically, archaeology at its beginning started with the system of three periods which Thomsen and Danneil published in 1836, inspired by a rough classification of ancient material into stone, bronze, and iron — or early, middle, and late periods. This system of obligatory chronological currencies has survived, in increasingly complicated forms, to the present (Montelius 1885, 1900, 1903, 1917; Müller-Karpe 1974, 1975; Reinecke 1911). In a permanent vicious circle this system has proved itself by presupposing evolution to present the idea of cultural progess. After all, prehistory nowadays succeeds in filling up the apparent vacuum of unattested times with dates by new dating methods (cf. Jaguttis-Emden 1977). This consolidating network of dates is going to open, and even partially contradict, inflexible periodical systems. This is particularly true where they intend to mark material or conceptual indicators of progess.

To return to Habermas: his theory of evolution fails to analyse the structure of intellectual effort and social formations such as those represented by palaeolithic art. Already in 1929 E. Dennert had compared palaeolithic paintings with drawings of recent people as children, so called primitives, and European adults, too. Even the untrained eye distinguishes the ancient artisan to be more skilled than the uneducated individual of today. Therefore even Dennert had to admit that "early man, as far as available facts permit any conclusion, was a fully qualified human being with respect to his intellectual development" (1929: 477, unauthorized translation). In an evolutionary perspective it is surprising indeed to note that the various examples of palaeolithic art simply invite comparisons with modern art (cf. Giedion 1962).

But if we consider the palaeolithic artisan to be an educated specialist, then in terms of historical materialism this means that there had been a society with a producing base and a superstructure at least partially liberated from food production in the glacial period (cf. Adorno 1970; Engelhardt 1978). Of course the quantity and quality of the acquired archaeological finds are limited. This borders the area within which science tries to obtain insights into social complexity and cultural diversification by means of new methods.

Doubtless the people who decorated the franco-cantabric caves lived in a pre-neolithic world. Obviously these complicated rock-paintings do not cover the first of Habermas' steps of progess, but the next or even the third. The consequence is that the first step is suspended in a dark space of speculation about the oldest unexplored — if not unexplorable — cultures before the early art. Habermas talks of a "logical scope of possible structural changes which appeared parallel to the natural innovation of a linguistically produced intersubjectivity at the threshold to a socio-cultural way of life" (cf. Habermas 1976: 248). There remains the problem of whether this thesis becomes meaningless if one assumes that these structural changes were extensively carried out at a much earlier date than that accepted by the evolutionary theory. It appears that this evolutionary theory equates — not quite without subjectivity in our view — a technological primitiveness with an intellectual one.

It is not surprising that the expression "neolithic revolution" — introduced by V. G. Childe (1973, 1975) — was received without criticism in the theory of Habermas and Eder: it sounds too good in relation to a theory which pretends to represent classical historical materialism. The term "neolithic revolution" is of little help even in illustrating phenomena of a "discrete sequence" of production procedures. These procedures have articulated themselves in a view fascinated by cultural steps as signals of a permanent prehistoric and historical revolution. Therefore in this sense other great categories could be called: 'The metallic revolution', 'the hill-fort revolution', 'the feudal revolution', 'the great soviet October revolution,', or — originally — 'the osteodontoceratic revolution'.

It would be of secondary importance to quarrel about this matter, if Habermas and Eder had not given this expression a mystical element, when they state that "since the 'neolithic revolution' great technological investions did not introduce but only accompanied new eras" (Habermas 1976: 164, unauthorized translation). This statement should simply be contradicted. On the one hand, the innovations of the so-called neolithic period did not signify a new epoch in that stylized manner. On the other hand, certain single technological inventions <u>have</u> been as important as the production facilities by which we used to define ancient societies. Two arguments may serve to explain this view:

1) People deciding to alter slowly their mode of acquisition from marauding to cultivation and/or from hunting wild animals to herding learned to live by experimenting with their environment. But they had no reason to alter their behaviour in communication, interaction, social distribution and redistribution of products (<u>cf.</u> Leone 1968).

2) Without the invention of stirrups the iron-clanking knights of the occident, and the related history and social structure would never have developed.

Such theories are not intended to ignore facts, but to relativate them. The transition from looking where the crops had grown so well last year to sowing grains did not necessarily bring about significant changes in consciousness. There is no archaeological basis for burdening this innocent first step with complicated theories.

So the term "neolithic" — used as a <u>terminus technicus</u> — in the historical sense dissolves into what it had previously assigned to science: a series of chronological and geographical facts and phenomena. If it is correct that an increasing data base "softens" periodical systems fixed by standards of technological and aesthetic skilfulness, there must be consequences for a description of sequential structures of consciousness. Such a system loses its explanatory value, if the achieved evolutionary steps can hardly or never be identified in "pure" form. They could still serve as an experimental model of explanation, but it would also be necessary to seek a higher level of explanation, capable of accounting for the unexplained residue from such a model.

Perhaps the next question is to what extent one is dealing with relativism when constructing a theory about history without attempting to discover the hidden elements of its development. Surely, Habermas knows that the present as we know it was not inevitable. The role of chance in setting processes of development into motion is hidden in the categories of the "influencing factors" (Randbedingungen).[1] Finally, what is the purpose of a theory of evolution or historical materialism, even as a reconstruction? It would be equally possible, for instance, to imagine a model of history that represents a complete antithesis to this schema. Such an approach has been one of the great themes of Critical Sociology (cf. Scott 1978).

Almost every sociologically relevant insight Habermas and Eder use is developed with the aid of ethnological structuralist science. Historical data become implanted like dots into a network of explanations elaborated by Lévi-Strauss, Godelier, Piaget, Kohlberg and, finally, Marx. This abstraction of social theories contains certain dangers. Firstly, systems-theoretical and structuralist hypotheses lack the necessary material with which to analyse prehistoric societies. The preferred approach is then to observe existing or recently disappeared ethnic groups with very different ways of life. Many prehistorians are concerned about these methods, because they know of similar attempts from their own scientific history and the dubiousness of any conditionally acceptable results. Dealing with prehistoric matters is bound and indebted to the facilities of prehistoric research and must not involve an impatient sifting of recent historical material.[2] Secondly, there are the problems connected with the appropriation of a scientific language originally developed for use in other kinds of research. Of course there has existed in the past an "archaic society" with its "systemic crises" and "leadership problems", as Habermas suggests. However, language is capable of proving everything and its opposite: although such terms may be universally applied, they do not necessarily have the same meaning in different contexts.[3]

The search for unmistakable individual structures of consciousness which limit possible lines of historical development can be understood as a sociological answer to the problem of objectivism in historical theory. Habermas no longer has any illusion that it could be possible to discover natural laws in the history of human species. Others in the historical and social sciences still may hope that the results of their research could be laws like those of "nomothetic" sciences. Against the background of current epistemological discussion. Habermas knows that history has no immutable laws other than banal ones. Nevertheless, the sociological endeavour to comprehend history with the parameters of systems theory or structuralism is an attempt to serve objectivism, even if there are considerable differences in detail. The level of abstraction on which Habermas places his structures of consciousness indicates the difficulties of trying to objectivise historical sciences.

Anyhow, in spite of the confusion in which archaeologists are left by the arguments of Habermas and Eder, they should use these hypotheses to continue critical discussion. Perhaps some first tentative suggestions are permitted.

It would be worthwhile to consider Habermas' theory in the light of the problem of whether and how evolutionary models are to be proven or falsified by archaeological reality. Of course, nearly all prehistoric analysis of cultural changes is interpreted in terms of the basic ideas of evolution. Change is simply characterised as development and its reverse. Today one cannot deny the impression that there might be something wrong with this simple schema. Again two brief examples should demonstrate that the theory of evolution is evidently imperfect standing by itself. One should conduct a morphognostic comparison[4] of early middle bronze age pottery of Hungary[5] with one classified to the final bronze age of southwest Germany[6] and the pottery of the Early Iron Age in the southern parts of France.[7] The pottery shapes are related to the well-known funeral rites. It is to be expected that by a Single Link Cluster Analysis[8] the three mentioned varieties have more in common with each other than with nearly any other culture. The question arises as to the reason for this similarity. Is it caused by those "influencing factors" mentioned above or did this pottery together with its funeral rites result inevitably from original shapes and customs? The first solution can be excluded mathematically, the latter by trivial archaeological arguments. The assumption that the producers of such easily comparable complexes can be connected through time and space might be perhaps more attractive. The second example reiterates this point. J. Boardman (1971: 121ff.) compares the thoreutic representations of early Etruscan Situla art (Lucke and Frey 1962) with those of orientalizing Greek bronze belts. Encouraged by this it is possible to draw attention to even more distant parallels. M. Böse has published old Babylonian consecration plates, probably produced in the middle of the third millenium (1971). Even at a glance one can recognise the great similarity between those complicated scenes across 2000 miles and 2000 years. Whatever the reason may be, the nearly identical arrangements cannot be understood other than by supposing that somewhere and somehow there must be a connection between the intentional backgrounds. A mechanistic interpretation by a pure theory of evolution, however, seems to fail in confrontation with this kind of fact. We cannot go into the unfortunate discussion about diffusionism and evolutionism here. But many facts indicate that both theories remain imperfect without each other and are not completed by others. So it seems that discussion starves in a dead end, respecting only certain points of view among the yet unknown number of factors responsible for historical processes and their results. To provoke constructive dialogue, let's gather all those diverging expressions concerned with processing history — evolution, diffusion, convergence, and so on. Why not — to gain a new perspective of objectivity — refer to past and future change by the Greek term Metaplasis — as an expression of continuous alteration?

Footnotes

1. In sociological literature the German term "Randbedingungen" is also translated as " marginal conditions".

2. We are grateful to E. Sangmeister for discussing basic ideas in his lectures. See Sangmeister 1967.

3. We cannot deal here with the important question of whether categories such as "sense", "legitimation", or "systems of identification which guarantee identity" play a prominent role in world history as Habermas supposes. It is obvious that the principles underlying this theory of evolution are not sufficient for grasping history in its tremendous diversity. Cf. Nelson 1977: xiv; Döbert 1977: 528ff.

4. The term "morphognostic" is borrowed from K. Gerhardt.

5. E.g. Bóna 1975: Plate 7.14.

6. Kimmig 1940: e.g. Plate 12, A2.

7. Guilaine (ed.), 1976: 468, Fig. 6.8.

8. Concerning this problem see Gebühr and Kunow 1976.

References

Adorno, T. W., 1970. Negative Dialektik. Frankfurt/Main: Suhrkamp.

Bayard, D., 1978. "15 Jahre 'New Archaeology', eine kritische Ubersicht." Saeculum 29: 69-106.

Böse, J., 1971. Altmesopotamische Weihplatten, Eine Sumerische Denkmalsgattung des 3. Jahrtausends vor Christ. Untersuchungen zur Assyriologie und zur vorderasiatischen Archäologie 6. New York: De Gruyter.

Boardman, J., 1971. " A southern view of situal art" in The European Community in Later Prehistory, eds. J. Boardman, M. A. Brown and T. G. E. Powell. London: Routledge and Kegan Paul; 121-140.

Bóna, I., 1975. Die Mittlere Bronzezeit Ungarns und ihre Südöstlichen Beziehungen. Budapest: Akad. Kiadó.

Childe, V. G., 1973. " Die neolithische Revolution" in Die Entstehung von Klassengesellschaften, ed. K. Eder. Frankfurt/Main: Suhrkamp; 176-185.

Childe, V. G., 1975. Soziale Evolution. Frankfurt/Main: Suhrkamp.

Danneil, J. F., 1836. "Generalbericht über die Ausgrabungen in der Umgegend von Salzwedel" in Neuen Mitteilungen aus dem Gebiet Historisch-Antiquarischer Forschungen, ed. K. E. Förstemann. Halle: Thüringisch-Sächsischer Gesamtverein für Erdkunde.

Dennert, E., 1929. Das Geistige Erwachen des Urmenschen. Weimar: Verlag für Urgeschichte und Menschheitsforschung G.m.b.H.

Döbert, R., 1977. " Methodologische und forschungsstrategische Implikationen von evolutionstheoretischen Stadienmodellen" in Theorien des Historischen Materialismus, eds. U. Jäggi and A. Honneth. Frankfurt/Main: Suhrkamp; 524.

Eder, K. (ed.), 1973. Die Enstehung von Klassengesellschaften. Frankfurt/ Main: Suhrkamp.

Eder, K., 1976. Die Entstehung Staatlich Organisierter Gesellschaften, Ein Beitrag zu einer Theorie der Sozialen Evolution. Frankfurt/Main: Suhrkamp.

Eder, K., 1977. "Zum Problem der logischen Periodisierung von Produktionsweisen. Ein Beitrag zu einer evolutionstheoretischen Rekonstruktion des Historischen Materialismus" in Theorien des Historischen Materialismus, eds. U. Jäggi and A. Honneth. Frankfurt/Main: Suhrkamp.

Engelhardt, H., 1978. "Ein Programm". Frankfurter Hefte 33 (2): 73-75.

Fleischer, H., 1970. Marxismus und Geschichte. Frankfurt/Main: Suhrkamp.

Gebühr, M. and Kunow, J., 1976. "Der Urnenfriedhof von Kemnitz, Kr. Potsdam-Land, Untersuchungen zur anthropologischen Bestimmung, Fibeltracht, sozialen Gliederung und "Depot" sitte". Jahrgang für Archäologie 10.

Gerhardt, K., 1975. "Spuren der Menschwerdung im Lichte anthropologisch-urgeschichtlicher Forschung". Scheidewege 5.

Giedion, S., 1962. Die Entstehung der Kunst. Köln: Du Mont Schauberg.

Guilaine, J. (ed), 1976. La Préhistoire Francaise, Tome II: Civilisations Néolithiques et Protohistoriques. Paris: Centre National de la Recherche Scientifique.

Habermas, J., 1975. " Towards a reconstruction of Historical Materialism". Theory and Society 2: 287-300.

Habermas, J., 1976. Zur Rekonstruktion des Historischen Materialismus. Frankfurt/Main: Suhrkamp.

Ignatow, A., 1977. "Jürgen Habermas, Zur Rekonstruktion des Historischen Materialismus". Philosophischer Literaturanzeiger 30.

Jäggi, U. and Honneth, A., 1977. Theorien des Historischen Materialismus. Frankfurt/Main: Suhrkamp.

Jaguttis-Emden, M., 1977. "Zur Präzision archaologischer Datierung". Archaeologica Venatoria 4.

Kimmig, W., 1940. Die Urnenfelderkultur in Baden. Berlin: Römisch-Germanische Forschungen 14.

Leone, M. P., 1968. " Neolithic economic autonomy and social distance". Science 162: 1150-1151.

Leakey, R. E. and Isaac, G. L. L., 1978. Koobi Foora, Researches into Geology, Palaeontology and Human Origins. Oxford: Oxford University Press.

Lucke, W. and Frey, O. H., 1962. Die Situla in Providence (Rhode Island), Ein Beitrag zur Situlenkunst des Osthallstatkreis. Berlin: Römisch-Germanische Forschungen 26.

Marcuse, H. and Habermas, J., 1978. "Gespräch uber anthropologische Grundlagen der Gesellschaften". Merkur 32: 479-592.

Montelius, O., 1885. " Om tidsbestämning inom bronsoldern, med särskildt afseende pa Skandinavien". K. Vittersheds Historie och Antiqvitets Akademiens Handlingar 30. Stockholm: P. A. Norstedt och Sön Förlag.

Montelius, O., 1900. Die Chronologie der Altesten Bronzezeit in Norddeutschland und Skandinavien. Braunschweig: Verlag Friedrich Vieweg und Sohn

Montelius, O., 1903. Die Alternen Kulturperioden im Orient und in Europa, I: Die Methode. Stockholm: O. Montelius.

Montelius, O., 1917. Minnen fran var Forntid, Ordnade och Beskrifna, I: Stenaldern och Bronsaldern. Stockholm: P. A. Norstedt och Son Forlag.

Müller-Karpe, H., 1974. " Zur Definition und Benennung chronologischer Stufen der Kugferzeit, Bronzezeit und alteren Eisenzeit". Jahresbericht des Instituts für Vorgeschichte der Universität Frankfurt am Main: 7-

Müller-Karpe, H., 1975. Einführung in die Vorgeschichte. München: C. H. Beck.

Nelson, B., 1977. Der Ursprung der Moderne. Frankfurt/Main: Suhrkamp.

Reinecke, P., 1911. Articles in Die Altertümer unserer Heidnischen Vorzeit, eds. Römisch-Germanisches Zentralmuseum. Mainz: Römisch-Germanisches Zentralmuseum.

Sangmeister, E., 1967. "Methoden der Urgeschichtswissenschaften". Saeculum 18: 199-244.

Scott, J. P., 1978. "Critical social theory: an introduction and critique". Brit. J. Sociol. 29: 1-21.

Thomsen, C., 1836. Leitfaden zur Nordischen Altertumskunde. Kopenhagen: C. Thomsen.

8. BONE REFUSE—POSSIBILITIES FOR THE FUTURE

Henrietta Moore

Introduction

This paper reviews some of the theoretical assumptions underlying current ethnoarchaeological work, which has consistently failed to account successfully for the processes which generate patterning in material remains.

In general there has been a very functional approach to an understanding of how 'cultural' factors affect deposition and formation processes. In the first section I discuss some theoretical problems arising from this functional approach, while the second section deals with bone refuse and the difficulties of interpretation.

Theory—its pitfalls and progress

It is often stated by archaeologists that the quality of their data base is such that certain types of past human behaviour are more amenable to study than others. For instance, it is argued that the economic basis of a particular society is more easily reconstructible from the distorted mirror image that is the archaeological record, than are the cognitive schemes, religious beliefs and social organization of the members of that society. This notion has a number of origins, but can be traced back to the predominant dichotomy in western philosophical thought, that between mind and body, thought and experience, belief and action.

In anthropology the clearest expression of this dichotomy is to be found in the varying types of ecological approach that have developed in the last twenty years, and usually takes the form of whether human behaviour is environmentally or culturally determined. In social anthropology this problem is often considered analogous to the controversy between practical and cultural reason, embodied for many in the dialogue between structuralism and Marxism. Proponents of both views can be found covering every available inch of ground between environmental determinism and idealism. One form that the opposition often takes is between the synchrony of structuralism and the diachrony of Marxism—that is, between the idealism of the former and the materialism of the latter. In many ways this debate has been extremely productive: some authors, usually neo-Marxist, have attempted to provide a more integrated approach and this has led to a consideration of the relation between practice (—for some, this just means productive action—) and the conceptual organisation of experience (Firth 1964; Habermas 1974; Feuchtwang 1975).

Archaeology has made little effort to understand the role of belief in action. The notion that areas of belief or thought (extending into religion and social organisation) are not available for analysis or interpretation because of the fragmentary and biased nature of the archaeological record has prevailed. Wittingly or unwittingly, archaeologists have perpetuated the dichotomy between mind and body (and other correlates of these, i.e. culture and environment). It is this dichotomy which, until recently, has underlain much of British palaeoeconomy and is the main source of this approach's failure to consider the importance of social and cognitive factors with regard to resource exploitation, subsistence needs, site location etc. (Higgs 1972, 1975).

Within the paradigm of the 'New Archaeology' the dichotomy has been extended. A genuine need for a more rigorous approach encouraged the development of a mode of scientific discourse based on deductive reasoning. The generation of hypotheses, and from these, models which can be tested against the data leads to explanations based on notions of 'best fit', although it is conceded that more than one explanation may be equally plausible. Deductive reasoning of this type encouraged work in areas of archaeology where archaeologists felt they could best elucidate the workings of general laws, and it is from this sort of perspective that Schiffer developed his behavioural archaeology (Schiffer 1976).

Under the auspices of the deductive mode of analysis, archaeologists first ventured into experimental and ethnoarchaeology. The resultant approach has, in some ways, prevented ethnoarchaeology from realising its full potential. This is because it has been primarily used to suggest possible analogies and point up the fallacies and misunderstandings of earlier archaeological work. In other words, it has concentrated on its negative aspects—i.e. showing that the spatial patterning of archaeological data does not directly reflect the spatial patterning of past human activity. Work, such as that of Diane Gifford with the Dassanetch, has concentrated on the problems of destruction of artifacts and sites after deposition and the resulting bias in the archaeological record (Gifford 1978). Yellen's work among the !Kung emphasises the bias inherent in bone refuse due to off-site butchering and the problems of designating activity areas on a site using the traditional assumption that spatial association equals functional association (Yellen 1977b). Work has also been done on factors affecting discard and has concentrated on problems such as how the availability of material influences the discard rate of particular artifacts and how consumption of different parts of an animal by people of different sex/age/status could affect the distribution of bone on a site (Gifford ibid.; Yellen 1977a, 1977b). Archaeologists have despaired of being able to generate general hypotheses that could be tested archaeologically because of the very variable nature of depositional and post-depositional factors and because their effects, while being very specific, have a very low predictability.

This despair is a product, not so much of poor quality data or of 'methodological naivité,' as of an insufficient theoretical base which itself has developed in response to the apparent need for a more rigorous, scientific approach. Archaeologists have failed to explain or understand the nature of the relationship between patterning in material culture and past human activities, because the approach is one that concentrates on function to the detriment of form, on action to the detriment of belief, and on the economic to the detriment of the symbolic. I would wish to make a plea for the re-integration of practice and symbol, action and belief. It should be pointed out that this is by no means a new idea: in social anthropology there is the work of Sahlins and Bourdieu, an in ecology a similar type of approach is developing (Sahlins 1976; Bourdieu 1977; Ellen 1978; Rappaport 1967, 1979). Without this re-integration, ethnoarchaeology would fast become little more than a description of material culture in an ethnographic context. What is required is an understanding of how patterns in material culture are generated. It has been emphasised that the formation of the archaeological record is the result of the integration of cultural and natural factors; but there has been a very functional approach to the comprehension of how cultural factors influence the processes of formation. Utilitarian functionalism sees the form of any object under study as explained in terms of its instrumental effects. This Malinowskian hangover has proceeded into archaeology, via anthropology, embodied in the notion that the economic and the political have some sort of primacy over the social and the religious (although it is claimed by some authors that such arbitrary divisions are no longer valid). It is under the influence of this notion, implicitly or explicitly, that much ethnoarchaeological fieldwork has been carried out.

In some senses it could be argued that the archaeologist has been too busy applying the conclusions of anthropology to his data, and the application of the method is only now beginning to come to the fore—principally in two fields that might loosely be termed 'ecological' and 'structuralist' archaeology. For example, Ellen's work on the Nualu suggests that the natural world is socially constructed. Men do not organise themselves in relation to 'nature' per se but in relation to the natural world as they perceive and conceive of it (Ellen ibid.). Bulmer shows this in relation to the disposal of animal bone by the Kalam (Bulmer 1976). Here he points out that the two major factors which affect the intensity with which particular animals are hunted are: 1) the extent to which they are considered appropriate for consumption by men and boys within the dietary rules; 2) the extent to which they are required or desired for ritual cooking and ceremonial distribution. He goes on to discuss the specialised nature of bone preservation and distribution, but makes it clear that although these are seriously affected by scavengers and localisation of particular activities, the specific effects of these factors are translated through the belief system. For example, bone remnants of animals cooked and eaten ritually are placed in the branches of shrubs and cannot be reached by scavengers; therefore it cannot be assumed that anomalies in the distribution of such bones are related to post-depositional distortion due to natural agencies, or to depositional distortion due to functional requirements.

There is no question of archaeology being able to elucidate particular cognitive schemes by an analysis of material remains. However, this is not really the point at issue and is rather like banging one's head against a brick wall when that wall could be circumnavigated. The reinstatement of the importance of belief in relation to social action could highlight the generative factors that are responsible for the cultural processes which form the archaeological record.

Boundaries and bones—their interrelation

One way in which I would like to suggest this could be done is by a consideration of the concept of boundaries as an analytical and interpretative tool for the understanding of formation processes and the interpretation of the archaeological record. By boundary I do not mean a hedge or a stone wall—although physical boundaries are both important and relevant, and in this context, inside/outside a structure would, for example, be a physical boundary. The 'boundaries' to which I am referring are conceptual notions that have a spatial referent in the way they act upon and reflect the real world. For example, prescriptive beliefs about women are common in a number of societies, and they are often first recognised by anthropologists because they have a spatial referent. Beliefs are translated into action and experience: this is done in a number of ways but space is the most important from the point of view of the archaeologist. The spatial referent of these ideas/notions is most commonly expressed in terms of boundaries. It is not necessary to think of these boundaries as being very distinct; they may be areas of 'greyness', rather than a dividing line between black and white. It is equally important to realise that boundaries no only separate, they also conjoin; that is, they create relational statements between things.

For the archaeologist, such an approach has obvious advantages. Quantitative methods for the determination of patterning in material remains can elucidate 'boundaries' in the archaeological record. This has been amply demonstrated in the past; what has been lacking has been an understanding of what generates the observed pattern. For example, the role of the negative is only just beginning to come into its own in archaeology, but only really with reference to various analytical spatial techniques (Hodder and Orton 1976). Areas on sites that are apparently devoid of artifacts may have particular importance. Anthropological work has indicated that pollution beliefs could be one way in which blank or 'barren' areas on a site may be explained. Dr. Okley's work among the gypsies emphasises that the caravan and the area immediately around it are kept spotlessly clean, but outside this conceptually clean area, all sorts of rubbish are deposited. As a result the gypsies consider themselves free of all possible pollution by dirt, but outsiders consider them extremely dirty. It is rare that a conceptual boundary of this type will have quite such a strong physical manifestation, but it suggests that much may be wrong with the way archaeologists have traditionally supposed patterning in material remains is generated (Okley 1974).

Work such as Dr. Okley's also casts much suspicion on the notion of primary and secondary refuse—particularly if they are defined in the narrow sense of objects discarded at the location of use and objects discarded away from their location of use. Concepts of boundaries do not, of course, elucidate problems relating to re-use, natural disturbance and other such factors. However, the explanatory value of these two categories is called into question. While archaeologists were concerned with isolating specific areas related to specific activities on a site, an understanding of primary and secondary refuse was essential, but such categories are of little value in any attempt to elucidate formation processes. Classifying material remains in respect of whether they are or are not found in their use location is another example of what Sahlins has called 'the cannibalism of form by function' (Sahlins ibid.). For example, the placing of certain artifacts in specific positions in a house may well say something about their function, but it says very little about their meaning in any relevant social context. In other words, to interpret their findspots in terms of their function might explain why kitchen utensils are found inside a house, but it fails to explain the processes that generated the observed pattern. The interior arrangement of houses is one field in which much anthropological work has been done, and although the boundaries which are expressed in such contexts are extremely complex, they are often available for study in the archaeological record. Their neglect, until quite recently, is a result of the constraints of the functionalist paradigm.

One of the possible ways in which these ideas about 'boundaries' could be used is in relation to the patterning of bone refuse. This has three main advantages: 1) there has been a number of studies on the biases produced by butchering techniques, preservation problems, scavengers, special utility locations, etc.; 2) with bone, unlike pottery, there are not so many problems relating to 'use-life' and subsequent possible re-use. Worked bone is often easily recognisable and would form a separate category; 3) and more importantly, much anthropological work has been done on the prevalence of systems of animal classification in societies and the apparently almost universal presence of animal symbols. It has been suggested that this symbolism arises naturally, for any system of classification seeks to impose order on the world, and if man begins with a consideration of himself and society, an understanding of this consideration must arise from an understanding of what is not man or society. The obvious candidates for this are animals, 'since they are most nearly man but not man' (Willis 1974; Douglas 1966, 1975:276-318). Tambiah's work on the classification of animals in Thailand is concerned with two main questions: 1) what kind of fit is there between dietary taboos relating to certain animals and their position in the scheme of classificatory categories? 2) what is the relation between rules concerning the eating of animals and the rules pertaining to sex and marriage? (Tambiah 1973). This, and other work, shows how the classification of the animal world is a mirror image of the classification of the human world (Willis ibid., Bulmer 1973). So that it is quite common to find specific animals associated with either men or women, old or young and 'member of the group' or 'non-member of the group'. Systems of classification of this kind may be recognisable in the archaeological record. For example, in some Durotrigian burials it is possible to see that although sheep bones are found in graves regardless of the age or sex of the dead, ox bones are only found with mature men (although there is one case of an ox bone found with an infant) and pig bones only with women. It may also be important to note that sheep bones are always placed on or near the lower half of the body, while ox and pig bones are placed near the head. Certain early Irish texts mention that particular animals or parts of animals were offered to people of particular status (Chambers 1978). But the Durotrigian burial material suggests, although the sample is small, that oxen and pig bones were separated spatially, and therefore conceptually, from sheep bones. If this were the case then archaeologists might expect to find differences between the distribution of ox/pig bones and the distribution of sheep bones on Durotrigian settlements. Work of this type has yet to be undertaken.

I would suggest that it is in the boundaries produced by bone refuse that archaeology could most easily become aware of the interaction between the practicalities of man's existence and a system of beliefs which acts as a medium through which man experiences the world. In other words, bone refuse is one aspect of the archaeological record which, of its very nature, brings together man's productive relation with the world and his symbolic relation with that world. This is not to suggest that a 'cognised' model of nature leads people to behave in ways that are conducive to the maintenance of ecosystems—in my opinion this is not the case—but to emphasise that any system of beliefs provides constraints within which practical action must operate. These constraints, in themselves, have no adaptive significance although the strategies carried out within them might be considered adaptive.

Conclusion

Ian Hodder has written "beyond the functioning of the 'economy' is a conceptual schems and meaning, but until this is accepted and the relevant models developed, the archaeologist will remain unable to provide a complete interpretation of his 'economic' evidence of the past" (Hodder, in press). I agree, but would like to stress that this integration of the'social' with the 'economic' is not common in archaeological interpretation; it is far more usual for authors to maintain that both ecological and social approaches are valid so long as they remain confined to their proper spheres of influence. As a result it is often emphasised that: a) these approaches are orientated towards answering different questions and b) they are only relevant with reference to certain time scales. The second point is particularly crucial because, in my opinion, it has adversely affected the development of the concept of change in archaeology, a concept which has been surprisingly poorly developed. Notions of 'long-term' change have dominated the discipline and the role of 'short-term' change has been neglected, both with regard to its role and importance in processes of 'long-term' change and with regard to its importance in the 'day-to-day' maintenance and generation of social and ecological systems. This is partly because 'short-term'change is considered less amenable to archaeological study and stands in the same relation to 'long-term' change as do minor perturbations in relation to long-term ecosystems development! The equation of change with 'long-term' change is just another facet of the dichotomy between synchrony and diachrony. What is required is an approach that not only integrates the social and the economic but which also stresses the proper role of belief in action. Until such an approach is developed there will never be an adequate understanding of the processes which generate patterning in material culture. This is not, as Sahlins has said, that "utility must be forgotten but it must not be fetishised" (Sahlins ibid.).

Archaeology, like anthropology, finds itself "mid-way between the unintelligible and the commonplace" (Geertz 1973)—but this is no reason to concentrate on the commonplace: rather, there should be every incentive to understand how the commonplace elucidates the apparently unintelligible, and how that normally considered unintelligible informs us of the real nature of the commonplace.

Acknowledgements

Grateful thanks are expressed to Ian Hodder and Sheena Crawford.

References

Bourdieu, P., 1977. Outline of a Theory of Practice. Cambridge: Cambridge University Press.

Bulmer, R., 1973. "Why the cassowary is not a bird" in Rules and Meanings, ed. M. Douglas. Harmondsworth: Penguin; 167-193.

Bulmer, R., 1976. "Selectivity in hunting and in disposal of animal bone by the Kalam of the New Guinea Highlands" in Problems in Economic and Social Archaeology, eds. G. de. G. Sieveking, I. Longworth and K. Wilson. London: Duckworth; 169-186.

Chambers, S. A., 1978. An Analysis of Iron Age Inhumation Burials in the Durotriges Area and an Assessment of their Value as Indicators of Social Organisation. Unpublished Certificate dissertation, Department of Extra-Mural Studies, University of Leeds.

Douglas, M., 1966. Purity and Danger. London: Routledge and Kegan Paul.

Douglas, M., 1975. Implicit Meanings. London: Routledge and Kegan Paul.

Ellen, R. F., 1978. "Ecological perspectives on social behaviour" in Social Organisation and Settlement, eds. D. Green, C. Haselgrove and M. Spriggs. Oxford: B.A.R. Suppl. Ser. 47: 121-127.

Feuchtwang, S., 1975. "Investigating religion" in Marxist Analyses and Social Anthropology, ed. M. Bloch. A.S.A. Monograph 2. London: Malaby Press; 61-82.

Firth, R., 1964. Essays on Social Organisation and Values. London: Athlone Press.

Geertz, C., 1973. "Thick description: toward an interpretive theory of culture" in The Interpretation of Cultures, ed. C. Geertz. New York: Basic Books; 3-30.

Gifford, D., 1978. "Ethnoarchaeological observations of natural processes affecting cultural materials" in Explorations in Ethnoarchaeology, ed. R. Gould. Albuquerque: University of New Mexico Press; 77-101.

Habermas, J., 1974. Theory and Practice. London: Heinemann.

Higgs, E. S. (ed.), 1972. Papers in Economic Prehistory. London: Cambridge University Press.

Higgs, E. S. (ed.), 1975. Palaeoeconomy. London: Cambridge University Press.

Hodder, I. (in press). Material Symbols.

Hodder, I. and Orton, C., 1976. Spatial Analysis in Archaeology. Cambridge: Cambridge University Press.

Okley, J., 1974. Gorgios and Gypsies: Public Health and Inner Purity. Paper read at the Institute of Social Anthropology, Oxford.

Rappaport, R., 1967. Pigs for the Ancestors. New Haven: Yale University Press.

Rappaport, R., 1979. Ecology, Meaning and Religion. Richmond: North Atlantic Books.

Sahlins, M. D., 1976. Culture and Practical Reason. Chicago University Press.

Schiffer, M. B., 1976. Behavioural Archaeology. New York: Academic Press.

Tambiah, S. J., 1973. "Classification of animals in Thailand" in Rules and Meanings, ed. M. Douglas. Harmondsworth: Penguin; 127-166.

Willis, R., 1974. Man and Beast. St. Albans: Paladin.

Yellen, J. E., 1977a. Archaeological Approaches to the Present. London: Academic Press.

Yellen, J. E., 1977b. "Cultural patterning in faunal remains: evidence from the !Kung Bushmen" in Experimental Archaeology, eds. D. W. Ingersoll, J. E. Yellen and W. MacDonald. New York: Columbia University Press; 271-331.

SECTION II

THEORETICAL APPROACHES TO INTEGRATION

9. CONCEPTS, TIME-SCALES AND EXPLANATIONS IN ECONOMIC PREHISTORY

Geoff Bailey

Introduction

Examination of the literature of economic prehistory[1] during the past forty years illustrates the extent to which the emphasis in interpretation has tended to fluctuate between 'social' and 'ecological' explanations. An implicit feature of the various arguments advanced in favour of one or another point of view has been the differing nature of assumptions about the effect of time-scale and time duration on the processes under study. In this paper I shall argue that an essential step towards an integrated approach lies in appreciating the historical character of economic prehistory, historical in the sense of a discipline concerned with processes and relationships over time, and hence with the effect of time duration on behaviour patterns and our observation of them. Economic prehistory is capable of revealing processes operating over long time spans as well as shorter ones, and hence of specifying the difference of perspective and focus imposed by different time-scales. Much of the opposition between 'economic' and 'social' archaeology involves argument at cross-purposes through failure to clarify this effect. Palaeoeconomic theories, stressing biological and ecological factors, are concerned primarily with long-term trends and the long-run consequences of human behaviour; sociological theories have concentrated mainly on behaviour over short time-scales, particularly the motivations, values and thought processes that lie behind observed behaviour patterns, or else with attempts to extrapolate to the longer term record of prehistory theories and concepts designed for the study of contemporary behaviour.

What is Economic Prehistory?

Economic prehistory has been formally recognised as an explicit approach to the study of the prehistoric past for over thirty years (Clark 1946; Heyman 1944), while a more general interest in economic matters can be traced in earlier writings (Daniel 1975). The term economic prehistory has been used in a general sense to characterise all attempts to describe and understand the economic life of prehistoric communities. As such, it is not a clearly bounded field of study, since its interests cut across ecological and evolutionary concerns on the one hand, and social, cultural and historical ones on the other; some, at least, of its objectives and methods have been shared by those who would not regard themselves as economic prehistorians or even archaeologists; and self-styled economic prehistorians, notably Grahame Clark himself, have made contributions to many other problems of archaeological importance. Nevertheless, economic prehistory as a central focus of study has been advocated perhaps most consistently and explicitly during the past forty years by Cambridge-based or Cambridge-trained archaeologists. This is not to overlook the influence or importance of similar work elsewhere, especially in the Americas or the Soviet Union, or the West European tradition of environmental archaeology, or to deny the other achievements of Cambridge archaeology during this period, but rather to single out a local tradition which highlights some of the issues raised in studying prehistoric economies.

Broadly two distinct tendencies can be discerned in this development. The first is exemplified in the founding work of Grahame Clark, whose interest in economy reaches back to at least as early as 1939 according to his own account (Clark 1939, 1944:1), although his 'economic approach' (Clark 1953, 1954a) was not fully elaborated until later, in a series of studies which ranged widely across the spectrum of economic life from descriptions of basic diet and subsistence to land use and agricultural production, and processes of trade and exchange (Clark 1945, 1946, 1947a, 1947b, 1948, 1952, 1954b, 1965). In keeping with the general preoccupations of this period, his interpretations focused on the detailed reconstruction of economic activities from the residual traces of the material record and on imaginative synthesis and the use of anthropological insight, rather than on theoretical issues. However, he took considerable pains to emphasise economy as an aspect of culture and to stress the influence of social behaviour and 'social choice' on economic patterning. His approach might be loosely described as substantive in the social anthropologists' sense of that term (LeClair and Schneider 1968), although his comprehensiveness of interests defies easy categorisation particularly in view of the emphasis not only on social organisation, but on the relationship with the natural environment and 'the wider economy of nature' (Clark 1952:6).

Palaeoeconomy

A more 'formal' study of economic prehistory, placing greater emphasis on cross-cultural regularities and general laws or principles shaped by biological and ecological relationships, was initiated in the late 1960s under the banner of 'palaeoeconomy' by Eric Higgs (see also Davidson, this volume). Higgs' interests were strongly influenced by his former careers as a London businessman and a Shropshire hill farmer and by his early archaeological work on faunas (Higgs 1961; Higgs and White 1963), and the main outlines of palaeoeconomy as a coherent group of ideas and methods had crystallised out by 1967. This was the year that saw the shift of emphasis in Higgs' palaeolithic researches in Epirus towards off-site archaeology and the definition of territorial concepts (Higgs et al. 1967), and the publication of some of the work of his earliest students, notably Higham's (1966, 1967) analysis of mortality patterns in neolithic and bronze age faunal assemblages and Shawcross' (1967) reconsideration of the issues involved in quantifying diet from midden refuse. It also saw the establishment of the British Academy Major Research Project in the Early History of Agriculture, which acted as the main vehicle for the development of palaeoeconomic ideas during the next ten years, the results of which are summarised in the Project's three principal reports (Higgs 1972, 1975; Jarman et al. forthcoming). Palaeoeconomic research, while it represented a change of direction, was clearly related to earlier work, and indeed developed and flourished under

Clark's patronage, deriving much of its momentum from the creative tension between Clark's more humanistic and traditional outlook and Higgs' iconoclastic emphasis on animal ethology and basic economics.

The relationship of palaeoeconomy to other developments in the 'New Archaeology' of the 1960s can scarcely be touched on here, although it may be noted that, by rejecting early on the study of artifacts, palaeoeconomists placed themselves outside many of the most polemical debates of the time, and beyond even the definitions of those who see the primary concern of theoretical archaeology as the explanation of patterns of material culture. Klejn in his masterly survey noted only (without supplying the reference) that Higgs was an archaeologist who "from Australia asked ..... 'Archaeology—Where Now?'" (Higgs 1968; Klejn 1977:12). In common with other trends of the period, however, the early development of palaeoeconomy was characterised not only by a more explicit interest in theory but by a renewed concern for methodological rigour in the retrieval and analysis of primary data. It is important to recognise this duality of palaeoeconomy, both as a particular stance about the determinants of economic behaviour and economic change, and as a general corpus of methods for improving the detail and reliability of reconstructions of economic activities, lest dissatisfaction with the former should encourage wholesale rejection of the latter.

The theoretical issues that stimulated the development of palaeoeconomy and both sharpened and narrowed its focus of interest centred around the problem of the origins of agriculture. Research was devoted to a critical analysis of the inadequacies of 'wild' and 'domesticated' as classificatory categories of food resources, and of 'hunter-gatherer' and 'herder-farmer' as categories of economic behaviour. The main thrust of investigation was over the nature and identification of domestication and agricultural development, and about the sorts of processes necessary to account for overall patterns of long-term economic change and intensification apparent in the prehistoric record. The principal challenge to an integrated approach was thus seen to lie in the attempt to resolve the apparently disparate principles of economic organisation implied by the distinct categories of hunter-gatherer/herder-farmer, according to a more general theory of economic behaviour. Research interest broadened into a general study of economies far beyond the limits of agricultural origins as traditionally conceived, in which the initial emphasis was necessarily on attempts to assess productive capacity (in terms of food) rather than patterns of distribution and exchange, and hence on the relationship between economy and environment rather than economy and society—or, in palaeoeconomic terminology, the relationship between population, resources and technology. Population pressure was emphasised as a recurrent feature of this triadic equation and therefore an important source of change in explanations of long-term patterns, and considerable emphasis was placed on long-term continuities in economic behaviour, particularly in the use of the concept of resource husbandry as an alternative to the wild/domesticated dichotomy.

Early controversies arose mainly with those who viewed the man-ment relationship through the concepts of the natural sciences, and took two forms. The first involved a fundamental break with zoological approaches to early agriculture which rested on an assumed correlation between morphological changes in plants and animals and changes in human economy. A second divergence was from the assumption of much environmental archaeology that prehistoric environments could be objectively reconstructed by the techniques of the natural scientist without necessarily referring to the specific limiting factors relevant to the particular economic systems and archaeological sites under scrutiny. In contrast to the natural scientists' conception of the issues, the objectives of palaeoeconomy were defined as anthropological ones in which human behaviour should occupy a central position rather than a peripheral or incidental factor in ecosystem behaviour. A further distinctive feature was the rejection of certain ecological concepts. This stemmed not so much from a rejection of ecological principles, which are deeply embedded in palaeoeconomic thinking, as from a belief that specific concepts such as the ecosystem or the ecological niche cannot be used without modification to analyse developmental processes over long periods of time, or to cope with the peculiarities of the human species, in particular its flexibility in the exploitation of the natural environment and its capacity artificially to modify environmental resources for its own benefit (or detriment).

Social Relations

At a time when these earlier debates are beginning to recede and to be resolved in the light of subsequent research, the focus of controversy has shifted away from environmental and ecological relations to the role of social behaviour and cognition in prehistoric economies. This is an issue which the palaeoeconomic literature has generally excluded from consideration, partly for practical reasons, partly as a matter of belief, and in so doing has done much to stimulate the current polarity between 'economic' and 'social' archaeology, a measure of which may be seen in Clark's more recent re-emphasis on social values and social archaeology (Clark 1972, 1975, 1977:xviii). Palaeoeconomic writings have often been expressed in controversial terms, perhaps none more so than the eponymous paper of 1975 (Higgs and Jarman 1975), whose succinctness and quite deliberate provocation were well calculated to inflame lurking accusations of environmental determinism, ecological functionalism, biological reductionism, or vulgar materialism.

Two examples will briefly indicate something of the nature of this sociological reaction. Bender (1978, see also this volume) emphasised the social matrix of economic behaviour, and suggested that evolving social institutions such as reciprocal exchange mechanisms, hierarchical social structures and trade networks are the principal stimuli to long-term economic development, providing the essential motivation for the production of surplus and increased demands on the resource base. One difficulty here is that the social relations described by Bender are widely in evidence in the ethnography of surviving hunters and gatherers, and in the archaeological record of at least the last 30,000 years. We are thus brought no closer to an explanation of why the development of prehistoric agriculture, at least in Bender's conception of it, should be so highly localised in time and space. Indeed it is not at all clear what changes in the prehistoric subsistence record the alleged development in social relations is intended to explain. Ingold (1979, 1980, see also this volume) elaborated a different approach by emphasising the reciprocal interplay between social and ecological systems, in which the exploitation of the environment is organised in accordance with premises which are socially given. The social system is seen as dominant, in that it specifies the way in which the environment is to be exploited, whereas the ecological relations are determinant only in the negative sense of setting the limits of viability. In seeking to explain the particular social transformations involved in the development of animal pastoralism and plant cultivation, however, Ingold invoked episodes of resource crisis brought about by environmental change or population pressure, an appeal to variables operating on a time-scale well beyond the range of focus of his analysis. This raises the possibility that the social reationality which is 'given' as an independent variable over the short time span of his analysis might turn out to be a more strongly dependent variable over longer time spans.

It seems that there may be a number of different types of 'social' explanation, some of which do not differ from those that would be advanced by palaeoeconomists themselves. Perhaps this is no more than to underline the artificiality of the polarity between social and economic factors. Both Bender and Ingold draw attention to the apparent contradiction between the Higgs-Jarman emphasis on continuity and the evidence of discontinuities in economic behaviour. However, this contradiction can be reconciled in other ways without necessarily having to resort to elaborate discussions of differential social behaviour (Bailey in press). If the aim of these sociological excursions is to demonstrate that certain sorts of social formations are necessary to facilitate certain patterns of economic production, or to emphasise social flexibility as a general property inherent in human behaviour which allows the possibility of economic transformations unique at the species level, then these are scarcely matters of great contention. If, however, the aim is to demonstrate that changing social relations are an independent variable of sufficient force to deter or initiate long-term economic changes, this remains a hypothesis in need of testing against the prehistoric record.

Part of the difficulty seems to lie in the very definition of the term economy. For social anthropologists, whatever their particular theoretical persuasion, economy is generally defined in terms of relations between persons, whether these be social relations of production or of distribution, rather than in terms of relations between persons and things (e.g. environmental resources). From this point of view it is no doubt logical to redefine palaeoeconomic interests as being concerned with ecology or to write them off as descriptive studies of subsistence. While appropriation of the terminology in this way may be justified in relation to problems which loom large in the study of contemporary behaviour, its importation into archaeological thinking should immediately call into question the definition of basic terms. Subsistence refers to those resources, principally food supply but including other materials, that are necessary to support life (Dennell 1979). Economy refers to the way in which the consumer population organises, integrates and manages those resources for its own benefit. It may be granted that this is simply an alternative definition of economy (albeit one sanctioned by the Oxford English Dictionary), and a definition, moreover, which subsumes and certainly does not exclude the social relations involved. From this alternative point of view, however, the issue is not whether palaeoeconomic studies are in fact about the integration and management of subsistence resources, but whether their treatment of social behaviour as being implicit in the relations under study rather than an explicit objective of analysis is crucially detrimental to the explanations offered of prehistoric change.

The confusion between subsistence and economy is perhaps understandable in view of one practical and unavoidable difficulty in prehistoric archaeology, namely the necessity of having to approach the analysis of economy, however defined, largely through the analysis of environmental and subsistence data in the first instance, rather than through the analysis of prehistoric social relations. The latter can be inferred, at best, only in an indirect fashion from material remains, and it would be fair to argue that their study has scarcely moved beyond the level of 'conjectural sociology' (Clark 1954a:28).

Much of the reaction to palaeoeconomy, with its emphasis on animal behaviour and ecology, has been supported by recourse to anthropological thinking on contemporary or near-contemporary societies. The benefits of thorough acquaintance with this literature are indubitable, but the danger here is that recent trends in economic prehistory will be forced into a priori categories of anthropological thought, and that the literature of economic prehistory may become burdened with a re-run of controversies which properly belong to the context of anthropological debate about contemporary societies—such as the opposition between formalism and substantivism, functionalism and structuralism, cultural ecology and structural-Marxism, or sociobiology and social action theory. Indeed, many such debates have already been superseded.

Nevertheless, as will be apparent from other studies in this volume, the major challenge to an integrated approach is currently seen by many as residing in the re-instatement of social behaviour, a redefinition of an archaeology "..... whose prime concern..... is the study of how men have lived in society, of how within the social framework they have striven to satisfy and multiply their wants" (Clark 1942:208). The challenge merits a response not simply because of its importance in the development of economic archaeology, but because it has wider implications for an integrated view of human behaviour.

Time Perspectivism in Archaeology[2]

As a discipline which expends a large part of its resources on dating and chronology, archaeology has made remarkably little contribution to the elaboration of time concepts, perhaps all the more surprising in a discipline concerned with time spans far beyond what is customary in the studies of the anthropologist or the historian. Although frequent emphasis has been placed on the importance of archaeology's extended time dimension, the value of this is usually perceived in terms of providing a framework for the study of change, and relatively little discussion has been devoted to the possible effects that varying time-scales may have on our basic concepts. Fletcher, in a comprehensive analysis of the human perception and use of space in archaeological and ethnographic contexts, concluded that individual and social variation which has a significant impact within and between settlements ceases to be relevant at the larger scale of adaptations to the macro-environment or in the study of long-term economic patterns, and that "the nature of social cause and effect operates differently at different scales of space and time" (Fletcher 1977a:53, 1977b). A similar point has been made by Holly (1978), who questioned whether behaviour at different spatio-temporal scales could be logically linked, and suggested that "Time must be considered a multidimensional entity, which can be defined in terms of a hierarchy of scale levels .....Too often the languages we employ are either incapable of distinguishing one level from another, or we use more than one language at a time, thus mixing up scales" (Holly 1978:14).

There are in fact two contrasting assumptions about the effects of time-scale involved in archaeological interpretation. One, which is more or less implicit in all archaeological practice, I shall characterise as behavioural uniformitarianism. By this I mean the belief that patterns of behaviour revealed in the prehistoric record can be explained in terms of processes visible at the present day—in effect that long-term patterns are simply the summation of short-term events. Such a belief is implicit in the archaeological application of theories and concepts derived from the study of contemporary behaviour, whether of functionalist, structuralist or Marxist orientation. The second sort of assumption—time perspectivism—is based on the belief that differing time-scales bring into focus different features of behaviour, requiring different sorts of explanatory principles. Processes and relationships visible at one time-scale, say over a period of years or decades, are not necessarily visible at time-scales measured in hundreds or thousands of years. Hence categories, concepts and explanations appropriate to the study of contemporary behaviour—necessarily a study of short time-scales—may not be appropriate or sufficient at the longer time-scales through which much of the prehistoric record is filtered. The converse, of course, also applies, that concepts applicable to long time-scales may not be suitable or adequate for the study of contemporary behaviour.

At first sight, it is true, these two approaches appear to be mutually exclusive. But this need not be so. Behavioural uniformitarianism, unless it is expressed in a particularly narrow form, does not specify that past patterns are to be explained only in terms of presently visible processes, while time perspectivism does not stipulate that contemporary processes are wholly or necessarily inappropriate. Some element of behavioural uniformitarianism is inescapable in archaeological interpretation, and without some such assumption a systematic knowledge of the past is scarcely conceivable. This especially applies at the level of Binford's (1977) middle-range theory—the level of interpretation which attempts to reconstruct behaviour patterns from the material record by a study of the natural and cultural processes that affect the deposition and preservation of artifacts. It is rather at the level of general theory—the interpretation of the reconstructed behaviour patterns in terms of general principles of behaviour, thought or action—that the distinction between uniformitarian and time-perspective assumptions becomes critical.

Whatever the degree of mutual complementarity between these two approaches, what most sets them apart are their respective conceptions of time. For behavioural uniformitarianism the passage of time can, in effect, be ignored, or at least regarded as a constant in the sense that the study of short-term processes is treated as being sufficient to provide explanations for long-term trends. For time perspectivism, time duration is a key variable in the interpretation of past behaviour patterns; the interpretation of macro-temporal trends in terms of micro-temporal processes is seen as an assumption, and one which can scarcely be submitted to any sort of test until analysis is extended to include a span of time which can only be supplied by archaeological study. If archaeological data are interpreted only in terms of presently visible processes, that assumption remains untestable, unrecognised even, and archaeological study is condemned to apply concepts and theories derived from elsewhere rather than to formulate its own, and is thus reduced to an appendix—at best entertaining, at worst dispensable—of ecology, sociology or whichever study of contemporary behaviour happens to be the current fashion.

There is, however, a detectable reluctance among prehistoric archaeologists to face up to this paradox. An underlying reason for this seems to be an unwillingness to abandon the basic tenets of behavioural uniformitarianism. This stems, in part, from a dependence on ideas and theories drawn from studies of contemporary behaviour in which consideration of time-scaling plays no part, and in economic prehistory in particular from the limiting effect of an interdisciplinary approach on the formulation of theory. This attitude is also influenced by reaction to evolutionary theories of social and cultural development, a reaction sometimes expressed as a preference for an historical archaeology emphasising idiographic objectives. These two approaches in their turn are reinforced by a limited conception of uniformitarianism based on analogies with outdated concepts in the historical branches of the natural sciences: geology, palaeontology and cosmology. A further inhibition may be the difficulty we experience as time-bounded observers in visualising what behaviour patterns might look like from different points of view in time.

Uniformitarianism and Interdisciplinary Studies

In economic prehistory, lack of clarity about time-scales is strongly influenced by the inter-disciplinary nature of many of the central issues. A problem such as the origins of agriculture, for example, lies at the intersection of the boundaries of at least three well-established disciplines outside archaeology itself, namely biology, particularly the zoological and botanical study of the food resources themselves, ecology, with its emphasis on transfers of materials, energy and information between the constituent populations of biotic communities, and social anthropology, with its focus on the structural forms and ideological premises of particular human societies. The developing science of human ethology, with its interest in the evolutionary development of behaviour through processes of natural selection should perhaps be recognised as a fourth potential claimant on this area of study (Blurton Jones 1976).

In this intellectual no-man's-land archaeologists sit as uneasy and sometimes bewildered arbiters between the rival claims of competing and powerfully-voiced conceptual schemes. Short of abandoning their interest in this sort of problem altogether, or of succumbing to the role of mere technicians supplying data for others to interpret, they can seek to resolve the dilemmas posed by these conflicting claims in one of several ways. One attitude is to emphasise the perspective of a single discipline—biology, ecology, social anthropology, or ethology, according to preference and intellectual background. The shifting currents of controversy in the development of economic prehistory outlined above clearly reflect the varying influence of one or other of these disciplines. A second attitude is to seek some sort of inter-disciplinary compromise aimed at a hybridisation of terms and concepts. Much of the appeal of systems theory lies in the prospect of integrating different sectors of behaviour as interacting subsystems of a larger whole, although recent criticisms indicate that such a prospect may well be illusory (Salmon 1978).

A third attitude—one characteristic of the palaeoeconomic approach—represents an alternative attempt at integration and involves making the problem of agricultural origins the central focus of a distinctive archaeological field of study, developing its own concepts in relation to the particular needs and problems of those data most relevant to the problem. Amongst the various features which are held to justify this definition of an archaeological perspective, perhaps the most important is the claim that prehistoric archaeology is confronted above all with problems of origins and development over time and with the evidence of long-term processes. From this point of view the limitations of the other disciplines which bear on the problem is that they are essentially ahistorical disciplines founded on observations of recent or present-day events and short-term processes. They are constrained by their very terms of reference and the nature of their data to exclude any consideration of long-term processes except by an exercise in more or less tenuous extrapolation from an ethnographic or ecological present.

One impediment to the development of a distinctively archaeological approach of this sort is the very number, diversity and constantly changing nature of ideas and concepts available in contingent disciplines, and the belief that the possibilities that can be derived from studies of contemporary behaviour should be fully explored before alternative solutions are sought to the problems posed by the prehistoric record. This in its turn is symptomatic of deeply ingrained uniformitarian assumptions that knowledge should be acquired by proceeding from the known to the unknown, and hence from the better known present to the less well known past—that events in the past should be explained by reference to presently observable processes. The relative view implied by the palaeoeconomic approach, that different sorts of processes operated in the past from those visible at the present day, appears to require the rejection of uniformitarian assumptions.

Uniformitarianism and 'Historical' Archaeology

An alternative approach to archaeological explanation, which appears to avoid excessive dependence on the study of contemporary behaviour and the reduction of archaeological study to a pale and ineffective imitation of anthropology or ecology, is the espousal of an historical approach as advocated by Trigger (1970, 1973). He quoted the work of historians in support of his argument that the proper role for archaeology is an idiographic, or particularising, discipline concerned with the explanation of particular events, rather than a nomothetic or generalising discipline concerned with the establishment of general laws. The latter objective he considered was best left to students of contemporary behaviour such as sociologists. He emphasised the inadequacies of evolutionism with its over-deterministic or over-simplified theories of historical development, and further supported his case by an appeal to the principle of uniformitarianism. However, his approach, like the over-enthusiastic urgings of the 'archaeology as anthropology' (ecology etc.) school, also seems to condemn archaeology to the role of a second class discipline, compelled to consume the generalisations of others, but never able to produce its own. Several critics pointed out the dangers of over-exaggerating the contrast between idiographic and nomothetic goals, but without being able to offer a serious alternative to the uniformitarian premise of Trigger's argument (Harriss 1971; Tuggle et al. 1971; Watson 1973; Watson et al. 1971).

Disciplines other than archaeology have debated over whether their goals can or should be nomothetic rather than idiographic, including history, sociology, geology and geography (Harvey 1969). The example of history is especially instructive. For, although Trigger quoted the practice of historians in support of his argument, it appears that the contrast between nomothetic and idiographic approaches, and the identification of historical explanation with the latter, owes more to the work of Sir Karl Popper (1945, 1957) than to a generally accepted consensus among historians. As Carr (1961:85) pointed out, Popper's attack on so-called historical laws represented a reaction against the supposedly deterministic philosophies of Hegel and Marx. Evans-Pritchard (1961) also rejected the contrast between generalising and particularising sciences as a false distinction devised by functionalist anthropologists to justify their disregard of history. Here, too, the reaction was inspired by the evolutionist inheritance of the nineteenth century, but not so much because it was deterministic but because it produced conjectural history. The French sociological historians of the Annales school such as Febvre, Bloch and Braudel exemplify the search for historical generalisations. One might also cite the various attempts of their successors to integrate the surface interplay of 'events' with the persistent underlying patterns, or 'structures', of the long term, although there is clearly room for wide-ranging differences of approach within this broad position (compare, for example, Chesneaux 1978:97-104 and Le Roy Ladurie 1979:111-131, or Foucault 1972). It is true that historians have been rather wary of labelling their generalisations as 'laws' (Atkinson 1978), and that the attempt to formulate explicit laws has been as vulnerable to the attentions of Mickey Mouse as in archaeology (Flannery 1973). However, this has not deterred them from making comparisons and contrasts in the search for patterns, regularities and causes, even if the balance of emphasis has tended towards greater understanding of the particular, rather than a precise definition of the generalities under which the particulars are subsumed.

Perhaps the most important comment in the archaeological debate initiated by Trigger was his own statement made in defence of his views (in Tuggle et al. 1971:134). While reiterating his belief that the general laws of culture process were best studied in the present, he noted in passing that "If one assumes that there are certain processes that can be studied only over long periods of time, then a special role for archaeological data may be justified .....".

Uniformitarianism outside Archaeology

At this point it may be helpful to consider how the concept of uniformitarianism has fared in the discipline that first gave birth to it in the early nineteenth century. Lyell's assertion that spectacular, large-scale episodes in earth history could, given a sufficient length of time, be accounted for in terms of small-scale processes going on at the present day was essential to the removal of divine intervention from geological explanation and the development of a scientific approach. This idea was taken over by Darwin in his theory of organic evolution. However, the uniformitarian basis of Lyell's geology is really a dual conception (Gould 1965). 'Methodological' uniformitarianism, a belief in invariant laws of nature, has remained a central principle of scientific method. 'Substantive' uniformitarianism, a belief in uniform rates of change, has not stood the test of subsequent work. Not only is it clear that rates of change vary, but that different sorts of processes tend to operate at different rates, requiring different time-scales for their effective observation (Vita-Finzi 1973). Mountain building, for example, is only visible and amenable to analysis on a time-scale of tens of millions of years. For other geological processes, such as cycles of sedimentation and erosion, a time-scale of tens of thousands of years may be more appropriate. This is not to say that these processes are not going on at the present day, or that an on-the-spot observer might not detect their operation if he possessed sufficiently sensitive instruments, only that no effective analysis or interpretation would be possible of the very slight changes visible over such a short time span.

A second modification of the uniformitarian principle is that different principles of causality may apply at different time-scales, so that what appears to be a cause at one time-scale may turn out to be an effect at another time-scale. For example, over a short time span, the morphology of a river channel may appear to be a relatively fixed and independent feature, which determines the hydraulic properties of the river water. Over a longer time span the nature of the river flow will affect channel morphology. What appears relatively constant at one time-scale becomes highly variable at another, an independent or a dependent variable according to the spatial and temporal frame of reference (Schumm and Lichty 1965).

In theories of biological evolution, on the other hand, substantive uniformitarianism seems to have remained relatively intact. Slobodkin (1976), for example, has asserted that there are no trends in the evolutionary process, apart from a conservative tendency to do nothing, or to respond to disturbance in the smallest possible steps, and it is a widely held feature of the neo-Darwinian synthesis that such trends as are apparent in the long-term record are no more than an incidental outcome of the small-scale processes of natural selection (Schopf 1977, see also Foley, this volume). However, Gould (1977) has recently raised the serious possibility that the patterns of macro-evolution observable in the palaeontological record depend on processes not visible in ecological time.

Some of the clearest examples of time perspectivism are to be found in cosmological studies and the seemingly bizarre concepts of space-time (Davies 1977). For example, Einstein's theories deal with the vast distances of galactic and inter-galactic space, distances over which the finite speed of light becomes a variable of the greatest significance. On the more modest scale of our own solar system the effect of this variable is so small that it can be ignored for most purposes. The older mechanical view of Newton explains most of the features of the system, barring minor anomalies such as the irregularity in Mercury's orbit, and is quite sufficient to place men on the moon. On yet a smaller scale again, pre-Copernican conceptions persist. The assumption of a flat earth is perfectly adequate at scales where the curvature of the earth's surface is so small as to be irrelevant, for example in non-geodetic distance reckoning, Euclidean geometry and civil engineering. The development of ideas about the universe has involved not so much a replacement of one theory by a more advanced one, but rather the unification of an existing view within a larger whole which specifies the limits of scale within which the older assumptions work and beyond which they cease to be effective.

There is, then, in these historical disciplines no inherent conflict between time perspectivism and methodological uniformitarianism. The growth of a unified body of knowledge does not consist of establishing a single set of principles, which is then held to be absolutely and universally valid, but rather depends on establishing the existence of different sets of principles, each valid relative to its particular scale of focus. There is no absolute temporal frame of reference, only a relative frame of reference. While the concepts that work within these different frames of reference should be mutually compatible (if methodological uniformitarianism is to have any meaning), they cannot be transferred without modification from one frame to another.

Time Perspectivism in Human Behaviour

Developments in the natural sciences offer no guarantee of the correct approach in archaeology, and it may be asked what relevance these rather remote geological and cosmological perspectives have to human affairs. Let us then bring the argument down to earth again to consider what variables in economic behaviour might operate differently at different time-scales. Two brief examples may help to illustrate the possibilities. The first refers to the much discussed concept of population pressure as an explanation of prehistoric economic trends. This can be applied in at least two different ways. According to one school of thought, which takes its inspiration from Boserup's studies of modern and recent agricultural practice, population pressure can be treated as an independent variable (Spooner 1972). Periods of economic stagnation or decline can be attributed to stable or declining population levels, periods of economic growth to population increase which pushes against the existing resource ceiling, depending on the inherent balance between levels of natality and mortality. An alternative view is that on the larger time-scales of prehistory, these small-scale fluctuations become smoothed out, and population pressure becomes, in effect, a constant, so that explanations of economic change visible at this time-scale must be sought in other factors (Bailey in press; Bronson 1977; Cohen 1977; Higgs and Jarman 1975). What appears to be a variable on a small time-scale becomes a constant on a large time-scale.

The second example illustrates the reverse principle. Extreme climatic and environmental fluctuations tend only to occur and to have an impact on human behaviour patterns over fairly long time spans. Strictly speaking, we should recognise a number of different periodicities ranging from the extreme amplitude of glacial-interglacial fluctuations operating over tens of thousands of years, to the lesser fluctuations of centuries, to the minor changes from day to day and year to year (see O'Shea and Halstead, this volume). For the ethnographic observer working at the short end of the time-scale, environmental factors can be and are treated for many purposes as constants. Over longer time spans these may be variables of considerable significance in their potential effects on economic behaviour, although they are often ignored because of the lack of independent palaeoenvironmental data, or the fear of being tainted with the extreme oversimplifications of environmental determinism (Le Roy Ladurie 1972; Vita-Finzi 1978). Similarly the assessment of genetic influence on the development of cultural adaptations requires long time spans for its effective investigation (Durham 1976).

The use of the term 'adaptation' exposes some of the difficulties of ignoring time-scaling factors. Much of the conflict between cultural-ecological and structural-Marxist approaches to human behaviour centres on the use of this term. Both parties in the dispute seem to assume that adaptive behaviour is behaviour that exists. Structural-Marxists can point out that if all behaviour that exists (including social structures and beliefs) is adaptive, this is either self-evident or absurd (Godelier 1972; Sahlins 1974). Cultural ecologists can reply that not all behaviour that exists need be adaptive, but thereby undermine much of the explanatory power of their approach. There is, however, an implicit assumption here, that behaviour that exists within the time span of anthropological observation is behaviour that has persisted for some indeterminate time previously. This assumption may be acceptable in biological and ethological studies, where the viability of genetically-based behaviour is determined by the reproductive process. Traits that are maladaptive in relation to existing conditions are swiftly eliminated and cannot be recalled should conditions subsequently change. Cultural transmission, however, represents an accumulation of behaviour patterns, ideas and techniques which persist to some extent independently of their originators. Maladaptive or non-adaptive patterns may persist, in store as it were, alongside the adaptive, ready for more widespread adoption if conditions change. The greater flexibility and speed of response that this confers also entails a greater looseness of fit between behaviour and environment, in which factors on either side of the relationship may be varying at different rates and thus appear to be out of phase over short time spans.

Another factor that should reinforce the exploration of time perspectivism in prehistoric investigations is the very nature of much of the available data. A sample of archaeological sites, animal bones, molluscs, or of any other type of subsistence data, large enough for reliable interpretation, often represents a palimpsest of activities ranging over a period of at least a hundred years to several thousand or more. It refers not to the activities of individuals, or even individual societies, but to larger aggregates of behaviour, reflecting average tendencies which persisted over long periods of time. This coarseness of resolution is further accentuated by the margins of error inherent in radiometric dating. This is not to say that a finer resolution of short-term variations may not be possible in favourable circumstances, for example in the dendrochronological study of neolithic lake settlement (Sakellaridis 1979), or that some features of the material record cannot be usefully referred to individual actions, as in the culture-symbolical study of stylistic variation in artifacts (Hodder 1979). But much of the palaeoeconomic record refers, by definition, to long-term trends. While this may seem a severe limitation, it also offers an opportunity to focus on a different scale of behaviour and imposes a requirement to adjust one's conceptual framework accordingly.

Time Boundedness

A final deterrent to exploring the implications of time perspectivism lies in the tendency to view historical processes from a single, fixed observer position in time, that of the present. From this time-bounded perspective, events and processes near to us in time appear more detailed and complex than those further back in time, and it is natural to see in this the evidence of a directional historical process. The concept of directional or sequential time is strongly rooted in the Western scientific tradition, and contrasts with the conception dominant in Greek or Mediaeval thought of time as cyclical or eternal (Tuan 1978), differing conceptions which reflect two fundamentally distinct notions of time: repetitive or reversible time, and directional or irreversible time (Leach 1966:124-136).

Some of the most far-reaching questions raised in historical studies centre on whether the time trends under study are directional, implying a beginning and an end, or part of an endlessly repeating series of oscillations. In cosmogony the contrast is between big-bang and steady-state or oscillating models of the universe, in palaeontology between directional and steady-state theories of organic evolution, and in human history between the conception of progress and the rise and fall of civilisations.

Archaeological theories of prehistoric development, in contrast, are almost entirely directional. If the nineteenth century notions of progress and unilinearity have long since been abandoned, current theories of social evolution addressed to such problems as the origins of agriculture and urbanisation rely more or less implicitly on the idea of multilinear directionality. A fully articulated steady-state theory of social evolution scarcely exists, although a significant element of such thinking enters into the Higgs-Jarman palaeoeconomic theory of agricultural development. As against almost all other theories, which regard the origins of agriculture as a progressive development in the terminal Pleistocene and Early Holocene, they see the technical and cognitive skills of resource husbandry implied by the conception of agriculture as being universally inherent in human exploitation of the environment, although subject to variations according to local circumstances; directionality, according to their view, is confined to long-term overall increases in the gross level of economic output.

The choice between emphasising directional and steady-state aspects of development is partly dependent on the point of view adopted, and is further complicated by the effects of varying the time perspective. A directional trend at one time-scale may turn out to be part of a steady-state oscillation at a larger time-scale. This in its turn may appear as part of an overriding directional trend at a yet larger time-scale again.

It is an inevitable part of our status as individual observers and our time-bounded condition that we tend to understand most easily what happens close to us, whether that closeness is in terms of personal experience, space or time, and that the extension of our understanding involves projecting outwards the familiar categories of our own experience until confrontation with more remote or less familiar data requires their modification. The dominance of this egocentric or ethnocentric view is easily corrected in terms of personal or social experience because we can observe and question other people and appreciate their 'point of view'. The application of this corrective is almost a truism of anthropological research, and finds its expression in economic anthropology in the rejection of the formal models of Western capitalist economies as appropriate analogues for all economic systems (Godelier 1972). In spatial terms also we can change our position at will and appreciate the different perspective offered by different observer positions in space. We know that the earth's surface is not really flat because we can take photographs from an orbiting satellite; we know that the convergence of parallel railway lines at a point on the horizon is an optical illusion because we can travel along the railway track. Our time-bounded perspective is less easily corrected because we cannot easily travel through time. At best we can only move backwards in time, and then only through the vicarious and highly imperfect methods of historical and archaeological research.

Conclusion

I have emphasised time perspectivism here, not because I believe it is necessarily the only approach to archaeological explanation, but in order to highlight a set of assumptions that has always been implicit in palaeoeconomic thinking. Moreover, time perspectivism has three general virtues which are worth emphasising. First, it reasserts the importance of the historical dimension in archaeological data, without committing us to the fate of an idiographic discipline. Secondly, it allows for the co-existence of a diversity of theoretical points of view without undermining the search for integration. Thirdly, it challenges us to justify our theories in archaeological terms regardless of the support they may derive from adjacent disciplines.

Equally, a number of objections may be raised against the time perspective view of human behaviour that I have sketched out above. One obvious point is that its implications are far more complex than I have indicated. Time perspectivism is not simply a question of distinguishing the short term from the long term, the present from the past, existence from persistence. There is a multiplicity of scales, and more detailed consideration is required to define the limits of these different scales, the way in which they mesh together, and the residual effects at one scale of processes which are more clearly in focus at another scale. Even activities played out in the ethnographic present are influenced by longer term decisions (Holly 1978), while the long term record of prehistory comprises a number of different scales ranging from the one hundred thousand year time-scales of the Lower Pleistocene to one hundred year time-scales in the later periods of prehistory.

A more fundamental objection may be that since behaviour patterns are mediated through the actions of individuals as members of corporate societies, explanations that leave these factors out of account in an appeal to a different order of scale are somehow incomplete explanations. If we leave aside the notion of completeness as being—like the notion of absolute truth—beyond the scope of the present discussion, the nub of this objection seems to be a reluctance to abandon an egocentric view of the world which requires that even the remotest features of reality be reduced to, and explained in terms of, the familiar categories of everyday experience. Time perspectivism is no more than an extension along a particular dimension of the quite unremarkable principle that group behaviour is more than a simple sum of the individual actions and behaviour patterns of which it is constituted, and cannot be inferred from or reduced to a study of its individual members.

Another sort of objection may be that time perspectivism is simply an elaborate justification for the perpetuation of palaeoeconomic dogma. If the counter to this sounds like an appeal to realism, nevertheless it may not be inappropriate to reassert the practical value of accepting the limitations of time-scale and concentrating on those variables that are most sharply in focus in the prehistoric record, rather than striving in vain for an elusive type of data. The crucial question is not what features of human thought and behaviour are relevant to explanations in economic prehistory, but what time-scale is best suited to the study of the particular variables which interest the analyst, and where in the total span of human behaviour the necessary chronological resolution and the necessary data are most easily to be found. If the interest is in the relationship between economic exploitation and social and ideological values, then short time-scales in the present or recent past would seem to offer the most suitable frame of reference. For effective studies of the ecological relationship between economy and environment, longer time spans would seem to be necessary. It is no coincidence that classic palaeoeconomic theories tend to be most popular with those who work mainly with the archaeology of the Late Pleistocene and Early Holocene; sociological theories with specialists whose interests centre on the Late Neolithic and Bronze Age or later (in European terms); and more strictly ecological and genetic theories with specialists in the earlier phases of the Palaeolithic.

If the proposition is to be taken seriously, that socially given premises or culturally determined perceptions of environment are independent variables on the longer time-scales of prehistory, capable of exerting a significant differential impact on long term economic trends, then their effect must surely be manifest in the material record of prehistoric subsistence, and the inadequacy of current palaeoeconomic explanations made apparent. Archaeological data may be patchy, ambiguous and difficult to analyse, but only the most abject pessimist would deny that the prehistoric record can be made to speak on this issue if interrogated with suitably framed hypotheses. If, however, the main message of the sociological polemic is that social behaviour and social action represent autonomous fields of study, that they cannot be reduced to or inferred from economic or ecological data, that they develop, at least in part, according to a logic of their own, or that different social solutions may be found to similar economic problems, these points may all be valid and even interesting, but their relevance to the central concerns of economic prehistory has yet to be demonstrated. It would be mistaken to exclude any hypothesis or concept *a priori*, except as a matter of personal preference or as an act of faith. But if it be granted that the polemical confrontation within archaeology of different assumptions about human behaviour has stimulated the perception of new problems in recent years, it should also be recognised that the resolution of these problems cannot be achieved without recourse to the prehistoric record.

Footnotes

1. The term 'economic prehistory' is used here in preference to economic archaeology, partly as a matter of convention as the term most commonly used in the literature cited, partly to express the emphasis on the earlier periods of the archaeological record.
2. The term 'perspectivism' is preferred here, following Walsh (1951) and von Bertalanffy (1968), rather than 'relativism'. The latter term is widely used in anthroplogy, e.g. cultural relativism (Harris 1968), but may refer to the study of relations rather than the relativity of knowledge.

Acknowledgements

I would like to thank Iain Davidson, Tim Ingold and Claudio Vita-Finzi for helpful comments on an earlier draft.

References

Atkinson, R. F., 1978. *Knowledge and Explanation in History*. London: Macmillan.

Bailey, G. N. (in press). "Concepts of resource exploitation: continuity and discontinuity in palaeoeconomy." *World Archaeology*.

Bender, B., 1978. "Gatherer-hunter to farmer: a social perspective." *World Archaeology* 10:204-222.

Bertalanffy, L. von, 1968. *General Systems Theory*. New York: Braziller.

Binford, L. R., 1977. General introduction. In *For Theory Building in Archaeology*, ed. L. R. Binford. New York: Academic Press; 1-10.

Blurton Jones, N. G., 1976. "Growing points in ethology: another link between ethology and the social sciences?" in *Growing Points in Ethology*, eds. P.P.G. Bateson and R. A. Hinde. Cambridge: Cambridge University Press; 427-450.

Bronson, B., 1977. "The earliest farming: demography as cause and consequence" in *Origins of Agriculture*, ed. C. A. Reed. The Hague: Mouton; 23-48.

Carr, E. H., 1961. What is History? London: Macmillan.

Chesneaux, J., 1978. Pasts and Futures or What is History For? London: Thames and Hudson.

Clark, J. G. D., 1939. Archaeology and Society. London: Methuen.

Clark, J. G. D., 1942. "Bees in antiquity." Antiquity 16:208-215.

Clark, J. G. D., 1944. "Water in antiquity." Antiquity 18:1-15.

Clark, J. G. D., 1945. "Farmers and forests in neolithic Europe." Antiquity 19:57-71.

Clark, J. G. D., 1946. "Seal-hunting in the Stone Age of North-Western Europe: a study in economic prehistory." P.P.S.12:12-48.

Clark, J. G. D., 1947a. "Sheep and swine in the husbandry of prehistoric Europe." Antiquity 21:122-136.

Clark, J. G. D., 1947b. "Whales as an economic factor in prehistoric Europe." Antiquity 22:84-104.

Clark, J. G. D., 1948. "The development of fishing in prehistoric Europe." Antiq. J. 27:45-85.

Clark, J. G. D., 1952. Prehistoric Europe: The Economic Basis. London: Methuen.

Clark, J. G. D., 1953. "The economic approach to prehistory." Proc. Brit. Acad. 39:215-238.

Clark, J. G. D., 1954a. The Study of Prehistory. Cambridge: Cambridge University Press.

Clark, J. G. D., 1954b. Excavations at Star Carr. Cambridge: Cambridge University Press.

Clark, J. G. D., 1965. "Traffic in stone axe and hand blades." Econ. Hist. Rev. 18:1-28.

Clark, J. G. D., 1972. "The archaeology of stone age settlement." U.J.A. 35:3-16.

Clark, J. G. D., 1975. The Earlier Stone Age Settlement of Scandinavia. London: Cambridge University Press.

Clark, J. G. D., 1977. World Archaeology (3rd. ed.). Cambridge: Cambridge University Press.

Cohen, M. N., 1977. The Food Crisis in Prehistory. New Haven: Yale University Press.

Daniel, G. E. D., 1975. A Hundred and Fifty Years of Archaeology. London: Duckworth.

Davies, P. C. W., 1977. Space and Time in the Modern Universe. Cambridge: Cambridge University Press.

Dennell, R. W., 1979. "Prehistoric diet and nutrition: some food for thought." World Archaeology 11:121-135.

Durham, W. H., 1976. "The adaptive significance of cultural behaviour." Human Ecology 4:89-121.

Evans-Pritchard, E. E., 1961. Anthropology and History. Manchester: Manchester University Press.

Flannery, K. V., 1973. "Archaeology with a capital S" in Research and Theory in Current Archaeology, ed. C. L. Redman. New York: Wiley; 47-53.

Fletcher, R. J., 1977a. "Alternatives and differences" in Archaeology and Anthropology: Areas of Mutual Interest, ed. M. Spriggs. Oxford: B.A.R. Suppl. Ser. 19; 49-68.

Fletcher, R. J., 1977b. "Settlement studies (micro and semi-micro)" in Spatial Archaeology, ed. D. L. Clarke. London: Academic Press; 47-162.

Foucault, M., 1972. The Archaeology of Knowledge. London: Tavistock.

Godelier, M., 1972. Rationality and Irrationality in Economics. London: New Left Books.

Gould, S. J., 1965. "Is uniformitarianism necessary?" Amer. J. Sci. 263:223-228.

Gould, S. J., 1977. "Eternal metaphors of palaeontology" in Patterns of Evolution as Illustrated by the Fossil Record, ed. A. Hallam. Developments in Palaeontology and Stratigraphy 5. Amsterdam: Elsevier; 1-26.

Harris, M., 1968. The Rise of Anthropological Theory. London: Routledge and Kegan Paul.

Harriss, J. C., 1971. "Explanation in prehistory." P.P.S. 37:38-55.

Harvey, D. W., 1969. Explanation in Geography. London: Arnold.

Heyman, G., 1944. Préhistoire Economique Général. Bruxelles, Vromont.

Higgs, E. S., 1961. "Some Pleistocene faunas of the Mediterranean coastal areas." P.P.S. 27:144-154.

Higgs, E. S., 1968. "Archaeology—where now?" Mankind 6:617-620.

Higgs, E. S. (ed.), 1972. Papers in Economic Prehistory. London: Cambridge University Press.

Higgs, E. S. (ed.), 1975. Palaeoeconomy. London: Cambridge University Press.

Higgs, E. S. and Jarman, M. R., 1975. "Palaeoeconomy" in Palaeoeconomy, ed. E. S. Higgs. London: Cambridge University Press; 1-8.

Higgs, E. S. and White, J. P., 1963. "Autumn killing." Antiquity 37:282-9.

Higgs, E. S., Vita-Finzi, C., Harris, D. R. and Fagg, A. E., 1967. "The climate, environment and industries of stone age Greece, part III." P.P.S. 33:1-29.

Higham, C. F. W., 1966. Stock Rearing in Prehistoric Europe with Special Reference to the Danish Islands and the Alpine Foreland. Unpublished Ph.D. thesis, Cambridge University.

Higham, C. F. W., 1967. "Stock rearing as a cultural factor in prehistoric Europe." P.P.S. 33:84-106.

Hodder, I., 1979. "Economic and social stress and material culture patterning." Amer. Ant. 44:446-454.

Holly, B. P., 1978. "The problem of scale in time-space research" in Timing Space and Spacing Time, Vol. 3: Time and Regional Dynamics, eds. T. Carlstein, D. Parkes and N. Thrift. London: Arnold; 5-18.

Ingold, T., 1979. "The social and ecological relations of culture-bearing organisms: an essay in evolutionary dynamics" in Social and Ecological Systems, eds. P. C. Burnham and R. F. Ellen. A.S.A. Monograph 18. London: Academic Press; 271-291.

Ingold, T., 1980. Hunters, Pastoralists and Ranchers: Reindeer Economies and their Transformations. Cambridge: Cambridge University Press.

Jarman, M. R., Bailey, G. N. and Jarman, H. N. (eds.), (forthcoming). The Early History of European Agriculture. Cambridge: Cambridge University Press.

Klejn, L. S., 1977. "A panorama of theoretical archaeology." Curr. Anth. 18:1-42.

Leach, E. R., 1966 (2nd. impression). Rethinking Anthropology. London: Athlone Press.

LeClair, E. E. and Schneider, H. K. (eds.), 1968. Economic Anthropology. New York: Holt, Rinehart and Winston.

Le Roy Ladurie, E., 1972. Times of Feast, Times of Famine. London: Allen and Unwin.

Le Roy Ladurie, E., 1979. The Territory of the Historian. Hassocks: Harvester Press.

Popper, K. R., 1945. The Open Society and its Enemies. London: Routledge and Kegan Paul.

Popper, K. R., 1957. The Poverty of Historicism. London: Routledge and Kegan Paul.

Sahlins, M. D., 1974. Stone Age Economics. London: Tavistock.

Sakellaridis, M., 1979. The Economic Exploitation of the Swiss Area in the Mesolithic and Neolithic Periods. Oxford: B.A.R. Suppl. Ser. 67.

Salmon, M. H., 1978. "What can systems theory do for archaeology?" Amer. Ant. 43:174-183.

Schopf, T. J. M., 1977. "Patterns of evolution: a summary and discussion" in Patterns of Evolution as Illustrated by the Fossil Record, ed. A. Hallam. Developments in Palaeontology and Stratigraphy 5. Amsterdam; Elsevier; 547-561.

Schumm, S. A. and Lichty, R. W., 1965. " Time, space and causality in geomorphology." Amer. J. Sci. 263:110-119.

Shawcross, F. W., 1967. "An investigation of prehistoric diet and economy on a coastal site at Galatea Bay, New Zealand." P.P.S. 33:107-131.

Slobodkin, L. B., 1976. "Evolution is no help." World Archaeology 8:332-343.

Spooner, B, (ed.). 1972. Population Growth: Anthropological Implications Cambridge, Mass.: M. I. T. Press.

Tuan, Yi-Fu, 1978. "Space, time, place: a humanistic frame" in Timing Space and Spacing Time, Vol. I: Making Sense of Time, eds. T. Carlstein, D. Parkes and N. Thrift. London: Arnold; 7-16.

Trigger, B. G., 1970. "Aims in prehistoric archaeology." Antiquity 44: 26-37.

Trigger, B. G., 1973. "The future of archaeology is the past" in Research and Theory in Current Archaeology, ed. C. L. Redman. New York: Wiley; 95-111.

Tuggle, H. D., Stanley Price, N.P. and Trigger, B. G., 1971. 'Trigger and prehistoric archaeology." Antiquity 45: 103-104.

Vita-Finzi, C., 1973. Recent Earth History. London: Macmillan.

Vita-Finzi, C., 1978. Archaeological Sites in their Setting. London: Thames and Hudson.

Walsh, W. H., 1951. An Introduction to Philosophy of History. London: Hutchinson.

Watson, P. J., 1973. "The future of archaeology in anthropology: culture history and social science" in Research and Theory in Current Archaeology, ed. C. L. Redman. New York: Wiley; 113-124.

Watson, P. J., LeBlanc, S. A. and Redman, C. L., 1971. Explanation in Archaeology: An Explicitly Scientific Approach. New York: Columbia University Press.

10. THE HUNTER AND HIS SPEAR: NOTES ON THE CULTURAL MEDIATION OF SOCIAL AND ECOLOGICAL SYSTEMS

Tim Ingold

A review of the anthropological literature concerning the material conditions of social life would yield a number of competing theoretical paradigms, under such various labels as cultural ecology, cultural materialism, neo-Marxism, neofunctionalism, and many more. Much of the debate surrounding these alternatives centres on the juxtaposition of four grand terms — ecology, technology, society and culture — and the connections between them. We enclose our terms in boxes with arrows going this way or that, or sometimes in all directions at once (e.g. Cohen 1974:65). Depending upon the source of inspiration, there is talk of selective pressure, dialectical process, or a labyrinth of 'multiple feedback loops'. Colossal, poly-hyphenated, multi-systemic monsters stalk the pages of this debate: there are techno-environmental and socio-cultural systems, somehow exchanging heads and tails with socio-environments and techno-cultural complexes. It is all very confusing, and not a little imprecise. I think it might be helpful, in the circumstances, to abandon these monsters to their fate, and to start again by considering the simplest of situations, which in fact embodies all the ingredients of a complex argument. I hope, in so doing, to re-examine the import of certain basic terms, and to suggest a theoretical approach which I find more satisfactory than the alternatives on offer, if not without problems of its own.

Ecology and society

Let us imagine, then, a hunter, armed with a spear, out in pursuit of game. He is, of course, a man, equipped with head and hands, arms and legs. But he also belongs to a social group, or a band, amongst whose members the products of his hunting will eventually be distributed. Though he encounters his prey physically as an individual, socially his action in making a kill constitutes just one event in the collective appropriation of a natural resource. Bearing in mind this dual — physical and social — existence of our subject, we may observe him in stalking and dispatching his quarry, in transporting the meat to camp, in preparing it for consumption, and together with his fellows in actually eating it. Suppose that we could somehow wire him up so as to measure his total expenditure of energy in all these activities. The figure thus obtained could then be compared with an estimate of the calorific content of the game consumed, yielding a ratio of 'techno-environmental efficiency' (Harris 1971: 203 ff.). Clearly, if the hunter is to survive the latter quantity must exceed the former, normally by a large margin.

Yet it would be quite mistaken to suppose that any intrinsic relation exists between these quantities. When the hunter throws his spear, muscular energy is converted to kinetic energy in the motion of the spear, all of which is ultimately expended in the friction of impact. There is no physical sense in which the energy of the hunter might be said to be incorporated into his quarry. He will not necessarily obtain more by throwing more spears, or by throwing them harder. Likewise, there is no relation between the electric current required to flick a switch and the heat generated by the boiler it controls. In hunting as in control engineering, precision rather than power is of the essence. Pressing the mechanical analogy, we could perhaps view the act of hunting in terms of the transmission of information, by which the state of one system effects changes in the state of another, linked system. Thus the thrust of the spear establishes the conditions for a trophic exchange of materials and energy from the victim to the humans who eventually consume it, just as the triggering of the switch initiates a conversion of boiler fuel into heat.

Such an exchange, by which animal tissues are organically assimilated into human bodies, may perfectly well be regarded as a form of energy conversion, whose efficiency may be measured in thermodynamic terms. It forms a part of the process of ecological production, by which I mean the creation of organic material by reactions going on in Nature, fuelled ultimately by solar radiation. The action of the hunter in throwing his spear functions to 'switch off' a process of ecological production in the game, and his action in processing and eating the meat functions to 'switch on' a process of ecological production in his own body. But these actions are wilful, and involve the expenditure of labour in order to obtain from Nature the means of subsistence. I refer to this as economic production. If we wish to measure the efficiency of economic production, the values assigned to labour and to the products of labour must be socially rather than physically defined, for it is only in a social sense that we can speak of labour being embodied in products. Essentially, therefore, the economically productive activity of the hunter is initiated and directed by the system of social relations in which he is involved, which determines the constituents of the environment that are to be valued as resources, and the rationality of their exploitation.

We may define the social system, in a general way, as consisting of the relations between people in respect of the resources and products of the environment. It specifies who should perform the work of economic production, how the fruits of that production are distributed, and who eventually consumes them. From an ecosystemic perspective, on the other hand, the human group appears as an undifferentiated population aggregate, dependent for its growth and reproduction on an input of materials and energy from its environment. We define the ecosystem in energy terms as a network of trophic exchanges linking the human population directly with the organic resources it consumes, and linking those resources with other components of the environment. Such exchanges, unlike the social transfers involved in distribution, have an immediate bearing on the physical state of the recipients. Thus the socially directed acts of economic production, distribution and consumption serve to effect a transduction from the social system to the ecosystem: food is ingested by humans, there is a direct conversion of energy. To return to the mechanical analogy: we might regard the motion of the hunter's spear as representing a signal from the social system, 'translating' the state of that system into a change in state of the ecosystem with which it is articulated (cf. Rappaport 1968: 229). In this sense, the social system could be said to 'drive', or dominate, the ecosystem.

A brief digression is necessary at this stage, in order to indicate how the theoretical position advanced here diverges from the 'new' (though now somewhat dated) ecology advocated most forcibly by Vayda and Rappaport (1968). The essence of their view is that the human economy can be reduced to ecological relations of production, and that the total system thus constituted has homeostatic properties of self-maintenance, hence perpetuating itself in a qualitatively steady state over indefinite periods of time. This view is erroneous in two critical respects. Firstly, as I have already shown, the purposive action of men (or indeed of animals — see Ingold 1979) in extracting food from the environment cannot be comprehended purely in terms of trophic energetics. Economic and ecological production must be held distinct. This point should not require further elaboration. Secondly, there is no justification for the arbitrary invocation of a rationality of long-term ecosystem maintenance. It is true that the ecosystem can only function within certain limits, defined in the extreme case by the onset of negative energy balances. Once the limit is approached, either the social system must be returned to its point of origin — thus yielding a series of repetitive cycles — or a transformation must ensue in both social and ecological conditions of production. The ecosystem therefore imposes a kind of <u>negative determination</u> upon the development of the social system which drives it: it can only be driven so far without breaking down. But there is nothing intrinsic to the ecosystem itself which ensures that its limits of functioning cannot be exceeded. Of course it is possible that the social system may impose constraints of its own on the intensification of economic production that come into play before the ecosystemic threshold is reached, but there is no necessary reason why this should be so (Friedman 1974: 459-60).

Let us be clear about the distinction between ecosystem and environment, for the two are often confused. The environment can only be defined relative to the subject whose environment it is, be it a single individual, a local or regional population, or an entire species. It does not therefore exist as a system, but rather as a set of possibilities. The environment does not itself specify the manner or intensity of its exploitation, but it does impose physical and organic constraints on the realization of the socially defined objectives of the subject population. For example, the environment of steppe or tundra does not specify that men should be hunters rather than, say, pastoralists. The distinction here is a <u>social</u> one: hunters appropriate the herds collectively, pastoralists individually; and this difference in turn generates the contrasting rationalities of sharing and accumulation respectively (Ingold 1980). But <u>given</u> the social relations of hunting, the environment naturally places restrictions on <u>what</u> may be hunted and, up to a point, on <u>how</u> it is done. The application of a social rationality to the possibilities presented by the environment generates a certain constellation of ecological associations between men, animals and plants. These associations, characterized by trophic exchanges of materials and energy, constitute the ecosystem.

It is to the 'what' and 'how' of environmental exploitation that the method of cultural ecology has classically directed its attention. As outlined by Steward, the method begins with an analysis of 'the interrelationship of exploitative or productive technology and environment'; and then proceeds to analyse 'the behaviour patterns involved in the exploitation of a particular environment by means of a particular technology' (Steward 1955: 40-1). This is legitimate as far as it goes; but there is no provision in this procedure for the comprehension of social relations of production unless, as Steward seems to imply, they are constituted on the basis of 'behaviour patterns'. Now it is quite evident that forms of co-operation, along with skills and equipment, form a part of the means whereby a population adapts to its environment. However, the objectives of this adaptation, as I have shown, can only be defined in terms of the rationality of the social system in which that population is involved. It is thus fundamentally mistaken to compound the social relations of production with the technical organization of work under the general rubric of 'social organization' (Harris 1968:221-3). Rather, as Friedman puts it, we should say that 'a number of necessary technical activities are organized socially' (1975: 168). It is not possible to deduce the form of the social system from the interaction between environment and technology. Where, then, does technology belong in this scheme of things? To consider this question, let me return to the example of the hunter and his spear.

Technology and culture

Our first observation must be that the spear itself, however elegant its construction, forms but a small part of the hunter's equipment. Far more important is his knowledge about the different species of animals available to him, where they may be located, how they reproduce, and how they may best be approached and captured. And again, for certain kinds of hunting which involve the co-operation of a number of people, an effective allocation of tasks among the participants may be more crucial for the success of the hunt than the sophistication of their material equipment. The adaptive repertoire of the hunter must therefore be broadened to include such immaterial factors as skills, organizational techniques, and knowledge about the natural world and the way it behaves. But behind every tool or technique there lies a conscious model, or blueprint, which the hunter carries in his imagination, and which he can communicate symbolically (Marx 1930: 170). It would appear, therefore, that no rigid boundary can be drawn between technology and ideology. If any distinction can be made, it is between models of and models for, between representations of reality and instructions for action: yet it is characteristic of human symboling that these kinds of models are inter-transposable (Geertz 1966: 7-8).

In these terms, technology — alongside organizational and ideological aspects of culture — may be seen to mediate relations both between man in society, and between men and components of the natural environment (Cook 1973: 39). The actual use of technology represents an aspect of the functioning of the social system, whilst the physical or organic consequences of that use are embodied in the state of the ecosystem. It is through technology that the transduction between these two kinds of system is effected, from the social to the physical domain of human existence. The hunter's spear, as I have argued above, represents the instrumental conductor of signals from one domain to the other. Now, it is important to recognize that the properties of technology are not autonomous, but are derived from the combination of underlying social and environmental conditions; for it is these that define the practical problems that technology is brought in to solve. We must therefore reject the notion of the 'techno-environmental' or 'techno-ecological system' that is encountered so commonly in the literature. Even if the ecosystem is, to a great extent, 'engineered' by human action, we should not confuse the artificial result with the instrumental means. The ecosystemic consequences of the use of technology, and not the technology itself, impose limits on the development of the associated social system. Or to put it another way, the social is dialectically opposed not to the technological but to the ecological.

These conclusions require us to rethink the classic Marxian concept of 'productive forces', as well as the conventional dichotomy between infrastructure and superstructure. If we are to regard the 'forces' as a component of the material conditions of existence, they cannot consist of a mere inventory of the tools and techniques available to a population (Terray 1972: 98; see Balibar 1970: 233-5). They should rather be conceived as the physical relations that men establish with the natural environment through the mediation of their ideas and techniques. Thus the hunter's spear is in itself inert, it may conduct a force, but does not constitute it. But then, are the 'forces' those of economic or ecological production? The direct action of human producers upon the natural environment, since it is governed by the social system, cannot oppose it. There can be no contradiction between the hunter's pursuit of game and the social rationality that leads him to do it. On the other hand, a critical point may be approached at which the hunter must expend more in procuring his food than he can derive from its consumption. Here there is a real contradiction between the functioning of the social system and the dynamics of the associated ecosystem: hunting simply ceases to be ecologically viable. It follows that if we are to retain the notion of a dialectic between 'relations' and 'forces', the latter must be defined as those of ecological production.

I think it would be more appropriate, however, to visualize an opposition not between relations and forces, but between two distinct systems of relations, social and ecological, to each of which there corresponds a notion of force — of economic production in the one case and ecological production in the other. The intensification of economic production beyond the limits of functioning of the ecosystem brings these forces to a point at which they can no longer operate in conjunction: there is, in other words, an emergent contradiction between social action and ecological reaction, or between the use of technology and the consequences of its use. But I have suggested that technology cannot rigidly be separated from other aspects of culture. If that is so, it is as important to distinguish these other (organizational and ideological) aspects from their social application as it is to distinguish technology from its ecological impact. In other words, the notion of the 'sociocultural system' must be abandoned, along with its counterpart, the 'techno-ecological system'. To justify my rejection of these constructs, it is necessary at this stage to elaborate a little on the concept of culture.

I hesitate to give a definition of culture when there are so many alternatives already on offer, yet it seems that I must. Culture may be regarded as an ordered system of knowledge and values for explaining and acting upon the real world, carried in the consciousness of individuals, and amenable to symbolic transmission and storage. As such, of course, it includes both organizational and technological capabilities. But if the form of a culture is conditioned by the social reality which it symbolically constructs, we cannot regard that reality as an extension of the symbolic process. This is the fallacy of cultural reason, illustrated so well by the recent commentary by Sahlins on Marx. According to Sahlins, Marx apprehends ideology as 'the model of a given system in consciousness, while ignoring that the system so symbolized is itself symbolic' (1976: 139). Symbolic, one may ask, of what? The grafting of the social onto the cultural makes a nonsense of the symbolic constitution of culture, since there is nothing left to symbolize. Consider the implications of such a position. Either we would have to suppose that the entire 'sociocultural system' forms an adaptive response to environmental objectives that are somehow given in advance — a 'cognized model' of Nature that leads people to behave in ways conducive to ecosystem maintenance (Rappaport 1968: 238–41). Or we would have to follow Sahlins in taking the opposite view, rejecting altogether the idea of culture as a means of adaptation, and supposing rather that it conforms to a logic all of its own.

I would insist to the contrary that culture, divorced from social rationality, is practically inert. Words and symbols cannot think, any more than spears can hunt. However, so long as we are prepared to accept the distinction between society as the reality and culture as its intellectual representation, it is possible to take a thoroughly pragmatic view of the functions of culture without falling for the fallacies of organic or environmental reductionism. In brief, I would argue that culture serves to translate a social rationality into practical effectiveness. Note that this is no more than a generalization to culture as a whole of the transducing property of technology which I have already illustrated by the example of the hunter and his spear.

Let me now return to the problem of the dichotomy between infrastructure and superstructure. This has recently come in for a good deal of criticism, notably from within the ranks of Marxist anthropology itself. The point is made that it is impossible to conceive of either 'forces' or 'relations' of production without introducing elements of a normative or ideal character. Thus, if the 'forces' are regarded in the traditional sense as a set of technical capabilities, it is obvious — as we have remarked above — that these must include non-material elements such as knowledge, skills, and organizational arrangements. And if relations of production are apparently structured, for example, by kinship, then we must conclude that the same kinship structure functions both as relations of production and as normative ideology, and hence that it registers at all levels of the total social formation (Godelier 1972: 93–5).

I would argue rather differently. Firstly, I hold that it is essential to retain some kind of dichotomy to denote the distinction between the ecological and social dimensions of material reality, on the one hand, and the intellectual representations of that reality by acting, thinking individuals, on the other. This distinction seems to me to be a necessary logical corollary of the supposition that the symbolic process is constrained within a reality 'out there', which is no mere construct of the mind. Let us denote that reality, at least provisionally, by the term 'infrastructure'. Then it should be clear that technology — as distinct from its application (the force of economic production) and the consequences of its application (the force of ecological production) — does not belong to it. In other words, we should recognize the ideal component of technological capability not by collapsing the distinction between infrastructure and superstructure, but by taking technology out of the infrastructure altogether. Technology is essentially a corpus of culturally transmitted knowledge, expressed in manufacture and use, and as such it belongs with ideology in the domain of human consciousness.

So, too, do structures of kinship (Lévi-Strauss 1968: 50). The argument that kinship functions both as productive relations and as ideology, though an ingenious device for reconciling the alleged dominance of kinship in primitive societies with the ultimate determinacy of the economy, is logically fallacious. The fallacy stems from the notion of 'structure' itself. People use kinship paradigms in order to construct models, or to impose a cultural ordering on real relations of production. To be effective, such models must be compatible with the reality represented. But compatibility must not be rendered as identity. The same structure cannot appear both as a representation and as the reality beneath, both as a model and what is modelled. On the infrastructural level, we should be seeking elementary structures of production, not of kinship, whilst the kinship systems that are constructed on this base should be regarded as so many different ways of encoding or enacting these elementary structures, not as the structures themselves (cf. Turner 1978).

Both kinship systems and technological systems, therefore, belong to the domain that I have called cultural. Should we, then, equate culture with superstructure? Yes, if it were not that 'superstructure' is such an unfortunate term. The architectural image it conveys is not apt to portray the cultural mediation of social and ecological relations. Culture, in effect, is not imposed 'on top', but 'in between' — perhaps we should call it a 'medistructure'. It constitutes a vital link between the components of the base, a condition for the effectiveness of social production, and hence of ecological reproduction. But of course it is not only culture that intervenes in this way between the social and the ecological. So, too, do the genetically fashioned, instrumental attributes of Man. The spear of the hunter, for example, is no more than a detachable extension of the arm, and would be useless without the mechanical leverage of the arm and the grip of the hand to throw it. There is no behaviour that is not conducted by both genetically and culturally transmitted attributes, even though — in the course of human evolution — cultural transmission has assumed such a dominant role as to render hereditary attributes almost immune to direct selective pressures. Nevertheless, it is impossible to define any kind of qualitative jump from the instinctive to the symbolic, for the conscious blueprint (model of) is never more than a partial representation of subsequent performance.

Evolution and adaptation

This brings me to the twin problems of social evolution and cultural adaptation. First, let me make a clear distinction between organic and social evolution. We may readily accept the Darwinian theory that organisms evolve through a process of adaptation under natural selection. It is commonplace, moreover, to posit an analogy between organic and cultural adaptation, likening the genetic phenomena of mutation and drift to the cultural phenomena of invention and diffusion (Carneiro 1968, Rappaport 1971: 246). Now this analogy is valid only insofar as it is possible to specify the criteria, and mechanisms, by which cultural attributes are selected. Since the transmission of culture proceeds quite independently of biological reproduction, natural selection does not provide such a mechanism (Burnham 1973: 94-5). Rather, if we conceive of culture — as I have done in this paper — as a repertoire of technological, organizational and ideological models, then the acceptance or rejection of alternative models will depend upon their perceived efficacy for members of a human population in either explaining or acting upon the real world, in accordance with a set of premises that are socially given. In other words, the rationality of cultural adaptation is embodied in the system of social relations through which men reproduce their material existence.

It follows that 'selective pressure' can only be defined in terms of the conjunction of social and ecological systems within which men are simultaneously involved as bearers of culturally transmitted attributes. Hence, too, the evolution of society cannot be regarded as a process of adaptation. This conclusion radically refutes the cultural materialist argument, according to which 'sociocultural systems' are brought forth under the deterministic influence of 'techno-environmental' pressures (Harris 1968: 4). As a principle of positive determination, the Darwinian analogue is in any case invalid, for environmental constraints can operate only on what has already been created; they cannot therefore be held responsible for the appearance of social forms. To say that one or another form is 'adapted' is no more than to affirm the possibility of its existence (Godelier 1972: xxxiv). It cannot be emphasised too strongly that the concept of adaptation loses all significance unless it is combined with a demonstrable principle of selection (cf. Stern 1970). If this principle is contained within the social system, it is evident that the latter cannot be the object of a selective process.

When, therefore, I speak of social evolution, I refer to the succession of qualitative transformations in the social relations of production, each of which generates a corresponding transformation in the ecological conditions of reproduction. Since each conjunction of social and ecological systems contains within itself the conditions of its future development, the course of social evolution is determinate, or law-like (though not necessarily unilinear). In this, it contrasts with organic evolution, which is essentially indeterminate — since mutations appear at random, there is no way of predicting the direction of phylogenesis. Now within each phase of social evolution, men are faced with particular problems, which they attempt to solve by cultural means. The hunter, for example, needs to locate his prey; the pastoralist needs to protect his herd — in each case the problem is one of realizing certain socially defined objectives under given environmental conditions. It is on this level of cultural adaptation that invention and diffusion may play a part. Every innovation, whether of local origin or introduced from outside, represents just one of a potentially infinite range of possible solutions to a given problem. Thus the course of cultural adaptation, like that of organic evolution, is indeterminate. But my basic point is this: social evolution does not consist in the cumulative record of cultural innovations, but involves a series of transformations in the very conditions to which they emerge as functional responses.

We may conclude that cultural adaptation under selective pressure, through invention and diffusion, represents the superstructural (or medistructural) correlate of evolutionary transformations in the productive infrastructure, both introducing the conditions for, and in turn being conditioned by, such transformations. However, the actual dynamic of social evolution lies not in the domain of culture, but in the reciprocal interplay between social and ecological systems, the former dominant in that it specifies the way in which the environment is to be used, the latter determinant in the negative sense of imposing the limits of viability. In short, whereas an analogue of natural selection — with reservations that I have outlined elsewhere (Ingold 1979) — is appropriate on the level of culture, an ecological version of dialectical materialism is required to account for the evolution of society itself. The Darwinian and Marxian paradigms are not opposed but complementary, for Darwinian 'pressures' are in fact generated by Marxian 'contradictions'. The intensity of 'selective pressure' to which the individuals of a population are subject is itself an indication of the degree of strain between the social and ecological systems in which they are involved. As I have already pointed out, the environment does not specify the manner or intensity of its exploitation, and therefore, taken on its own, exerts no selective pressure at all.

My argument is summed up — as well as it can be in two dimensions — in the accompanying diagram (Fig.10.1), illustrating schematically the way in which I would conceptualize the linkages between social, ecological and cultural systems. I should end, perhaps, with an apology: for I have given no hint as to how these heady generalizations could be translated into practical research strategy. However, I have noticed a disturbing tendency among archaeologists to make up for the inevitable paucity of their data on social relations by allowing themselves to be lured into the fallacies of environmental or ecological reductionism. To take an extreme case, the approach of palaeoeconomy (Higgs and Jarman 1975:4-5), in directing its attention to what are regarded as 'the major factors which direct and determine human behaviour and development' is theoretically crippled by its failure to realize that these factors are social as well as ecological. A genuinely palaeoeconomic approach must take account of both dimensions, viewing the 'basic necessities' of existence in terms of the conjunction of the two. To dismiss the dominance of the social in shaping the relationship between populations and resources is to deem irrelevant the entire evolutionary process which I take it to be the task of economic prehistory to explain. For this reason alone, I think an effort of theoretical clarification is worthwhile, even if it is not immediately suggestive of new hypotheses.

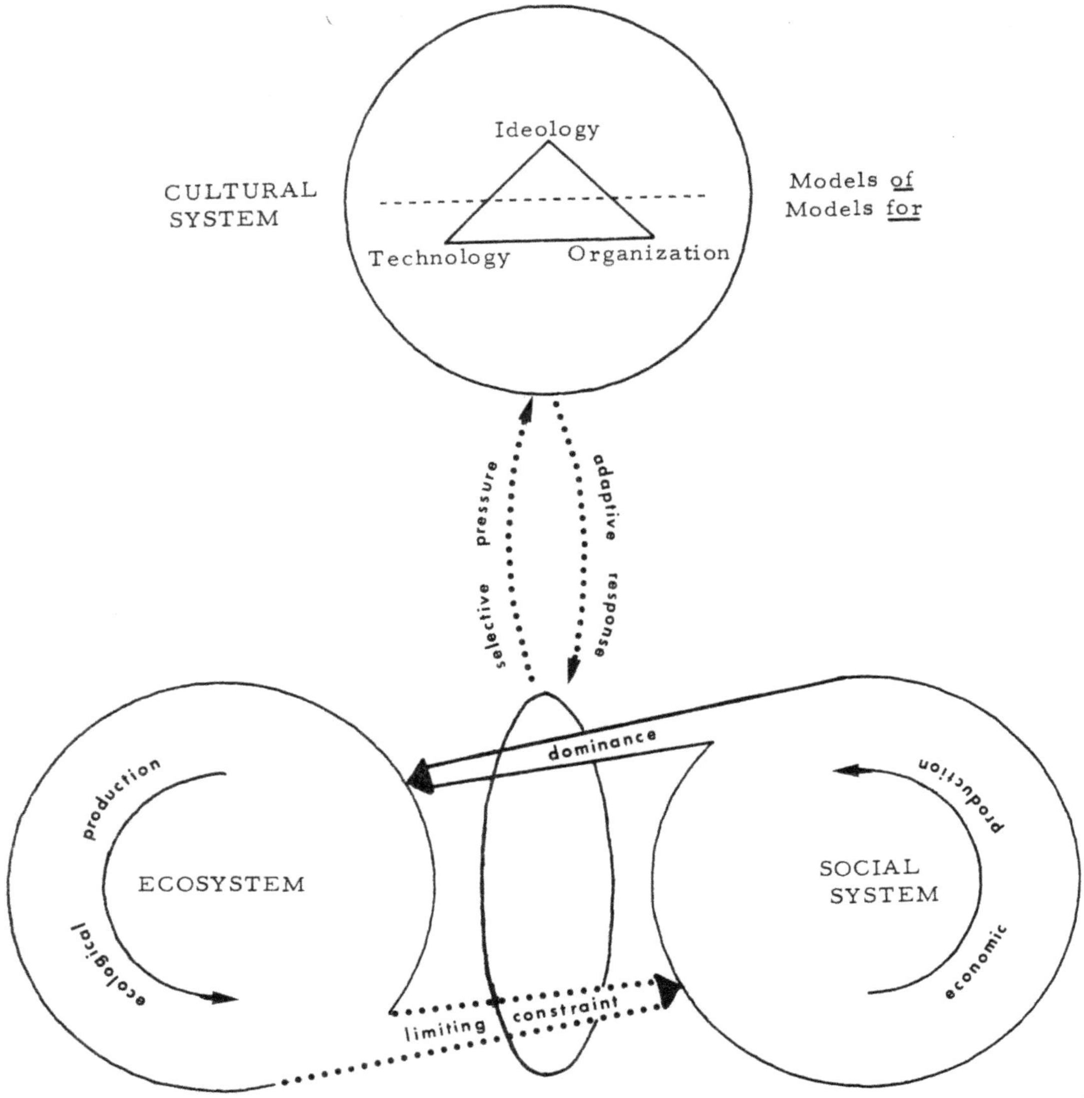
CULTURAL SYSTEM
Ideology
Technology
Organization
Models of
Models for
selective pressure
adaptive response
dominance
production
ECOSYSTEM
ecological
SOCIAL SYSTEM
production
economic
limiting constraint

Fig. 10.1

References

Balibar, E., 1970. "The basic concepts of historical materialism" in Reading Capital, eds. L. Althusser and E. Balibar. London: New Left Books; 199-308.

Burnham, P., 1973. "The explanatory value of the concept of adaptation in studies of culture change" in The Explanation of Culture Change, ed. A. C. Renfrew. London: Duckworth; 93-102.

Carneiro, R., 1968. "Cultural adaptation." Int. Enc. Soc. Sci. 3: 551-554.

Cohen, Y. A., 1974. "Culture as adaptation" in Man in Adaptation: the Cultural Present, 2nd Edition ed. Y. A. Cohen. Chicago: Aldine; 45-68.

Cook, S., 1973. "Production, ecology and economic anthropology: notes towards an integrated frame of reference." Soc. Sci. Info. 12: 25-52.

Friedman, J., 1974. " Marxism, structuralism and vulgar materialism." Man 9: 444-469.

Friedman, J., 1975. "Tribes, states and transformations" in Marxist Analyses and Social Anthropology, ed. M. Bloch. A.S.A. Studies 2. London: Malaby; 161-202.

Geertz, C., 1966. "Religion as a cultural system" in Anthropological Approaches to the Study of Religion, ed. M. Banton. A.S.A. Monograph 3. London: Tavistock; 1-46.

Godelier, M., 1972. Rationality and Irrationality in Economics. London: New Left Books.

Harris, M., 1968. The Rise of Anthropological Theory. New York: Crowell.

Harris, M., 1971. Culture, Man and Nature. New York: Crowell.

Higgs, E. S. and Jarman, M. R., 1975. "Palaeoeconomy" in Palaeoeconomy, ed. E. S. Higgs. London: Cambridge University Press; 1-7.

Ingold, T., 1979. "The social and ecological relations of culture-bearing organisms: an essay in evolutionary dynamics" in Social and Ecological Systems, eds. P. Burnham and R. Ellen. A.S.A. Monograph 18. London: Academic Press; 271-291.

Ingold, T., 1980. Hunters, Pastoralists and Ranchers: Reindeer Economies and their Transformations. Cambridge: Cambridge University Press.

Lévi-Strauss, C., 1968. Structural Anthropology Vol. 1. London: Allen Lane.

Marx, K., 1930. Capital. London: Dent.

Rappaport, R. A., 1968. Pigs for the Ancestors. New Haven: Yale University Press.

Rappaport, R. A., 1971. "Nature, culture and ecological anthropology" in Man, Culture and Society (revised edition), ed. H. L. Shapiro. New York: Oxford University Press; 237-267.

Sahlins, M. D., 1976. Culture and Practical Reason. Chicago: University of Chicago Press.

Stern, J. T., 1970. "The meaning of 'adaptation' and its relation to the phenomenon of natural selection" in Evolutionary Biology Vol. 4, eds. Th. Dobzhansky, M. K. Hecht and E. C. Steere. New York: Appleton-Century-Crofts; 38-66.

Steward, J. H., 1955. Theory of Culture Change. Urbana: University of Illinois Press.

Terray, E., 1972. Marxism and "Primitive" Societies. New York: Monthly Review Press.

Turner, D. H., 1978. "Ideology and elementary structures." Anthropologica 20: 223-247.

Vayda, A. P. and Rappaport, R. A., 1968. "Ecology: cultural and non-cultural" in Introduction to Cultural Anthropology, ed. J. Clifton. Boston: Houghton Mifflin; 477-497.

11. ECONOMY AND SOCIETY: WHAT RELATIONSHIP?

Christopher Tilley

Introduction

This paper examines the conceptual structure of the economic approach to archaeology as presented in some of the recent literature. It attempts to formulate a rigorous conception and critique of the positions adopted and briefly sketches an alternative approach. In Part I the intention is to draw out and discuss the assumptions and presuppositions underpinning contemporary archaeological conceptualisations of the economy. The paper attempts to show that such approaches tend to be both reductive and theoretically suspect, and without reformulation would seem to be an inadequate foundation for future research. Part II presents some elements of an alternative theory of dialectical-structuralism which suggests that theories of human action and structuralist thought are not incompatible and may provide a fruitful characterisation of the relationship between economy and society.

Part I: Archaeological approaches to the economy

Positivism and empiricism

It is possible to discern in the recent literature a number of lines of approach which share common assumptions to a greater or lesser degree:

(i) The Cambridge Palaeoeconomic school (Higgs 1972, 1975)

(ii) more ecologically orientated discussions (Anderson 1978; Clarke 1976; 1979; Foley 1977; Yellen and Harpending 1972)

(iii) incorporation within a systemic framework (Clarke 1968: 114-119, 490-503; Flannery 1968; 1972; Jochim 1976; Plog 1974: 43-78; Redman 1978; Renfrew 1972).

All these approaches are based on a positivist epistemology which, while discredited in many other fields of intellectual inquiry, remains the dominant perspective within the archaeological literature. The extension of this position to fields of sociological inquiry, and here we include archaeology, logically results in a particular model of man which Hollis (1977) terms 'plastic man'. The actors in social systems necessarily become reified, helpless spectators always subject to external forces over which they have very little control. Human intentions, motivations and meanings become dependent variables, functions of social, psychological or biological forces. The individual or the social group cannot be *causa sui* in the explanation of their actions. Social actions become the product of antecedent factors operating in a law-like way. This perspective (naturalism) denies that man is in any way unique and goes hand in hand with determinism which asserts explanatory monism. However, man is not a natural entity if we accept the primacy of sentience, intentionality, linguistic and symbolic communication. We clearly need to distinguish between bodily movement which may be readily assimilated under such a model and actions involving choices, intentions and motivations which may not. Behaviour may have its causes but actions have their reasons. This is a fundamental dichotomy overlooked in the majority of the archaeological literature. The question is not whether science is applicable to the study of man but what sort of science it should be. Significantly the prototype of Humean causality is one billiard ball striking another. Much of human action, however, does not take the character of things happening but things which people make happen for a variety of reasons.

A commitment to a positivist perspective reduces knowledge of the world to the narrow domain of agreed sense experience. The senses supposedly provide us with direct acquaintance of the world and knowledge is thought to be susceptible to evaluation in terms of statements which designate what is given to the experience of human subjects, i.e. data available to sense — perception. The sensory data and their transaltion into the form of an observation language are epistemically privileged, and as a consequence, the theoretical language and the ontological structure which it seeks to represent have no true validity of their own. They must always remain parasitic on the observation language and have to be related back to it by means of correspondence rules. This is because in the light of Popper's (1959: 78-93) falsification criterion the theoretical language must be open, at least in principle, to being impugned by observed 'facts'. Consequently internal connections between elements of the theoretical structure can only play a secondary role and theory construction becomes dependent upon practice (Fig. 11.1). To Marx all science would be superfluous if the forms and essence of things really coincided. In the structuralist approach put forward in Part II of this paper, knowledge is conceived as being a product of a form of discourse governed by a specific set of concepts or a scientific problematic. The epistemological notion of 'knowledge' is not a necessary one so the relationship between theoretical and ontological structures does not have to be presented in terms of correspondences between theoretical discourse and observation statements. Knowledge is not solely discovered by reference to 'reality' but is actively produced. It follows from this that the real world structure cannot be opposed to the theoretical structure built to represent it as in the hypothethico-deductive method. The latter operates on a purely phenomenological level dealing only with apparent appearances which frequently contradict the theoretical structures built to represent them. Both the ontological structure and the theoretical structure are objects to be constructed, so they must be isomorphic and the relationship between theory and practice becomes dialectical (Fig. 11.1). This very brief cussion of some aspects of positivism is necessary to the following discussion of economic archaeology since the positions adopted are all founded upon variants of it, whilst a dialectical-structuralist viewpoint opposes this conception.

Appearances ⇄ Observation Language ⇄ Theoretical Language ⇄ Ontological Structure

Practice ⇄ Theory

Positivist Approach

Appearances

Theoretical Structure ↗ ↖ Ontological Structure

Practice ⟷ Theory

Structuralist Approach (source: Gregory 1978)

Fig. 11.1 Positivist and structuralist approaches to theory construction

Economic behaviour and systemic perspectives

Current perspectives, with differing emphases, connect human behaviour with the environment in terms of calorific input and output regulated by the specific nature of local trophic systems in terms of primary and secondary productivity. Subsistence techniques are either constrained or determined by the nature of the local ecosystem and by levels of technological sophistication and/or population densities. The basic question under consideration is how specific populations fit in, as biological entities, into environmental settings. The environment, to a greater or lesser extent, determines the nature of possible cultural configurations and firmly sets the boundaries to human existence. The dominant conception of culture is as an adaptive system which maintains human populations as viable ongoing units. Social systems become concomitants of economic activities and must always conform to and satisfy overriding economic directives defined as being basic biological requirements for survival.

The conceptualisation of the economy as a functional subsystem of the overall social system is one of the most frequently adopted approaches in the contemporary literature. This approach is an explicit attempt to relate economic processes to the realm of the social which is largely lacking from the palaeoeconomic and ecological approaches.

An essential element in the explanation and understanding of economic behaviour is deemed to be its place in an overall system. What is of essential importance is the relationship between the economic subsystem and the other subsystems, on the one hand, and the external environment on the other. The changing relationship between man and the resources he exploits is regarded as one of the primary causative situations promoting sociocultural change.

Clarke provides us with an initial definition: the economic subsystem is "the integrated strategy of component subsistence methods and extraction processes which feed and equip the society" (1968: 103). Four factors are of essential importance in order to maintain the overall viability of the system:

a) adaptation,
b) goal attainment,
c) integration,
d) overall pattern maintenance.

This is achieved by the flow of information through and between the subsystems and the natural and social environment. All of these might be conceived as being fairly automatic processes which maintain the system in equilibrium, apart from the second factor, goal attainment. Logically, in all systemic approaches this requirement must be elevated to a position of central importance because it establishes the specific relationship of the system to its environment and orientates the overall trajectory:

> "The social system does not consist of the objective ties by descent or consanguinity that obtain among individuals; it exists only in human consciousness, it is an arbitrary system of ideas, not the spontaneous development of a factual situation'. This commonly held information causes the individuals in a group to repeatedly act according to an explicit or tacit pattern. On the basis of these ideational patterns human groups are everywhere ..... orientated towards proscribed sets of activities within the system" (Clarke, 1968: 105, citing Lévi-Strauss, 1945).

Consequently economic activity can only be explained and understood by reference to an understanding of the environment as cognised by the actors in specific sociocultural systems. In practice Clarke never acheives this objective and much of his methodological and theoretical perspective directly eschews such an attempt. As Gregory (1978) notes systems theory has a theoretical structure which describes how a system is maintained but not how it is transformed. The theoretical structure is not isomorphic with the ontological structure it seeks to represent. Change (<u>via</u> positive feedback mechanisms) is always circumscribed and does not really penetrate the internal structure. The whole position becomes little more than an ideology of universal harmonies. Consequently the model, in order to explain social and economic change, resorts to a position of exogenous causality (Flannery 1968; Hill 1977) and fails to avoid reductionism and hence the reification of social relations (Tilley in press: 364-70). A further dangerous tendency in Clarke's conception and that of Plog (1974) is that of double determination which follows from the characterisation of systems as having emergent properties and also changing adaptively in relation to their environments. Plog (1974: 62-5) suggests there is a tendency towards the increasing efficiency of the system, "an evolution from multifunctional role structures to more specialised ones " (1974: 62; <u>cf.</u> Clarke 1968: 87) whilst also stating that "Changes in the loci of resources being utilised by an adaptation and experimentation with new resources may account for changes in differentiation." (1974: 64). The analysis would seem to suffer from a contradiction between two incompatible modes of determination. On the one hand it is teleological, an inherent capacity to change inbuilt into the system, yet on the other hand change takes place as a result of interactions with an environmental milieu. The effectiveness of one would seem to preclude the effectiveness of the other.

There would appear to be a tension running through most systemic discussions of the economy and its relation to the non-economic periphery. On the one hand the importance of symbolic and conceptual orientations towards the environment by human groups is recognized yet in practice the explanatory model employed reduces the social and symbolic to the status of epiphenomena which are effectively screened out from the analysis. This is an inevitable consequence of a positivist explanatory structure.

Palaeoeconomy

Perhaps the most extreme position is the Palaeoeconomic approach as advocated by Higgs and Jarman (1975) with the exhortation that we need to "formulate models with specifically archaeological objectives and data in mind" (ibid:I). This perspective attempts to relate population, resources and technology and to see how these factors are related over long time periods. However, the only resources considered are categories of potential land use and animal and vegetable foodstuffs. There is no detailed consideration of resources which do not have direct subsistence potential or any reference to the exchange of commodities or intra-and intercommunity relationships except in relationship to transhumance systems (Dennell and Webley 1975; Barker 1975). This extremely restricted arena for discussion is predicated on the assumption that archaeologists can deal only ineffectively with social and ideological parameters of human behaviour which in the long run have little significance. Similarly, discussions of the origins of agriculture (Higgs and Jarman 1969, 1972; Jarman 1971), whilst useful in questioning the validity of the blanket terms 'mesolithic' and 'neolithic' as an apt way of describing particular forms of material culture, settlement and subsistence patterns remains unsatisfactory as changing social relationships and their effect upon economic change is not considered. Anything beyond basic subsistence behaviour must be regarded as random noise, "short term trivia in the historic or anthropological record" (Higgs and Jarman 1975: 2). The locus of the research resides in the search for natural laws which govern the relationship between human behaviour and the natural environment. All this is, apparently, compatible with the belief that "archaeology is, or should be, a discipline concerned first and foremost with the study of man" (ibid: 4). Any characteristics which we might regard as essentially human — cognition, thought, intentional activity, the ability to classify and categorise the world — become subsumed under a supposedly universal logic which demands specific limited responses to biological exigencies. Consequently ethological studies and the application of such concepts as territory, home range, ecological niche, natural selection and adaptation are of relevance. The emphasis placed on ethological studies is based on the premise that if we study the behaviour of animals it is possible to predict much of the behaviour of human groups exploiting them. This statement might have some element of truth if we persist in taking such marginal and extreme cases as the Nunamiut Eskimo or the !Kung Bushmen as our major examples. Higgs and Jarman (1975) also suggest that it is only by studying the similarities between human and animal behaviour that we may identify the major differences.

It is suggested here that the superficial resemblances between human and animal behaviour conceal fundamental differences. There is a categorical distinction between such concepts as production and foraging, ethnicity and ecological niche, property and territoriality. One set of concepts does not elucidate the other since they belong to fundamentally different frames of reference. Culture is not a part of nature, but a transformation of it and what we may have in common with animal populations enters into our lives as social and cultural structures which mediate the nature of our action in the environment.

Protagonists of this viewpoint defend this reductionism by a) denying that much more can be achieved from the archaeological record b) suggesting that while, in the short term, the social and ideological parameters of human existence may conflict with or override basic economic directives such fluctuations, although recurrent, can only be short lived. Over long time periods environmental change can be considered to be a norm and consequently will have an important, if not the most important, effect upon social and economic change. If we take prehistoric Europe as an example the major changes are those that man has induced himself so altering the conditions for his own existence. Furthermore culturally mediated and apparently irrational economic strategies may last very long periods of time (the Jewish taboo on pork or the Hindu holy cow).

Adaptation and rationality

The concept of adaptation plays a central role in most discussions of economic archaeology. In practice the concept is theoretically vacuous since anything that does not destroy the system may be said to be adaptive, while to say that adaptive traits are present is tautological. The use of the concept of adaptation goes hand in hand with one of rationality which is not unambiguously applied. Jochim states that "the major assumption underlying all theories of choice is that of the rational decision maker" (Jochim 1976: 4). Despite his discussion of the logical principles of decision theory, which defines for him the nature of rational choice, we are told that "the primary determination of what is 'rational' would seem to be the structure of the preference order. This, in turn, depends on the culturally defined goals and value systems" (ibid: 5). This implies that "those factors important in structuring the behaviour of one group may be of little significance to another" (ibid: 8) yet despite this the whole of Jochim's book is concerned with erecting a general predictive model. (Fig. 11.2).

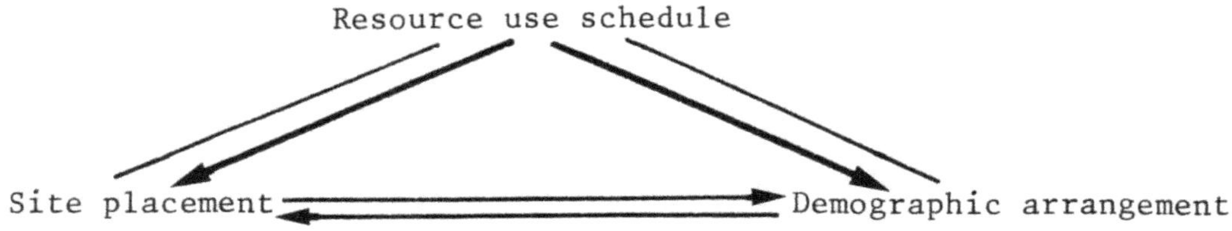

Fig. 11.2 Jochim's model for hunter-gatherer subsistence and settlement (Jochim 1976: 13)

Social and ideological factors play an insignificant role since "culture is commensurable as far as ecological relations are concerned with the behaviour of populations of non-human animals" (ibid: 9, citing Rappaport 1969: 181). Consequently "it would be expected .... that identical natural environments would encourage identical or very similar solutions" (ibid: 77-8). The model runs into very serious difficulties when he considers the case of the Mbuti pygmies. Different groups, the archers and the net hunters, live in an identical environment and yet practice different economic strategies. The only way that these differences can be explained is by reference to socio-political factors. What is of essential importance for these different pygmy groups is that economic patterns are mediated and orientated by a conceptual and symbolic order. Innumerable cases of this sort could be cited from the anthropological literature which would seem to indicate that the production process is a symbolic and social process and runs counter to formal predictive schemes. In effect both the palaeoeconomic and systemic approaches reduce the non-economic to the status of a random or a dependent variable. They depend on a postulate of the intrinsic rationality of economic action. The means-ends relationship is considered in a perspective which militates against the consideration of ends at all in the last analysis. The ends of economic action either become random or can only be conceived of at a metaphysical level as fulfilling 'needs' such as biological survival. It is an assertion of the '*Homo economicus*' of 'human nature', where little else is of real importance. Ultimately this leads us to the position that "when we are dealing with large population aggregates and long periods of time, one can adequately account for the goals and aspirations of individuals in statistical, cumulative, behaviourist terms" (Redman 1978: 330-1).

Economic activity is always the allocation of resources among alternate but given ends. If the ends of economic activity were to be determined within that activity then it could no longer be properly called economic. Unless we attempt to specify the social and ideological parameters of action there is no way in which we can explain behaviour which we may properly call economic. To assert that the end of economic behaviour is to satisfy basic biological requirements remains indeterminate since it does not explain why those ends were met in one way rather than another.

Part II: Economy and society: A dialectical-structuralist approach

In so far as archaeology is concerned with a study of man as a sentient social being it becomes a part of social science and should contribute towards it. Our substantive studies must be firmly located within the realm of social theory or they can have little validity. We should contribute to that theory by considering it in its own terms, not by attempting to discern specifically archaeological ramifications and implications of that theory. Unless we adopt a theoretical problematic which provides an adequate characterisation of the social world and social change, our substantive studies will be inadequate. The economy cannot be understood apart from that which gives it its specificity, the structures of the social world and the structuring principles orientating social action. In order to understand economic change we must consider social change in general. Theoretical discussion should not be limited by *a priori* views which stress the inadequacy of our data base. Archaeological data are essentially meaningless. We give them meaning by relating them to theory. The nature of this relationship should be a dialectical one between theoretical discourse and the empirical data rather than the refutation or falsification of theories by the data. 'Facts' are not in themselves sufficient to disprove theories, since our theories decide what is or is not a 'fact'. Theories can only be completely discredited as a result of internal contradictions and inconsistencies. The future of archaeology as a social science must "lie with those theories which do not attempt to give the phenomena of experience the form of reason but seek to explain objects not given in experience, objects constituted in knowledge" (Hirst 1975: 7). This entails adopting a structuralist approach and the rejection of positivist epistemologies (briefly discussed above, Tilley forthcoming).

Structuralism

The literature concerned with structuralism may be broadly divided into two approaches which differ most fundamentally in their characterisation of change. A categorial approach is adopted by Saussure (1960) in structural linguistics and in the work of Lévi-Strauss (1955, 1966, 1968) in anthropology. This approach emphasises stability and synchrony and, in essence, denies that there can be real qualitative historical change. The actors in sociocultural systems are merely involved in an endless series of combinations and recombinations of the same fundamental elements. A dialectical approach may be seen in Marx (1967, 1970, 1971) and Piaget (1970, 1971, 1972) and emphasises that structures are dynamic relational entities. There can be no structures common to all mankind but only particular structures with a specific locus in space and time. However, both versions overlap at many points and share a number of very important elements in common. The general approach to social structures is in direct opposition to what Althusser termed 'the empiricism of the object'; that our object of study must be immediately present to the senses, can be isolated as such and constitutes the correct unit of study. Human actions are conceived as being mediated by structures or abstract sets of relations by means of which the fields of interactions between individuals at an empirical level may be explained. Actions are given meaning by structuring principles such as notions of purity and pollution.

Structural Marxism and dialectical-structuralism

Recent work within the spheres of anthropology and sociology has attempted to build upon and extend basic Marxian concepts and elucidate Marx's conception of social structure in the terms of contemporary structuralist thought (Althusser 1977; Althusser and Balibar 1970; Friedman 1974, 1975; Godelier 1977; Hindess and Hirst 1975). This structural-Marxist framework would appear to be inadequate and may be criticised on the grounds that it fails to consider the subjective meanings actors place upon their experiences within given structures. The individual becomes powerless in the face of general structural causality and his existential being becomes denigrated: "the structure of the relations of production determines the places and functions occupied and adopted by the agents of production, who are never anything more than the occupants of these places, insofar as they are the supports (Träger) of these functions" (Althusser and Balibar 1970: 180). However, between the structures of a given social situation and the action of individual actors lie shared meanings by means of which the actors interpret, identify and evaluate the significance of events, objects and interpersonal encounters in their social world. The term dialectical-structuralism is adopted in this paper to distinguish the general approach from the categorial perspective of Lévi-Strauss and from structural Marxism. An action frame of reference is of crucial importance and requires the integration of action philosophy and structuralism if we are to understand the nature of social and, as a concomitant of this, economic change. Human action may take place within a framework of social structures but these structures are themselves created by human action within and on the social world. This perspective requires a dialectical emphasis between conceptions of structures and the process of structuration or structural change (Giddens 1979: 49-95).

Social formations cannot simply reproduce the conditions of their own existence as some recent structural Marxist writings have presupposed. We should employ, rather, the notion of continuous self-production rather than reproduction. Society has "the capacity to define itself and thus, through the knowledge and investment it has achieved, to transform its relations with its environment, to constitute its own milieu" (Touraine 1977: 3-4). Godelier's (1977) and Friedman's (1974, 1975) interpretation of the mode of production artificially separates the organisation function of kinship systems in organising production as the social relations of production, from their ideological features which take place in other spheres. This sets up a damaging theoretical barrier to our understanding of the relationship between the ideological and the economic in human action. It is suggested here that all societies involve a unity of the economic and the ideological instances. The term 'instance' rather than level is used in order to avoid the problems involved with Marx's base-superstructure analogy, in which the base consisting of the relations and forces of production might be conceived to be in some sense primary, and ideology merely an expression of phenomena emanating from the economic. The object of our analysis cannot simply be the mode of production, consisting of the articulated combination of the social relations of production (the social relationships between individuals in the production process, mode of appropriation and distribution of surplus, division of productive labour) and the forces of production (the technical conditions of production). The connection between them can only be understood in terms of their own conditions of existence in the overall social formation (Hindess and Hirst 1977: 50). The mode of production is inextricably bound up with other social relationships and social practices and cannot be understood apart from these. This would appear to be closer to Marx's project when he writes: "at the end of every labour process we get a result that already existed in the imagination of the labourers at its commencement" (1967:I, 178).

Economic action and the objects of economic action are characterised solely by the meaning they have for human action in such roles as means, ends, obstacles and by-products. This alone defines the realm of the economic and the nature of the processes involved and enables such processes to be successfully explained (Weber 1964: 158). The economic aspect of social action may only be defined in relation to the total socio-cultural system or cognitively informed order of things. In a production relation the product becomes the goal of that activity. Resources or factors of production are the means by which that product is realized but that product is an irretrievably social product and obtains its specific meaning by its place in an overall structure of action. The natural world is appropriated in order to meet ends defined within the social and ideological order. It follows from this that the nature of the economic and the object of economic activity may not be predicted or defined on a priori grounds. This is not an idealist thesis, merely a relational perspective for the characterisation of economic activity and its objects. Economic action is mediated and structured in relation to the overall social formation which assumes the aspect of an expressive totality of experience and action. As such the nature of that action becomes both reflexive and symbolic.

Economic activities form the conditions of existence for any society in that resources must be extracted from the environment in order to maintain it. However, the environment and the nature of the resources to be exploited cannot be objectively defined. The specific nature of environmental constraint is given its specificity and effectiveness by the social and ideological order. The nature of the available resources and the technological capacity determine the manner of extraction and appropriation of resources in only a minimal sense, that is only in terms of existence or non-existence: "nature is to culture as the constituted is to the constituting. Culture is not merely nature expressed in another form. Rather the reverse: the action of nature unfolds in terms of culture, that is in a form no longer its own but embodied as meaning" (Sahlins 1976:211). It is the articulated combination of the ideological and the economic instances which constrain economic action and the nature of social change. This is because societies embrace a capacity for symbolic creation, the constitution of meaning structures between particular contexts and social actions, which orientate and reorientate conduct as part of the continuous process of the social construction of reality. It follows from this perspective that economic and social change may not be considered a product of the non-social, of the environment or a determinant economic base, but as a result of the nature of social action, defined in terms of the meaning structures of their ideological base. Economic action is consequently only intelligible in the context of ways of living, modes of social life. The rationality of action, therefore, becomes both relative and relational from one context to another. As economic action is mediated by social relationships which take their meaning from the overall social formation attention shifts from production or distribution per se to the social concomitants of production and distribution. However this position does not go far enough as we need to analyse the nature of social action in terms of its ideological base.

Behaviour, action and social action

Here it is important to make three distinctions; those between behaviour, action and social action. Wittgenstein raised the question "What is left over if you subtract the fact that my arm goes up from the fact that I raise my arm?" (1953: I, sec. 621). The implication of this statement is that there is something far more important in the action of raising an arm than mere bodily movement. Behaviourist theories which have dominated economic archaeology do not take into account meaning structures involved in economic activities. Behaviour becomes action when it has a meaning structure attached to it. Behaviour is movement through space and time largely governed by external stimuli, it is purely passive in form. Action includes "all behaviour when and insofar as the acting individual attaches a subjective meaning to it" (Weber 1964: 88). We subsume action not under general laws connecting it nomically with antecedent conditions but in terms of a meaning structure through which that behaviour is mediated and directed. Action, as opposed to behaviour, goes beyond itself. Action becomes social action when the articulation of the act is to a socially shared meaning or goal or end. Social action takes a number of forms including, most fundamentally, reflective and pre-reflective action. Reflective action or intentional activity can be explained and articulated between actors in speech acts. Pre-reflective action involves practical consciousness or habitual and other motivational referents which are not consciously formulated or discussed. This is by no means a mutually exclusive dichotomy. These together relate to an epistemic attitude or an ideological schema composed of structuring principles by means of which the actors in sociocultural systems orientate themselves to their natural and social environment and in collective actions. This orientational focus defines the rationality of action which can have no other referent (Fig. 11.3).

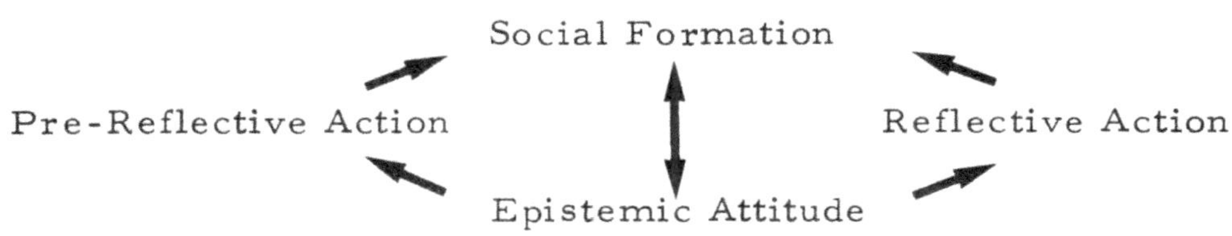

Fig. 11.3 The nature of social action

The epistemic attitude is relational between the natural and social environment and the social formation. The social formation is conceived as the objective social situation in which individuals find themselves. Socially mediated and defined constraints from the natural environment and other social groups outside the system under consideration operate dialectically in relationship with the social formation which is, as a consequence, in a state of constant movement and change. This results in a relational change in the epistemic attitude providing new principles for social action (Fig. 11.4) and conditions for social existence.

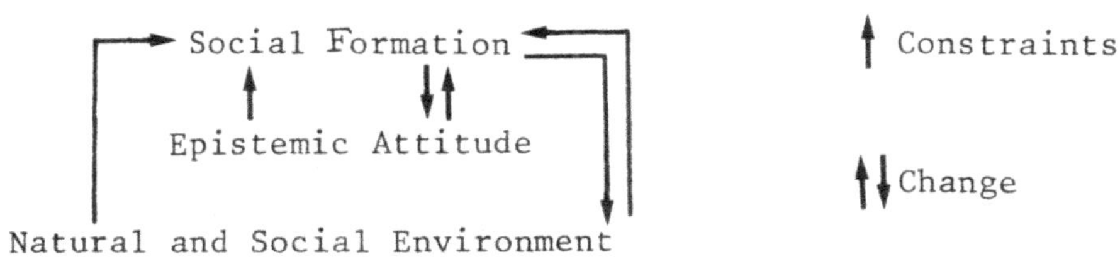

Fig. 11.4 The change process

Socioeconomic change and social structures

This dialectical viewpoint is, in essence, a view of the social world as a world in constant movement, between being and becoming. We are able to reject the synchrony/diachrony distinction besetting a positivist analysis of change. The categories and meaning structures which go to make up the epistemic attitude change relationally and coherently in dialectical fashion with the changing conditions of social existence. The social formation refers to a totality of experience and action, but in a very different way from the systemic perspective in which explanation has to focus on the laws which govern the behaviour of the totality and can effectively proceed without reference to the parts. In the approach offered here the important relationships are those between the elements and the way in which they structure the totality: "the logical processes or natural processes by which the whole is formed are primary, not the whole, which is consequent on the systems laws of composition, or the elements" (Piaget 1970: 9). The social formation, embracing distinctive types of social action, as defined above, is constituted by structures. These structures may not be perceived but nevertheless they are real. Structures may be conceived as sets of transformations. The elements of a structure may be related to one another in complex sets of linkages involving relative degrees of autonomy and independence (metynomic causality). Inbuilt into a dialectical form of structuralism is a conception of change such that no structure may be considered apart from structuration or construction. This follows from the notion of the essential duality of structures (Giddens 1975:120-5, 1970:77-8, 255-6). Structures mediate the interactions of actors in social life, but they are given their specific effect by the actions of individuals and are consequently in a state of transformation. The totality of structures which go to make up social life, but which by themselves do not constitute the social formation (which only exists in the observable relationships between individuals), may be conceived to be in a state of continual change because every collective or individual social act is not fixed or static but entails a renegotiation of the content and meaning of action.

Hence, social action can be considered as the production of something new and yet at the same time it exists in a continuum with past systems of action. So, structures form a medium for action and yet by the very nature of that action are transformed.

Structures forming the totality may exist in opposition to each other or in compatible identity relationships. Opposition may lead to structural disjunction when a number of conflicting structures and structuring principles with competing motivational referents come into contradiction with each other, resulting in disjunction and rapid social and economic change. Relations of identity or compatability result in continuous processes of structuration, entailing a gradual transformation of social and economic relations (Fig. 11.5). It follows from the above considerations that dialectical-structuralism has a conceptual apparatus which enables us to theorise the kinds of processes involved in both continuous and rapid change. The approach requires us to look for paradox as much as complementarity, for opposition as much as accomodation and for dissonance underlying apparent order (Moore 1978: 38).

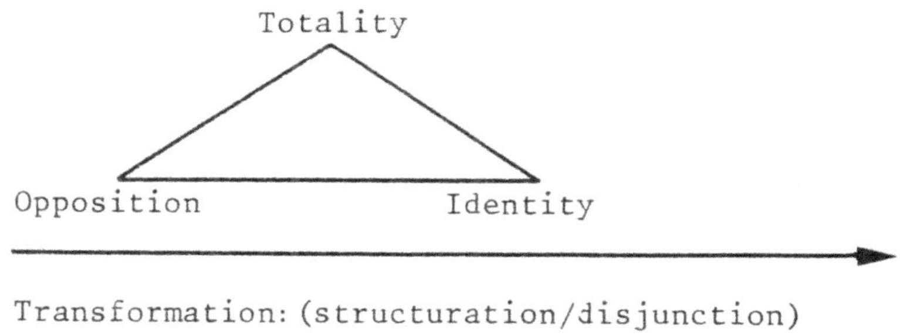

Fig. 11.5 Structural transformations

In relating the analysis to economic change it is insufficient just to stress the dominance of social relations (Bender 1979). It is necessary to examine the changing conditions for these relations in the epistemic attitude and in the dialectical relationship that must exist between activity in the world and consciousness of the world. Obviously this paper cannot develop the details of such a project in relation to economic archaeology, but it may indicate some implications and general directions. The transformational character of structures can enable us to understand the oscillation of economic strategies in relation to resources in an environment which is not itself rapidly changing. The notion of structural contradiction enables us to explain changes in economic strategies in relation to both exogenous variables (a rapidly changing natural and social environment) and internal variables (contradiction between structures mediated by competing motivational referents).

We can only hope to analyse determinate social situations and the particular role of economic action in such contexts. To compare cross-culturally and hope to arrive at some general model of the relationship between economy and society is like trying to compare the worth of different commodities where no common standard of value is applicable. In short we should not expect explanations of any particular case to be applicable elsewhere, although they may provide insights into the kinds of relationships we might look for in other situations. In archaeology this is best realised by a regional approach as advocated by Binford (1964), Struever (1968, 1971), Tilley (1979).

Dialectical-structuralism and economic archaeology

Our analyses must be more sensitive to variations in the form and content of artifacts and ecofacts in particular contexts. Economic archaeology has, in general, concentrated its attention on estimating the minimum numbers of different species of animals on archaeological sites, their calorific value, the inference of seasonal or continuous occupation and whether the site could be categorised as a kill site or as a home base where the food was actually consumed. Insufficient attention has been paid to the consumption of food as an inherently social and symbolic process which goes far beyond biological exigencies. As Douglas (1966: 41-57, 1975: 249) argues, if food is treated as a code, the messages it encodes should relate to the patterns of social relationships being expressed. The messages will relate to degrees of inclusion and exclusiveness, social boundaries, transactions across these boundaries and power relations between individuals and groups. Eating is a patterned activity and is likely to vary in its social importance from one context and occasion to another. The division of body parts of animals may provide a framework for social classification and a powerful source of symbolism. The cultural use of body parts may become a part of a society's social construction of reality and provide a restricted yet rich set of metaphorical possibilities for non-verbal communication. Social meanings become attached to the physical medium of the carcase. To understand such meanings it would seem to be necessary to go beyond them and investigate the classificatory structures on which they are based. Lévi-Strauss (1966: 135-90) suggests that it is only through classificatory schemes that the natural and social universe may be grasped as an organised and coherent whole.

To translate these notions into archaeological practice we need to pay detailed attention to the patterning of skeletal remains of animals on archaeological sites, to look at the relations between classes of bones on a number of levels rather than to investigate the aggregate pattern morphology. The physical make-up of the body would seem to provide a natural set of classificatory possibilities which can be exploited. It also acts to constrain the total number of possible members of a set. Any change in the cultural definition of the body is incapable of separating physically or symbolically the integral association of different parts of the body or the skeleton (skull, ribs, limbs etc.). They form an integral part of an irreducible whole. The total system consists of whole/part relations and there are a limited number of anatomical contrasts both within and between species which may be manipulated symbolically. At an analytic level the body may be broken down into formally analogous units: limbs/head/trunk/feet. In relation to skeletal anatomy this will take on a slightly different form: hind and fore limbs, skull, ribs, vertebrae and foot or hoof bones. However, joints would appear to remain ambiguous areas of transition. For instance the pelvis might be grouped with the vertebrae as part of the trunk or with the hind limbs. Similarly the scapula might be grouped either with the fore limbs or with the ribs. We might expect, therefore, that the arrangements of these bones would be variable from context to context. At the synthethic level the bones, once broken down analytically, might be grouped on another plane. At one level there is likely to be an exploitation of basic body symmetries, between right and left halves or between front and back body halves. If basic left/right body symmetries are being exploited we might expect spatial separation of body halves on sites or significant statistical differences between numbers of bones from the left and right halves of the body. This may be variable from species to species and relate to differences in their social and symbolic importance. Analysis might take the following form:

1) We should pay attention to relations between different classes of bones on an inter- and intra-species basis.

2) Are different classes of bones being grouped spatially in discrete groups on the site or at its periphery?

3) Are front/back or left/right distinctions being exploited?

4) Are all species being broken down for consumption, in terms of body parts, in the same manner or is this variable?

5) Are mature or immature animals being treated differently?

6) How do these relationships vary over time or from site to site?

7) Are certain species particularly variable from context to context either on a presence/absence basis or in terms of classes of bones being represented?

By means of a careful consideration of these relationships we may be able to suggest the operation of specific generative or structural principles which regulate the social use of body parts of animals and gain considerable insight into the relationship between ideological expression and economic activities. It is interesting to note in connection with the above discussion the presence of large numbers of incised ox scapula at many later Cypriote sanctuary sites indicating the special significance of the bull forelimb over more than 700 years (Webb 1977) and it would be interesting to tie in this evidence with detailed faunal analyses from domestic sites along the lines indicated above.

Conclusions

The justification for this somewhat abstract theoretical discussion, which many will consider bears little relationship to the flesh and blood of substantive studies in economic archaeology, is to suggest that economic activities can only be explained by the non-economic. Calorific estimates and lists of animal and plant species exploited at a particular series of sites in themselves tell us very little about the specific content of the activities. Perhaps more importantly current perspectives have failed to realise in large measure the potential of economic analyses for gaining significant insights into the social and ideological principles underlying these activities. If we continue to categorise the economic as a separate functional subsystem, simply concerned with the procurement of food and other resources, then of course we will have difficulties trying to integrate it with other aspects of social systems and the perspective offered will always be rather limited. An integrated approach to the economy necessarily presupposes an integrated approach to the social world of which the economic is just one part.

Acknowledgements

I would like to thank Geoff Bailey, Paul Halstead, Ian Hodder, Mike Shanks and Alison Sheridan for their comments on an earlier draft of this paper.

References

Althusser, L., 1977. For Marx. London: New Left Books.

Althusser, L. and Balibar, E., 1970. Reading Capital. London: New Left Books.

Anderson, A., 1978. "The role of a competition model in the archaeological explanation of culture change" in Social Organisation and Settlement, eds. D. Green, C. Haselgrove and M. Spriggs. Oxford: B.A.R. Suppl. Ser. 47: 31-46.

Barker, G. W., 1975. "Prehistoric territories and economies in central Italy" in Palaeoeconomy, ed. E. S. Higgs. London: Cambridge University Press; 111-176.

Bender, B., 1979. "Gatherer-hunter to farmer: a social perspective." World Archaeology 10: 204-222.

Binford, L. R., 1964. "A consideration of archaeological research design." Amer. Ant. 29: 425-441.

Clarke, D. L., 1968. Analytical Archaeology. London: Methuen.

Clarke, D. L., 1976. "Mesolithic Europe: the economic basis" in Problems in Economic and Social Archaeology, eds. G. de G. Sieveking, I. Longworth and K. Wilson. London: Duckworth; 449-481.

Clarke, D. L., 1979. "The economic context of trade and industry in barbarian Europe till Roman times" in Analytical Archaeologist, ed. N. Hammond. London: Academic Press; 263-332.

Dennell, R. W. and Webley, D., 1975. "Prehistoric settlement and land use in southern Bulgaria" in Palaeoeconomy, ed. E. S. Higgs. London: Cambridge University Press; 97-110.

Douglas, M., 1966. Purity and Danger. London: Routledge and Kegan Paul.

Douglas, M., 1975. Implicit Meanings. London: Routledge and Kegan Paul.

Flannery, K. V., 1968. "Archaeological systems theory and early Mesoamerica" in Anthropological Archaeology in the Americas, ed. B. J. Meggers. Washington D. C.: Anthropological Society of Washington; 67-87.

Flannery, K. V., 1972. "The cultural evolution of civilizations." Ann. Rev. Ecology and Systematics 3: 399-426.

Foley, R., 1977. "Space and energy: a method for analysing habitat value and utilisation in relation to archaeological sites" in Spatial Archaeology, ed. D. L. Clarke. London: Academic Press; 163-88.

Friedman, J., 1974. "Marxism, structuralism and vulgar materialism." Man 9: 444-469.

Friedman, J., 1975. "Tribes, states and transformations" in Marxist Analyses in Social Anthropology, ed. M. Bloch. A.S.A. Monograph 2. London Malaby; 161-202.

Giddens, A., 1975. New Rules of Sociological Method. London: Hutchinson.

Giddens, A., 1979. Central Problems in Social Theory. London: Macmillan.

Godelier, M., 1977. Perspectives in Marxist Anthropology. Cambridge: Cambridge University Press.

Gregory, D., 1978. "Social change and spatial structures" in Making Sense of Time, eds. T. Carlstein, D. Parkes and N. Thrift. London: Arnold; 38-46.

Higgs, E. S. (ed.), 1972. Papers in Economic Prehistory. London: Cambridge University Press.

Higgs, E. S. (ed.), 1975. Palaeoeconomy. London: Cambridge University Press.

Higgs, E. S. and Jarman, M. R., 1969. "The origins of agriculture: a reconsideration." Antiquity 43: 31-44.

Higgs, E. S. and Jarman, M. R., 1972. "The origins of animal and plant husbandry" in Papers in Economic Prehistury, ed. E. S. Higgs. London: Cambridge University Press; 3-13.

Higgs, E. S. and Jarman, M. R., 1975. "Palaeoeconomy" in Palaeoeconomy, ed. E. S. Higgs. London: Cambridge University Press; 1-8.

Hill, J. N., 1977. "Systems theory and the explanation of change" in Explanation of Prehistoric Change, ed. J. N. Hill. Albuquerque: University of New Mexico Press; 59-104.

Hindess, B. and Hirst, P., 1975. Pre-Capitalist Modes of Production. London: Routledge and Kegan Paul.

Hindess, B. and Hirst, P., 1977. Mode of Production and Social Formation: An Autocritique of Pre-Capitalist Modes of Production. London: Macmillan.

Hirst, P., 1975. Durkheim, Bernard and Epistemology. London: Routledge and Kegan Paul.

Hollis, M., 1977. Models of Man. Cambridge: Cambridge University Press.

Jarman, M. R., 1971. "Culture and economy in the north Italian Neolithic." World Archaeology 2: 255-265.

Jochim, M. A., 1976. Hunter-Gatherer Subsistence and Settlement: A Predictive Model. London: Academic Press.

Lévi-Strauss, C., 1945. " L'analyse structurale en linguistique et en anthropologie." Word 1: 33-53.

Lévi-Strauss, C., 1955. Tristes Tropiques. Paris: Plon.

Lévi-Strauss, C., 1966. The Savage Mind. London: Weidenfeld and Nicholson.

Lévi-Strauss, C., 1968. Structural Anthropology. London: Allen Lane.

Marx, K., 1967. Capital. New York: International Publishers Edition.

Marx, K., 1970. A Contribution to the Critique of Political Economy. New York: International Publishers Edition.

Marx, K., 1971. The Grundrisse (ed. D. Mc. Lellan). London: Macmillan.

Moore, S. F., 1978. Law as Process. London: Routledge and Kegan Paul.

Piaget, J., 1970. Structuralism. London: Routledge and Kegan Paul.

Piaget, J., 1971. Biology and Knowledge. Edinburgh. Edinburgh University Press.

Piaget, J., 1972. The Principles of Genetic Epistemology. London: Routledge and Kegan Paul.

Plog, F., 1974. The Study of Prehistoric Change. London: Academic Press.

Popper, K. R., 1959. The Logic of Scientific Discovery. London: Hutchinson.

Rappaport, R., 1969. "Some suggestions concerning concept and method in ecological anthropology." Nat. Mus. Canada Bull. 230.

Redman, C. L., 1978. "Mesopotamian urban ecology: the systemic context of the emergence of urbanism" in Social Archaeology: Beyond Subsistence and Dating, eds. C. L. Redman, M. J. Berman, E. V. Curtin, W. T. Langhorne, N. M. Versaggi and J. E. Wanser. London: Academic Press; 329-347.

Renfrew, C., 1972. The Emergence of Civilisation. London: Methuen.

Sahlins, M. D., 1976. Culture and Practical Reason. Chicago: Chicago University Press.

Saussure, F. de., 1960. Course in General Linguistics. London: Peter Owen.

Struever, S., 1968. "Woodland subsistence-settlement systems in the lower Illinois valley" in New Perspectives in Archaeology, eds. L. R. and S. R. Binford. Chicago: Aldine; 285-312.

Struever, S., 1971. "Comments on archaeological data requirements and research strategy." Amer. Ant. 36: 9-19.

Tilley, C. Y., 1979. Post-Glacial Communities in the Cambridge Region: Some Theoretical Approaches to Settlement and Subsistence. Oxford: B.A.R. 66.

Tilley, C. Y., (in press). "Conceptual frameworks for the explanation of sociocultural change" in The Pattern in the Past, eds. N. Hammond, G. Isaac and I. Hodder. Cambridge: Cambridge University Press; 363-86.

Tilley, C. Y. (forthcoming). "Explanatory structure and theory construction in archaeology."

Touraine, A., 1977. The Self Production of Society. Chicago: University of Chicago Press.

Webb, J., 1977. "A scapula from Limassol-Komissariato" in Two Cypriote Sanctuaries of the End of the Cypro-Archaic Period, ed. V. Karageorghis.

Weber, M., 1964. The Theory of Social and Economic Organisation. New York: Free Press.

Wittgenstein, L., 1953. Philosophical Investigations. Oxford: Blackwell.

Yellen, J. and Harpending, H., 1972. "Hunter-gatherer populations and archaeological inference." World Archaeology 4: 244-253.

12. GATHERER-HUNTER INTENSIFICATION

Barbara Bender

The evolution of gatherer-hunter societies has usually been viewed as a long process of economic and technological innovation and adaptation, of increasingly sophisticated tool-kits and techniques geared to extracting a more successful living from a wider variety of environments. Social development has been relegated to second place, responding to ecological and technological imperatives. Interestingly, in some recent writings on human origins the focus has shifted from 'man the tool-maker' and 'man the hunter' to 'people' as food-sharers, homebase occupiers, child-rearers, thus to a more balanced social perspective (Leakey and Lewin 1979: 103-90). This shift is less noticeable in studies of later gatherer-hunter societies which continue to operate within the currently pervasive systemic ecological-functionalist paradigm. In the following section some of the problems associated with this orientation are reviewed, followed by a discussion of an alternative Marxist perspective. This retains the systemic element but moves away from techno-environmental adaptiveness to evolving social relations of production, to the way these structure the productive forces, and to the potential for change imbedded in the tensions set up between social demand and technological response.

The archaeological version of ecological functionalism, found in the writings of British Ecological and many American Processual archaeologists, concentrates on eco-systemic interactions, primarily between the environment, which is given an unwarranted autonomy, and the technological sub-system, which is assumed to be largely directed by, and responsive to, the environment. In turn, this techno-environmental (matter-energy) core is assumed to dominate, and often determine, much of the social form. So, in the case of gatherer-hunters, the emphasis is on the variability, seasonality and unpredictability of the wild resources, which, in conjunction with a limited technology, supposedly set the conditions for band mobility, autonomy, size, and patterns of seasonal aggregation and dispersion. While it is self-evident that a dependence on wild resources places constraints on the social organisation of gatherer-hunters, it will be shown later in this paper that such constraints explain neither structure nor variation in social form.

This eco-systemic orientation is combined with a heavy emphasis on feedback as a regulatory homeostatic mechanism: feedback functioning to promote and maintain the stability of the system (Hill 1977). The question arises 'what system?' and the answer is usually in terms of population reproduction, or a more ambiguous conflation of population and social reproduction (Bailey this vol.; Rappaport 1977. For an alternative viewpoint Faris 1975; Blanton 1975). Particularly in the case of gatherer-hunters, it is the ability of populations to regulate themselves well below carrying capacity that is stressed.

Binford and Chasko (1976), for example, working within such an adaptive framework, offer an environmental gloss to variability in gatherer-hunter birthrates. In reality, however, their data demonstrate more clearly the significant role of social relations in the organisation of procurement systems, division of labour, processes of accumulation and distribution, and, ultimately, demographic variability. What we see is not societies adapting for population sur-survival but societies attempting to ensure social reproduction, which may not involve the entire population, nor be ecologically adaptive in the long-run.

With an ecological-functionalist orientation, the problem of explaining change and variation becomes acute, for if the system is there to maintain the system (a teleological proposition at the best of times) and if the system is primarily homeostatic, why and how does it get to be that way, and why and how does it evolve? If, in addition, social organisation is largely geared to meeting subsistence requirements (the Domestic Mode of Production) then there can be no question of invoking the specifics of the social form and its interaction with the productive forces, nor potential contradictions between social demands on production and productive capacity, in any explanation of change. Thus, at best, a systemic analysis serves to describe the working of a given system, it neither explains the genesis of the system, nor its subsequent transformation. Flannery's (1972) account of the structure of control hierarchies, while significant because it focuses on information rather than matter and energy flows, describes a relatively invariant structure. Neither the content of the various control levels within a specific social formation, nor variation in content between differing formations can be derived from the model. Again, while Flannery's *The Early Mesoamerican Village* is a masterly methodological compilation which finally lays to rest the hoary archaeological myth that material culture can provide little evidence of social organisation, the ultimate 'explanation' offered for the evolution of Mesoamerican chiefdoms falls back on notions of economic rationality. The evening out of regional variability, a necessary economic symbiosis, requires increased hierarchisation. Ritual is no more than a superstructure that masks the increasing inequities of the system (Drennan 1976). Ecological — or in other instances demographic — imperatives, forces outside the system, have to be called upon to break through the functionalist strait-jacket.

A Marxist approach offers an alternative to such mechanistic explanations. The 'core' is no longer the articulation of environment and technology but rather the articulation between relations of production, that is the relations by which society reproduces itself as a social and economic unit, and the forces of production — the resources, techniques, work-units that constitute the productive capacity. Clearly the level of the productive forces constrain the possible social permutations and in that — negative — sense they are determinant. But they only determine what cannot happen, not what does, and are themselves dominated by the social relations of production. It is these that set the pattern of the productive forces and at the same time make demands upon them. Potential disequilibrium between escalating demand and productive capacity provides at least one internal source of change and intensification.

Before continuing this theme within the context of gatherer-hunter intensification, some general points about Marxist analyses of Pre-Capitalist formations must be made. First, there is no unitary Marxist theory. Particularly in the case of Pre-Capitalist societies, most of the work is of very recent date. French Marxist anthropology began in the aftermath of the Twentieth Congress of the Soviet Communist Party and the denunciation of Stalin (1956), and took off with the publication, in 1965, of Althusser's For Marx and Reading Capital. Since Marx himself offered only general comments on Pre-Capitalist societies, there has been room for many readings and interpretations, to which have been added theoretical insights gained from other sources. There is, thus, considerable variation in the approaches offered by Meillassoux, by Godelier and early Friedman, and by Rey and Terray. (For a selection of French writings translated into English see Seddon 1978; Critique of Anthropology 13-14, 1979; and, for a discussion of the French developments, Kahn and Llobera in press).

Not only is there variation between Marxist anthropologists but also — as befits any dynamic theoretical development — there is considerable development within each individual's writings. As Kahn and Llobera (in press) note, the early works were often ham-strung by a less than radical break with traditional anthropology, by a too easy acceptance of categories such as 'economics', 'politics', 'ideology', which may obscure an understanding of the structuring of Pre-Capitalist societies. There has also been a fear of moving too far away from Marx's analysis of Capitalist societies, a tendency to view Pre-Capitalist societies as simply non-Capitalist, rather than as something in their own right. A term such as Mode of Production, taken from the analysis of Capital, which stresses production and control of production as the key to variation and development in social form, is often inoperative for societies where there is no division between producer and means of production and where control of reproduction via control of exchange is a more critical variable. More recent writings have begun to come to grips with these problems (Kahn and Llobera in press; Gledhill in press).

Another difficulty has been a tendency, among some French Marxists, to fall back on the comparative method, assuming that contemporary tribal societies are genuinely pre-Capitalist in form, and opting for a rather static structural analysis that avoids the question of historical development. Kahn and Llobera (in press) and Gledhill (in press) have been particularly critical of Godelier in this respect, for his failure to move beyond generalisations about the role of kinship in structuring Pre-Capitalist economies towards a closer analysis of the historical conditions that explain the dominance and variation in kinship structure. The sort of analysis appropriate to a Marxist study of society requires that the anthropologist turn historian and join forces with the archaeologist (or that these disciplinary categories be abandoned altogether). The Friedman-Rowlands (1978) epigenetic model of emergent social formations demonstrates the dynamic possibilities of a reintegration of the social sciences.

One further general consideration relates both to the lack of historical perspective and to the constraints of traditional anthropological divisions. Marxist anthropologists have usually retained as the unit of study a specific, bounded, society or groupings within a society, creating an areal vacuum around them. In part this reflects the desire to screen out the effects upon

Pre-Capitalist societies of contact or articulation with market-economies (Wobst 1978). In the case of gatherer-hunters this screening process leads, once again, to an emphasis on band autonomy or minimal interaction spheres. Yet it is obvious that inter-societal interaction among gatherer-hunters is not a post-contact phenomenon. Long before the end of the Pleistocene groups exchanged goods, sought access to exotic raw materials, made contacts across tribal boundaries. Twenty thousand years ago in Europe fine quality flints and highly valued shells were passed between groups over vast distances. The impact of such exchanges on social relations between and within societies must be considered. Moreover, by the Late Palaeolithic there was undoubtedly considerable variation in the level of development between different gatherer-hunter societies. In southern France, for example, there was a degree of social differentiation, craft specialisation, and economic intensification not found throughout most of Europe. Unequal development must also have repercussions on the form of inter-societal exchange.

A detailed discussion by Gledhill (1978) of the impact of trade and exchange between the state-organised Toltec of Mesoamerica, the Pueblo food producers of the American Southwest, and the peripheral southwestern gatherer-hunter societies sheds a good deal more light on developments in both core and periphery than does the currently favoured ecological 'explanation' (Plog 1978). This core-periphery interaction is not a matter of passive acceptance or rejection, rather that peripheral groups, within the context of their specific social configuration, are affected by the opportunities and constraints of being incorporated into, and responding to the demands of a larger, more highly developed system, while the core, in turn, is affected by the form and stability of the peripheral integration. It should be stressed that the variations in social complexity and thus in patterns of accumulation and exchange are not simply reflections of different modes of subsistence, of food producers v. food procurers. We have noted variation in complexity among gatherer-hunter societies in Europe, and many other instances could be developed: the American northwest coast chiefdoms articulate with the less highly organized Californian groups, the northeast North American Hopewellian chiefdoms with far-flung egalitarian gatherer-hunter groups (Struever and Houart 1972). 'World-systems theory' may sound too grandiose a concept for gatherer-hunter societies, but we need to move towards such an enlarged perspective and to abandon the current parochial models (Wallerstein 1976).

To move then from this general discussion of Marxist developments to the specifics of gatherer-hunter intensification, I suggested in an earlier paper that the focus of study should not be the on-the-ground band but rather that larger structure within which the band operates (Bender 1978). This larger structure is the alliance network imbedded in kinship and other cross-cutting relationships. The alliance network cannot be explained as merely a response to ecological imperatives. Groups must, of course, be able to move around, to coalesce and fragment, in order to cope with seasonality and variable resource distribution, but they have also to respond to social dictates. At one level movement and alliance are means of resolving social tensions in societies that have few other alleviating mechanisms, and Lee and Woodburn have discussed how large groups often disperse long before subsistence stress sets in. But we need to take this analysis further, to move towards an understanding of the emergence and development of alliance systems, which must be associated with the emergence of increasingly closed breeding networks. It is clear that closed networks are not feasible until a certain demographic density is reached, a stuation which may not have occurred until the Middle or Late Palaeolithic (Wobst 1976). However the fact that they can emerge, that the demographic constraint has been removed, does not explain why they do emerge, for it is clear that a closed breeding network involves both increased risk and inequality of access — those on the periphery having further to go to tap the breeding pool than those more centrally placed. Wobst opts for a 'technological' explanation, suggesting that the closed network arises from the need for co-operative, regulated partnerships in late palaeolithic big game hunting. This would mean that only in areas where such co-operation in hunting had an adaptive advantage would closed networks emerge. It also means that we face the same old problem of the system calling forth its own conditions of existence. An alternative is to view the 'closed system' as a response to emergent self- and group identity, itself a product of long-term developments associated with food sharing, home-base occupation, prolonged infant dependency, increasing social transmission of skills and a corresponding need for improved communication and conceptual ordering. Such improved conceptualisation and communication feeds into technology, including improved hunting skills. In turn, increased hunting and meat procurement creates further problems of distribution and sharing and involves delays in return that further promote social cohesion. With developing group-identity come increasingly closed networks bound by more intensive interaction, and from this derives the possibility of more systematic co-operation, more systematic exploitation of game. As Leakey and Lewin (1979) point out, brain size increases far more rapidly among lower and middle palaeolithic hominids than the slowly accumulating tool inventory would seem to warrant. It is not technological advance that leads to social consciousness, but rather that evolving social skills promote more successful adaptations, including improvements in technology.

It seems reasonable to accept that by the Late Palaeolithic we can talk of alliance systems, probably associated with relatively closed breeding networks, regional identities, which I have called tribal configurations, although perhaps some less loaded term would be more suitable. These are the structures that underwrite social reproduction. Alliance is about circulation and exchange, marital and material. To a greater or lesser degree this circulation makes demands upon productivity and production.

In my earlier paper I tended to dismiss increased productivity as a development (series of developments: inventions, different ways of scheduling activities) that required less explanation than increased production (Bender 1978). Productivity, I suggested, meant that you produced the same amount of food more effectively, and enjoyed more 'leisure'. It did not involve increased labour or much social adjustment. In contrast increased production meant people producing more <u>per capita</u>, and probably involved more work, social costs, etc. Pressure to work harder had to be explained, pressure to work less hard did not. This is clearly a unsatisfactory situation since productivity then seems to result from some indeterminate vitalism, 'man's play instinct' or 'innate drive'. More informatively, increased productivity, permitting a cut-back in time spent in food procurement, should be seen as a concomitant of social intensification, in terms of increased interaction and obligations. More time to visit relatives, more time for ritual, more time to gamble, and out of the emergent 'non-subsistence' activities new relations, new demands arise. When Sahlins writes that Australian aborigines simply use their increased leisure to intensify their ceremonial life it's not 'simple' at all (Sahlins 1974). In that ceremonial life lie the seeds of increased demands, more food for feasting, more goods for exchange, more intensive relations between elder and initiate, and between elder and wives. And the productive efficiency, the techniques used which permit more intensive ritual etc. can then, as the social relations intensify, as demands increase, be used to produce more. The gerontocratic elder can manipulate the labour of his many wives because they can produce more than their immediate requirements. Thus we can envisage not only the intermeshing of the social relations of production and the forces of production, but also how the engagement at any particular time takes its form from what went before. We see also how social demands realise the potential surplus, converting it into a medium of exchange and transaction via feasting, marital or initiate payments. These material exchanges, like marital exchanges, create obligations, ties of delayed reciprocity. They are part of the social reproduction.

The perspective offered here is not specific to a particular mode of subsistence, for the properties of an alliance (tribal) system are not generated by the form of subsistence. Nonetheless since the alliance configuration is constrained by the level of the productive forces there is no way in which an analysis can ignore the mode of subsistence. So on the one hand the analysis must focus on the emergent properties of specific alliance structures and the internal dynamics underwriting social demand on production, whether it be simply to produce more effectively or to produce more abundantly; on the other, on the way the social relations of production structure the productive forces and on the resultant productive capacity and potential. The range of resources available and exploited, their responsiveness to manipulation, long-term ecological tolerance to human interference etc. must be taken into account. We are then in a position to assess to what degree and how social demands on production may be met, and the feedback between intensification of the technological base — or inability to intensify — and further social development. In such an analysis no part of the system is determinant, but the social relations of production are dominant.

Evolutionary studies must focus on specific social configurations, specific trajectories set within a wider historical (and pre-historical) context. In a forthcoming paper such a study is attempted for Archaic and post-Archaic gatherer-hunter societies in northeast North America and California (Bender in press). Without going into details, an initial analysis of the northeast North American material suggests slow widespread social and economic intensification through the Archaic involving increasing material exchange, increasing amounts of exotic materials in circulation, increasing ritual elaboration with associated shaman roles, increasing manufacture of non-utilitarian goods often used as burial offerings, and — in response to demands on production — increasingly intensive procurement strategies (Tuck 1978; Dragoo 1975;

Ford 1974). But in much of the more northerly coniferous-deciduous Great Lakes-St. Lawrence region these developments were constrained by the relatively limited amount of edible plant foods. Potential for surplus production was limited and while role variation emerged there is relatively little evidence of developing status variation.

In contrast, further South, in the deciduous regions, with patches of savanna, rich boundary eco-tones, abundant seed and nut, shell-fish and fish resources, the productive constraints were mainly in terms of labour investment and organisation. Once these were overcome large surpluses could be realised. In this region there is, within the Early Woodland, a move from role- to status differentiation and a shift from productive efficiency to increased per capita production. In large part emergent status seems to have been invested in ritual authority sustained by control of the circulation of items considered essential to social transactions, and hence to social reproduction. The maintenance and further development of such systems requires an ever expanding production and circulation of prestige items, and there is ample evidence for the emergence of a complex network of inter- and intra-regional production and exchange (Struever and Houart 1976; Tainter 1977). There is evidence also that peripheral groups supplying the necessary exotic materials were in turn affected. For example, the western Great Lakes copper-producing societies begin to show more evidence of status variation, with individuals gaining prestige through their control of trade, and considerable caches of trade items are found in selected graves.

The elaboration of the Hopewell chiefdoms was founded on very intensive food procurement, processing and storage, with a slight element of food production. Certain archaeologists have over-emphasised the significance of maize production mainly, one suspects, to permit a technological explanation of the social intensification (Prufer 1967). More evident is the strain that the social demands made on an economy based mainly on wild procurement, and the probability that the system began to collapse under the pressure. An additional, very important, factor in the decline, requiring much closer analysis, is the effect of the burgeoning Mississipian culture to the South. This southerly development is strongly linked into the expanding Mesoamerican Toltec system and there is little doubt that in the process of siphoning exotic commodities towards the south and ultimately to Mesoamerica, many of the supply regions on which the Hopewellian centres depended were cut off and their products re-diverted. The Hopewell core became peripheralised and it is as much the breakdown of exchange and thus the loss of the transactional medium that underwrote the reproduction of the society, as the ecological and technological pressures that led to a social transformation.

References

Althusser, L., 1969. For Marx. Harmondsworth: Penguin.

Althusser, L. and Balibar, E., 1970. Reading Capital. London: New Left Books.

Bender, B., 1978. "Gatherer-hunter to farmer: a social perspective." World Arch. 10: 204-222.

Bender, B., (in press). " North American hunter-gatherer societies" in Marxist Perspectives in Archaeology, ed. M. Spriggs. Cambridge: Cambridge University Press.

Binford, L. and Chasko, W. Jr., 1976. "Nunamiut demographic history: a provocative case" in Demographic Anthropology: a Quantitative Approach, ed. E. B. Zubrow. Albuquerque: University of New Mexico Press; 63-143.

Blanton, R. E., 1975. "The cybernetic analysis of human population growth" in Population Studies in Archaeology and Biological Anthropology: a Symposium, ed. A. C. Swedlund. Memoirs of the Society for American Archaeology 30: 116-126.

Dragoo, D. W., 1975. "Some aspects of eastern North American prehistory: a review." Amer. Ant. 41: 3-27.

Drennan, R. D., 1976. " Religion and social evolution in Formative Mesoamerica" in The Early Mesoamerican Village, ed. K. V. Flannery. New York: Academic Press; 345-368.

Faris, J. C., 1975. "Social evolution, population and production" in Population, Ecology, and Social Evolution, ed. S. Polgar. The Hague: Mouton; 235-271.

Flannery, K. V., 1972. "The cultural evolution of civilisation." Ann. Rev. Ecology and Systematics 3: 399-426.

Flannery, K. V. (ed.), 1976. The Early Mesoamerican Village. New York: Academic Press.

Ford, A., 1974. "Northeastern archaeology: past and future directions." Ann. Rev. Anth. 3: 385-413.

Friedman, J. and Rowlands, M. J., 1978. "Notes towards an epigenetic model of the evolution of 'civilisation'" in The Evolution of Social Systems, eds. J. Friedman and M. J. Rowlands. London: Duckworth; 201-276.

Gledhill, J., 1978. " Formative development in the North American southwest" in Social Organisation and Settlement, eds. D. Green, C. Haselgrove and M. Spriggs. Oxford: B.A.R. Suppl. Ser. 47; 241-290.

Gledhill, J., (in press). "Time's arrow." Critique of Anthropology 16.

Hill, J. N., 1977. "Systems theory and the explanation of change" in Explanation of Prehistoric Change, ed. J. N. Hill. Albuquerque: University of New Mexico Press; 59-103.

Kahn, J. and Llobera, J. R., (in press). "Towards a new Marxism or a new anthropology?" in The Anthropology of Pre-Capitalist Societies, eds. J. Kahn and J. R. Llobera. London: Macmillan.

Leakey, R. and Lewin, R., 1979. People of the Lake. London: Morrison and Gibb.

Lee, R. B., 1968. "What hunters do for a living, or how to make out on scarce resources" in Man the Hunter, eds. R. B. Lee and I. DeVore. Chicago: Aldine; 30-48.

Plog, F., 1978. "The Keresan Bridge: an ecological and archaeological account" in Social Archaeology: Beyond Subsistence and Dating, eds. C. D. Redman, M. J. Berman, E. V. Curtin, W. T. Langhorne, N. M. Versaggi and J. E. Wanser. New York: Academic Press; 349-372.

Prufer, O., 1967. "The Hopewell Culture." Sci. Amer. 211: 90-102.

Rappaport, R., 1977. "Ecology, adaptation and the ills of functionalism." Discussions in Anthropology, Dept. of Anthropology, University of Michigan, 2: 138-190.

Sahlins, M. D., 1974. Stone Age Economics. London: Tavistock.

Seddon, D. (ed.), 1978. Relations of Production. London: Frank Cass.

Struever, S. and Houart, G., 1972. "An analysis of the Hopewell interaction sphere" in Social Exchange and Interaction, ed. E. N. Wilmsen. Ann Arbor: University of Michigan, Museum of Anthropology; 47-79.

Tainter, J. A., 1977. "Modeling change in prehistoric social systems" in For Theory Building in Archaeology, ed. L. Binford. New York: Academic Press; 327-351.

Tuck, J. A., 1978. "Regional cultural development, 3000 to 300 B.C." in The Northeast. Handbook of North American Indians, Vol. 15, ed. B. B. Trigger. Washington: Smithsonian Institution; 28-43.

Wallerstein, I., 1976. "A world-system perspective on the social sciences." Brit. J. Sociol. 27: 343-352.

Wobst, H. M., 1976. "Locational relationships in paleolithic society" in The Demographic Evolution of Human Populations, eds. R. H. Ward and K. M. Weiss. London: Academic Press; 49-58.

Wobst, H. M., 1978. "The archaeo-ethnology of hunter-gatherers or the tyranny of the ethnographic record in archaeology." Amer. Ant. 43: 303-309.

Woodburn, J., 1968. "An introduction to Hadza ecology" in Man the Hunter, eds. R. B. Lee and I. DeVore. Chicago: Aldine; 49-55.

13. EXCHANGE AND HIERARCHY

Carol P. MacCormack

Introduction

In his recent paper "Alternative models for exchange and spatial distribution", Renfrew concludes with the advice that we look closely at the range of organizational devices in human exchange systems, particularly those which are hierarchically structured (1977:88). This paper will look at exchange and emergent hierarchy under two complementary theoretical headings: 1) a materialist historical view, and 2) a social/cognitive view.

Marxist materialists are interested in exchange as a component in a theory of history, while the intellectual descendents of Mauss are concerned with exchange patterns for a different reason. They are still working on the Durkheimian problem of explaining how societies are integrated. How are we to account for social solidarity?

Materialist view of exchange relations, and appearance of hierarchy

Where Hindess and Hirst (1975) have begun with concepts about industrial society and worked "backward", attempting to fill out a scheme of pre-capitalist modes of production, Meillassoux (1972) has begun at the other end. His theoretical formulations are stimulated by field work in a west African agricultural society, and one might say he builds theory from the ground upward. He notes the distinction Marx made between land being regarded by members of a society as a subject of their labour, and land being regarded by members of a society as an instrument of their labour.

Hunters and gatherers regard land as a subject of their labour, taking from it what they need each day. They enjoy an instantaneous "product", and share it out immediately, being free from any further reciprocal obligation in regard to that day's labour. If there is a dispute, the aggrieved party simply goes away to another social group, taking subsistence from the land in another area. Hunters and gatherers tend to have a simple kinship structure of ego-centred bilateral kindreds (like ours), which ramify infinitely on a person's mother's and father's side. There is no hierarchy in a kindred, no ancestral sanctions, and the number of potential kin is enormous. It is not a socially bounded group.

Meillassoux then looks at sedentary agriculturalists. Men and women invest their labour in the land, hoeing and planting in one season, expecting a return on their labour investment in a later season, with the harvest. They may even terrace, irrigate, fertilize, or modify the land in other ways. Thus, land is an instrument of their labour. The population is bound together until the harvest is in, and after that they are tied to the granary for subsistence and for seed corn to initiate the next yearly cycle. Disputes must be settled, within authority structures, and in accordance with agreed procedures.

As Meillassoux notes, lineages have hierarchy built into them. A lineage often originates with a founding ancestor who, in the Sherbro area of Sierra Leone, subdued the bush spirits and achieved abundant harvests and good health for his dependants. First fruits are offered to the bush spirits, but in time these become ceremonies to "feed the dead": ancestors who are the ultimate source of blessings and sanctions (MacCormack 1978a, 1978b). Elders are about to become ancestors, the sacred mediators between the living and the dead. On a more materialist level of analysis, they have produced crops over many, many agricultural cycles, sustaining junior members of the lineage. Thus, Meillassoux identifies, through the way land is used, the material and temporal basis for the emergence of lineage and hierarchy.

It is also important to note that because lineages are ancestor-focused, they create bounded social groups. For example, in a matrilineal society, only the children of females, in line of descent from an ancestor, have the ascribed right to use the property of the group. All others are automatically excluded. It is a social device for restricting access to valued resources such as terraced or irrigated land. By way of contrast, Bushmen, Pygmy, or Eskimo bilateral kindreds do not embody any ideology of exclusiveness, nor do they divide people into discrete social units as unilineal descent groups do.

With the emergence of a dominant lineage, prestations to elders often become tribute to a chief. That tribute may be in kind, in labour, or in people. If the chief has many wives in a patrilineal society, they provide both labour in production and progeny, strengthening the dynasty in material wealth and descendants, a point I shall return to later.

Categories of exchange and reciprocity, and appearance of hierarchy

Human societies cannot exchange without first having cultural categories. Lévi-Strauss, influenced by both Freudian theory and linguistic theory, notes that the primary binary contrasts we make are between self and not-self, extended to "us" and "other" (1969). The incest taboo, a uniquely human cultural rule, defines the boundary of "us" against "other". Human society originated, according to Lévi-Strauss, with rules of category discrimination between "us" and "other", and rules of marriage exogamy forcing us to make on-going social relations outside our own incest-defined group. That incest-defined group may be a family, a lineage, an enormous clan, or a moiety (that is, the other half of the population, however that population is defined).

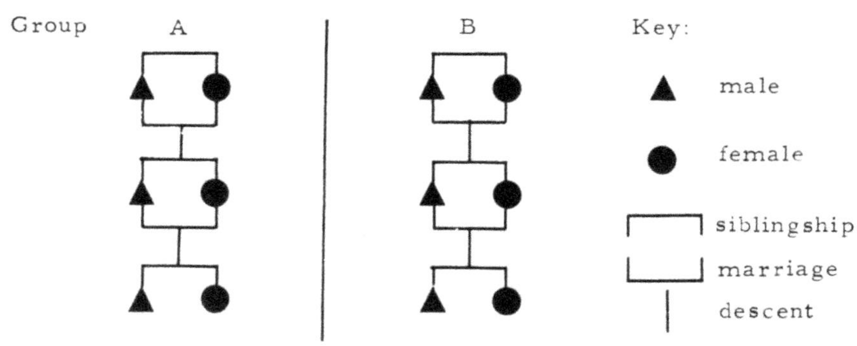

Fig. 13.1 Non-society. Without incest taboo and rules of exogamy

Marriage rules may make a difference in regard to hierarchy. If a man should marry his father's sister's daughter, an egalitarian integration of lineages may result:

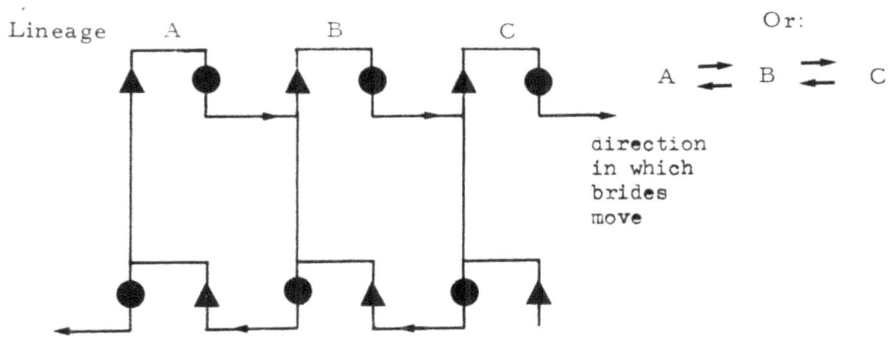

Fig. 13.2

But if the marriage rule states that a man should marry his mother's brother's daughter, one lineage may perpetually be in the superior position of "wife givers" to another lineage:

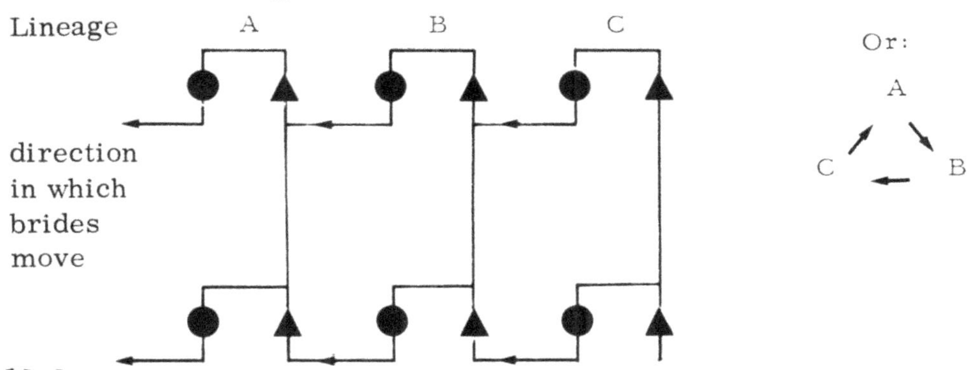

Fig. 13.3

The essential feature of rules of marriage exogamy is that they serve to integrate social groups, causing us to query Renfrew's assumption that exogamy and marriage rules "lead to a higher degree of intermarriage among 'us' and hence a greater information flow, leading to an effective, operational difference in the culture of 'them' and 'us' " (1975:18-19). If I have understood him correctly, he uses the concept of marriage exogamy and marriage exchange rules to explain the origin not of social integration over social and geographical space, but the origin of the exclusive or autonomous Early State Module. It is important for the archaeologist to discriminate types of marriage rules. With patrilateral cross-cousin marriage there is direct reciprocity among equals and no hierarchy. But with matrilateral cross-cousin marriage some lineages may have a constant dominant position as wife givers over other lineages who remain perpetually in their debt. Thus, the possible emergence of hierarchy and perhaps an Early State Module (Leach 1954).

Mauss (1954) proposed that to give a gift is to give oneself. If the gift is accepted, there is a social relationship between giver and receiver which is sustained over time as the gift is reciprocated. When reciprocity is delayed, as it is in the ceremonial <u>kula</u> trade in the Trobriand Islands, for example, an umbrella of peace is created to enable ordinarily hostile people to engage in utilitarian trade while they wait for ceremonial gifts to be reciprocated in the following year.

Polanyi (1957) developed two basic categories of exchange, those which were reciprocated directly between partners or groups, and those that flowed to a central person (and place) and were then reciprocated outward again. The second category is clearly associated with hierarchy. Cynthia Irwin-Williams has suggested (1977) that archaeologists formulate predictions of the attributes to be found in these two kinds of exchange systems and test them in the field. She then went on to list some of the characteristics of each system which might be observed in present-day populations and discerned from the archaeological remains of past populations.

Sahlins has correlated types of reciprocity with social distance (1974: 185-275). Close kin give and receive small gifts and services, frequently, often altruistically, in a spirit of generalized reciprocity. Much ceremonial exchange between groups which intermarry, or between trade partners, is quite formal and correct, the reciprocity being balanced with the receiver returning equivalent value. Those at the greatest social distance, for example strangers in a market, try to make a profit, receiving more than they reciprocate, in a mode of negative reciprocity.

Richard Salisbury, in his work with the Siane of New Guinea, charted out these levels of reciprocity in subsistence goods, luxury items, ceremonial exchange, and rules of marriage alliance (1962). He, as Bohannan had done for the Tiv of Nigeria, identified three moral spheres of conveyance. Vegetable food, for example, could be conveyed for help in garden work, but could not be converted into luxury trinkets or shell valuables. Where there are spheres of conveyance, food is always found in the category characterized by altruistic generalized reciprocity. Food is life-giving, urgent, domestic. It is readily available and necessarily shared. As Sahlins has commented, it "has far too much social value—ultimately because it has too much use value—to have exchange value" (1974:215). (See Fig. 13.4.)

In New Guinea, inter-clan exchange networks are built up by ambitious men who make trade partnerships with others. The resultant networks differ from patron-client networks in that all participants start out as social equals in their attempts to use exchange and debt to achieve status enhancement. Several authors, notably Rappaport and Strathern, have commented on the restrictions in geographical scope of exchange which result from these chain-like structures of partnerships. These narrow chains of exchange in objects like stone axes tend to occur throughout the New Guinea highlands wherever there are 1) few sources of production, 2) the sources are widely spaced, and 3) hostile political relations between groups make it impossible for people in many local groups to have personal ties with people in groups which control production (Strathern 1971:112).

Rappaport, for the Maring area of New Guinea, describes exchange of two main items: salt from one valley and stone axes from another (1967). Both are classified by the Maring as utilitarian goods but circulate in the same sphere of conveyance with prestige goods such as feathers and shells. If utilitarian goods are restricted to a single sphere of conveyance, as the

Sphere of conveyance (nexus)	Type of goods and services	Mode of reciprocity	Social relationships (social distance)
Subsistence	Veg. food Help in garden	Generalized	Intra-clan relationships
Luxury	Pandanus mats Trinkets	Balanced	Inter-clan individual relationships
Ceremonial	Pigs	Balanced	Inter-clan group relationships

Fig. 13.4 Siane exchange (Salisbury 1962)

Bohannans describe for the Tiv (1968), then the supply of these necessary goods is kept down by limited demand. When people in Jimi Valley have enough salt for their sweet potatoes they don't want any more. With utilitarian goods, "more" is not "better". Demand is inelastic. The number of axes produced for exchange by people in Jimi Valley is limited by their inelastic demand for salt. However, demand for prestige goods is quite elastic. With feathers and shells, "more" is "better". Therefore, with utilitarian and prestige goods combined in a single sphere of conveyance, combined demand will draw out more production and utilitarian goods will be exchanged over a wider social field and geographical area. (See discussion in Pires-Ferreira and Flannery 1976, and Renfrew 1975:28.)

Rappaport has also noted that utilitarian exchange can be jeopardized by demographic variability. If population in the salt-consuming valley drops, fewer axes will be produced for exchange, but this disadvantage is overcome by enhanced demand when utilitarian and prestige goods are combined in a single sphere of conveyance.

The Tiv case suggests that merged spheres of conveyance may possibly lead to greater production, and may account for intensified social hierarchy (Bohannan and Bohannan 1968:220ff.). Or, rather than greater production and social hierarchy, it may only lead to inflation and famine. In the historical case of the Tiv, there was a subsistence sphere of conveyance, a prestige sphere, and thirdly, the exchange of persons in marriage through a rule of sister exchange:

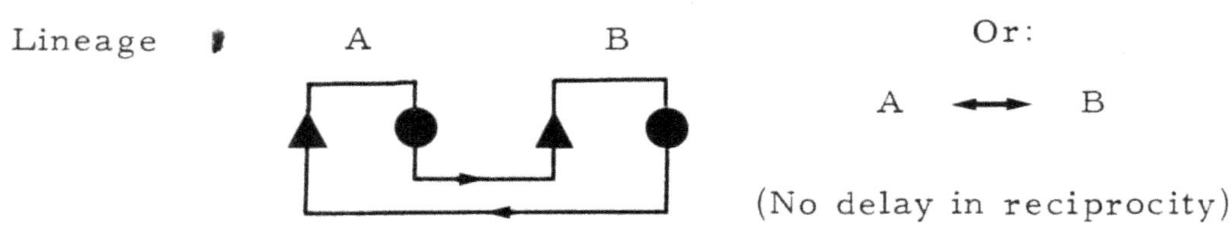

Fig. 13.5

The physical reproduction of each lineage depended primarily upon demography, not upon wealth for exchange. It was possible to do some converting upward, from one sphere to another. Prestige goods could be used for obtaining marriage rights in a woman and her children, but ideally marriage should be reciprocal exchange of brides between two lineages. However, when general-purpose money was introduced it functioned as a medium of exchange cutting across the three spheres of conveyance, allowing literally anything to be converted into anything else. Subsistence foods could be sold in the market for money for bridewealth, brides being the most prestigious and morally superior thing to acquire. Tiv are a patrilineal society, with an economy based upon hoe cultivation. Women do most of the farm labour. Controlling women is the way to control both production and the reproduction of patrilineages. Where the Tiv had been an economically egalitarian society, it was now possible for one person to sell food, cows, etc. to make many marriages, thus increasing his number of potential political alliances, acquiring many wives and children as farm labourers, and many descendents to guarantee dynasty:

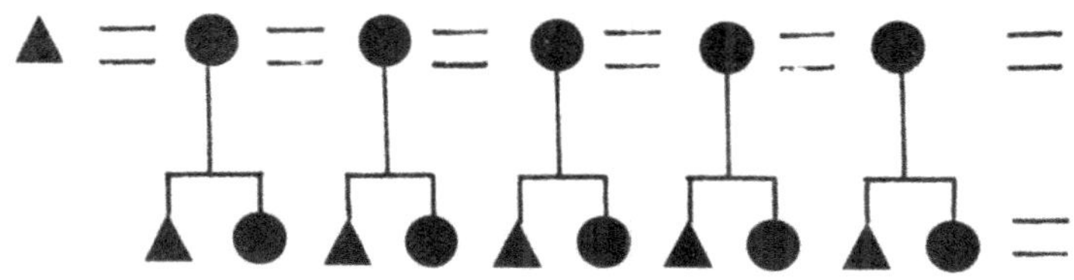

Fig. 13.6

(See MacCormack 1978b for uses of surpluses in acquiring clients and slaves as well.) In the rush to acquire wives, the Tiv sold too much food, resulting in famine and inflation in bridewealth. Had not colonial authorities intervened, some individuals with economically strong households may have succeeded to social and political prominence by the new rules of the game (see Chayanov 1966). Then, the point at which an acephalous political system of segmentary lineages transforms itself into a system of ranked lineages and chiefs might have been reached. That might have been the point where an exchange system of reciprocity gave way to a centralized redistribution system. One might also speculate that the pre-colonial exchange system, by insulating subsistence goods in a single sphere of conveyance, enhanced the survival chances of the many against the accumulating wealth of the few; given the possibility that incipient chiefs may not always redistribute generously.

I might conclude by noting that although there is much altruistic generalized exchange in societies without monetized economies, many are as commercial as any Western economy, especially in New Guinea. But as Mary Douglas has noted, although there is abundant entrepreneurial ability, those societies are incapable of long-term accumulation of capital. They do not produce anything which will yield over a longer time than the life cycle of a pig. These are not systems of primitive capitalism, but merely primitive commerce (Douglas 1967:126).

References

Bohannan, P. and L., 1968. Tiv Economy. Evanston: Northwestern University Press.

Chayanov, A. V., 1966. The Theory of Peasant Economy. Homewood, Ill.: American Economic Association.

Douglas, M., 1967. "Primitive rationing" in Themes in Economic Anthropology, ed. R. Firth. A. S.A. Monograph 6. London: Tavistock; 119-148.

Hindess, B. and Hirst, P. Q., 1975. Pre-Capitalist Modes of Production. London: Routledge and Kegan Paul.

Irwin-Williams, C., 1977. "A network model for the analysis of prehistoric trade" in Exchange Systems in Prehistory, eds. T. K. Earle and J. E. Ericson. New York: Academic Press; 141-152.

Leach, E. R., 1954. Political Systems of Highland Burma. London: Bell.

Lévi-Strauss, C., 1969. The Elementary Structures of Kinship. Boston: Beacon Press.

MacCormack, C. P., 1978a. "The cultural ecology of production: Sherbro Coast and hinterland" in Social Organisation and Settlement, eds. D. Green, C. Haselgrove and M. Spriggs. Oxford: B.A.R. Suppl. Ser. 47:197-210.

MacCormack, C. P., 1978b. "Wono: institutionalized dependency in Sherbro descent groups" in Slavery in Africa, eds. S. Miers and I. Kopytoff. Madison: University of Wisconsin Press; 181-204.

Mauss, M., 1954. The Gift. London: Cohen and West.

Meillassoux, C., 1972. "From reproduction to production." Economy and Society 1:93-105.

Pires-Ferreira, J. W. and Flannery, K. V., 1976. "Ethnographic models for Formative exchange" in The Early Mesoamerican Village, ed. K.V. Flannery. New York: Academic Press; 286-292.

Polanyi, K., 1957. "The economy as institutionalised process" in Trade and Market in the Early Empires, eds. K. Polanyi, C. M. Arensberg and H. W. Pearson. Glencoe, Ill.: Free Press; 243-270.

Rappaport, R., 1967. Pigs for the Ancestors. New Haven: Yale University Press.

Renfrew, A. C., 1975. "Trade as action at a distance: questions of integration and communication" in Ancient Civilization and Trade, eds. J. A. Sabloff and C. C. Lamberg-Karlovsky. Albuquerque: University of New Mexico Press; 3-59.

Renfrew, A. C., 1977. "Alternative models for exchange and spatial distribution" in Exchange Systems in Prehistory, eds. T. K. Earle and J. E. Ericson. New York: Academic Press; 71-89.

Sahlins, M. D., 1974. Stone Age Economics. London: Tavistock.

Salisbury, R. F., 1962. From Stone to Steel. Cambridge: Cambridge University Press.

Strathern, A., 1971. The Rope of Moka. Cambridge: Cambridge University Press.

14. COPING WITH SCARCITY: EXCHANGE AND SOCIAL STORAGE

John O'Shea

> Variation in the environment is a fact of life for all plants and animals, except perhaps for inhabitants of the abyssal depths of the sea.
>
> Ricklefs 1979: 159.

> The people still definitely prefer their ruler to have a big granary. It gives them, I think, a sense of security.
>
> Richards 1939: 214

The study of economic archaeology is similar to the anthropological analysis of current native economies in the sense that the object of study, the 'economy', is inextricably bound up with the social, political and religious activities of the society under examination. Only in the most complex societies are these aspects of culture differentiated sufficiently to be studied as self-standing entities (and even then, it is often impossible to appreciate the working of one aspect in isolation from the others). Yet, as it is impossible to analyse all aspects simultaneously, studies tend to focus on a particular component of culture as a device for study, emphasising particular functional roles of human social interaction, so as to highlight one or another aspect of the operation of the culture system.

The Palaeoeconomic approach has been critised, often rightly so, for assuming that economy can be somehow divorced from other cultural activities, or that it even dictates social formations. Such assertions are clearly untenable. Similarly, however, anthropological economics often appears so intent on stressing the 'social' content of exchange, that the concomitant economic aspects of such transactions are often ignored or even denied. Such a non-economic bias can seriously distort our view of the multi-functional character of social institutions, and obscure the essential organisation of cultural behaviour as an adaptive system. Such distortion is a serious shortcoming for archaeology, where the concept of adaptation has both long and short term implications.

In this paper I am concerned with the inherent uncertainty surrounding human food procuring activities and the resulting strategies employed by societies for coping with periodic scarcity. In particular, the ways in which exchange is used on a regional basis as a means for the indirect storage of perishable food surplus will be considered. In doing so, the economic aspects of such exchange relationships will be highlighted. This is not to deny the other social and political functions which exchange simultaneously fulfills, but rather to emphasise the latent economic and adaptive content of such transactions. It will be argued that the working of regional exchange systems, capable of mobilising food in times of scarcity, is a regular feature of semi- and fully-sedentary adaptations, and a phenomenon with important implications for the study of prehistoric economies.

Shortage and uncertainty:

Few societies lead the dire "hand-to-mouth" existence which has traditionally been seen as the plight of all but the most advanced civilisations. Indeed, recent studies have reversed this proposition, identifying the simplest hunter-gatherers as the original affluent societies (Sahlins 1974: 1). Yet, neither the stark view of tradition nor the idyllic image of Sahlins accurately portrays the true nature of primitive subsistence. For most groups, be they hunter-gatherers or agriculturalists, the acquisition of necessary food is unproblematic in good years, but they are faced with mortal deficiencies in the occasional 'bad year'. The problem which must be solved by any primitive economic system is how to utilise the abundance which may be available in any given year as a defence against scarcity in poor years.

Some periods of scarcity are predictable and regular, and as such their effects can be anticipated. For hunter-gatherer groups this may be a cycle of resources which are available for harvesting for only a limited period of time, or for farmers is the regular delay between planting and harvesting.

Unpredictable scarcity can be the result of a wide range of phenomena; biological, climatological or cultural, which result in the interruption of the normal scheduling of resources. Such resource failures may be periodic or cyclical, as in the case of anadromous fish or the successive size of olive harvests; they may be catastrophic, as with hail, flooding, frost, or insect plagues; or they may be the purposive result of unfriendly human interaction (cf. raiding of agricultural fields among the Yanomamö, Chagnon 1968). Shortages of this kind present radically different problems to the economy of primitive groups precisely because they cannot be predicted, nor is their duration known. It is in these times of severe, unanticipated shortage, that the true carrying capacity of an environment is determined, and where Liebig's law of the minimum (Bartholomew and Birdsell 1953; Suttles 1968: 60) operates most directly on the size and density of human population.

Human societies employ three strategies for lessening their vulnerability to such periods of scarcity: movement, diversification, and storage. Movement as a response to scarcity exploits the fact that failures are frequently very localised in character. The use of such a strategy necessitates, however, that the landscape as a whole is being under-exploited. In such situations, a group can usually move away from an area of scarcity. However, the more densely a region is populated, the less viable will be movement as a strategy for ensuring subsistence. In situations where groups occupy well defined and intensively exploited territories, movement may have grave consequences and will usually occur only as a last resort.

Diversifying strategies, such as movement, take advantage of the localised character of most resource failure, which may be restricted to a small area or a particular class of food resource. Diversifying strategies are used to 'cover-the-bets' by exploiting a broad range of food resources. Diversifying practices are common among both sedentary and non-sedentary groups and, as we shall see below, frequently provide a community with a first line of defence against shortage.

The final strategy countering scarcity is storage. With reference to food procurement and uncertainty, two varieties of storage can be defined. Direct storage is any process which serves to stabilise actual foodstuffs such that they can be consumed at a later time. Following this definition, salting, drying, freezing, smoking, and caching all represent types of direct storage. Storage of this kind may be undertaken by individual households or may involve the participation of whole communities, but generally does not require further economic transactions. The usefulness of direct storage is determined in large part by the types of foods, the climate and the existing technology.

The second variety of storage is termed indirect. Indirect storage encompasses all those processes which transform foodstuffs into a more stable, alternative form, from which food value may later be recovered. A particularly elegant form of indirect storage is the dual strategy of agriculture and animal husbandry. When agriculturalists also maintain livestock, crop surplus can be converted into a more stable animal form, which can later be consumed in time of need. Since animals can also make use of foodstuffs that are totally unusable to the human population, and they reproduce, they offer a great potential for buffering the effects of agricultural failure. Excluding animal husbandry, the transformations which are characteristic of indirect storage are cultural, and involve the equivalencing of foodstuffs and non-food items through exchange. Within a community, food may be exchanged against a moral obligation of reciprocity, but when such exchange is extended between corporate groups or villages, some manner of physical token usually enters the transaction n. In such a transaction, food is exchanged for some non-food token with at least the implicit understanding that such tokens can later be re-exchanged for food. This type of exchange transaction is here referred to as social storage. The nature of such transactions may vary widely in their frequency and formality, as may the kind and number of durable items moving through the exchange network. The characterisation of such social storage systems will be considered in detail below.

The storage of food as insurance against anticipated or unanticipated scarcity can occur either through the stabilisation of existing foodstuffs, or by exchanging foodstuffs for obligations or tokens which may be later reconverted into food. The first process tends to be atomising, involving only the primary productive units within a given community, while the second process tends to be integrative, linking different productive units within the same community, and linking one community to another.

These three basic strategies for coping with scarcity are not mutually exclusive and frequently will be employed by the same community. The usefulness of these strategies, however, is determined in most cases by the organisation of the society's productive system. This interrelationship can be illustrated by contrasting, in a general way, non-sedentary and sedentary adaptations.

Scarcity: non-sedentary strategies

In adapting to predictable shortages, the principal non-sedentary strategy is movement. A resource is exploited as it becomes available and some attempt may be made to store a portion of it, then the band moves on to be in line for harvesting the next resource (cf. Feit 1973: 120). Movement, in this case, may mean simply a shift in the resources being exploited within a particular area, or it might entail moving some distance to exploit a new ecological zone. The necessity of movement will often limit the degree to which available surplus can effectively be stored. Therefore, in many cases such societies are unable to utilise the full potential of a resource when it becomes available. The gathering of large populations in a particular season, as with the communal rabbit hunts among the Great Basin Shoshoni (Steward 1938) has undeniable social value, but is a clear admission that the technological and economic systems of the society are incapable of making more direct use of the abundance. This inability to make full use of existing abundance is not limited to simpler or non-sedentary societies, as Oberg (1973) illustrates among the Tlingit, where again it is not the number of salmon which can be caught which is the limiting factor, but rather the number which can be processed and stored in the time available.

In the event of major resource failure, the options for a non-sedentary society are limited. If the failure is such as to disrupt only a single food source, the community may be able to procure sufficient food through the use of secondary or 'fall-back' resources (Colson 1979). The existence of such resources is largely a product of the low level of environmental exploitation practiced by non-sedentary groups, which in this instance serves as a kind of passive storage (Cohen 1977: 29). Lee (1972: 343) has shown how the !Kung bushmen employ food preferences as a means of leaving secondary food resources unexploited as long as supplies are plentiful. If, however, the resource failure is more general in spread or severity, as indeed is fluctuating rainfall among the !Kung (Yellen 1977: 31-32), then it is unlikely that a diversifying strategy alone would be sufficient. In such cases, the only option is movement. In this sense, too, the very low population densities maintained by mobile societies act as a passive form of storage. Indeed, that bands move into the territories of other bands, and are permitted to remain in such circumstances, can be claimed as a legitimate type of social storage (cf. Steward 1938: 27-28; Meggitt 1962: 52).

To summarise, two points seem crucial to an understanding of non-sedentary adaptations to scarcity: (a) a substantial proportion of the calorific value available to such societies in the course of a single year, given their level of technology, is never exploited; and (b) the principal response to generalised scarcity is migration.

Scarcity: sedentary strategies

The strategies employed by sedentary groups differ from those of non-sedentary groups in the degree to which available surplus food is actively manipulated. Whereas mobile societies tend to leave what is not required for immediate consumption and rely on a passive banking strategy of under-exploitation, sedentary groups exploit available resources more intensively, harvesting in quantities well beyond those needed for immediate consumption. This surplus produce is then actively manipulated through storage techniques. This strategy of over-production coupled with storage is the cornerstone of sedentary life.

For agriculturalists, like mobile hunter-gatherers, there is a distinct seasonal cycle, including times of predictable scarcity. Direct storage is the principal means of providing food during these seasons when fresh crops are not available for consumption. Even in modern agriculture, and despite a supposed 'cash economy', physical storage has retained an important role, with farmers frequently holding a crop in store for several years in an effort to receive a maximum price for its sale in a year of poor harvest. Among societies with less well-developed storage technologies, the ability to store produce directly is more limited and rarely will allow foods to be preserved for more than a single year. Such stores are usually sufficient to provide food for a community through the predictable non-producing season. Such stores are not sufficient, however, to protect the community against crop lure, i.e. unpredictable scarcity.

One approach to the contingency of crop failure is to diversify, either in terms of the varieties of crops grown; or spatially, by planting a number of discontinuous plots. This tendency towards agricultural diversification is well illustrated by the farming practices observed in northern Mexico:

> " Interestingly, the farmers view this arrangement (the division of land holdings among heirs into discontinuous miniplots) as an economic asset rather than liability, in spite of the additional travel time required to work the fields. In addition to soil characteristics, each plot is also perceived as unique with respect to microclimate and susceptibility to natural disasters such as winds, drought, frost, hail, insects and gophers. In a typical growing season it is not uncommon for the crops of one plot to be severely damaged while the other fields of the farmer escape with little or no loss."
>
> (Clawson and Hoy 1979: 375)

Such diversifying strategies, coupled with heightened levels of production, are often sufficient to level out differences in food availability among households within a community, but they are insufficient to protect the community against larger scale failures, and in severe cases a community may yet be forced to move or disperse.

An alternative strategy for coping with such scarcity is the operation of an indirect storage system on an inter-community level. Through the regular exchange of foodstuffs and other goods between communities it becomes possible to store or bank food value through exchange. Such exchange systems, as with diversifying strategies on a local level, exploit the localised character of most scarcity, and enable the surplus production of one community to become available to a second community during a period of acute shortage. Clearly, the operation of such an inter-community storage system is a complex cultural operation, even in its simplest form, and involves both the problems and dangers of travelling to foreign villages, and maintaining a 'willingness' to exchange foodstuffs in crucial situations. Yet, the frequency with which such systems of social storage occur, and the tenacity with which such exchange relations are maintained, serves to underline the critical nature of such relations to the continued security of sedentary communities. Although this discussion has concentrated on the occurrence of social storage among sedentary agriculturalists, it is worth noting that similar food exchange systems do occur among non-agriculturalists. Damas (1972) illustrates mechanisms for community-wide and inter-community exchange of food along lines similar to those discussed here, among three central Eskimo groups. Similar social storage mechanisms can also be seen in the elaborate inter-community exchange networks of the Northwest Coast Indians (Suttles 1968).

To summarise, three strategies have been identified for coping with scarcity: movement, diversification and storage. Whereas diversification is a nearly universal phenomenon, it has been suggested that the degree of sedentism practiced by a society will in large part determine the extent to which storage or movement are viable options for countering serious shortages. For sedentary societies, particularly agriculturalists, it is clear that systems of indirect storage are crucial. It is to these regional systems that the remainder of the paper will be devoted.

Varieties of social storage

Up to this point, systems of social storage have been described as regional networks of food exchange, but with little further specification as to how such systems are organized, or their variety. Any system of social storage can be considered in the light of the commodities being exchanged, the structure of relationships linking the communities within a region, or the organisational context into which the exchange system is embedded. The character of a social storage system will be determined by a series of cultural and environmental factors, which form the medium in which the system operates.

Three aspects of the natural environment exert a particularly strong influence on the existence and form of a social storage network. The first is the physical geography of a region, which influences the range of subsistence activities which can be undertaken, the efficiency of direct storage techniques, and the case of transport between communities. It also affects patterns of weather, and other potential causes of failure, and by doing so influences the scale of failure within the region, and the relative homogeneity of its effects (see Halstead this volume). The factors which most frequently produce scarcity within a given region are a second environmental input. The scale of such factors, for instance, will determine the minimum size which an exchange network must attain in order to level-out failure successfully. Similarly, the frequency of such resource or production failures will have a strong conditioning effect on the intensity and formality of the food exchange system. Finally, the distribution of resources within a region is the third major environmental variable. Such resources may relate directly to food production, as with the distribution of agriculturally suitable soils, or to the distribution of other commodities which could function as tokens moving against food in the exchange system.

One can, in a similar manner, specify a series of cultural variables which will influence the form and character of social storage systems. Perhaps the most important determinant is the distribution of subsistence practices within the region, and particularly the range of diversity which can be interconnected through such an exchange system. This will, in large part, determine the types of failures for which the system can compensate. A second cultural determinant is the existing technology, both for the direct storage of foodstuffs and for the transport of foods and other commodities. Finally, the levels of socio-cultural integration and complexity existing within a region will have an important effect on how such networks of exchange are organised and regulated.

Social storage systems can usefully be distinguished on the basis of the kinds of commodities moving through the exchange network, into complementary and redundant systems. Complementary systems are those in which different varieties of goods move directionally through the exchange network. These different items may be specific kinds of subsistence produce, or may reflect differentially distributed durable goods which function as markers of value in the exchange. Exchange systems of this kind are robust and their motivation is obvious, as the exchange system allows the goods from different ecological zones to move in respect to scarcity and abundance.

The exchange relations maintained by the Navajo of the American Southwest with neighbouring Pueblo groups during historic times provide a good case in point of a complementary exchange system. After the introduction of livestock by the Spaniards, animal husbandry became a major subsistence activity of the Navajo (Downs 1964; Kluckhohn and Leighton 1951: 8). Yet they continued to consume large quantities of maize, which was obtained, in part, from their Pueblo neighbours (Hill 1938: 189). The social storage system of the Navajo focused on three basic commodities: sheep, maize and silver jewelry (see Fig. 14.1). In normal years, individual Navajo families or whole outfits would journey to the Pueblo, where they would exchange a portion of their sheep either for maize or for silver jewelry (Dyk 1938: 50-52). Silver thus obtained by the Navajo served both as a sign of individual prestige and as a repository of stored value to be used to meet economic emergency, particularly during the lean months of winter (Downs 1972: 118). In times of shortage, these same silver ornaments were traded back to the Pueblo for maize. Thus the exchange meets the requirements for indirect storage. By keeping silver, the Navajo were able to bank their surplus production for use in time of need. During the reservation period the focus of the Navajo social storage system shifted from the Pueblo communities to the white-run trading post. Yet, the system continued to function in much the same manner. Sheep, other livestock, and craft objects were used to purchase both normal goods and to purchase silver jewelry from the trading post. These silver ornaments could later be temporarily pawned in time of shortage for vital necessities from the trader (Bedinger 1973: 113).

The second variety of exchange system is termed redundant. In such systems, the main traffic of goods moving through the system is in items which are more or less available to all participants and do not have any regular directional nature to their flow (i.e. the trade does not cross a major resource boundary). Identical goods are not exchanged in the same transaction, but food may be traded for a craft good or other durable item which either group could (and probably did) itself manufacture. In normal years an approxi-

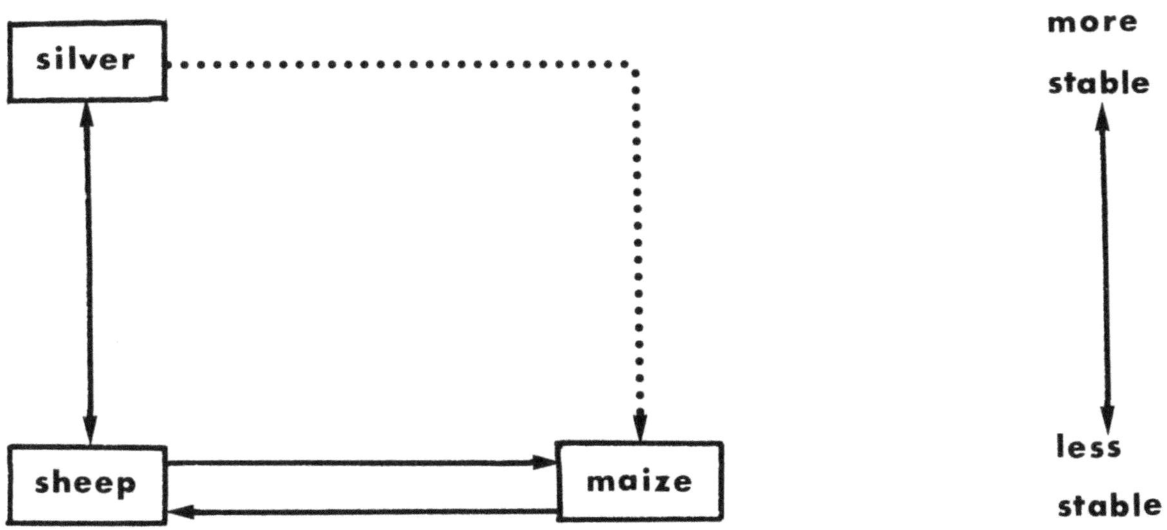

Fig. 14.1 Schematic model of Navajo exchange pathways

mate symmetry is maintained in the items traded between any two groups participating in a redundant exchange network, but with a greater emphasis on non-food commodities. In times of scarcity, however, the exchange becomes distinctly asymmetrical, with foodstuffs moving in one direction and durables in the other. Frequently a kind of informal specialisation occurs among such groups to enhance the complementarity of such exchange situations. Such specialisation, however, rarely has any basis in the actual distribution of resources among the groups (cf. Chagnon 1968: 100).

Exchange systems of this kind are most characteristic of broad and undifferentiated environments. Because of the limited diversity in subsistence activities which are linked through redundant systems, they can only function in those instances when the failures are localised relative to the size of the exchange network. For this reason, redundant systems may be more extensive in size than complementary systems. It is also likely, however, that in most years they will carry a lower density of exchange transactions.

An example of such a redundant exchange network can be found in the exchange system of the agricultural villages of the Great Plains of North America. These communities employed a mixed subsistence economy, consisting of riverine horticulture of maize, beans, squash and sunflower, and of taking large game, principally bison (Willey 1966: 320). It is well documented in historic times how each village diversified its subsistence base by planting a number of small, discontinuous garden plots as protection against freak weather, insects, and raiders (Lottinville 1973: 335) and how they employed a highly developed storage technology based on deep, bell-shaped cache pits (Will and Hyde 1917: 134-135). Such techniques enabled these communities to survive localised shortages, but were clearly insufficient to protect the community against large-scale disturbances, such as the crucial level of rainfall (Wedel 1961: 24) and the timing of frosts. Shortages of this kind could only be evened out through exchange over a much wider area.

Two types of commodity commonly moved in these exchange transactions: agricultural produce and craft goods (most often items fashioned from animal hides), but without any more formalised valuable tokens. In historic times these transactions were frequently conducted under the ritual cover of the Calumet ceremony, and it seems likely that similar types of ritual activity helped to maintain such trade relationships in prehistoric times (Blakeslee 1975; Hall 1977). Trading visits also occurred in good years, and on such occasions less food was actively traded and more emphasis was placed on the exchange of durables and, in later times, on horses. Such visits played an important role in reinforcing the trade relationships between communities, so that they could be called upon in time of need (Will and Hyde 1917: 174).

In later times a more complementary system developed between the sedentary villages and the new equestrian nomads (Ewers 1968: 20). The village tribes participated less in the hunt (although not always on a voluntary basis, cf. Will and Hyde 1917: 189), and concentrated on intensive maize production. The large surpluses of maize were exchanged to the hunting groups for meat and hides. Similar maize exchange systems, but on an even greater scale, were known among the more easterly, woodland tribes, such as that of the Huron on the Great Lakes waterways (cf. Hunt 1960). The village groups were also situated to act as middlemen in the trade of horses and other manufactured goods, an option they vigorously exercised. The shift in the orientation of the Plains village exchange system illustrates the greater attractiveness and stability of complementary networks.

These two patterns of exchange, as was suggested by the last example, are not mutually exclusive, and a given community may maintain both complementary and redundant links. Ford's study of the Tewa Pueblos provides a good case in point. These Pueblos maintained complementary exchange relationships with the Plains Apache and other hunter-gatherer groups to the north (Winship 1896: 527-528). In addition, they employed a diversified strategy in their local agriculture, with discontinuous fields and discrete maize strains (Ford 1977: 157), and participated in a redundant exchange network with other Pueblos. The workings of this complex set of exchange networks has been described by Ford:

> "The social environment constitutes one determinant of trade, but the adaptation of the respective parties is another. The subsistence differences that distinguish nomadic from Pueblo life point to food as a major trade commodity. While craft objects were always part of the transactions, foodstuffs were paramount. Quite the opposite characterized the relations between Tewa and Southern Pueblos. These groups had similar subsistence and technological bases. Consequently, we find craft items and services exchanged more often than food. Infrequently, corn, wheat, and other foods were exchanged in some quantity, but this was at times of crop failure."
>
> (Ford 1972: 43)

In his summary of Tewa exchange systems, Ford makes what can serve here as a general statement of the crucial nature of social storage networks to sedentary agricultural communities:

> "...we must not interpret exchange for ritual goods as the only basis for exchange. For all parties, the constant demand for expendable sacred items maintained a valuable linkage between populations that, in the case of the Pueblos, tended towards closed, self-sustaining systems or, in the case of nomads, gravitated towards alternative means and markets. Once anthropologists rid themselves of the notion that corn, beans, and squash gave sedentary Southwestern Indians a lifetime of security, the necessity for these links can be understood. In times of famine when other regulatory mechanisms proved inadequate, contacts, perpetuated by ritual needs, gave the Pueblos access to the produce of other eco-systems."
>
> (Ford 1972: 45)

Ford's observations provide additional insight into the mechanics of such exchange systems, which is relevant to the interpretation of ethnographic reports. In complementary systems, food is a regularly-moving commodity in most exchange transactions, therefore it is highly visible to an observer. Redundant systems, on the other hand, only move food in quantity in times of shortage; yet as the trade links must be maintained, trade channels are kept open through the regular exchange of durables and services. As such, in a normal year, an ethnographer would be expected to view the movement of goods and services, but not food. Such limitations in the observation of exchange networks lie at the basis of many of the objections which could be raised against the concept of indirect storage presented here.

Objections are often raised against the equivalencing of foodstuffs and durables or prestige goods. Besides the more general belief that primitive exchange is non-economic (cf. Thurnwald 1932: 105), the most frequent objection is that foodstuffs and prestige goods, for example, exist in distinct social and economic spheres (Dalton 1977: 198-199; Sahlins 1974: 218). Yet such equivalencing does occur, and prestige goods are exchanged for food. Even among such classically studied groups as the Trobriand Islanders (cf. Bohannon and Dalton 1962), and the Indians of the Northwest Coast (cf. Vayda 1961; Piddocke 1965; Suttles 1960; 1968), we see the use of prestige goods as a means of both storing food value and of obtaining food in times of shortage. From this perspective, we see not the normative distinction between "primitive valuables", "primitive money" and "cash", as envisioned by Dalton (1977: 197-199), but rather a continuum, on which all valuables have an exchange potential, although some may be more regularly converted than others. The potential for such exchange, and at the same time the friction working against such downward conversion of prestige goods for food, is aptly described by Gould in his re-evaluation of Tolowa economics:

> "It is certainly true ... that a Tolowa Indian was quite reluctant to part with his dentalia or other 'treasures' for food. He would try hard to obtain his own food, and at most times this was not hard to do. But if he had few wives, daughters or sisters, he would find it difficult to store up enough food to last over periods of shortage... When shortages arose there were always individuals in the community who were only too glad to obtain hard-won dentalia and other currency in exchange for the food which their wives had stored away."
>
> (Gould 1966: 77).

The crucial factor is variation. In good years, little food is exchanged and most transactions are limited to prestige goods and other durables. These are the times which are observed by most anthropologists, and the basis for the normative view of primitive economics. Yet, in lean years the story is different. Unfortunately, this necessary long-term view of exchange behaviour, particularly during times of stress and shortage, is the type of observation which is lacking in most ethnographic studies of native economies (Colson 1979: 18). I would argue that the persistent and high value placed on inter-community exchange in good years reflects the importance of such trade links as a safeguard against shortage — the channels must continue to be used and reinforced in good years, so that obligations will be sufficiently strong to be honoured in times of shortage. Thus, we view not the sudden shift in food exchange rules in lean years which ethnography suggests, but rather the logical extension of a single adaptive economic system.

This crucial convertibility of non-food tokens has some major implications for the study of prehistoric economy and social ranking. The use of tokens as a means of storing food value introduces a new dimension into primitive economic systems, the ability to accumulate wealth. By definition, such tokens are more 'stable' than foodstuffs, yet they retain, in a symbolic manner, food value. Because of this greater stability and the constant social pressure to convert foodstuffs into such valuables, the unequal accumulation of wealth becomes possible. Furthermore, it provides a mechanism through which wealth can be retained and transmitted across generations within corporate units. This, in turn, makes possible the symbolic and active manipulation of wealth by such groups and so provides the critical pre-conditions for the emergence of institutionalised social differentiation. In addition, since the use of tokens permits the development of far more ramified systems of social storage than can be maintained purely on the basis of direct reciprocity, such networks are, by virtue of their complexity, predisposed to simplification through some form of centralisation, particularly in complementary networks where the produce of diverse zones can be more efficiently drawn to together and mobilised.

However, the very stability which allows tokens to be accumulated also threatens to destroy their value. Clearly, the food value which can be obtained through the reconversion of valuables is strictly limited by the system's ability to produce and mobilise surplus. If too many valuables exist relative to the potential of the system, the value of such tokens will decrease. In other words, indirect storage networks can be faced with an inflationary problem. Because such valuables usually are consumed at a slower rate than food, such an imbalance is inevitable unless some mechanism exists to remove or further transform these tokens.

The interrelationship between the potential for the accumulation of valuables and the system's capacity to maintain their value can be illustrated by returning to the use of silver jewelry among the Navajo. Downs (1972: 118-119) noted that prior to the reservation period, it was customary to bury an individual with his silver jewelry, but that since the reservation period this practice has ceased and the family of the deceased now retain the silver as much needed capital.

Clearly, the capital represented by the silver jewelry would have been an important asset even in pre-reservation times, so why did the change occur with the advent of the white-run trading post? One explanation is that prior to the reservation period it was necessary to protect the value of silver jewelry as an exchange commodity, and that this could only be done by progressively removing a portion of it from the exchange system to compensate for the new jewelry being produced by the Pueblos. This was perceived as sufficiently crucial to the exchange network's continued operation that it off-set the immediate financial loss suffered by the deceased's relatives. With the advent of the trading post, however, the Navajo became integrated into the immense economy of the United States, and in these new circumstances the amount of silver maintained by the Navajo was too insignificant to affect its worth in the larger economic system. As such, it was no longer necessary to remove silver from the exchange network and its accumulation was allowed to proceed unhindered.

In general, two possibilities exist for curbing the inflationary tendencies of indirect storage systems. The first, as has just been suggested by the Navajo example, is to remove the valuable tokens from the exchange system.

This may be done by their active destruction (as in the rivalry potlatch), by their being placed out of reach by inclusion in burials, hoards, or river offerings, or they may be exchanged outside of the regional network through long-distance trade. The second possibility is the formation of a hierarchy of increasingly scarce items, wherein a quantity of lower level goods may be exchanged for a more highly valued item. Again the objective is to tie up valuable tokens and limit their downward conversion for food. Vayda, in his discussion of the exchange system of the Southern Kwakiutl, describes just such a process:

> "Among the Kwakiutl, as among the Coastal Salish, relatively perishable subsistence goods could be 'converted' into more durable wealth. The wealth, if not reconverted at a later time into food, could be converted at Potlatches into prestige."
>
> (Vayda 1961: 622).

Such a hierarchy tends to produce a constant upwards conversion of wealth, with each successive level being less likely to be reconverted into food — although in fact all levels still retain such potential. In this manner, an even distribution of food can be maintained within a community, although if some social groups regularly produce a surplus and others regularly consume it, such an even distribution will only be achieved at the expense of an uneven distribution of tokens. The need to tie up tokens in order to maintain the integrity of indirect storage systems may account for frequent claims by natives that their valuables are nor convertible for food, even though close observation clearly demonstrates that they, indeed, are (cf. Gould 1966).

Hierarchical systems of valuable tokens, of the kind described here, are most typically encountered in association with societies organised at a high level of complexity. In such situations, the basic economic motivation for exchange at these higher levels may be overshadowed by the manipulation of prestige goods for social or political ends. Social storage systems may then 'take-off' with the focus shifting from the redistribution of food to the upwards mobilisation of resources and manpower for consumption by an institutionalised élite.

Social storage: implications for archaeology

The working of regional exchange systems as a defence against periodic scarcity and its prevalence among sedentary societies has important implications for the study of prehistoric economy. Firstly, it emphasises two shortcomings in the approaches used by archaeologists for studying past economies. It brings home, forcefully, the importance of fluctuations in the availability of resources, both from year to year, and from place to place. It is this inter-annual fluctuation, and not the average availability, which sets the limits for human subsistence activities. Clearly, it is a difficult task to reconstruct even the average environment and its productive potential in remote prehistory, but further efforts are necessary. In particular, it is crucial to estimate the magnitude and frequency of inter-annual fluctuations which would have had an impact on food production. To a certain extent this must be done by extrapolation from recent environments, but it is also possible to make direct estimates of at least gross fluctuations in rainfall and sunlight. This can be done through the study of tree-ring width (Fritts 1976) and varve thickness and composition (West 1968: 168-169), both of which provide an inter-annual record from which both frequency and severity can be modelled.

The second shortcoming which this discussion of social storage has accented is the inadequacy of the 'site' approach to prehistoric subsistence. Although in most cases, the evidence of food remains on a settlement will reflect the foods which were consumed on the site, it does not specify where the food was produced, nor how it got to the site. As has been argued, although the household may be the primary unit of food production, the region, in terms of the area over which food exchange occurs, is the principal economic entity. Therefore, whether one is considering a region with an obvious hierarchy of sites, or a region of relatively homogeneous settlement, it is the certainty and efficiency of production within the region which must be considered.

If regional exchange systems serve to complicate the life of the economic archaeologist, they also offer important insights into the workings of past economies. This is most clearly shown with reference to the occurrence of exotic goods. The close relationship between food production (and over-production), indirect storage, and the movement of exotic goods, allows the archaeologist a rare glimpse of the structure of past socio-economic systems. This is particularly true since exotic goods are often durable and so survive archaeologically, and are highly visible by virtue of their raw material or workmanship. They also can frequently be traced to a particular source through independent physical or chemical analysis (cf. Earle and Ericson 1977). Long-distance trade has long been a concern of archaeology, but the concept of indirect storage opens new possibilities for the analysis of exchange on a regional level. Such goods can serve to delimit the boundaries of exchange networks, as evidenced by differences in the use of such goods, while the elaboration of such symbols into hierarchies of value, and the degree to which accumulation of such items is unequal, can similarly suggest much about the structure and complexity of the socio-economic system. Finally, through archaeological investigation it is possible to identify deflationary behaviour, i.e. the conscious removal of exotic or valuable materials from the economic system. The scale of such activities provides valuable insight into the intensity of exchange and differential access to production within the economic system.

The recognition of regional food exchange systems, and their importance to sedentary economies, does not invalidate the useful work which has been done to reconstruct past environments and subsistence practices. It does suggest, however, perhaps a next step which should be taken in the study of economic archaeology.

Acknowledgements

I am grateful to Ann Lynch, Glynis Jones and Sue O'Shea, who corrected at least the most glaring errors in this manuscript, and particularly to Paul Halstead, who in numerous discussions helped clarify many of the ideas which have been presented here.

References

Bartholemew, G. and Birdsell, J., 1953. "Ecology and the protohominids." Amer. Anthropologist 55: 481-98.

Bedinger, M., 1973. Indian Silver. Albuquerque: University of New Mexico Press.

Blakeslee, D., 1975. The Plains Interband Trade System: an Ethnohistoric and Archaeological Investigation. Unpublished Ph.D. dissertation at the University of Wisconsin-Milwaukee.

Bohannan, P. and Dalton, G., 1962. Markets in Africa (introduction). Evanston: Northwestern University Press.

Chagnon, N., 1968. Yanomamö: the Fierce People. New York: Holt, Rinehart and Winston.

Clawson, D. and Hoy, R., 1979. "Nealtican, Mexico: a peasant community that rejected the 'green revolution'." Amer. J. Economics and Sociology 38(4): 371-87.

Cohen, M., 1977. The Food Crisis in Prehistory. New Haven: Yale University Press.

Colson, E., 1979. "In good years and bad: food strategies of self-reliant societies." J. of Anthropological Research 35(1): 18-29.

Dalton, G., 1977. "Aboriginal economies in stateless societies" in Exchange Systems in Prehistory, eds. T. Earle and J. Ericson. New York: Academic Press; 191-212.

Damas, D., 1972. "Central Eskimo systems of food sharing." Ethnology 11 (3): 220-40.

Downs, J., 1964. Animal husbandry in Navajo society and culture. University of California Publications in Anthropology 1. Berkeley: University of California Press.

Downs, J., 1972. The Navajo. New York: Holt, Rinehart and Winston.

Dyk, W., 1938. Son of Old Man Hat. New York: Harcourt, Brace and Co.

Earle, T. and Ericson, J., eds., 1977. Exchange Systems in Prehistory. New York: Academic Press.

Ewers, J., 1968. Indian Life on the Upper Missouri. Norman: University of Oklahoma Press.

Feit, H., 1973. "The ethnoecology of the Waswanipi Cree: or how hunters can manage their resources" in Cultural Ecology, ed. B. Cox. Toronto: Carlton Library.

Ford, R., 1972. "Barter, gift, or violence: an analysis of Tewa intertribal exchange." Anthropological Papers, Museum of Anthropology, University of Michigan 46: 21-45.

Ford, R., 1977. "Evolutionary ecology and the evolution of human ecosystems: a case study from the midwestern USA" in Explanation of Prehistoric Change, ed. J. Hill. Alburquerque: University of New Mexico Press.

Fritts, H., 1976. Tree Rings and Climate. New York: Academic Press.

Gould, R., 1966. "The wealth quest among the Tolowa Indians of northwestern California." Procs. of the Amer. Philosophical Soc. 110(1): 67-89.

Hall, R., 1977. "An anthropocentric perspective for Eastern United States prehistory." Amer. Antiq. 42(4): 499-518.

Hill, W., 1938. The Agriculture and Hunting Methods of the Navajo Indians. Yale University Publications in Anthropology 18. New Haven: Yale University Press.

Hunt, G., 1960. The Wars of the Iroquois. Madison: University of Wisconsin Press.

Kluckholn, C. and Leighton, D., 1951. The Navajo. Cambridge: Harvard University Press.

Lee, R., 1972. "The !Kung Bushmen of Botswana" in Hunters and Gatherers Today, ed. M. Bicchieri. New York: Holt; 326-368.

Lottinville, S. ed., 1973. Paul Wilhelm, Duke of Wurttenberg Travels in North America 1822-1824. Norman: University of Oklahoma Press.

Meggitt, M., 1962. Desert People. Sydney: Angus and Robertson.

Oberg, K., 1973. The Social Economy of the Tlingit. Seattle: University of Washington Press.

Piddocke, S., 1965. "The potlatch system of the Southern Kwakiutl: a new perspective." Southwestern J. Anth. 21: 244-64.

Richards, A., 1961. Land, Labour and Diet in Northern Rhodesia. London: Oxford University Press.

Ricklefs, R., 1979. Ecology (2nd edn.). New York: Chiron.

Sahlins, M., 1974. Stone Age Economics. London: Tavistock.

Steward, J., 1938. Basin-Plateau Aboriginal Sociopolitical Groups. Bureau of American Ethnography Bulletin 171. Washington: US Government Printing Office.

Suttles, W., 1960. "Affinal ties, subsistence and prestige among the Coast Salish." Amer. Anth. 62: 296-305.

Suttles, W., 1968. "Coping with abundance: subsistence on the Northwest Coast" in Man the Hunter, eds. R. Lee and I. De Vore. Chicago: Aldine; 56-68.

Thurnwald, R., 1932. Economics in Primitive Communities. London: Oxford University Press.

Vayda, A., 1961. "A re-examination of Northwest Coast economic systems." Transactions of the New York Academy of Sciences, Series II 23: 618-24.

Wedel, W., 1961. "Plains archaeology, 1935-1960." Amer. Antiq. 27: 24-32.

West, R., 1968. Pleistocene Geology and Biology. London: Longman.

Will, G. and Hyde, G., 1917. Corn Among the Indians of the Upper Missouri. Lincoln: University of Nebraska Press.

Willey, G., 1966. An Introduction to American Archaeology, Volume I. New York: Prentice-Hall.

Winship, G., ed., 1896. The Coronado Expedition, 1540-1542. Bureau of American Ethnology 14th Annual Report. Washington: US Government Printing Office.

Yellen, J., 1977. Archaeological Approaches to the Present: Models for Reconstructing the Past. New York: Academic Press.

SECTION III

ARCHAEOLOGICAL CASE STUDIES

15. FROM DETERMINISM TO UNCERTAINTY: SOCIAL STORAGE AND THE RISE OF THE MINOAN PALACE

Paul Halstead

Economic Archaeology—making a virtue of necessity

On the face of it, the 1970s have been a good decade for economic archaeologists. The importance of investigating the economic basis of past societies is now widely recognised and studies of animal bones, plant remains and commodity provenances now abound. Moreover, the battery of techniques and models available to economic archaeologists to acquire, analyse and interpret their data is continually being expanded and refined. And yet recently, doubts have been expressed about the value of economic archaeology. These criticisms, however, vary in their source, nature and relevance, and some seem to mirror confusion as to the aims and assumptions of economic archaeology.

For example, Hodder (1979) has rightly pointed out, with the aid of a suitably chosen ethnographic example, that 'economic' data are not free of symbolic content and that they are not, in consequence, amenable to complete interpretation in purely economic terms. The implication that we should be concerned at this state of affairs, however, rests on the definition of archaeology as 'the study of the relationships between human behavior and material culture' (Schiffer 1976:4). This definition is salutary in stressing the paramount importance of considering the very complex relationship between past human behaviour and surviving material remains, but archae-ologists must remember that they are also historians or prehistorians. As 'economic archaeologists' we must be careful to distinguish our aims—the study of past economies—and our methods—the analysis of surviving bones, seeds, coins and the like. And though Hodder is right to remind us that our economic data are affected by the thoughts of men, as well as by the actions of dogs, earthworms and soil pH values, we are no more obliged to interpret man's symbolic behaviour *per se* than is an economic historian to explain why generations of inscription carvers chose to alter the forms of their letters.

Turning from confusion about aims to confusion about assumptions, it should first be noted that an interest in past economies does not imply a belief that the human past can be explained entirely in economic terms. Nor would most practitioners insist that they are studying 'the major factors which direct and determine human behaviour and development' (Higgs and Jarman 1975:4-5). Reaction to such rash claims, however, should not blind us to the usefulness of the generalisation that, over the last 2,000,000 years, a growing human population has been arranged in increasingly large communi-ties and supported by economies which extract more and more energy per unit area, often at the price of higher labour costs. Significantly, this generalisation has lost its explanatory power more by familiarity than by falsification (e.g. Bender 1978).

It is often argued that archaeological studies of past economies take twentieth century western rationality as being a universal feature of mankind or assume human economies to be directed towards the long-term maintenance of an equilibrium between population and resources. Clearly, man is capable of rational thought and economies often do exhibit directional (teleonomic) tendencies, but it is not necessary to assume either great foresight on the part of mankind or a teleological purpose on the part of an abstract economic subsystem. More simply, human beings have certain nutritional requirements and, whenever a particular level of population density or aggregation survives over a period of time, it can be assumed that the economy is meeting these requirements. The strength of economic archaeology is that it can make a present virtue of such past necessity.

A more pressing cause for concern is the need for economic archaeology to provide interesting questions and answers at a time when the initial mapping of past economies, in terms of the range of species which were utilised or the sources of the commodities which were exchanged, is nearing completion for some areas. Inevitably, yesterday's revealing explanations have become today's superficial descriptions. Attempts to focus more finely on the subject, however, must cope with the social dimension of economy, but several contributors to this volume mention the difficulty of assessing the relationship between production, on the one hand, and exchange, cooperation and exploitation, on the other. Awareness of this difficulty does not, however, necessitate acceptance of the extreme substantivist argument that the economy, though blithely autonomous in our own society, is so thoroughly embedded in the fabric of simple societies as to be inextricable for analysis. This claim reflects a myopic view of our own society, rather than an insight into the past, and ignores the fundamental role of categorisation as a tool for simplifying the infinite complexity of the real world.

The solution of this problem requires the integration of many different classes of evidence, for which a spatial framework provides a suitable context. The spatial organisation of settlement is partly determined by economic relationships, both within and between communities (e.g. Clarke 1972a; Hodder 1972), and so may be used to develop hypotheses about the social dimension of the economy. These can then be tested against the quantitative distribution, within this spatial framework, of commodities—principally of craft products or raw materials (e.g. Hodder 1974) but also potentially of foodstuffs (Rowley-Conwy this volume; Maltby 1979). This approach caters adequately for the role of economy in mediating between spatial variability in the availability (or production) and consumption of resources. It has even lent itself to a theory of the origin of 'civilisation', whereby social complexity develops to handle the importing of raw materials into resource deficient lowland areas (e.g. Rathje 1971).

Economies have to cope, of course, with temporal as well as spatial variability in resources—particularly food resources. Archaeologists have commonly allowed for this at two levels: short-term variability has stimulated studies of seasonality of economic activities, and long-term environmental change was, for a time, a popular quarry for explanations of the origins of agriculture. The intermediate level, of periodic or inter-annual fluctuations, is also a fundamental aspect of economy, but has received far less attention (Clarke 1972b:38-39). In fact, given some knowledge of the physical environment and subsistence economy of a particular community, it should be possible to predict, not only the frequency and severity of inter-annual fluctuations in food resources, but also the possible range of alternative strategies. This paper considers briefly some of the causes of, and possible solutions to, these fluctuations. It is suggested that these factors have implications for the development of exchange, cooperation and exploitation in prehistory, and that the social dimension of the economy is not a random variable, but rather one which exhibits a significant degree of patterned behaviour. This hypothesis is then examined in a case study of neolithic and bronze age Greece.

Predicting Uncertainty

A host of factors governs inter-annual variation in the abundance of plant and animal species from which man derives his food, but, for the sake of simplicity, this initial model will consider two of the most basic limitations on terrestrial biological activity—temperature and rainfall. Annual average temperatures decrease from the equator to the poles (Ricklefs 1979:33-34) while, in the case of rainfall, wet belts around the equator and in the middle latitudes alternate with arid belts around the tropics and at the poles (Trewartha 1954:141-42). Broadly speaking, the productivity of terrestrial ecosystems is very high at the equator, high in the moist-temperate mid-latitudes and low in the tropical and polar deserts (Odum 1975:81). Moreover, both temperature and rainfall exhibit an inverse correlation between average level and inter-annual variability, so that they are least dependable in just those areas where they are most likely to be the limiting factor on biological activity (Ricklefs 1979:847-49, Trewartha 1954). In consequence, man's food supply is naturally subject to the greatest fluctuations in the arid or cold areas of the world.

The abundance of plant and animal species varies in space as well as time. Differences of altitude, latitude, aspect and soil may all radically affect the amount and timing of an organism's water and temperature requirements, while rainfall is itself partly determined by the distribution of land and sea and by the position of mountains. So, for example, inter-annual variation in wheat yields is considerably greater for a small island like Cyprus (area 9000 sq. km) than for either Greece (area 130,000 sq. km) or W. Germany (area 250,000 sq. km); Europe as a whole embraces even more environmental diversity and fluctuations in average yields are therefore even lower (Fig. 15.1). Of course, the severity of fluctuations in regional yields depends not only on the size of the region but also on the degree of topographic diversity which it displays. This point is illustrated in detail below for two different regions within Greece.

Coping with Uncertainty: diversification, storage and mobility

As a species which matures slowly and reproduces infrequently, man is ill-adapted to varying his own numbers simply in tune with fluctuations in

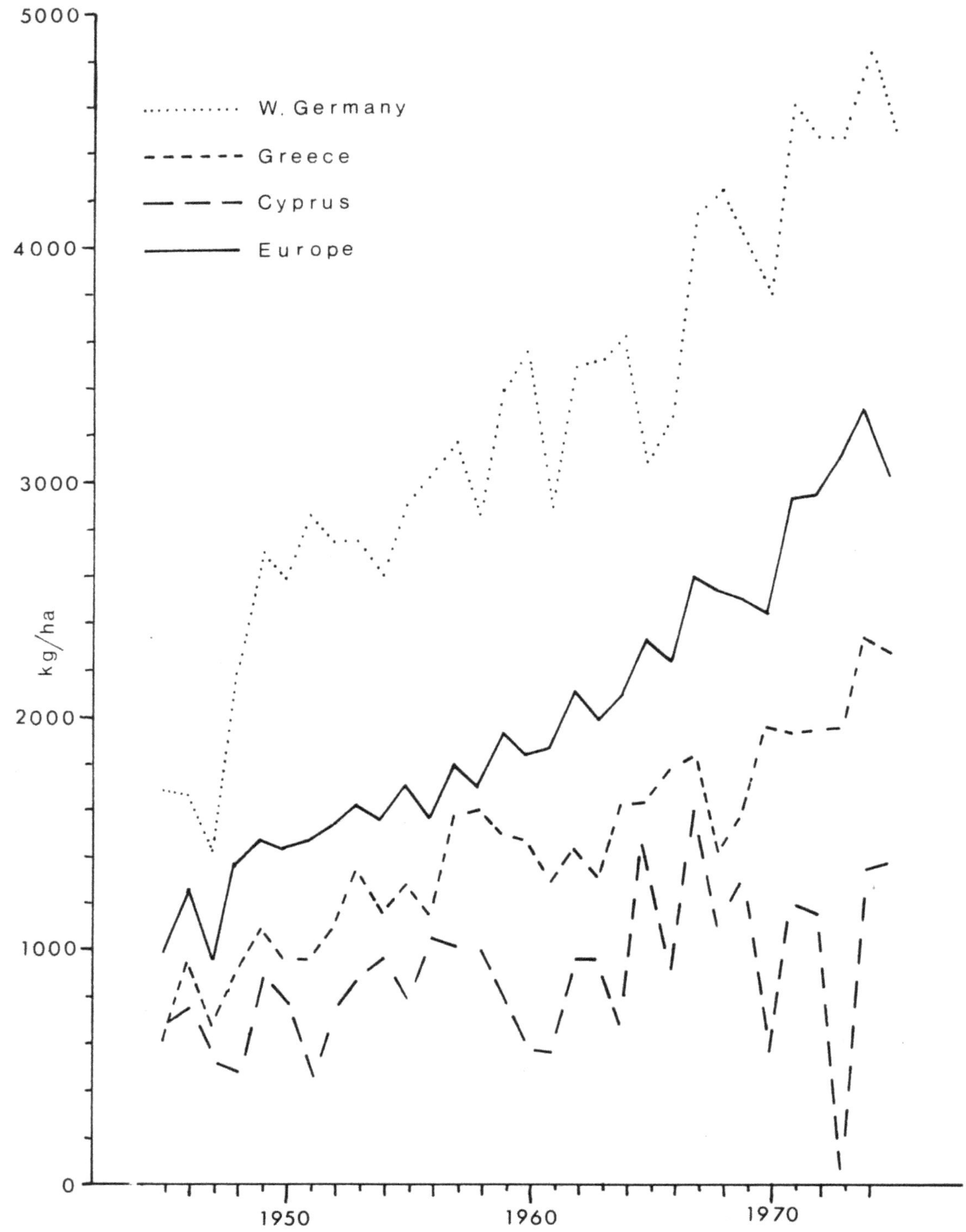

Fig. 15.1 Wheat yields (data from F.A.O. 1946-74)

his food supply, and he is left with essentially four alternative strategies—diversification, storage, mobility and exchange. Different plant and animal species have different levels of tolerance to environmental variation, so that man may cushion himself against all but the most severe fluctuations by varying his diet. A more active strategy is to store present abundance for use in the case of future shortage. Storage is most viable with abundant, dense resources such as cereal stands, nut groves, banks of shellfish, anadromous fish, migratory fowl or herd mammals.

Diversification and storage may be contrasted in two important respects. The number of species in an environment is roughly proportional to its productivity (Ricklefs 1979:687), so that the potential for diversification is greatest in areas of high and relatively stable productivity, while dense and abundant resources suitable for storage are generally available in poorer, less stable environments. Obviously, the low productivity of the deserts is as big a barrier to storage as is the diversity of the equatorial rain forests, but the semi-arid regions, where agriculture, for example, developed at an early stage, provide both the stimulus and the opportunity for storage. The second point is that, with increasing density and aggregation of human population, fewer species are available in sufficient abundance to make an effective contribution to man's nutrition, whether in normal or bad years. As a result, diversification is most viable for sparse, scattered populations while storage tends to be necessary for the maintenance of dense, aggregated populations.

At this juncture, it may be worth noting that agriculture involves intensive exploitation of a few resources which are not only particularly productive but also eminently storable. Thus the origins of agriculture may reflect short-term attempts by man to stabilise a fluctuating food supply rather than the long-term implications of inexorably burgeoning population numbers (Cohen 1977). Indeed, given the short-term advantages of expanding the labour force in intensive economies (cf. Athens 1977:366), any causal relationship between population growth and economic intensification is likely to have been two-way.

In areas of sufficient topographic diversity man may also use his mobility to play off spatial against temporal variability and so buffer himself against local shortages. Mobility is widely practised by modern gatherer-hunters, who also commonly allow free access to each others' territories (Lee and DeVore 1968). As with diversification, mobility has most potential for small groups while large communities, which exploit the environment intensively, will have to travel much further to find an alternative source of food. The problem is most acute for sedentary farmers or fishers whose mobility is often compromised by the need to guard stored foods and vital installations (fields, fish-weirs etc.) or to tend crops with a prolonged growing period. When Mohammed cannot go to the mountain, then the mountain must be brought to Mohammed: storage and mobility are combined in exchange.

Coping with Uncertainty: exchange and social storage

The particular advantage of exchange to food-producing communities is that surpluses from good years may be exchanged to needy neighbours in the expectation of reciprocation when circumstances are reversed. Since the time elapsing between giving and receiving may well be longer than the effective storage life of the food in question, exchange may function as an indirect form of storage (Flannery 1969:87), or what O'Shea (this volume) has termed 'social storage'. In fact social storage is commonly attested in the ethnographic record, as an important mechanism for buffering communities against periodic shortage, and it provides a framework within which 'social' motives for the production and storage of surplus (Bender 1978-79) might fruitfully be re-embedded in an environmental context.

A point of importance to archaeologist (although it is often obscured by overemphasis of the substantive context of transactions—O'Shea this volume) is that food is frequently exchanged against more durable tokens, whose possession may confer prestige. These tokens can be reconverted for food in time of need and so provide a vehicle for vital exchanges of food between a far wider network of communities than can be maintained by direct, reciprocal relationships alone (O'Shea this volume). Moreover, because of their greater complexity, these expanded networks may be predisposed to simplification through centralisation; at a sufficiently intensive level, therefore, social storage may be a factor favouring the concentration of population or the development of centralised redistribution under a managerial élite.

Coping with Uncertainty in the Aegean: the spread of farming

The crop and livestock components of a mixed farming economy (cereals, pulses, sheep, goats, cows and pigs) are attested in the Aegean from the seventh millennium B.C. and it is often assumed that both farmers and domesticates were immigrants from Anatolia. However, although early farming settlements do tend to occupy the most favourable soils for agriculture (Bintliff 1977a), within this framework they are heavily concentrated in the arid, eastern half of Greece and are barely known in the wetter lowlands of western Greece (see Fig. 15.2). In view of the rapidity with which farming spread into the more temperate climate of the north Balkans (Ammerman and Cavalli-Sforza 1971), it seems unlikely that the apparent paucity of farming settlements on the fertile soils of western Greece simply reflects the failure of the domesticates to adapt to wetter conditions.

As an alternative to the immigration hypothesis, indigenous gatherer-hunter groups may initially have adopted cultivation on an small scale in order to have a storable resource for use in the event of scarcity (cf. Lewthwaite forthcoming). In eastern Greece, where low and uncertain rainfall will frequently have restricted the productivity of both plants and animals, such a stored resource would have been particularly important. Moreover, because sowing and harvesting may clash with the seasonal procurement of other resources, while storage conflicts with mobility, the cultivation of crops might rapidly have come to dominate the subsistence base (cf. Flannery 1968). In the wetter, western half of Greece, by contrast, the availability of wild resources will have been subject to less frequent and less severe fluctuations and so the adoption of farming may have been retarded accordingly.

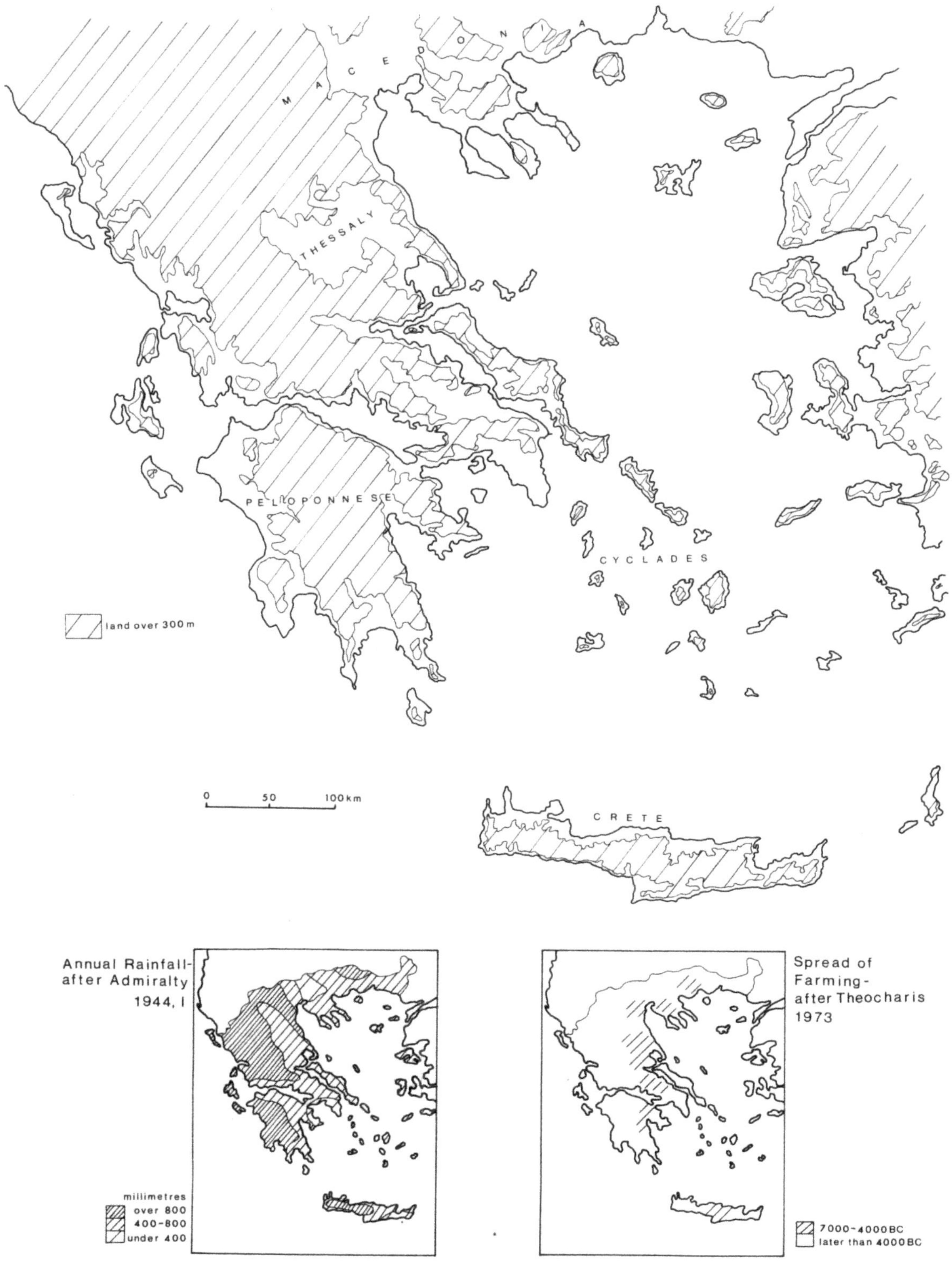

Fig. 15.2 Greece—topography

Within eastern Greece, a distinction may be drawn between the relatively fertile lowlands of central- and north-eastern Greece and of central Crete, on the one hand, where farming was established from the seventh millennium B.C., and those areas of the southern mainland and Crete, together with the Cycladic Islands, on the other hand, where arable land is poorer and more dispersed, where rainfall is especially low and where the spread of farming is not documented until the fourth or third millennium.

In the more fertile lowlands, the 'typical' settlement of the seventh, sixth and fifth millennia was a small village occupying between 0.4 and 0.8 hectares and housing a community of perhaps somewhere between 40 and 240 inhabitants (Renfrew 1972:238; Halstead 1980:312-13). In most cases, it is arguable that cultivated crops will have provided the bulk of the calorific requirements of these communities (Halstead 1980).

In the more marginal areas, where farming was a later development, however, early settlements tended to be considerably smaller. Many of the new fourth millennium sites on the southern mainland and Crete are caves (Theocharis 1973:90; Sakellarakis 1973) and so suggest occupation by just a few individuals, whether seasonally or not. Early open sites on Melos, in the Cycladic islands, also indicate small-scale and perhaps temporary occupation (Cherry 1979:33), and the penetration of some of these 'marginal' areas may have taken the form of seasonal herding or fishing activity (Bintliff 1977a:350-51; cf. Evans and Renfrew 1968). By the third millennium, open sites with rather more substantial remains of occupation are commonly found, but these settlements too are often very small. In upland Arcadia, in the central Peloponnese, many third millennium sites may have been no more than farmsteads or small hamlets (Howell 1970:111), while Debla (Warren and Tzedakis 1974) and Myrtos (Warren 1972), in western and eastern Crete respectively, covered no more than 0.1 hectare each. The latter site was excavated in toto and the suggestion, based on a detailed microspatial study (Whitelaw 1979), that five or six nuclear families lived there is probably the most reliable estimate of community size available for the prehistoric Aegean. Similarly small social groups are implied by the numbers of burials in the third millennium communal tombs of the Mesara basin in south-central Crete (Bintliff 1977b:83-84) and, in the nearby Ayiofarango valley at least, each of these tombs was probably associated with a small open settlement (Blackman and Branigan 1977). Much the same picture may have characterised the pattern of settlement in the Cycladic islands in the earlier third millennium (Cherry 1979:37-43). The economic base of these small farmsteads or hamlets was also apparently mixed farming, to judge from excavated remains (e.g. Warren 1972) and from the general association of the settlements with local pockets of arable soil (Wagstaff 1972:276; Bintliff 1977c:24-30; Cherry 1979).

Early farming communities in the Aegean, whatever their size, will have been subject to fluctuations in crop yields, not all of which could practicably have been countered by growing and storing a surplus. In these circumstances, they will have had to diversify the range of species or habitats from which they drew their food supply.

One possibility is to reduce the risk of shortage by growing a wide range of crops. There is a tendency to think of cultigens as being introduced to Europe in two waves—firstly by Neolithic Man in the seventh millennium B.C. and secondly by Sir Walter Raleigh in the sixteenth century A.D.—but the adoption of new species has in fact been an almost continuous process (e.g. Hubbard in press). In the Aegean, Renfrew (1972) has drawn attention to the diffusion of perennials, particularly the olive and vine, in the fourth and third millennium, and from the second millennium onwards chestnut and walnut were spreading across northern Greece (Bottema 1974; Wright 1972:198). Considerable diversity is also becoming apparent in the range of annuals exploited: three species of pulse are attested at seventh millennium Prodromos in western Thessaly (Halstead and Jones 1980), three at sixth millennium Servia in western Macedonia (Hubbard 1979:226) and no fewer than seven at fifth millennium Dimini in eastern Thessaly (Kroll 1979).

A wide range of wild foods is available in the Mediterranean, particularly in the more heterogeneous 'marginal' areas (Clarke 1976), and the potential of this source of diversity for small groups of people is illustrated by the story of a child in Evvia in the last century who kept himself alive by eating wild grasses (du Boulay 1974:7-8). However, wild foods were probably least abundant in the fertile lowlands favoured by the earliest farmers (Clarke 1976) and would not generally have been sufficient to feed a whole village for any length of time (Halstead 1980:314-16): certainly, although acorns and the like are often found on early settlements (Renfrew 1966), the extreme rarity of wild animal remains is notable (Bökönyi 1973:166-67; Payne 1975; Halstead and Jones 1980).

Domestic livestock are well attested on early farming settlements, both villages and hamlets, and may well have been an important source of nutrition in years of bad harvests. Moreover, as well as stabilising the subsistence base through diversification, domestic livestock were also able to convert to meat the otherwise unusable surpluses from exceptionally good harvests. The wide variation apparent in the age at which neolithic livestock were slaughtered may well, therefore, reflect a flexible response to variable harvests and the consequent alternation of abundance and scarcity (Halstead and Jones 1980). In the more fertile lowlands, tree-cover will have restricted the availability of grazing, so that the number of livestock maintained is likely to have been roughly proportional to the extent of fallow and stubble and so to the size of the human community (Halstead 1980). In 'marginal' areas, afforestation will often have been limited by poor soils or low rainfall and grazing will, in consequence, have been more plentiful. In this case, hamlets will have been able to maintain more livestock per head of population than villages—an important consideration if domestic animals were part of the key to survival in bad years.

Thus communities of just a few families are at an advantage in terms of the use of either wild resources or domestic livestock as a reserve food supply, but within villages sharing and exchange may iron out losses affecting individual households, such as when a garden is raided by deer or when a farmer misjudges the timing of his sowing. In marginal areas, such problems were probably insignificant compared to more general losses caused by drought, but in the more fertile areas the situation may have been rather different—a point which can be illustrated by some modern yield figures for wheat. In the Canadian Prairies, black soils retain more moisture than brown soils and give higher average yields, with less percentage variation from year to year: on the black soils only 57% of the inter-annual variability in yields can be accounted for by climate, whereas the corresponding figure for the brown soils is 86% (Ricklefs 1979: 850-52). In Greece, a similar contrast is often exacerbated because marginal areas, such as eastern Crete and the Cyclades, have both poor soils and low, unpredictable rainfall—and a similar pattern of rainfall in the third millennium, at least, is attested by annual growth rings in oak charcoal from Myrtos in southeast Crete (Rackham 1972:303). In the more fertile areas, however, small-scale losses will have been a major component of variability in yields and may consequently have been a factor in the emergence of the village, rather than the household, as the typical form of settlement.

More general, climatically-induced losses, on the other hand, call for the exploitation of diversity of habitat and we have already noted the possibility of seasonal movements to grazing or fishing grounds in the fourth millennium. The marginal areas tend, for topographic reasons, to offer the greatest range of habitats, and, of course, a small community will have to forage over shorter distances to find an alternative food supply. On the other hand, the use of distant resources by sedentary farmers favours communities large enough to provide both a seasonal 'task force' and a second group which stays to look after stored foods, seed corn and so on. It may be no coincidence, therefore, that the period of settlement nucleation in the fertile lowlands is also the period when many of the marginal areas may have been first exploited on a seasonal basis.

For sedentary communities, the movement of food rather than of people may be the most practicable way to exploit spatial diversity and the discovery on inland settlements of obsidian from the Cycladic island of Melos clearly indicates some exchange between communities (Renfrew 1973). However, contact is more apparent in the general similarity of widespread pottery styles (French 1972; Theocharis 1973; Sherratt 1972) than in the demonstrable movement of craft goods. We may speculate that social storage operated on the principle of reciprocity between kinsmen and exchange partners.

Diversification, storage, mobility and exchange were all apparently used by early farmers to cushion themselves against poor harvests, and regional differences in the potential of these strategies may partly account for the observed dichotomy between village settlements in the more fertile lowlands and hamlets in the more marginal areas. What concerns us now is how prehistoric farmers in Greece coped with poor harvests in the face of the additional difficulties raised by the radical shift in settlement pattern which was taking place in the fourth, third and second millennia B.C.

Coping with Uncertainty in the Aegean: the growth of social storage

During the Bronze Age, settlements regularly extended over more than one hectare and presumably contained rather more inhabitants than their neolithic predecessors. Generally speaking, these larger settlements appear as early as the fourth or third millennium in the areas where farming is attested from the seventh millennium, but only in the later third or second millennium in the areas to which farming spread rather later. In Thessaly, in north-eastern Greece, settlements of more than one hectare became the norm quite rapidly at the end of the Late Neolithic—perhaps in the early fourth millennium. In this case the changeover was contemporary with the abandonment of many earlier sites and so clearly reflects a process of nucleation (Halstead 1977). Knossos, on the other hand, an early foundation in a well-watered spot in central Crete (Roberts 1979), grew steadily throughout the Neolithic and Bronze Age (Evans 1971; Hood 1958) and covered five hectares by the fourth millennium. Elsewhere in Crete, however, settlements covering more than one hectare did not develop until the beginning of the second millennium B. C., at sites such as Gournia or Palaikastro in the east of the island (Branigan 1972). In the Mesara, in central Crete, the regular spacing and diminished numbers of the communal tombs in the early second millennium may also hint at some degree of settlement nucleation (Branigan 1970:124). In the Cycladic islands, the growth of larger settlements is clearly connected with nucleation and takes place slightly earlier, from the latter third millennium (Cherry 1979:43-46).

However, disregarding regional differences in the process of, and perhaps reasons for, nucleation, Gamble (1980) and Halstead (1980) have discussed some of its implications for food production in the Aegean Bronze Age. Although economies of scale, cooperative labour and specialisation may confer some benefits, the basic effect of living in larger communities is, for any given system of food procurement, to necessitate either expansion of the area exploited or intensification. Both alternatives involve higher labour costs, and of course, similar problems will have been encountered in coping with periodic scarcity. In fact, there is evidence from the period of settlement nucleation for increasing concern with measures to ensure survival through bad years, although such measures may have been as much stimuli for nucleation as responses to it.

A source of diversity apparently exploited more fully at mainland settlements in the third and second millennia is wild animals (Bökönyi 1973; Jordan 1975; Reichstein in press)—perhaps because of an increase in their numbers as man opened up the woodlands (Halstead 1980).

Progressive deforestation will also have allowed larger numbers of domestic livestock to be maintained and so may have made seasonal use of distant pastures more attractive (Halstead 1980; Lewthwaite this volume). Thus, whereas neolithic herds may largely have been grazed on stubble, fallow and in local clearings, more mobile bronze age herds may have been able to use spatial differences in the availability of grazing to enhance their reliability as a food supply. Agricultural communities can, in this way, combine diversification, storage and mobility. A further point is that the use of livestock primarily as a source of meat or milk involves a rapid turnover, with herds dominated by juveniles and breeding females. But juveniles would be most vulnerable to the sorts of extremes of weather which might also be ruining crops, while milk yields are very sensitive to checks in nutrition (Duckham 1963:276 and 295). The use of livestock as a reserve for bad years, therefore, favours a more stable herd structure, consisting predominantly of mature animals and providing relatively little meat or milk in good years. In this respect, sheep are attractive in that they can supply wool in the meantime, and it may therefore be significant that sheep and wool appear to assume increasing importance in Aegean economies from about the period of settlement nucleation (Halstead 1980).

There is also more evidence for storage in the enlarged settlements of the fourth, third and second millennia. The most dramatic examples are the great magazines of the second millennium Cretan palaces, but smaller built facilities and deep pits suitable for storing grain (cf. Reynolds 1974) are found at an earlier date, especially on the mainland (Marinatos 1946; Hutchinson 1936:61-64; Hourmouziadis 1979). However, storage of normal surpluses is unlikely to provide sufficient insurance against a run of bad harvests and the inadequacy of diversification for relieving large communities has already been discussed (see above). The area of real growth appears to have been social storage.

In Thessaly, whereas contact between early farming villages is largely seen in the general similarity of pots made from ubiquitous raw materials, in the later fifth and fourth millennia potential 'valuable tokens' are more in evidence—polychrome pottery with paints from rarer minerals (cf. Sherratt 1975), spondylus shell bracelets (e.g. Milojčić 1976), perhaps skins and furs (Halstead forthcoming) and a few metal objects (Tsountas 1908:350-54; Theocharis 1973, plate 125). Such tokens may have facilitated the proliferation of wider exchanges of foodstuffs and there is some evidence that such transactions were organised on a village rather than household basis: for the first time, some Thessalian settlements are now dominated by a large, central 'megaron' building (Theocharis 1973; Milojčić 1976; Hourmouziadis 1979), while bell-shaped storage pits are so dense in the centre of some mounds (e.g. Milojčić 1976) that they are virtually the only recognisable feature of the fourth millennium 'Larisa culture' (Theocharis 1973). Indeed, centralisation of an expanding social storage network may have been a major stimulus for the contemporary nucleation of settlement in the region.

More detailed evidence for an early community storehouse comes from Lerna, a third millennium settlement in the eastern Peloponnese: a large central structure, the 'House of Tiles', contained clay sealings from boxes and jars which preserved the impressions of seventy different seals (Heath 1958). At Knossos in Crete, a large underground chamber, the 'Hypogeum', dating from the end of the third millennium, may have served as a granary (Marinatos 1946:348); if so, with a capacity of 600 cubic metres, it could have held as much as 300-400 tonnes of grain, or enough to provide most of a year's food supply for as many as 1500 to 2000 people. This would clearly have been a community-wide, if not regional, undertaking.

The third millennium saw a dramatic upsurge in the volume and variety of craft goods exchanged in Crete, the Cycladic islands and the south-eastern mainland (Renfrew 1972). The coasts of Thessaly were evidently part of this essentially maritime network (Theocharis 1957; Schachermeyr 1976), but the great inland plains, which had been relatively precocious in the preceeding millennia, were now isolated backwaters (Hanschmann and Milojčić 1976). If the production of an increasing number and variety of craft goods was partly stimulated by the need for valuable tokens in an expanding social storage system, then the 'decline' of the Thessalian plains becomes comprehensible.

In Thessaly, exchange between households and even between neighbouring communities will have been a useful mechanism for dealing with small-scale crop losses (see above pp.195, 198) and may even have been a contributory factor in the fourth millennium nucleation of settlement. However, the uniformity of the inland plains is such that losses caused by drought would affect almost the whole region. Again, inter-annual variability in modern crop yields is illuminating, once allowance is made for the overall trend towards higher yields. Thessaly is divided administratively into four nomoi, covering an average of ca. 2500 sq. km each, and Table 1a shows the extent to which inter-annual fluctuations in wheat yields covary from one nomos to another. With the significant exception of the topographically heterogeneous, coastal nomos of Magnesia, fluctuations in yields are remarkably uniform across the whole extent of the plains. In other words, a social storage system in inland Thessaly would have to be effective over very long distances to deal with any serious, drought-inflicted losses—and, of course, the nucleation of settlement will have increased the dependence of prehistoric Thessalians on social storage. Topographically, the Thessalian plains offer no barrier to the exchange of small quantities of portable craft goods. If the movement of these goods was linked to the movement of bulky foodstuffs, however, then their absence from the inner plains need occasion no surprise.

In the south-eastern Aegean, by contrast, broken topography creates far greater local diversity in rainfall and crop yields, so that the likelihood of adjacent nomoi in Crete, for example, experiencing widespread crop losses in the same year is relatively low (Table 1b). By the third millennium, the donkey is attested on the mainland, at settlements as far apart as Lerna in the Peloponnese (Gejvall 1969) and Kastanas in Macedonia (Reichstein in press), and the availability of pack animals doubtless assisted the growth of regional social storage systems, but the movement of bulky foodstuffs will almost certainly have been easier by boat (cf. Hopkins 1978:43-44). Again, the south-eastern Aegean is topographically well-placed in that the vast majority of its arable land is not far from the sea and it is tempting to see the emphasis on coastal settlements in this area during the third millennium (Bintliff 1977a:120) in terms of the growing importance of exchange in foodstuffs. Bintliff has interpreted this phenomenon as evidence for fishing playing a major role in subsistence, but this assertion is not supported by the very sparse remains of fish from most excavated sites (Gamble 1979:125-27). This is not to deny that marine resources could play a vital role in times of scarcity and the very variable proportions of fish bones in successive levels at Franchthi cave (Gamble 1979) might be interpreted in such a light. However, the Mediterranean is not rich in fish (Coull 1972; Cushing 1975; Houston 1964) and, being virtually non-tidal, is particularly poor in shellfish. In fact, sea-fishermen in Greece in 1936 landed little over one metric tonne each as their year's catch (Admiralty 1944, II:93) and, while it is true that overfishing may adversely have affected these figures, the 1936 catches will have been inflated by some fishermen, at least, using more sophisticated technology than was available in prehistory. Now, one tonne of grain would provide the bulk of the energy requirements of a family of five persons (Clark and

Table 1 Inter-annual variation in wheat yields, 1961-76: partial correlations between regions, controlling for time. Data from N.S.S.G. 1961-76. (high values indicate a high level of correlation)

(a) Thessaly

	Trikala	Karditsa	Larisa	Magnesia
Trikala	-	.6266	.4715	.2576
Karditsa	.6266	-	.3644	.1419
Larisa	.4715	.3644	-	.7613
Magnesia	.2576	.1419	.7613	-

(b) Crete

	Chania	Rethymnon	Heraklion	Lasithi
Chania	-	.4235	.1706	.3293
Rethymnon	.4235	-	.4562	.2933
Heraklion	.1706	.4562	-	.1109
Lasithi	.3293	.2933	.1109	-

Haswell 1970; Hillman 1973; Halstead field notes) but the calorific content of fish (on average, say, 150 kcal. or less per 100 grams raw, edible portion—Pellet and Shadarevian 1970; as much as 30% of the catch, by weight, may be inedible—P. A. Rowley-Conwy pers. comm.) is much lower than that of grain (350 kcal. per 100 gram portion), while the preparation of fish for storage is extremely labour intensive (Zvelebil 1979). It seems likely, then, that fishing will only form the regular basis of subsistence in the Aegean if fish are exchanged to inland communities for farm produce on very favourable terms. In the context of the third millennium, the proliferation of coastal settlements is far more likely to represent the growth of exchange in foodstuffs in an attempt to take advantage of the local nature of periodic scarcity and surfeit. To take the example of the island of Melos, the second millennium concentration of population in the coastal settlement of Phylakopi, at the eastern end of the island, could be seen not as minimising access to arable land (cf. Gamble 1979; 1980), but as maximising access to a social storage system embracing the western Cycladic Islands.

The nucleation of settlement in the prehistoric Aegean may have been, in part, a response to the growth of social storage systems, and will certainly have led to greater dependence on them. Because of the convertibility of tokens, moreover, such systems have an inherent potential for growth in both extent and intensity and so may over-reach their capacity to mobilise food in bad years. Catastrophic droughts, such as that which hit Cyprus in 1973, devastating both grain and oil crops and decimating herds of livestock (Fig. 15.1), may well have brought on the collapse of early systems. Certainly, the later second millennium Mycenaean palace centres of the Peloponnese do not seem to have developed, without interruption, from their third millennium precursors, such as Lerna (Warren 1977:68). On Crete, however, there is no such disjunction, though the appearance of the Minoan palaces was far from gradual. The final section of this paper looks at the evidence for the changing function of the Cretan palaces during the first half of the second millennium.

"Redistribution" and the Minoan Palaces

The island of Crete is only 8000 sq. km in area, but is characterised by a very varied relief and, in consequence, "climatic variations in Crete are great for an island of its size" (Admiralty 1945, III, p.213). This point has already emerged in the comparison of Crete with Thessaly in terms of variation between relatively large units, the modern nomoi, in the timing of good and bad years (Table 1; Fig. 15.3a). From this it transpired that Crete, the more heterogeneous area, has greater potential for evening out local shortages by exchange within a developed, regional system of social storage. A series of annual crop yield figures is not available for smaller areas than the nomoi, but enquiries at the Agricultural Offices in both Chania and Heraklion in Crete suggested that, for the olive at least, good and bad years tend to cancel each other out to a significant degree even within the administrative subdivisions of the nomos, the eparchiai (Fig. 15.3a). As a result, although Cretan crop yields are very vulnerable to low and unpredictable rainfall, the resulting fluctuations can often be ironed out by exchange over quite modest distances. Whether the apparent nucleation of settlement shortly after 2000 B.C. is seen as cause or effect, it is suggested that the contemporaneous development of regional palace centres reflects the exploitation of this environmental potential.

Apart from their role as élite residences, the Minoan 'palaces' seem to have served a multiplicity of functions, combining under one roof the equivalents of Buckingham Palace, Whitehall, Westminster Abbey and, perhaps, even Wembley Stadium (cf. Graham 1962). Massively built magazine blocks and the written records of the palace bureaucracy, the 'Linear B' tablets, also testify to the part played by the palaces in the acquisition and storage of foodstuffs and raw materials and in the manufacture of goods.

Finley (1957) has further pointed out that the Linear B tablets do not record the equivalence of different commodities and concluded that they were dealing with centrally administered 'redistribution', rather than with market exchange; although the Linear B tablets date from literally the last year in the functioning life of the largest of the palaces, Knossos, the earlier and more widespread Linear A script preserves essentially the same system of accounting (Godart and Olivier 1976). However, the extent of this central interference in the economy is not beyond dispute (compare Finley 1957: 135 and Chadwick 1976:108-09), nor is it clear whether resources were literally redistributed or simply 'mobilised' upwards (cf. Earle 1977). The transactions recorded by the Linear B archives seem largely to concern the provision of rations and raw materials to the servant of the élite and to craftsmen who maintained their supply of luxuries (Chadwick 1976); benefits to the populace at large seem to have been of a strictly intangible nature— "what goes up, stays up" (Cherry 1978:425). On the other hand, the storage facilities for foodstuffs at the palaces (Graham 1962, pp. 129-37; Renfrew 1972:291-96) are too extensive to have been designed just to provision the élite and their retainers, while at Mallia it has been suggested that the storage capacity of the palace and surrounding settlement was sufficient to accommodate regional production (Dewolf et al. 1963).

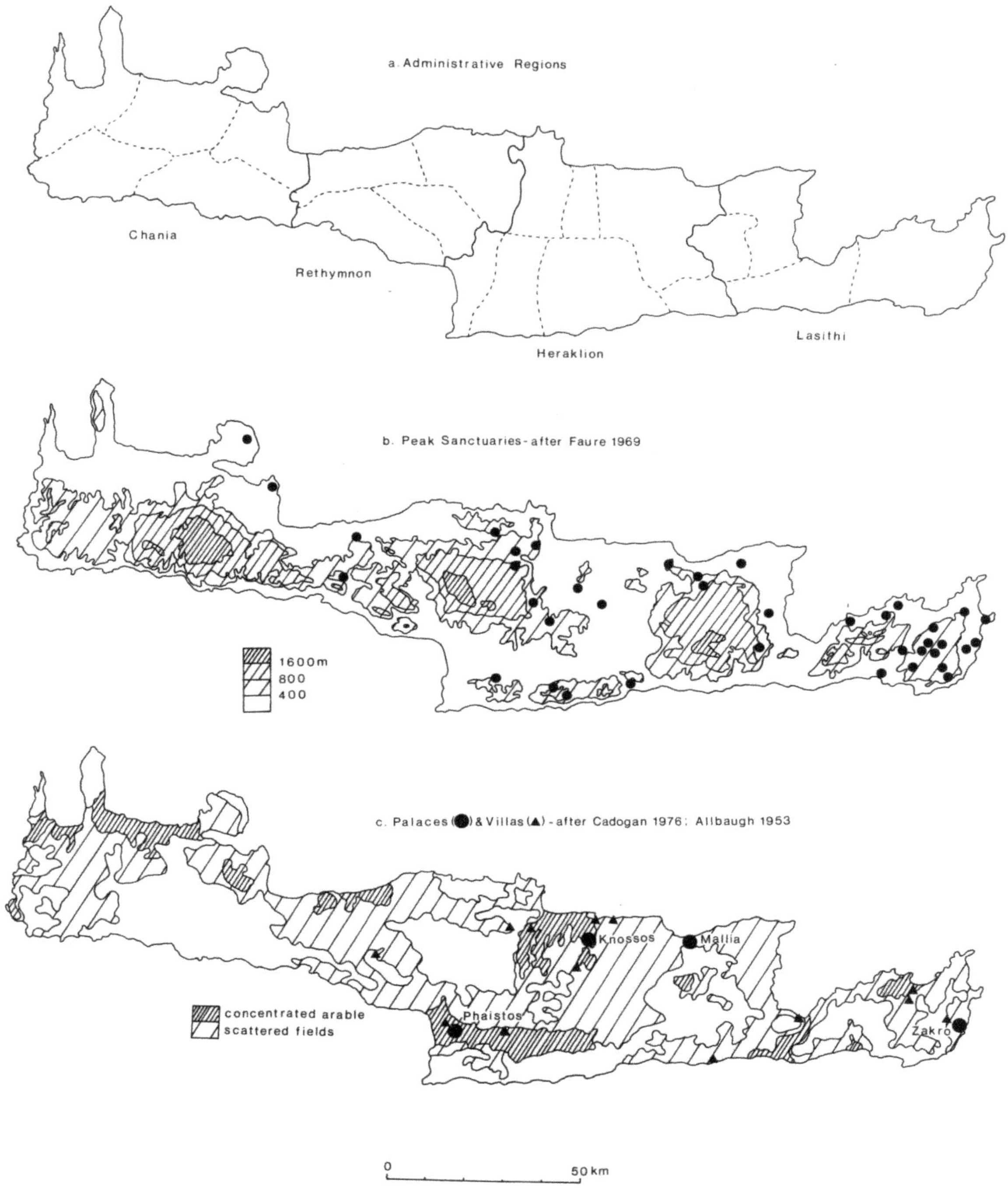

Fig. 15.3 Crete

In part, this contradiction between the documentary and archaeological evidence may be chronological in origin. Some 20-30% of the ground floor area of the early palaces at Knossos, Mallia and Phaistos seems to have been devoted to storage facilities (Graham 1962:129 and Figs. 2, 4 and 6), whereas the corresponding figure at the later foundation of Zakro is apparently about 5% (Platon 1971). Moreover, at much the same time, there is evidence for a reduction in the storage capacity of the early palaces: at Phaistos, and to a lesser extent at Knossos, remodelling ca. 1600 B.C. of the western façade encroached upon the magazine area (Pendlebury 1939:150-52), while at both Mallia and Knossos, new internal walls rendered some of the magazines effectively inaccessible to bulky commodities (Evans 1935:630). At Knossos, the original banks of storage jars were now supplemented by lead-lined cists, which evidently contained treasure (Evans 1935:630), and on the eve of the final destruction (probably in the fourteenth century B.C.—Popham 1970; 1979) a large part of the magazines was given over to offices concerned primarily with the manufacture of textiles (Graham 1979).

The remodelling of the palaces and the reduction of their storage capacity coincides with the construction of the 'villas'. Although the distribution of these villas is incomplete and their definition perhaps rather arbitrary (in Fig. 15.3c the 'minor palaces' at Gournia and Agia Triadha are treated as villas), finds of Linear A tablets indicate that some of them, at least, fulfilled the role of second order centres (cf. Cherry 1978:429). Moreover, some of the villas, and especially the 'minor palaces', contained substantial storage facilities, so the reduction of storage capacity in the remodelled major palaces probably reflects the decentralisation of this function. By the fourteenth century, the villas had been destroyed and Knossos administered the central third of the island, including what had previously been the territory of Phaistos (Killen 1977). However, the Linear B tablets record quantities of grain which could not have been stored at Knossos—for instance, the 775 tons from Dawo (Chadwick 1976:118) would have filled as many as 2500-3000 of the large Minoan storage jars or could have covered the entire central court at Knossos to a depth of one metre or more. Clearly some degree of decentralisation must have persisted and the apparent contradiction between the documentary and archaeological evidence is indeed partly the result of a change in the function of the palace.

Another source of confusion is that the Linear B archives are not only incompletely preserved, but were probably very selective in terms of the transactions they recorded. For example, although both pulses and grain are represented archaeologically in the palaces of Crete (Dewolf et al. 1963: 43; Evans 1899-1900:21; Haussoulier 1880:127; cf. also Cadogan 1978:83), and likewise in their Greek mainland counterparts, nowhere is there documentary evidence for pulses. It has been suggested elsewhere that the pulses (and perhaps the grain) which reached the palace storerooms were the surplus from small-scale garden cultivation, while the large grain returns, such as that from Dawo mentioned above, may have been the total produce of consolidated palace estates (Halstead 1980:332-33). However, there are two further implications. Firstly, that there was a 'private sector' in the Minoan economy, which was at least partly responsible for the provisioning of the palaces and perhaps received in return some of the craft products of the palace—for the disposal of which there is very little evidence (Killen forthcoming). Secondly, that the large grain returns were available for redistribution to artisan dependents of the palace, who may originally have been drawn from communities facing occasional shortfalls in their food supply.

Both points may be illuminated by consideration of another of the features of the Knosses Linear B archives: the extraordinary emphasis on sheep-raising, wool-production and textile manufacture. The bureaucracy used tablets of unfired clay which were only preserved, by chance, in the final destruction, but tablets concerned with sheep, wool and textile manufacture came from several different offices located throughout the palace (Olivier 1967a). Differences from one office to another in the severity of the conflagration cannot, therefore, account for this emphasis. Nor does the season at which the conflagration took place adequately explain the phenomenon, because the tablets tended to record transactions which were repeated at regular intervals and so they would generally not have been thrown away until replaced in the following year or at a later stage in the seasonal cycle.

The number of sheep controlled by the palace was of the order of 100,000 (Killen 1964), ranging probably over the central third of Crete (Killen 1977). The total area involved is about 300,000 hectares and so can theoretically support something like 250,000–430,000 head of sheep and goats (pers. comm. of Mr. S. Piperakis, of the Heraklion Inspectorate of Agriculture). However, even in the second millennium B.C. some of these 300,000 hectares will have been built over and some will have been under perennial crops, some will have been grazed by animals other than sheep and some will have been relatively inaccessible because of tree cover or rough terrain. The proportions of different grazing species may be clarified in the near future by the analysis of faunal remains from settlements of the period, but the scale of deforestation, which might also give some idea of the extent of grazing, is more difficult to assess. Nonetheless, in a region of broken topography and, doubtless, with quite considerable areas of tree cover, the most extensive, accessible and consolidated grazing will surely have been in the arable lowlands—fallow in winter and spring and stubble in summer—and perhaps in some of the high mountain basins. It is interesting to note that, in the Linear B archives, the localities with the largest numbers of sheep also tend to have the largest flocks (J. T. Killen, pers. comm.), suggesting the concentration of sheep grazing on these consolidated pastures. Moreover, two of these localities with large flocks, Phaistos and Dawo, can be located with confidence and they evidently lay in the extensive Mesara basin. Lowland Mediterranean fallow with an average annual rainfall of between 400 and 600 mm, as in central Crete, can support roughly one sheep per hectare (le Houerou 1977), but the area under cereals, vines and fallow in this part of Crete in the 1930s was less than 80,000 hectares (Allbaugh 1953). Thus, even with fallowing in alternate years and the use of stubble and upland grazing for six to eight months of the year, the carrying capacity of the lowland arable areas could not have exceeded 80,000 to 120,000 sheep. Of course, some flocks may have been grazed on the lower, uncultivated slopes during the winter but, on the other hand, some goats and cattle must also have been maintained. These calculations involve a number of possible sources of error, but even so it is clear that the 100,000 sheep controlled by the palace at Knossos must have been a very large proportion of the total sheep population of central Crete and it may not be entirely inappropriate to think in terms of a monopoly.

Evidence for the antiquity of this emphasis on sheep is scanty, but the Minoan 'peak sanctuaries' may provide a clue. These sites are clearly associated with the palace centres, both by contemporaneity of construction and by certain iconographic and artefactual connections (Cherry 1978:429-30), while Rutkowski (1972:184) has pointed out that they are generally located next to upland grazing areas. Again, faunal studies might clarify the position. However, from the point of view of the preceding discussion of sheep carrying capacity, it is interesting to note that the sanctuaries are generally sited on low peaks, near the arable lowlands, rather than near the high mountain pastures (Figs. 15.3a and 15.3b).

Reasons for the importance of sheep are rather easier to find. As meat producers, sheep make efficient use of fallow, stubble and upland grazing (Halstead 1980) and can also be fattened on surplus grain. The use of domestic livestock as a mobile 'bank', for consumption in the event of crop failure, entails the maintenance of mature animals, with a low turnover in meat and milk: mature sheep provide a regular crop of wool instead. Furthermore, the contradiction between the short-term interests of individuals (which may favour killing an animal for meat or fattening it up on surplus grain) and the long-term interests of the community (which may require keeping the animal alive and retaining the surplus grain for exchange purposes) makes central control of sheep flocks advantageous.

In fact, there is some evidence that the sheep flocks recorded in the Linear B archives were part of a social storage system (Killen 1963; 1964; Chadwick _et al_. 1971; Olivier 1967b). Wool yields from individual flocks seem to have varied enormously and this may reflect differences in nutritional status, with some flocks being fed local grain surpluses and others subsisting on poor quality graze. There was also variation in sex ratio between flocks. Separate ewe flocks were run for breeding, while the wool flocks consisted primarily of wethers, which give more wool than ewes. The minority of females (_ca_. 15%) in the wool flocks were clearly substitutes for wethers as they were not set lambing targets. This is not surprising because the production of replacement wethers by the breeding flocks may have been finely tuned to the normal (_ca_. 20%) rate of wastage in the wool flocks. However, the substitute females are not spread evenly among the flocks, as might be expected in the case of natural wastage, but are heavily concentrated in just a few flocks. It is suggested that certain flocks had been slaughtered wholesale in response to local crop failures and that they were only gradually being built back up to full strength.

It seems, then, that the sheep recorded in the Linear B archives at Knossos may still have been used as a direct source of relief in cases of local food shortage, but the main emphasis was clearly on wool production. As in the case of olive oil, with which the palaces also dealt in large quantities (Evans 1935:632-33), sheep had the great virtue that in bad years they could be consumed directly, while in good years they provided the raw material for craft production: surplus oil or wool could then be converted to perfumed oil or ornate textiles, doubtless using the labour of victims of crop failure who had been recipients of relief from the palace-centred social storage system. These craft products may then have been exchanged, both locally for foodstuffs, in the case of the more commonplace items, and at a distance for more exotic raw materials and foreign craft products (Alexiou 1961: Catling 1979; Davis 1979), in the case of the rarer items whose possession may often have carried connotations of high status.

To summarise, then, two major developments seem to have taken place in the Minoan palace economies of the second millennium B.C.: firstly, the decentralisation of their redistributive role to a local level more suited to the transport capability of the time: secondly, concentration in the palace centres on the conversion of surplus resources into craft products which could then be used to stimulate the flow of further raw materials. This emphasis on craft production may have led to the maintenance of large numbers of permanent artisans (Chadwick 1976:79) with a consequent reduction in the ability of the palace to mobilise surplus in bad years. In closing, we might note that all these developments can be seen in a more extreme form in the Linear B archives of ca. 1200 B.C. from Pylos on the Greek mainland (Chadwick 1976)—but that is another story.

Conclusion

Studies of past economies do run the risk of simply reaffirming, in an uninformative fashion, the existence of environmental constraints on human behaviour, but emotional appeals to man's social instincts or conceptual abilities are hardly an improvement. In stressing uncertainty in the availability of resources, this paper not only identifies a vital area of subsistence economy but also addresses itself to the social dimension of economy—exchange, cooperation and exploitation. In the light of these considerations, some radical, long-term changes in the distribution, organisation and sustinence of human populations may be seen as the results of short-term measures to stabilise an inherently unstable subsistence base, rather than as blind reactions to environmental and demographic stress or as inspired but inexplicable searching after social and ideological goals. The severity and frequency of uncertainty (but not its precise timing) is essentially predictable, as is the range of available counter-measures, so this approach is highly amenable to cross-cultural investigation. For the present, however, it is surely fitting that the 'Palace of Minos' at Knossos should provide a suitable arena for grasping the economic bull a little more firmly by the horns.

Acknowledgements

Some of this paper would not have seemed necessary without the goading of Ian Hodder; none of it would have been possible without the help and encouragement of Glynis Jones, John Killen and John O'Shea. I am also indebted, for a variety of stimulating discussions, to Pete Callaghan, Hector Catling, Bill Cavanagh, Andy Garrard, Jim Lewthwaite, Chris Mee, Mike Parker Pearson, Pete Rowley-Conwy, Dan Rubenstein and Anthony Snodgrass.

This research is partly based on fieldwork (to be presented in greater detail elsewhere), which was financed by the British Academy Small Grants Research Fund in the Humanities.

References

Admiralty, 1944-45. Greece (Geographical Handbook Series). Admiralty, Naval Intelligence Division.

Alexiou, S., 1961. "Zitimata tou proistorikou viou. Kritomykinaikon emporion." Arkhaiologiki Ephimeris 1953-54, III:135-45.

Allbaugh, L. G., 1953. Crete: a Case Study of an Underdeveloped Area. Princeton: Princeton University Press.

Ammerman, A. J. and Cavalli-Sforza, L. L., 1971. "Measuring the rate of spread of early farming in Europe." Man 6:674-88.

Athens, J. S., 1977. "Theory building and the study of evolutionary process in complex societies" in For Theory Building in Archaeology, ed. L. R. Binford. New York: Academic Press; 353-84.

Bender, B., 1978. Review of "The Food Crisis in Prehistory", M. N. Cohen. Antiquity 52:77-78.

Bender, B., 1978-79. "Gatherer-hunter to farmer: a social perspective." World Arch. 10:204-22.

Bintliff, J. L., 1977a. Natural Environment and Human Settlement in Prehistoric Greece. Oxford: B.A.R. Suppl. Ser. 28.

Bintliff, J. L., 1977b. "The number of burials in the Mesara tholoi" in "An archaeological survey of the lower catchment of the Ayiofarango valley", D. Blackman and K. Branigan. Ann. Brit. Sch. Athens 72: 83-84.

Bintliff, J. L., 1977c. "Pedology and land use" in "An archaeological survey of the lower catchment of the Ayiofarango valley", D. Blackman and K. Branigan. Ann. Brit. Sch. Athens 72:24-30.

Blackman, D. and Branigan, K., 1977. "An archaeological survey of the lower catchment of the Ayiofarango valley." Ann. Brit. Sch. Athens 72:13-84.

Bökönyi, S., 1973. "Stock breeding" in Neolithic Greece, D. R. Theocharis. National Bank of Greece; 165-78.

Bottema, S., 1974. Late Quaternary Vegetation History of Northwestern Greece. Groningen: University of Groningen.

Boulay, J. du, 1974. Portrait of a Greek Mountain Village. Oxford: Oxford University Press.

Branigan, K., 1970. The Tombs of Mesara. London: Duckworth.

Branigan, K., 1972. "Minoan settlements in east Crete" in Man, Settlement and Urbanism, eds. P. J. Ucko, R. Tringham and G. W. Dimbleby. London: Duckworth; 751-59.

Cadogan, G., 1976. Palaces of Minoan Crete. London: Barrie and Jenkins.

Cadogan, G., 1978. "Pyrgos, Crete, 1970-77". Archaeological Reports 1977-78:70-84.

Catling, H. W., 1979. "Copper in Cyprus, bronze in Crete: some economic problems" in Acts of the International Archaeological Symposium "The Relations Between Cyprus and Crete, ca. 2000-500 B.C.". Nicosia: Department of Antiquities, Cyprus; 69-75.

Chadwick, J., 1976. The Mycenaean World. Cambridge: Cambridge University Press.

Chadwick, J., Killen, J. T.and Olivier, J-P., 1971. The Knossos Tablets (4th edn.). Cambridge: Cambridge University Press.

Cherry, J. F., 1978. "Generalization and the archaeology of the state" in Social Organisation and Settlement, eds. D. Green, C. Haselgrove and M. Spriggs. Oxford: B.A.R. Suppl. Ser. 47:411-37.

Cherry, J., 1979. "Four problems in Cycladic prehistory" in Papers in Cycladic Prehistory, eds. J. L. Davis and J. F. Cherry. U.C.L.A. Institute of Archaeology Monograph 14. Los Angeles: U.C.L.A.; 22-47.

Clark, C. and Haswell, M., 1970. The Economics of Subsistence Agriculture (4th edn.). London:MacMillan.

Clarke, D. L., 1972a. "A provisional model of an Iron Age society and its settlement system" in Models in Archaeology, ed. D. L. Clarke. London: Methuen; 801-69.

Clarke, D. L., 1972b. "Models and paradigms in archaeology" in Models in Archaeology, ed. D. L. Clarke. London: Methuen; 1-60.

Clarke, D. L., 1976. "Mesolithic Europe: the economic basis" in Problems in Economic and Social Archaeology, eds. G. de G. Sieveking, I. Longworth and K. Wilson. London: Duckworth; 449-81.

Cohen, M. N., 1977. The Food Crisis in Prehistory. New Haven and London: Yale University Press.

Coull, J. R., 1972. The Fisheries of Europe. An Economic Geography. London: Bell.

Cushing, D. H. 1975. Marine Ecology and Fisheries. Cambridge: Cambridge University Press.

Davis, J. L., 1979. "Minos and Dexithea: Crete and the Cyclades in the Later Bronze Age." in Papers in Cycladic Prehistory, eds. J. L. Davis and J. F. Cherry. U.C.L.A. Institute of Archaeology Monograph 14. Los Angeles: U.C.L.A.; 143-57.

Dewolf, Y., Postel, F. and Effenterre, H. van, 1963. "Géographie préhistorique de la région de Mallia" in Fouilles Executées à Mallia: Site et Nécropoles 2 (Études crétoises 13), eds. H. and M. van Effenterre. Paris: Paul Geuthner; 28-53.

Duckham, A. N., 1963. The Farming Year. London: Chatto and Windus.

Earle, T. K., 1977. "A reappraisal of redistribution: complex Hawaiian chiefdoms" in Exchange Systems in Prehistory, eds. T. K. Earle and J. E. Ericson. New York: Academic Press; 213-29.

Evans, A. J., 1899-1900. "Knossos, I: the palace". Ann. Brit. Sch. Athens 6:3-70.

Evans, A. J., 1935. The Palace of Minos at Knossos, 4 (2). London: MacMillan.

Evans, J. D., 1971. "Neolithic Knossos—the growth of a settlement." P.P.S. 37 (2):95-117.

Evans, J. D. and Renfrew, C., 1968. Excavations at Saliagos. British School at Athens.

F.A.O. 1946-74. Production Yearbook 1-28. Rome: United Nations, Food and Agriculture Organisation.

Faure, P., 1969. "Sur trois sortes de sanctuaries crétois." Bulletin de Correspondance Héllenique 93:174-213.

Finley, M. I., 1957. "The Mycenaean tablets and economic history." Econ. Hist. Rev. 10:128-41.

Flannery, K. V., 1968. "Archaeological systems theory and early Meso-america" in Anthropological Archeology in the Americas, ed. B. J. Meggers. Washington: Anthropological Society of Washington; 67-87.

Flannery, K. V., 1969. "Origins and ecological effects of early Near Eastern domestication" in The Domestication and Exploitation of Plants and Animals, eds. P. J. Ucko and G. W. Dimbleby. London: Duckworth; 73-100.

French, D. H., 1972. Notes on Prehistoric Pottery Groups from Central Greece. Athens: privately circulated.

Gamble, C. S., 1979. "Surplus and self-sufficiency in the Cycladic subsistence economy" in Papers in Cycladic Prehistory, eds. J. L. Davis and J. F. Cherry. U.C.L.A. Institute of Archaeology Monograph 14. Los Angeles: U.C.L.A.; 122-34.

Gamble, C. S., 1980. "Animal husbandry, population and urbanisation" in An Island Polity: the Archaeology of Exploitation on Melos. eds. C. Renfrew and J. M. Wagstaff. Cambridge: Cambridge University Press.

Gejvall, N-G., 1969. Lerna I: the Fauna. Princeton: American School of Classical Studies at Athens.

Godart, L. and Olivier, J-P., 1976. Receuil des Inscriptions en Linéaire A (Etudes Crétoises 21). Paris: Paul Geuthner.

Graham, J. W., 1962. The Palaces of Crete. Princeton: Princeton University Press.

Graham, J. W., 1979. "Further notes on Minoan palace architecture, 1: west magazines and upper halls at Knossos and Mallia." Amer. J. Arch. 83:49-63.

Halstead, P., 1977. "Prehistoric Thessaly: the submergence of civilisation" in Mycenaean Geography, ed. J. L. Bintliff. Cambridge: British Association for Mycenaean Studies; 23-29.

Halstead, P., 1980. "Counting sheep in Neolithic and Bronze Age Greece" in Pattern of the Past: Studies in Honour of David Clarke, eds. I. R. Hodder, G. Isaac and N. Hammond. Cambridge: Cambridge University Press; 307-39.

Halstead, P., forthcoming. "Animal bones from Late Neolithic Dimini, Thessaly: evidence for subsistence and exchange".

Halstead, P. and Jones, G., 1980. "Early Neolithic Economy in Thessaly: some evidence from excavations at Prodromos." Anthropologika 1.

Hanschmann, E. and Milojčić, V., 1976. Die deutschen Ausgrabungen auf der Argissa-Magula in Thessalien, 3: die frühe und beginnende mittlere Bronzezeit. Bonn: Rudolf Habelt.

Haussoullier, B., 1880. "Vases peints archaiques découverts à Knossos." Bulletin de Correspondance Hellenique 4:124-27.

Heath, M. C., 1958. "Early Helladic clay sealings from the House of Tiles at Lerna". Hesperia 27:81-121.

Higgs, E.S. and Jarman, M. R., 1975. "Palaeoeconomy" in Palaeoeconomy, ed. E. S. Higgs. London: Cambridge University Press; 1-8.

Hillman, G., 1973. "Agricultural productivity at Aşvan." Anatolian Studies 23:225-40.

Hodder, I. R., 1972. "Locational models and the study of Romano-British settlement" in Models in Archaeology, ed. D. L. Clarke. London: Methuen; 887-909.

Hodder, I. R., 1974. "Regression analysis of some trade and marketing patterns." World Arch. 6: 172-89.

Hodder, I. R., 1979. "Economy, meaning and archaeology: a study from Sudan." Unpublished paper read at the Cambridge conference "Economic Archaeology: Towards an Integrated Approach".

Hood, M. S. F., 1958. Archaeological Survey of the Knossos Area. British School at Athens.

Hopkins, K., 1978. "Economic growth and towns in Classical Antiquity" in Towns in Societies, eds. P. Abrams and E. A. Wrigley. Cambridge: Cambridge University Press; 35-77.

Houerou, H. N. le, 1977. "Plant sociology and ecology applied to grazing lands research, survey and management in the Mediterranean basin" in Handbook of Vegetation Science 13: Application of Vegetation Science to Grassland Husbandry, ed. W. Krause. The Hague: Dr. W. Junk; 211-74.

Hourmouziadis, G., 1979. To Neolithiko Dimini. Volos: Society for Thessalian Studies.

Houston, J. M., 1964. The Western Mediterranean World. London: Longmans.

Howell, R., 1970. "A survey of eastern Arcadia in prehistory." Ann. Brit. Sch. Athens 65:79-127.

Hubbard, R. N. L. B., 1979. "Ancient agriculture and ecology at Servia" in "Rescue excavations at Servia 1971-1973: a preliminary report", C. Ridley and K. A. Wardle, Ann. Brit. Sch. Athens 74:226-28.

Hubbard, R.N. L. B., in press. "The development of agriculture in Europe and the Near East: the evidence of quantitative studies." Economic Botany 33.

Hutchinson, R. W., 1936. "Hearths and house pits" in Excavations at Thermi in Lesbos, W. Lamb. Cambridge: Cambridge University Press; 55-64.

Jordan, B., 1975. Iierknochenfunde aus der Magula Pevkakia in Thessalien. Munich: Institut für Palaeoanatomie, Domestikationsforschung und Geschichte der Tiermedizin der Universität München.

Killen, J. T., 1963. "Some adjuncts to the SHEEP ideogram on Knossos tablets." Eranos 61:69-93.

Killen, J. T., 1964. "The wool industry of Crete in the Late Bronze Age." Ann. Brit. Sch. Athens 59:1-15.

Killen, J. T., 1977. "The Knossos texts and the geography of Mycenaean Crete" in Mycenaean Geography, ed. J. L. Bintliff. Cambridge: British Association for Mycenaean Studies; 40-47.

Killen, J. T., forthcoming. A Mycenaean Industry.

Kroll, H., 1979. "Kulturpflanzen aus Dimini." Archaeo-Physika 8: 173-89.

Lee, R. B. and De Vore, I., eds. 1968. Man the Hunter. Chicago: Aldine.

Lewthwaite, J. G., forthcoming. "Cardial disorder? Aspects of cultural and economic change in the early postglacial of the west Mediterranean".

Maltby, M., 1979. Faunal Studies on Urban Sites: the Animal Bones from Exeter, 1971-1975. Sheffield: Department of Prehistory and Archaeology.

Marinatos, S., 1946. "Greniers de l'Helladique Ancien." Bulletin de Correspondance Hellénique 70:337-51.

Milojčić, V., 1976. "Die Grabung auf der Agia Sofia-Magula" in Magulen um Larisa, 1966, V. Milojčić, A. von den Driesch, K. Enderle, J. Milojčić-v.Zumbusch and K. Kilian. Bonn: Rudolf Habelt; 4-14.

N.S.S.G. 1961-76. Agricultural Statistics of Greece. Athens: National Statistical Service of Greece.

Odum, E. P., 1975. Ecology (2nd edn.). London: Holt, Rinehart and Winston.

Olivier, J-P., 1967a. Les Scribes de Cnossos (Incunabula Graeca 17). Rome: Edizioni dell'Ateneo.

Olivier, J-P., 1967b. "La série Dn de Cnossos." Studi Micenei ed Egeo-Anatolici 2 (Incunabula Graeca 18): 71-93.

Payne, S., 1975. "Faunal change at Franchthi cave from 20,000 B.C. to 3,000 B.C." in Archaeozoological Studies, ed. A. T. Clason. Amsterdam and New York: North-Holland and American Elsevier; 120-31.

Pellet, P. L. and Shadarevian, S., 1970. Food Composition Tables for Use in the Near East. Beirut: American University.

Pendlebury, J. D. S., 1939. The Archaeology of Crete: An Introduction. London: Methuen.

Platon. N., 1971. Zakros. New York: Scribner's.

Popham, M. R., 1970. The Destruction of the Palace at Knossos, Pottery of the Late Minoan IIIA Period. Goteborg: Paul Astrom.

Popham, M. R., 1979. Review of "The Mycenaean palace at Knossos: evidence for final destruction in the IIIB period", E. Hallager. J. Hellenic Studies 99:202-03.

Rackham, O., 1972. "Charcoal and plaster impressions" in Myrtos, P. Warren. British School at Athens; 299-304.

Rathje, W. L., 1971. "The origin and development of lowland Classic Maya civilisation." Amer. Ant. 36:275-85.

Reichstein, H., in press. "Erste Ergebnisse von Untersuchungen an Tierknochen aus bronzezeitlichen Siedlungsschichten" in "Ergebnisse der Grabungen bei Kastanas in Zentralmakedonien, 1975-78", B. Hänsel. Jahrbuch des Römisch-Germanischen Zentralmuseums Mainz.

Renfrew, C., 1972. The Emergence of Civilisation. London: Methuen.

Renfrew, C., 1973. "Trade and craft specialisation" in Neolithic Greece, D. R. Theocharis. National Bank of Greece; 179-91.

Renfrew, J. M., 1966. "A report on recent finds of carbonised cereal grains and seeds from prehistoric Thessaly." Thessalika 5:21-36.

Reynolds, P. J., 1974. "Experimental Iron Age storage pits." P.P.S. 40:118-31.

Ricklefs, R. E. , 1979. Ecology (2nd edn.). New York: Chiron.

Roberts, N., 1979. "The location and environment of Knossos." Ann. Brit. Sch. Athens 74:231-41.

Rutkowski, B., 1972. Cult Places in the Aegean World. Warsaw: Polish Academy of Sciences.

Sakellarakis, J., 1973. "Neolithic Crete" in Neolithic Greece, D. R. Theocharis. National Bank of Greece; 131-46.

Schachermeyr, F., 1976. Die Ägäische Frühzeit, I: die vormykenischen Perioden. Vienna: Austrian Academy of Sciences.

Schiffer, M. B., 1976. Behavioral Archaeology. New York: Academic Press.

Sherratt, A. G., 1972. "Socioeconomic and demographic models for Europe" in Models in Archaeology, ed. D. L. Clarke. London: Methuen; 477-542.

Sherratt, A. G., 1975. The Beginning of the Bronze Age in the Area between the Middle Danube and the North Aegean. Cambridge: unpublished Ph.D. dissertation in the Department of Archaeology.

Theocharis, D. R., 1957. "Iolkos." Ergon:43-50.

Theocharis, D. R., 1973. Neolithic Greece. National Bank of Greece.

Trewartha, G. T., 1954. An Introduction to Climate. New York, Toronto, London: McGraw-Hill.

Tsountas, C., 1908. Ai Proistorikai Akropoleis Diminiou kai Sesklou. Athens: Athens Archaeological Society.

Wagstaff, J. M., 1972. "The physical geography of the Myrtos region: a preliminary appraisal" in Myrtos, P. Warren. British School at Athens; 273-82.

Warren, P. 1972. Myrtos. British School at Athens.

Warren, P. 1977."The emergence of Mycenaean palace civilisation" in Mycenaean Geography, ed. J. L. Bintliff. Cambridge: British Association for Mycenaean Studies; 68-72.

Warren, P. and Tzedakis, J., 1974. "Debla, an early Minoan settlement in western Crete." Ann. Brit. Sch. Athens 69:299-342.

Whitelaw, T. M., 1979. Community Structure and Social Organisation at Fournou Korifi, Myrtos. Southampton: unpublished M.A. dissertation in the Department of Archaeology.

Wright, H. E., 1972. "Vegetation history" in The Minnesota Messenia Expedition, eds. W. A. McDonald and G. R. Rapp. Minneapolis: University of Minnesota Press; 188-99.

Zvelebil, M., 1979. Prehistoric Subsistence and Settlement Patterns in the North-east Baltic. Cambridge: unpublished Ph.D. dissertation in the Department of Archaeology.

16. SOCIAL CONTROL AND THE ECONOMY

Clive Gamble

"The political economy cannot survive on that restrained use of resources which for the domestic economy is a satisfactory existence."
Marshall Sahlins (1974: 135).

Introduction

The concept of a dual economy, with production for use and production for exchange, is deeply embedded in archaeological thinking. This might arise in part from the nature of archaeological evidence — ecofacts speak directly to subsistence and use, artifacts to primitive valuables and exchange — but also from a view of 'economy' that owes more to the societies which produce archaeologists rather than to those which produced the archaeological remains they study. Thus subsistence and exchange form separate themes of analysis (Higgs 1975; Earle and Ericson 1977) although they may be addressing common questions of change and social development. The distinction is also based on a concern with examining patterns of distribution by means of spatial analysis (Hodder and Orton 1976) rather than considering systems of production. Moreover subsistence studies have frequently made the dubious assumption that by studying what people live on they are automatically engaged in an 'economic' analysis (Jarman 1972).

Ever since archaeologists began quarrying the works of Marshall Sahlins (1960, 1974) for appropriate economic models they should have been aware that the concept of the dual economy has little empirical support. An 'integrated approach' to economic archaeology should take this into account. Furthermore the sociohistorical writings of Karl Polanyi (et al., 1957), which have been widely incorporated into archaeology, stress that the study of economy can only proceed with a study of society. In a historical discipline such as archaeology the explanation of change in past societies requires that economy and society be treated as one, and not as separate spheres of development.

Polanyi however concentrated upon the circulation of goods and the systems of distribution within society. In this paper I want to take the theme of production and present an analysis of changes in bronze age Aegean politics. The development of social control through the management of agricultural production is the specific issue which will be investigated. This is not an integrated analysis since undue weight is placed upon subsistence but it is to be hoped that it will at least illustrate the potential of a social perspective (Bender 1978) that has generally been lacking in archaeological considerations of leadership, authority and factors of production such as intensification and 'surplus'.

Economy and society

The primitive economy, as pointed out by many people, lies embedded in the institutions of society (Polanyi et al. 1957). Thus the customary separation of economic activity into production for use and production for exchange is both arbitrary and misleading (Sahlins 1974: 82-3). Irrespective of whether production involves obsidian mirrors, pork sausages or feather headresses, and regardless of whether they are eaten or worn at home or given to someone else they still represent production for livelihood. No individual unit, nuclear family or domestic mode of production (Sahlins 1974), can exist in isolation and total autonomy from a wider social grouping. Production for livelihood involves feeding the immediate household and maintaining a place in a wider social aggregate. Moreover such units and aggregates are not in a constant state of change. They form a more or less stable set of institutions and social relationships whose definition is achieved through economic transactions.

This perpetuation of social order has been described by the term social reproduction.

> "A system of social reproduction is characterised by a socially determined set of productive relations ... that distribute the total labour input and output of a population and organise immediate work processes and the exploitation of the environment within limits established by a given level of technological development." (Friedman and Rowlands 1978: 203)

In discussing agricultural self-sustaining formations Meillassoux notes that their continuation depends upon 'control of the means of human reproduction: subsistence and women' (1972: 101) rather than upon any control over the means of material production.

> "Their end is reproduction of life as a precondition to production ... They represent comprehensive, integrated, economic, social and demographic systems ensuring the vital needs of all the members — productive and non-productive — of the community." (ibid: 101-2.)

Control over any member in a community is therefore quite simple. Dependent ties over any individual are forged because without the support of the community no member has access to the means of physiological reproduction. (ibid: 100).

One value of the concept of social reproduction is that it forces us to recognise the indivisible link between economy and society. The term 'agricultural self-sustaining formations' covers a very wide spectrum of economic, social and demographic systems and of course a variety of additional means by which control is exerted. Investment in ideology and the use of coercion can obviously be employed to control the means of reproduction. Economic resources of all kinds are mobilised to define the multivarious roles and positions which exist in such societies. The circulation of valuables and the monopoly over social knowledge (Bender 1978) combined with the obligations inherent in reciprocity and redistributive mechanisms serve to define such positions within society.

It follows therefore that such institutions as might be identified do not exist independently of the economy. In a very real sense they are the economy. For example, the maintenance of a chief requires certain demands on production so that food or goods are available for redistribution. Production, which most probably involves the creation of a surplus above subsistence requirements, is needed in order that society can reproduce the various roles, positions and institutions which are already in existence. The reason that a band society is very different from a chiefdom is not because one relies on hunting and the other on agriculture. It is because the economic resources available to both are utilised in totally different ways in the sphere of social activity. The institutions that need reproducing are very different and require different means of organising production in order to achieve this result.

The transformation of one mode of production into another is therefore an integral part of studies into the growth of institutions and hence the development of society (Bender 1978; Friedman and Rowlands 1978; Ingold 1980). My purpose in this short paper is not however to tackle such a broad theme but rather to examine a specific aspect of this social perspective. This concerns the relationship between the creation of a surplus in agricultural production and the development of society (Gamble 1979) which in this paper I want to explore from the perspective of social control.

Ranking and Surplus

A number of very great consequences have been drawn from the potential of prehistoric subsistence strategies to provide a surplus. As envisaged by Childe:

> "Society persuaded or compelled the farmers to produce a surplus of foodstuffs over and above their domestic requirements, and by concentrating this surplus used it to support a new urban population of specialized craftsmen, merchants, priests, officials, and clerks." (1954: 30-1).

This surplus came to form in the archaeological and anthropological mind the critical variable in allowing the development and emergence of more complex social and economic institutions (Pearson 1957: 322). Surplus production was characterised as a goal for the agricultural policy of emerging centralised polities.

From the perspective of social development Adams regards Childe's statement as little more than a truism (1966: 45). He asks whether it can be demonstrated that the exploitation of particular environments by particular technologies actually supports and enhances the ideological and institutional forces that are needed to organise a surplus in the first place. Moreover,

> "Is there an inherent tendency for agriculturalists to advance in productivity toward the highest potential level consistent with their technology, that is, to maximise their production above subsistence needs and so precipitate the growth of new patterns of appropriation and consumption involving élites freed from responsibilities for food production?" (1966: 45).

Substantivist economists such as Pearson (1957) also criticised Childe's view by pointing out that surpluses are relative. They require definition within a social context and that without this they remain unmeasurable. The concept of absolute surplus as employed by Childe and many archaeologists, and obtained by subtracting calorific needs from calorific yields, ultimately has little bearing on questions of organisation other than the purely heuristic. To sum up in Pearson's words,

> "There are always and everywhere potential surpluses available. What counts is the institutional means for bringing them to life." (1957: 339.)

However it is frequently maintained that changes in society spring from the possibilities offered by food resources. Thus we find Fried (1967: 111) arguing against environmental determinism as a major factor in social development but maintaining that

> "the pristine emergence of ranking is significantly dependent on the availability of food." (op. cit.)

The relation between a domesticated food supply and ranked societies

> "seems to be centered in the demographic effects of the more certain and more concentrated food supply: communities become large on the average and much more permanent." (ibid.: 115-6.)

The only exceptions to this relation are societies occupying 'windfall' environments (op. cit.), of which the North-West Coast Indians of America are the main example. Here ranking existed without domesticated food resources and was possible due to a predictable local abundance of fish. Put simply, the argument states that the surplus production of food is converted into more people and this requires changes in the social order to cope with this new circumstance.

Instead of comparing the relative richness of environments and the ease with which a surplus could be produced we might turn to considering the role between production and the institutions which organise it. This point of view is well put by Sahlins (1974: 140).

> "Too frequently and mechanically anthropologists attribute the appearance of chieftainship to the production of surplus. In the historic process, however, the relation has been at least mutual, and in the functioning of primitive society it is rather the other way around. Leadership continually generates domestic surplus. The development of rank and chieftainship becomes, *pari passu*, development of the productive forces."

One conclusion that stems from this point of view is that we no longer have to look for social developments only in those areas of either potentially productive, predictable or domesticated food supplies. While a relationship, as argued by Fried (1967), undoubtedly exists it is not determined by the effects of resources on society, but rather it is dependent upon the social relations of production leading to the development of the environment.

Leadership and Production

The role of élites or interest groups in the organisation of production has been extensively studied by anthropologists. The methods by which leadership can provide a stimulus to production and the outcomes of increased production are of some interest. We learn for example that

> " In Tikopia a chief has normally a greater command of economic resources than others of his clan." (Firth 1965: 190);

and that moreover,

> " The chief has an important integrative function because as primary intermediary with the clan gods he supplies the initiative and controls the correct utilization of most natural resources. Not only are the ceremonies he performs the pivotal points of the seasonal economic cycle, but by his imposition of taboos on crops and land he can make his people change their sphere and locality of production." (ibid.: 191.)

The Tikopian chief is however more than just a repository of all gardening wisdom and a check to ecological vandalism on the part of his clan. He is an instrument of stability in the system and while his prohibitions on production and the deployment of labour may reap ecological benefits, they are primarily designed to protect the status quo of the institutions, and hence fabric of society, that is defined through economic behaviour.

These powers over the organisation of production can also be used to achieve the effective integration of a geographically fragmented polity.

> " There were analogous but still more intensive contacts with Tetiaroa, a circlet of reefs and motus some eight leagues (26 miles) to the north (of Tahiti), but here the pattern of traffic was shaped by political considerations. It was part of the patrimony of the chief of the Pare district who forbade the cultivation of vegetable foods other than coconut and taro, compelling the inhabitants to seek their breadfruit from the mainland (Tahiti) and to produce a surplus of fish which were sent to Pare for local use or export." (Lewthwaite 1966: 49).

The integration of a dispersed polity of this nature is achieved through the artificially created dependence of the far flung settlements on the redistributive centre (Sahlins 1974: 141). This economic simplification and production of surplus for export provides a more secure basis for ensuring political control.

Sanctions in the form of taboos or prohibitions over production could be particularly effective because of the small spatial scale of such societies.

> " The material weight of this chiefly retinue (in Hawaii) and the sumptuary airs it affected fell, of course, on the ordinary people. It fell especially on those nearest the paramount, within a range that made transport worthwhile and the threat of sanctions effective."
> (Sahlins 1974: 145)

Force was a further sanction that could be most effectively employed at this spatial scale of political relations.

At a different social scale the prophet Muhammed appears to have appreciated the value of managing economic production in order to forge the state of Islam (Diener and Robkin 1978). While Harris (1975) has maintained that the Islamic prohibition on the pig was dictated by ecological necessity, Diener and Robkin have pointed out that

> " Pigs fit so ideally into local systems that they render peasant villages dangerously rich and autonomous; they provide a local standard of living which leads to a diminution of tax and tithe. Pig prohibition may result in decreased local consumption and increased appropriation. " (Ibid: 510.)

> " In his attempt to realize the political goals of Empire, Muhammed willingly compromised the ecological efficiency of local units. Indeed, the ecological efficiency of the nomad and peasant led them to self-sufficiency; the destruction of such autonomy became a conscious goal of Islamic political policy. " (ibid.: 503, emphasis mine.)

By prohibiting pigs to farmers Muhammed was able to ensure the much needed grain supply for Mecca. Diener and Robkin further suggest that periods of political instability in the Near East coincide with the lifting of the pig prohibition and it is re-introduced during periods of regional political stability when local autonomy is again broken (ibid: 503). This evolution of various animals from sacred, but eaten on special occasions, to prohibited (New Guinea pigs to Islamic prohibition: cattle using cultures in India prior to 600 B.C. to Hindu sacred cow prohibitions) is, the authors maintain, not a fact of environment but of the developing social field (ibid: 504) and coincides with political expansion over formerly autonomous units.

The means by which a surplus is produced is obviously important. The leadership can exhort people to work longer hours, to grow more crops and to cultivate more land. Such intensification runs counter to the characterisation of household economies where underproduction is a major feature (Sahlins 1974), and where effort ceases as soon as immediate demands are met. The authority of leadership in such contexts would tend to be charismatic and therefore likely to be of a temporary rather than a permanent nature. It could be backed up with ideological force and the threat of sanctions, but this is unlikely to increase the effective power of leadership when autonomy in subsistence remains the basic feature of either households or communities within such an alliance system.

The creation of surplus through specialisation on a single product and combined with the mechanism of redistribution provides another alternative. Deficiencies in household/community budgets under such a system of production (cf. the Tetitaroa example) would force dependent ties on the wider community in order to maintain access to the means of social reproduction. For such a system to function without continual failures there would be a need for some form of management. Redistribution could still provide the mechanism by which this was achieved. Factors of scale and cost suggest that such management would be centralised. The authority of the interest group responsible for such organisation would be based upon the importance of the dependent links. The permanence of such an institution based upon its managerial role and its effective power over decisions concerning production could therefore be considerable.

These two extremes point to the spectrum of response that must be expected when we consider the role of leadership in the organisation of production. The outcome of interest groups becoming involved in production can be seen in the permanence and scale of developing political formations. The development of polities is very much the development of the economy: not only because the latter allows changes in the demographic variables but because it provides a basis for effective authority as the erosion of formerly autonomous units is replaced by dependency, for the means of social reproduction, on a central agency.

Archaeological discussion

In order to illustrate some of the points made above I shall now turn to a discussion of the Aegean bronze age emergence.

Childe saw the palaces and citadels of Crete and the mainland as the hero's castle which acted as a nucleus for accumulating surplus wealth (1954: 205). More recently another authority has written that

> "The growth of the palaces has to be seen in the first instance as the development of redistribution centres for subsistence commodities, controlled by a well defined social hierarchy. The emergence of Aegean civilisation can be comprehended only if this central point is kept in view." (Renfrew 1972: 297).

Great stress has been placed upon the development of Mediterranean polyculture — with vines, olives, wheat and animal products — and the ability of the palaces to store the surplus wealth produced under this system.

Renfrew has been keen to point out also that

> "The innovations in the developing agriculture were thus largely cultural, with human control of these species the deciding factor ... The subsistence sub-system developed, along with other social and technical elements: it did not lead the way." (ibid: 304.)

However, he has also maintained

> "that in areas of productive diversity (in terms of Mediterranean polyculture: olive and vine as well as cereals) and only in such areas will such a redistributive system emerge." (ibid: 481-2.)

According to Renfrew's model the diversity of crops that was available to the prehistoric Aegean farmer led to local surplus that promoted redistribution. This emerged within the village and thus favoured social development in the form of local chieftains. The important factor seems to be a potentially highly productive environment which with a minimum of intensification produces a surplus. This in turn requires a change in social organisation in order to assimilate such a surplus into a new economic order.

One problem with this model concerns the surplus itself. Bintliff (1977b: 65) has pointed out that wine, wheat, olive products and wool are all locally available in the Aegean in some abundance. Surplus production should result in a 'coals to Newcastle' situation. The potential agricultural surplus consisted of goods which nobody wanted because everybody had them. Palmer has voiced a similar concern with reference to external trade.

> " It has always been a puzzle to know what so unproductive a country as Greece had to offer in exchange for the luxury goods for which the remains from the Mycenaean Age offer such striking evidence." (1961: 106-7.)

The answer has been to identify quality products such as perfumed olive oil (Palmer 1961: 108) and textiles as the possible exchange commodities.

Furthermore ethnoarchaeological work (Forbes 1976) has demonstrated that Greek farmers today diversify their agricultural base thereby spreading risk and achieving a measure of self-sufficiency. This philosophy of 'we have a little of everything' has the following result for social development.

> " Most of the villages tend to have territories exploiting a wide range of the environment, and in that situation the broader the base — one could argue — the more cushioned they are against the sort of situations demanding greater social organisation ... Only in situations where you get villages stuck exclusively on monocrop land might one expect a forced exchange of products between communities, ultimately encouraging more complex social organisation." (Halstead 1977: 63.)

There is no doubt that a surplus in agricultural foodstuffs could have been produced in the prehistoric Aegean. The problem is accounting for its use once it had been produced when evidence from economic strategies indicates self-sufficiency in the major essentials. But in that case how do we explain away the palaces with their storage facilities and bureaucratic archives which point to their primary function as administrative centres for agricultural production? (Chadwick 1976.)

Let us frame the problem differently. Instead of arguing about the place of a surplus in the Aegean emergence, it might be more profitable to turn to our themes of social development and political control and their relationship with organising the productive forces.

With the concept of Early State Modules (Renfrew 1975), the 'Asiatic' states of Friedman and Rowlands (1978: 220), we can provide some of the parameters for emergent ranked societies. These consist of autonomous central places spaced about 40 kms. apart and holding political sway over a territory of c. 1500 km^2 (Renfrew 1975: 13). The central place is characterised by frequent interactions between it and the hinterland and forms a redistributive focus. The size of territory described by Cherry (1978: 425) as a polity catchment area provides convenient travel distances between even the most far flung settlements in the polity and the redistributive centre. In terms of Sahlins' description of Polynesian chiefdoms (1974: 145) it is also a distance over which the intensity of interaction is such that sanctions will be effective. It is therefore reasonable to suggest that the élites could exert considerable influence over the organisation of rural production.

The Linear B archives from Pylos and Knossos provide some insight as to the form this took. The records from the ESM of Pylos testify to a complex system of land holding (Chadwick 1976) which has been likened to medieval feudal Europe. This is misleading (Finley 1957) since the historical analogy is inappropriate. The exact form of land holding is not clear but the evidence strongly suggests the unequal control of land by particular interest groups. The largest holdings appear to be closely connected with the central administration (Chadwick 1976: 116-7).

The system of land holding must also be viewed against the differential potential of agricultural land within the Pylian kingdom (van Wersch 1972). This has led Hutchinson to propose that

> "There would be specialization in different parts of the kingdom of Nestor so that the natural resources might be used to their best advantage. I have little doubt that certain areas of Messenia produced, say, flax, while others produced wheat or provided pasture (1977: 7). The mention of flax on the tablets is highly indicative of area specialisation because flax is labour intensive and its cultivation rapidly exhausts the soil. Therefore flax production is only profitable where there is a thickly populated region which can rely upon its grain supplies coming from elsewhere." (ibid.:16.)

However, it must be remembered that van Wersch's bronze age land use map only suggests a pattern of potential land use. As pointed out by Carothers and MacDonald (1979: 442), it should not be assumed that because an area within Messenia was, according to van Wersch, best suited to growing olives, no cereals were grown in that same area.

> "What our analysis does suggest is an interdependent economic situation in which communities of the same size produced greater or lesser amounts of the same commodities." (op. cit.)

This assessment modifies Hutchinson's view of monocropping but still allows for the creation of surplus at some expense to local community self-sufficiency.

> "We believe that the Messenian evidence suggests an essentially two-level, large-small size hierarchy ... Probably most of these small settlements were essentially self-sufficient. In addition, one or more of such products as barley, wheat, meat, wool, hides and other animal products may have constituted a modes surplus that, in sum, had a fairly important role in the overall redistributive system." (Carothers and McDonald 1979: 451.)

The large sites, such as Pylos itself, were more directly involved in creating surpluses under labour-intensive conditions (op. cit.) and in exchanging the products between equivalent sized partners. This is an interesting suggestion and if accepted narrows the effective authority of the large settlements such as Nestor's palace down to a very small area around the site itself. Outside this direct sphere of élite interest in production there would, according to Carothers and McDonald, be a large number of communities still with their subsistence autonomy. Their integration into the Pylian ESM would therefore be based upon a charismatic basis perhaps supported by religious controls and occasional coercion. This points to a comparatively fragile power structure within the Pylian Kingdom.

This conclusion based on Carothers and McDonald's assessment can be modified in the light of the evidence from the linear B tablets which deal with land holding. As suggested by Finley (1957: 139).

> "We must imagine a situation in which officials, soldiers, craftsmen, herders and farmers all held land (or worked on the land) on condition that they rendered either appropriate services or quotas of products, industrial or agricultural as the case may be."

In order to broaden the effective authority of the central administration some inroads into the productive and reproductive autonomy of the smaller communities would have to be made. The system of land holding with dispersed 'estates' within the ESM might have achieved this function as well as more direct control over the means of production.

One possible line that this took has been demonstrated by Killen (1964) with the SHEEP tablets from Knossos. In his analysis of these records Killen argues that sheep were allocated for herding to certain subjects by the palace administration (ibid: 8). The palace was responsible for maintaining herds at full strength while the shepherd fulfilled his side of the arrangement by meeting a target of fleece production that was set by the administration. The linear archive records the success or failure of the shepherds in meeting this quota production. Killen's analysis provides us with an insight into the way a surplus was produced and managed. We can infer further that the palace controlled the manufacture of the wool into textiles and that the quotas were geared to the capacity of this craft activity. The disposal of the finished products is not known although there are hints at foreign exchange in textiles (Killen 1964: 14) and redistribution within the Knossian polity is also a strong possibility. This example points to the control exerted over the means of production by the central administration and their precise management of the quantity of surplus output and its transformation into quality product. As with the Pylian example it is possible to see at least in one area of economic activity how dependent relations were constructed between the central interest group and those directly engaged in production. Note 1.)

These examples refer to a later stage of the Aegean emergence. If we turn to an earlier stage of the development of these central institutions we can observe alternative ways in which leadership exerted social control. A major feature of Aegean research has been concerned with the investiation of ritual monuments and religious behaviour. In an analysis of peak-top sanctuaries in Minoan Crete, Cherry (1978) has shown the close correspondence between the appearance of these specific ritual monuments and a palace élite. However, soon after their appearance many of the sanctuaries fall into decline which suggests that such sites were only needed when the social order was most precarious (Cherry 1978: 428).

> "There is, in fact, the suggestion of a general inverse relationship between the degree of investment in ideology and the strength of political authority/coercive power." (ibid: 429-431.)

The function of ceremonial cycles involving such sanctuaries has been used by Bintliff (1977a: 100) to account for political integration in a diverse economic landscape such as is found in Crete. He makes the important point that these monuments are found in areas of profitable but seasonal economic resources and therefore provide a focus for integrating fragmented demographic units into a wider social order.

The rapid decline in importance of these ritual monuments and the concentration of ideological authority in the palaces suggests that their function in a system of establishing authority was short lived. Social control has been transferred to a less fragile basis, although it still undoubtedly utilised much ideological authority. It seems reasonable to propose that the new basis of authority also rested on economic sanctions via the control of production.

In order to demonstrate this we must, however, demonstrate some of the conditions that have been outlined above. At the very least effective economic sanctions require a compact polity so that the authority of central leadership can be established. As suggested by Renfrew (1975: 18) it seems most probable that in the transition from a kinship-based polity of a chiefdom to that of a state there will be a reduction in the polity area in order to achieve effective control. The centralisation of authority in an ESM requires that the formerly dispersed power of leadership be nucleated. In economic terms I would suggest that what we are seeing is the growth of interest groups indirectly involved with the organisation of production. In the pre-palace stage there was no doubt a surplus that was related to the demands of leadership. However the effective control that the leadership exerted over its organisation was probably not great. We have no clear estimates for polity sizes in this Early Bronze Age period but the evidence suggests a pattern of small dispersed units maintaining alliances through prestation and exchange over extensive areas. In the later palace period of the Middle Bronze Age we are seeing a form of intensification that is achieved through the centralisation of the demands of leadership on production, and through the specialisation of certain products to meet the demands of social use. Changes in the demographic arrangement of population with, for example, a shift from a dispersed to a nucleated pattern of settlement, could result in a form of intensification (Gamble 1979: 132). This need not have involved population growth leading to pressure on resources and hence a change in production. Redistribution was essential to both systems but provided the leadership with different degrees of effective control.

The figure of 1500 km^2 for the ESM's of the Aegean has therefore to be seen as a diminution in previous polity size. Within this territory it is uncertain whether any major technical developments in intensification, such as irrigation works, occurred. However there were no doubt changes in the system of land ownership that resulted in greater productivity per unit area. This stimulus to production could also be controlled by a central leadership who must have derived their authority and position from their control over the means by which intensification could be achieved.

An example from Mesoamerica illustrates the further stage that is lacking in bronze age Greece. Earle has noted that Olmec centres lie 22 kms from the periphery of their territories (1976: 221) thus conforming, at least spatially, with expectations from the ESM model.

By contrast centres in the Valley of Mexico are only 4 kms from their territorial boundaries. Earle comments that,

> " this may be a partial answer to a perennial archaeological dilemma concerning the apparent inability of the Olmec to develop an urban state organisation. Development of the primary state may require a much more compact population, perhaps in a more nearly continual condition of interaction." (op. cit)

This does not appear to have happened in bronze age Greece where both the Minoan and Mycenaean polities were subject to systems collapse rather than further development (Renfrew 1979). The shrinkage in polity size that accompanies the appearance of city states is clearly linked to intensification of production and the opportunities this provides for extending social control. The limits to growth for an ESM have been summarised by Friedman and Rowlands (1978: 220):

> "The size of the political unit depends largely on the ability to centralise the economy and to prevent accumulation of labour and surplus in peripheral areas."

This process is often accompanied by new techniques of production, such as irrigation systems, and whose presence further underscores the erosion of household self-sufficiency and the creation of communal control. One consequence of such intensification is the extension of the authority of leadership over larger populations. It is noticeable that once achieved the political ambitions of Empire soon follow with rapid and substantial increases in the spatial size of polities.

Conclusion

The purpose of this paper has been to consider some of the implications of 'surplus' production. The aspect stressed here has been the relationship between increasing authority and changes in agricultural production. The growth of more complex polities is a response to the increasing control of political leadership upon the organisation of production. There is nothing particularly new about this observation. All economies are political economies. They serve to support and maintain the various requirements of a polity which may vary in complexity from a hunting band to an industrial state. Moreover it is polities and their institutions rather than economies which change; otherwise our present position might be that of the industrial band.

Society forms a network of alliances of variable permanence and commitment. The links and the nodes are defined through economic transactions that can express both equivalence and differentiation. But while this might encourage us to concentrate upon the distribution and circulation of goods around such alliance systems we should not forget the system of production which ultimately defines the network. The mobilisation of resources under the stimulus of leadership and the foundation of effective power through dependent links based on production are factors which can be traced archaeologically. With the development of more complex polities we expect changes in the manner that social control was exerted. The appearance of early states sees changes in demographic, spatial and social variables that point to the increased involvement of leadership in the organisation of production.

Acknowledgements

I should like to thank Hamish Forbes, Paul Halstead, Callum McFarlane and Todd Whitelaw for their comments and criticisms of earlier versions of this paper.

Note 1

It is worth comparing this analysis with Murra's (1962: 715) discussion of the role of cloth in the Inca state.

> " In Inca thinking there were two main economic obligations which the citizen had toward the state, and to each of them corresponded an enduring pre-Incaic right guaranteeing subsistence and traditional self-sufficiency to the peasant community; a right which the Inca found convenient to respect:

Obligation to work the crown and church lands	Right to continue to plant and harvest one's own crops on *ayllu* lands.
Obligation to weave cloth for crown and church needs	Right to wool or cotton from community stocks for the making of one's own clothes."

Murra emphasises the value of textiles in Inca and Andean display systems. They defined social position and were regarded as prestige items. Conquered groups were often obliged to receive large amounts of cloth from the Inca.

> " The compulsory issue of culturally valued commodities in a society without money and relatively small markets can be viewed as the initial pump-priming step in a dependent relationship, since the 'generosity' of the conqueror obligates one to reciprocate, to deliver on a regular, periodic basis, the results of one's own workmanship to the Cuzco warehouses." (*Ibid*: 721.)

I am not suggesting that here is a direct parallel for the Aegean situation. The Inca case provides an insight into the interests of the local community and the central power, and demonstrates how, through the organisation of production, the effective control of the central administration was extended over the new citizens of the state.

References

Adams, R. McC., 1966. *The Evolution of Urban Society.* Chicago: Aldine.

Bender, B., 1978. " Gatherer-hunter to farmer: a social perspective." *World Arch.* 10: 204-222.

Bintliff, J. L., 1977a. " New approaches to human geography. Prehistoric Greece: a case study" in *An Historical Geography of the Balkans*, ed. F. W. Carter. London: Academic Press; 59-114.

Bintliff, J. L., 1977b. Comments in discussion. In *Mycenaean Geograpy*, ed. J. L. Bintliff. Cambridge: British Association for Mycenaean Studies; 65.

Carothers, J. and McDonald, W. A., 1979. "Size and distribution of the population in late bronze age Messenia: some statistical approaches." J. Field Arch. 6: 433-454.

Chadwick, J., 1976. The Mycenaean World. Cambridge: Cambridge University Press.

Cherry, J. F., 1978. "Generalization and the archaeology of the state" in Social Organization and Settlement, eds. D. Green, C. Haselgrove and M. Spriggs. Oxford: B.A.R. Suppl. Ser. 47; 411-437.

Childe, V. G., 1954. What Happened in History. Harmondsworth: Pelican.

Diener, P. and Robkin, E. E., 1978. "Ecology, evolution, and the search for cultural origins: the question of Islamic pig prohibition." Curr. Anth. 19: 493-540.

Earle, T. K., 1976. "A nearest-neighbour analysis of two Formative settlement systems" in The Early Mesoamerican Village, ed. K. V. Flannery. New York: Academic Press. 196-223.

Earle, T. K. and Ericson, J. E. (eds.), 1977. Exchange Systems in Prehistory. New York: Academic Press.

Finley, M. I., 1957. "The Mycenaean tablets and economic history." Econ. Hist. Rev. 10: 128-141.

Firth, R., 1965. Primitive Polynesian Economy. London: Routledge and Kegan Paul.

Forbes, H. A., 1976. " 'We have a little of everything': the ecological basis of some agricultural practices in Methana, Trizinia" in Regional Variation in Modern Greece and Cyprus, eds. M. Dimen and E. Friedl. Annals of the New York Academy of Sciences 268. New York: Academy of Sciences; 236-250.

Fried, M. H., 1967. The Evolution of Political Society. New York: Random House.

Friedman, J. and Rowlands, M. J., 1977. "Notes towards an epigenetic model of the evolution of 'civilisation' " in The Evolution of Social Systems, eds. J. Friedman and M. J. Rowlands. London: Duckworth; 201-276.

Gamble, C. S., 1979. "Surplus and self-sufficiency in the Cycladic subsistence economy" in Papers in Cycladic Prehistory, eds. J. L. Davis and J. F. Cherry. U.C.L.A. Institute of Archaeology Monograph 14. L Los Angeles: U.C.L.A.; 122-133.

Halstead, P., 1977. Comments in discussion. In Mycenaean Geography, ed. J. L. Bintliff. Cambridge: British Association for Mycenaean Studies; 63.

Harris, M., 1975. Cows, Pigs, Wars and Witches: the Riddles of Culture. London: Hutchinson.

Higgs, E. S. (ed.), 1975. Palaeoeconomy. London: Cambridge University Press.

Hodder, I. and Orton, C., 1976. Spatial Analysis in Archaeology. Cambridge: Cambridge University Press.

Hutchinson, J. S., 1977. "Mycenaean kingdoms and medieval estates." Historia 26: 1-23.

Ingold, T., 1980. Hunters, Pastoralists and Ranchers: Reindeer Economies and their Transformations. Cambridge: Cambridge University Press.

Jarman, M. R., 1972. "European deer economies and the advent of the Neolithic" in Papers in Economic Prehistory, ed. E. S. Higgs. London: Cambridge University Press; 125-147.

Killen, J. T., 1964. "The wool industry of Crete in the Late Bronze Age." Ann. Brit. Sch. Athens 59: 1-15.

Lewthwaite, G. R., 1966. "Man and sea in early Tahiti: a maritime economy through European eyes." Pacific Viewpoint 7: 28-53.

Meillassoux, C., 1972. "From reproduction to production." Economy and Society 1: 93-105.

Murra, J. V., 1962. "Cloth and its functions in the Inca State." Amer. Anth. 64: 710-728.

Palmer, L. R., 1961. Mycenaeans and Minoans. London: Faber.

Pearson, H. W., 1957. "The economy has no surplus: critique of a theory of development" in Trade and Market in the Early Empires, eds. K. Polanyi, C. M. Arensberg and H. W. Pearson. Glencoe, Ill.: Free Press; 320-341.

Polanyi, K., Arensberg, C. M. and Pearson, H. W. (eds.), 1957. Trade and Market in the Early Empires. Glencoe, Ill.: Free Press.

Renfrew, A. C., 1972. The Emergence of Civilization, the Cyclades and the Aegean in the Third Millenium B.C. London: Methuen.

Renfrew, A. C., 1975. "Trade as action at a distance: questions of integration and communication" in Ancient Civilization and Trade, eds. J. A. Sabloff and C. C. Lamberg-Karlovsky. Albuquerque: University of New Mexico Press; 3-59.

Renfrew, A. C., 1979. "Systems collapse as social transformation: catastrophe and anastrophe in early state societies" in Transformations: Mathematical Approaches to Culture Change, eds. A. C. Renfrew and K. Cooke. New York: Academic Press; 481-506.

Sahlins, M. D., 1960. "Political power and the economy in primitive society" in Essays in the Science of Culture, eds. G. E. Dole and R. L. Carneiro. New York: Crowell; 390-415.

Sahlins, M. D., 1974. Stone Age Economics. London: Tavistock.

Wersch, H. J. van, 1972. "The agricultural economy" in The Minnesota Messenia Expedition, eds. W. A. McDonald and G. R. Rapp. Minneapolis: University of Minnesota Press; 177-187.

17. ECONOMIC GROWTH AND SOCIAL CHANGE: TWO EXAMPLES FROM PREHISTORIC EUROPE

Richard Bradley

"I think things draw to an end, the soil is stale.
And over-elaboration will nothing now avail."

Louis Macneice, 'An Eclogue for Christmas'.

John Alexander has recently interpreted the Urnfield Cultures of bronze age Europe as the outward manifestation of a prehistoric religion (1979). This view has undeniable attractions, but it would be wrong to suppose that the specific features that he discusses, concerned as they are with questions of funerary ritual, represent the whole extent of the Urnfield phenomenon. Adopting a broader definition, it is possible to point to a number of other patterns, which in different areas include the adoption of collective rather than individual burial, the proximity of settlements and cemeteries, and evidence of agricultural growth. It is this last feature which now needs emphasis, for the intensive study of single sites does not always reveal the reasons for wider economic change. The attraction of the Urnfield problem is precisely that it provides evidence of both social and economic changes and affords an opportunity to investigate their relationship. This short paper is concerned with later bronze age developments in two regions of Europe, southern England and north-west Bohemia. These are chosen because of the wealth of settlement evidence which is already available (Barrett and Bradley in press; Bouzek, Koutecký and Neustupný 1966).

Each area is documented in some detail and it is not necessary to repeat this material at any length. There are certain broad similarities in the settlement and cemetery evidence: a large number of domestic sites, which occupy a more prominent place in the archaeological record than those of the preceding phase; the intensification of crop production, marked by the development of field systems in England and the adoption of bell-shaped storage pits in Bohemia; the widespread use of bronze sickles, and also of loom weights and spindle whorls; evidence for intensive cattle raising; and the location of burials close to the settlement area. In both regions there are strong similarities in the later bronze age sequence: an initial concentration of rich metalwork close to the main rivers, despite the existence of a substantial agricultural hinterland; the recycling of bronze through the systematic collection of scrap; and, lastly, the gradual development of hill forts. Both areas show a peak of prosperity towards the end of the Bronze Age in Hallstatt B.

Certain parts of these sequences stand out. In southern England, land use was steadily intensified on both the chalk and the river gravels, and we see the development of Celtic Fields in both of these areas. But some of the fields on the Wessex downs were quite rapidly superseded by a network of more extensive territorial divisions. These may have been connected with increased cattle raising, whilst there is more evidence for textile production from the surrounding lowland, in which bronze sickles also occur. Towards the end of this period defended enclosures were constructed, sometimes at the junction of the two zones. There is reason to suppose that one function of these sites was to store surplus food. The bulk transport of grain would be much easier with the development of wheeled vehicles, the earliest evidence of which comes from this general period (Piggott 1979: 14). Throughout this sequence the re-organisation of food production is matched by the growth of the bronze industry, but the most elaborate metalwork is found mainly in the lowlands, and not in the peripheral areas in which so much economic evidence survives. These contrasts even extend to the river gravels. For example, the increasing deposition of metalwork in the River Thames matches the steady growth of cereal and livestock farming along its tributaries (Bradley, Lobb, Richards and Robinson in press).

In Bohemia, it again appears that hill forts and hill settlements may not be the richest sites. There is a gradual rise in the frequency of rich burials, weapons and ornaments. These match the increasing number of occupation sites, but are inversely related to the development of hill settlements: the main periods in which rich burials are known are the Early Middle and Late Middle Knovíz phases, whilst most hill settlements date from the Transitional and Late periods. Most of the rich burials are close to the River Ohre, despite clear evidence for settlement well beyond the river corridor. The same applies to the distribution of ornaments and weapons, and in both cases there is a tendency, which starts in the Late Middle phase, for metal finds to be more widely distributed. In the Late phase for example, the distribution of hoards leaves the area around the River Elbe and extends to inland settlements. Three other developments are important here: by the Late Middle period there seems to have been a new emphasis in the bronze industry, and the contents of the hoards change from scrap metal to ornaments and drinking vessels; richer graves are found, and, by the Late Knovíz period in Hallstatt B2 and B3, a number of sites show a significant increase in the capacity of corn storage pits. Some of these sites also increase in area.

In both sequences, then, there is evidence for an initial concentration of wealth in the river valleys, the regions which might be best placed to participate in long distance exchange, but intensive agriculture developed over a far wider area. In the hinterland, the development of the first hill settlements is not related directly to the overall growth of wealth. In each area some of the latest sites show evidence of increased food storage, although only in Bohemia does the distribution of rich metalwork extend very far beyond the river valleys or the most fertile lowlands.

The similarities between these two regional sequences suggest that rather similar processes were at work, but the available explanations are of an entirely determinist variety. The most common explanation is that economic reorganisation in these areas was achieved through a change of population. In England, the Deverel — Rimbury Culture has been interpreted as an intrusive phenomenon, although the arguments for this view are based almost entirely on pottery (*cf.* Hawkes 1972: 114-115). In Europe, interpretations of Urnfield origins vary widely and migration has again been suggested (Gimbutas 1965). But this raises the same objection that in some areas the distinctive burial rite might be a continuation, or even an elaboration, of existing local practice. The Knovíz Culture is supposed to have developed from the local Tumulus Culture 'under (the) simultaneous influence of the civilising changes of the Late Bronze Age and of cultural factors emanating from the Danube basin' (Bouzek *et al.*, 1966, 100), but there is nothing in this type of interpretation to account for economic growth.

A second suggestion is that the changes in subsistence might result from population pressures. This view is based on Boserup's work (1965), but arouses the uneasy suspicion that population growth is really being postulated on the evidence of subsistence agriculture. This leads to a circular argument. In fact, the major increase in site numbers in Bohemia *follows* the economic changes just described, just as in Britain the environmental evidence for land clearance shows its main increase *after* the new system had appeared. It seems more sensible to suggest that population growth — if this is what the evidence is showing — was *part* of the process of intensification and not its cause. As Macfarlane has argued, in most 'peasant' societies, where the family is the basic unit of peasant ownership, consumption and social life, in order to maximise production one must also maximise reproduction ... Where ... the basic unit of society is a family or kin group, each new child is an asset, contributing to the welfare of the group, increasing prestige and political power, as well as economic well-being" (1978). The British settlement and cemetery evidence has been interpreted as showing an extended family structure (Drewett and Ellison in Barrett and Bradley in press), and Bouzek and his colleagues note that a similar pattern of distinct 'family' burials may be recognised in the Knovíz Culture (1966: 84).

Lastly, there is the question of climate. This has been discussed for Britain rather than Bohemia, although the resettlement of the loess in the Upper Rhine after a prolonged interval of disuse has been attributed to the onset of damper conditions (Schaeffer 1928). It seems rather unlikely that climatic deterioration was comparable in Britain and in central Europe (Coles and Harding 1979:5), despite the broad similarity of the archaeological sequence; and even within the British Isles, it is difficult to relate the chronology of climatic change to significant changes in the settlement pattern except at a very local level.

Reference to the Upper Rhine may provide the clue to a different explanation, since Balkwill has shown that the reorganisation of settlement here follows a far more widespread pattern (1976). This renewed emphasis on productive land is a central ingredient in any interpretation of the Urnfield problem and may also be seen in Great Britain, where for the first time it is possible to find a significant relationship between the distribution of elaborate weaponry and the areas of first class soil (Gardiner in Barrett and Bradley in press). In both regions, the shift in the settled area was contemporary with the change in the burial record between 'tumulus' and 'urnfield' structures. The proximity of cemetery and settlement in Britain may have been a way of involving the ancestors in the holding of land, just as their involvement in agricultural production may be expressed by the burial of the dead on field boundaries in southern England, or in corn storage pits in Bohemia; the latter is a practice which developed independently in the British Iron Age. The emphasis on group, rather than individual, burial recalls Macfarlane's comments, quoted earlier, and such groups may represent the agricultural workforce, rather than a cross-section of contemporary society as a whole.

There is an additional aspect to the contrast between the Tumulus and Urnfield concepts. The Tumulus Culture in central Europe, like the Wessex Culture in southern England, can only be understood within a pattern of long-distance exchange, by means of which exotic and expensive items were distributed. Those items which still survive were 'consumed' in funerary ritual, and here it is often thought that the contents of different graves can be related to the social persona of the deceased, or more probably to the status of the mourners. This system was geographically extensive, and access to its products was perhaps restricted to a social élite, although there is a danger of circularity in this approach, since social rank is often inferred on the basis of grave goods in the first place. Individual artefacts were distributed, or were copied, over considerable distances, and the European Earlier Bronze Age possesses an essential unity which cross-cuts most local variation. Such an elaborate network seems to have developed alongside the increasing use of livestock products (Sherratt in press), and it seems inherently likely that these represented the opposite axis of exchange. In Wessex another aspect of external relations could have been control over ritual (Barrett and Bradley in press).

The change from the Tumulus to the Urnfield principle came about as part of a wider pattern. The end of the Wessex Culture has already been discussed by the writer (in Barrett and Bradley in press) and it is not intended to repeat this material here. Two separate factors seem to be important: the culmination of a process of soil deterioration which cut down the possibility of producing an agricultural surplus through the existing economic system; and widespread fluctuations in the scale and orientation of prestige trade. The first pattern is reflected by the development of heathland and moorland, even before the period of climatic change which seems to have brought further problems. The second can be seen in the transformation of the character of the European bronze industry. The balance of wealth and power changed on several scales. The movement of wealth within Britain now skirted Wessex in favour of the Thames Valley, just as much of central Europe fragmented into a series of regional groups. On the largest scale, the number of sites in central Europe increased as those in Greece declined (Bouzek 1969).

The ultimate forces behind these changes need not detain us here: what matter are the two general trends which appear through the empirical details. Competition for adequate soils would have gone on after the reorganisation of the landscape, especially if climatic change were of real significance; and there were apparently difficulties in maintaining and collecting a supply of prestige items through which to express individual wealth. The role of the latter material may have increased in this phase and is perhaps reflected by the different ways in which wealth was consumed. Elaborate artefacts, some of them unused, were withdrawn from circulation in graves, hoards and river finds, but these separate contexts conceal a common structure which is more important than the details of the different deposits. In each case we might think of the conspicuous consumption of wealth as a means of displaying power and of reinforcing social relations through patterns of reciprocity. In this respect the consumption of prestige items recalls the institution of potlatch, as well as similar practices in Big Man societies. Social status may have depended less on access to prestige items than on the capacity to discard them in quantity on public occasions (cf. Berthoud and Sabelli 1979).

Such a competitive approach to social relations is one consequence of the continuing pressures on agricultural land, since the renewal of political influence may have removed an élite from direct participation in food production. The reorganisation of the landscape in southern England may have been a way of rebuilding, or even maintaining, existing social relations through a period of recession. The extent to which we can talk of social change may be different between Wessex and the Thames Valley.

In fact both Britain and Bohemia show a similar outcome to these developments. In each case the distribution of fine metalwork was more clearly influenced by the distribution of good land, but these core areas were flanked by a considerable hinterland with evidence of intensive agriculture. In the Knoviz Culture there was a steady increase in the density of settlement and greater production of cattle, crops and textiles. It was only after these changes in the subsistence economy that much metalwork was consumed in burials. It is not clear whether this implies a change in social organisation or simply a changing attitude to wealth, but until a late stage of this sequence there is little evidence that these developments extended into the hinterland. When they did so, we find a wider distribution of hoards and the renewed growth of hill settlements. It is possible that by this time even the storage of grain was more carefully controlled.

In England, the sequence is equally revealing, with changes both in the main river valleys and in inland areas. As more items of weaponry were consumed, their detailed distribution appears to have changed from the best agricultural soils towards the river routes by which they first entered the system (Gardiner in Barrett and Bradley in press). And with these changes came corresponding adjustments in the hinterland, which must have introduced a range of other items into the sphere of exchange, including cattle and cattle products from the Wessex chalk and textiles from the surrounding areas. Again by the end of the period there is evidence for greater centralisation in inland areas, with a range of defended sites which may have controlled the movement of food, and have participated in regional exchange.

In both cases the same broad relationships can be seen in the archaeological evidence. In phases in which prestige trade took place within a fairly stable society there was no direct relationship between the distribution of material wealth and the most productive soils in the contemporary landscape. The élite may not have engaged directly in subsistence agriculture. But in periods when the social system was under strain the opposite relationship came to the fore and the distribution of prestigous artefacts was strongly influenced by the areas of more productive land. Thus there need be little relation between the material evidence of social complexity and the complexity of agricultural activity, and, far from symbolising a complex social scene, the reorganisation of subsistence farming described in this paper may have been an attempt to produce a sufficient surplus with which to engage more fully in the consumption of prestigous metalwork. That social groups felt any need to compete with one another reflects the continued instability of the agricultural regime. The major limiting factor still remained human ecology.

David Harris has recently provided an analogy for some of these arrangements (1979), and it is with his elegant case study that this paper will end. He describes an exchange system in the Torres Strait between Australia and New Guinea, an area which spans the whole range of economies from horticulture to hunting and gathering. On three small islands in the study area there was evidence for the development of horticulture, but there seemed to be no ecological reason why those islands, and only those islands, should undergo the change to sedentism. Instead Harris suggests that in these three cases the islanders were intensifying food production in order to participate in long distance trade. The evidence from Urnfield Europe suggests that a similar approach my be fruitful.

To return to my initial quotation. The archaeological record is full of apparent endings, and by the middle of the Bronze Age the soil of Europe was increasingly stale. It is tempting to make neat equations, but environmental determinism is always an easy option. I have tried to sketch a more complex pattern of change. Inevitably it runs a risk of over-elaboration.

References

Alexander, J., 1979. "Islam in Africa: the archaeological recognition of religion" in Space, Hierarchy and Society, eds. B. C. Burnham and J. Kingsbury. Oxford: B.A.R. Suppl. Ser. 59; 215-228.

Balkwill, C., 1976. "The evidence of cemeteries for later prehistoric development in the Upper Rhine Valley." P.P.S. 42: 187-214.

Barrett, J. and Bradley, R. (eds.), (in press). Settlement and Society in the British Later Bronze Age. Oxford: B.A.R.

Berthoud, G. and Sabelli, F., 1979. "Our obsolete production mentality: the heresy of the communal formation." Curr. Anth. 20: 745-760.

Boserup, E., 1965. The Conditions of Agricultural Growth. London: George Allen and Unwin.

Bouzek, J., 1969. "Zwei Hypothesen zu den Anfängen der Lausitzer Kultur" in Beiträge zur Lausitzer Kultur, ed. W. Coblenz. Berlin: Arbeits — Forschungsberichte zur Sächsischen Bodendenkmalpflege, Beiheft 7.

Bouzek, J., Koutecký, D. and Neustupný, E., 1966. The Knovíz Settlement of North-West Bohemia. Fontes Archaeologici Pragenses 10. Prague: National Museum.

Bradley, R., Lobb, S., Richards, J. and Robinson, M., (in press). "Two late bronze age settlements in the Kennet Valley." P. P. S. 46.

Coles, J. and Harding, A., 1979. The Bronze Age in Europe. London: Methuen.

Gimbutas, M., 1965. Bronze Age Cultures in Central and Eastern Europe. The Hague: Mouton.

Harris, D., 1979. "Foragers and farmers in the western Torres Strait islands: an historical analysis of economic, demographic and spatial differentiation" in Social and Ecological Systems, eds. P. Burham and R. Ellen. A. S. A. Monograph 18. London: Academic Press; 75-109.

Hawkes, C., 1972. "Europe and England: fact and fog." Helinium 12: 105-116.

Macfarlane, A., 1978. "Modes of reproduction." Man 13: 67-8.

Piggott, S., 1979. " 'The First Carts and Wagons': twenty five years later." Bull. Univ. London. Inst. Arch. 16: 3-17.

Schaeffer, F., 1928. "La question des variations du climat à l'Age du Bronze et du Fer." Bull. Arch. (1928-9): 451-458.

Sherratt, A., (in press). "Plough and pastoralism: aspects of the Secondary Products Revolution" in Pattern in the Past, eds. N. Hammond, G. Isaac and I. Hodder. Cambridge: Cambridge University Press.

18. ECONOMIC MODELS FOR BRONZE AGE SCANDINAVIA-TOWARDS AN INTEGRATED APPROACH

Kristian Kristiansen

1. Economic theory and archaeology

The application of a specific theory of economy creates two possible areas of theoretical debate. One is concerned with the nature of its underlying theoretical assumptions; this is the classical, but still alive " substantivist/ formalist" controversy, initiated by Karl Polanyi (e.g. 1971). Although these discussions are hardly reflected in archaeology, it is rather obvious that economic explanations based on systems theory/ecosystems theory to a wide extent reflect a " formalistic" approach (cf. in general Leclair and Schneider 1968, section 5). The second area of debate is concerned with the delineation of the economic sphere against other spheres in society — social, political etc. (in general Dalton 1971). This problem was most elegantly " solved" by the theoretical developments of structural-Marxism, represented in the works of Maurice Godelier, with the introduction of the concept of dominance — which, very simplified, means that economic relations may be embedded in kinship relations, political relations or even ideological relations (Godelier 1967: 111 ff.). Their specific combination defines the dominant relations of production (Godelier 1971, 1973:13-82, 1978; Friedman 1975). This elaborate approach has been given little attention in archaeology until quite recently (e.g. Friedman and Rowlands 1977). Normally a rather primitive separation into boxes, or subsystems, regulated by functional feedback mechanisms, has been employed. That goes not only for systems theory, but also for early neo-evolutionism and for vulgar materialism—although one should not forget that the scientific achievements of these approaches represented great improvements at their time.

Thus economic theory not only holds a large theoretical potential; the problems it raises are also crucial for understanding the dichotomy between the neopositivistic approach and the neo-Marxist approach in the study of society. On a more general level it should be stressed, however, that the development of an organized body of theoretical concepts, a formal system of theory — whether positivistic or Marxist — represents an important scientific achievement, as it creates a more unified theoretical basis for a scientific study of social and economic regularities. It also transcends the false contradictions between archaeological, historical and social sciences which have been rooted in their different source material. It should be added that one is only able to evaluate and discuss the possible place which the economy may occupy by applying a general theoretical framework, concerning societies in their structural and cultural totality, above the level of empirical analysis. Following from this, I regard economic theory both as an object of specific analysis and, at the same time, as inseparable from other aspects of society.

This is a warning against formalizing such terms and approaches as economic archaeology, social archaeology, behavioural archaeology etc. As an heuristic device, a strategy for solving certain types of questions, it may be fruitful — but as a formalized approach it tends to create barriers and distort the reality of its subject.

Having presented these more general aspects of economic theory I shall briefly explore some problems and possibilities arising from applying a Marxist economic perspective to archaeological analysis.

One crucial problem is concerned with the relationship between observed regularities in the archaeological record and their underlying structural properities. Here most explanations fail to transcend a purely empirical level, which reflects a widely held positivistic belief that there exists a testable, one-to-one relationship between empirical observations and the structural properties of prehistoric societies. However, a mode of production, or an economic system, is not constituted by the structure of the empirical evidence alone. It cannot simply be reconstructed through an intellectual process, using the formal system of theory as a helping tool. In the words of Lévi-Strauss, a structure represents a level of reality which is invisible but present behind the visible social relations.

Thus, in archaeology, the analytical and empirical gulf between separate levels of information — e.g. site catchment analyses in region x, distributional analyses of different commodities and the analysis of "princely graves" of the same region — has to be crossed by an explanatory bridge dependent on cultural and theoretical insights rather than on analytical and deductive techniques (despite multivariate analysis and other sophisticated techniques), in order to lead us towards an understanding of the structural reality — a system of social reproduction — that explains what happened between these levels. This may ultimately lead us to a determination of the dominant mode of production and a delineation of necessary and sufficient conditions of change, accounting for both intra- and intersystemic contradictions.

By this distinction between empirical reality and its hidden structural reality Marxism differs significantly from neopositivism and one can therefore expect that it will be vigorously rejected by most positivistic "law and order" archaeologists as unscientific. In my opinion, however, the combination of this distinction and the theoretical concepts of structural-Marxism holds a very great explanatory potential, far exceeding that of the systems theory-ecological approach. I shall not go into any debate on this or present an extentive description of the economic theory of structural-Marxism, but rather refer the reader to the original works of Godelier, Meillassoux, Friedman and others, which in later years have been extensively translated into English (e.g. Seddon 1978). Instead I will shortly discuss a few concepts of specific significance with respect to this article.

In the future much effort will probably be spent trying to establish the relations between local and supralocal levels of organization: what is the productive basis of wealth, who controls it and at what levels in the system. Local production is rarely autonomous, even in tribal societies. It is normally linked to a wider system of reproduction in various ways — exchange, trade, rent, tribute etc. Thus if we want to determine the relationship between local and supralocal levels of organization and production, then it is a necessary precondition that we are able to delineate the limits of the cultural systems within which these processes were operating. When only considering a local area, there is always a risk of overstressing the importance of the local level, and ignoring its place in a possible structural hierarchy of a wider area. One may also confuse a local or regional development with more general evolutionary change. The important question is: on what scale does evolution takes place? This leads me to stress the importance of looking for structural hierarchies and to consider the possibility that growth in one area and a simultaneous decline in another may be part of the reproduction of a single structure or a hierarchy of structures (Ekholm 1975, Friedman 1976).

Important when trying to determine the locus of evolutionary change is, then, the definition and the location of constraints, whose spatial and structural distribution may form a hierarchy of constraint, determining the limits and the potential of development within the larger system.

As a further help in distinguishing between local and supralocal levels of production and appropriation, the two concepts of expanded reproduction and accumulation should be mentioned. Expanded reproduction refers to growth which is internally derived, e.g. through intensified subsistence production or settlement expansion. Thus it represents an increase in scale, which can often be archaeologically detected when it is spatially expressed. Accumulation is the more general phenomenon, a surplus derived over and above the costs of reproduction. Accumulation may be derived from and correspond with expanded reproduction, or it may be derived through other means e.g. from outside through war, long distance trade etc. In the latter case it is derived from a larger system beyond its own productive basis, which means that it does not correspond with expanded reproduction. To establish the relationship between expanded reproduction and accumulation is an important task when trying to determine the relationship between local and supralocal levels of organization and their place within a larger system of social reproduction. This is often archaeologically possible when different types of accumulation are reflected in grave goods and hoards, whose distribution then may be related to their productive basis as reflected in the distribution of settlements and single finds. Thus the way in which wealth may concentrate in nodal points within a widely spaced settlement pattern is an important point of departure for discussing the relation between subsistence and appropriation of wealth, reflecting centres of political control and areas of production and exploitation. In more developed societies the geographical correspondence between expanded reproduction and accumulation is often small, and in less developed socities it may be greater.

From this point of departure I shall now explore a number of significant trends in the economic development of bronze age Scandinavia and present some generalizations concerning the relationship between subsistence production, exchange and the consumption of wealth within a tribal economy. But first a few words about the history of research.

2. A short history of research

Research on the Scandinavian Bronze Age has been dominated by two marked trends: specialized chronolgical investigations according to period and find group (graves/hoards), and religious interpretations favoured by the numerous rock carvings and other symbolic and ritual expressions in grave goods and hoards. Only in later years have settlement excavations and studies gained importance and attained their present dominant position.

This development is partly due to the richness and abundance of material. Thus the history of research has, on the one hand, been determined by the history of find accumulation. Fig. 18.1 shows that graves and hoards were the first classes of material to reach a representative level in the late 19th century; the peak period of their discovery centres round the years when the present chronological system was founded by Montelius (1885). The decreasing curve of hoards since the turn of the century suggests that this category of finds is now exhausted and, together with the grave finds, constitutes a representative sample (Kristiansen 1974 and forthcoming). Contrary to this, settlement finds only started to accumulate from the turn of the century (Fig. 18.2) and the present focus on settlement studies coincides with a steeply rising find curve. Thus settlement finds represent a growing but not yet representative sample (Thrane forthcoming). The analyses in this article will consequently be based on the evidence of burials and hoards.

On the other hand the history of research has also been linked to the theoretical and methodological development of Scandinavian archaeology (Klindt-Jensen 1975; Graslund 1974, 1976; Kristiansen forthcoming), dominated by a typological — chronological and culture-historical approach. The earliest research had been based on a comparison of associated and non-associated finds (e.g. stone axes and iron artefacts). This was the principle underlying the Three-Age System. Intermediate stages — finds combining e.g. stone axes and bronze artefacts, or bronze and iron — indicated the direction of development. With the growing interest in a finer chronological division, attention was increasingly focused on the gradual changes that could be observed in individual objects belonging to the same period. It was soon realized that such changes occurred fairly regularly, so that it was possible to establish whole " developmental series" of artefacts, which could be divided according to type. When these type series were compared with each other, in the context of closed finds, the main periods could now be subdivided with great accuracy. Formerly, divisions had primarily been based on differences. Now they were based on graduated similarity. This method had been developed in Sweden in the 1870's by H. Hildebrand and Oscar Montelius, who gave its methodologically most precise version under the name of " typology" (e.g. Montelius 1903). Thus by the end of the 19th century it had become possible to display type complexes forming consistent distributional patterns which were soon to be identified as cultures. From now on research took two directions which can essentially be linked to a Scandinavian and a continental tradition.

In Scandinavia chronological studies and the culture-historical reconstruction of past lifeways came to dominate. The latter is reflected in the appearance of the works of Müller (1898) and Montelius (1906) which represent the first major efforts to summarize the local prehistory of Denmark and Sweden. These books have had many successors, reflecting the consistency of this approach which is deeply imbedded in national ideology. That is also true of the continental direction, which, however, was strongly influenced by the thesis of Kossinna that cultural and ethnic distributions could be paralleled and studied through time and space, reflected in expansion, migrations or regressions of people (Eggers 1959: 210 ff.). This theoretical approach naturally favoured studies in cultural distributions, which for the Nordic Bronze Age were carried out very consistently by Ernst Sprockhoff in a number of important works. The basic approach was typological, but its focus was on spatial rather than chronological variations. The latter remained the main interest of Scandinavian archaeologists, following in the footsteps of Montelius, but in later years the focus was mainly on comparative studies of Nordic and European chronological systems and their interaction, as reflected in the distribution of imports (e.g. Thrane, 1975; Jensen 1965, 1966; Randsborg 1968, 1972. For a discussion see Kristiansen 1978a).

We may conclude, then, that until quite recently no convincing new interpretative and explanatory framework had been presented since the major efforts of research were carried out in the decades around the turn of the century. As there has existed no unifying theoretical framework since the abandonment of the Kossina approach after the Second World War, research has continued to reproduce itself within different spheres of specialization, but without any significant scientific progress in terms of explanation. Klejn very precisely characterized the archaeology of this epoch as " the sceptical tradition" (Klejn 1977: 3) — having lost the theoretical and explanatory foundations of its paradigm, but continuing its basic typological and chronological exercises.

Let us, however, for a moment return to the Kossinna/Sprockhoff interpretations, and present them in some detail, as they have not yet been replaced by new explanations. With that as a starting point I shall then in the following sections reconsider the evidence of the Nordic Bronze Age within the explanatory framework presented in the previous section.

When Kossinna in 1928 wrote his book " Ursprung und Verbreitung der Germanen in Vor- und Frühgeschichtlicher Zeit", the cultural distributions of the Nordic Bronze Age played a central role in his attempts to demonstrate the expansion of the Germans (Fig. 18.3). At the same time Jacob-Friesen concluded a critical analysis of the theoretical foundations of the Kossinna thesis with the following statement: " die Aufgabe der Fundgeographie auf etnischer Grundlage muss in der nächsten Zukunft die sein möglichst viele einzelne Formelkreise zu erschliessen, diese zu Kulturkreisen zu zusammenfassen und deren zeitliche Aufeinanderfolge zu ergründen" (Jacob-Friesen 1928: 145). This strategy was followed by Sprockhoff and his students in subsequent decades. In his early studies the geographical expansion of the Germans during the Bronze Age was clearly and convincingly demonstrated (Figs. 18.4a-d), and the general picture was further detailed by a number of studies showing regional groups or provinces in northern Germany (e.g. Sprockhoff 1937, 1941 and 1956) and southern Scandinavia (e.g. Oldeberg 1933, Baudou 1960, Jacob-Friesen 1967). They were generally interpreted as Germanic tribal groups, influenced in northern Germany by local groups during their expansion.

In the following I shall try to explain the very same cultural distributions from an economic point of view in terms of consumption, exchange and subsistence. I shall not go into much detail concerning the relations of production or the organization of exchange, but rather analyse the three variables on a regional level to see if spatial and temporal variations are predictable in terms of a systematic relationship between them. As a starting point I will briefly outline the level of social organization in bronze age Scandinavia according to our present state of knowledge.

3. Economic models for bronze age Scandinavia

The Nordic Bronze Age is subdivided into six periods spanning between c. 1800 B.C. and c. 500 B.C. In this article we are concerned with the periods II-VI, that is, the fully developed Bronze Age. This occupies the period from c. 1500 to c. 500 B.C., both according to calibrated 14C dates (mainly unpublished) and traditional archaeological dating.

The main evidence of the Nordic Bronze Age is derived from thousands of burials, often accompanied by personal objects in bronze and sometimes gold. To this are added several hundred hoards, mostly containing the same kind of prestigious objects as the graves. In the Early Bronze Age, inhumation burials below a mound, either in oak coffins or stone cists, predominates. In period III cremation is introduced and during the Late Bronze Age cremation graves in urns, deposited in the mounds of the Early Bronze Age, predominate. This shift in burial rites is accompanied by a reduction in grave goods, which now mainly consist of small personal objects, (pins, razors etc.) while prestigious objects are now mainly found in hoards, the frequency of which increases significantly. This is generally interpreted as an alternative way of depositing the traditional grave goods (Hundt 1955; in general Stjernquist 1962-1963).

Recent studies of the social structure of the Nordic Bronze Age have demonstrated unequal access to wealth, which can be systematically linked to variation in both population density and soil quality (Randsborg 1974). Randsborg interpreted the evidence as representing a chiefdom type of society, and certain symbols of rank, e.g. stools and staves, were suggested to represent chiefly status. Similar conclusions have been reached by other authors, based on hoards (Levy 1979) and local groups of burials (e.g. Strømberg 1974; Welinder 1977). Welinder also presented a model of the functioning of a chiefdom system (Welinder 1977; 151 ff.). It cannot be said, however, that this chiefdom model has been adequately tested or analysed, the method has rather been that of analogy to ethnography. We still need systematic studies of variations in burial equipment that are related to hypotheses about systems of rank and social groupings (e.g. Shennan 1975; for northern Germany see Bergmann 1968, Wüstemann 1978), just as we need systematic studies of the size of political units, means of political control, etc. (with respect to male equipment such studies are in preparation by the author). However, it is evident, from distribution maps of graves with full hilted swords for example (Ottenjahn 1969), that chiefdoms were numerous and small, probably forming competitive systems of shifting alliance networks between local chiefs, responsible for regional groups in the archaeological record. We should further expect to see the rise and fall of paramount chiefs, due to successful intra- and interregional manipulation of exchange and alliance politics. Such paramount chiefs, occupying extraordinary burial mounds and accompanied by rich grave goods, are known both in the Early Bronze Age (e.g. Kivik, Skallerup) and the Late Bronze Age (e.g. Voldtofte, Seddin).

We also need more systematic studies of economy and ecology. A regional analysis of the economy of the Bronze Age with an attempt to classify the different subsistence strategies has recently been presented by the author (Kristiansen 1978b, 1980), just as Welinder has presented an economic model of the Bronze Age in southern Sweden (1977). In these studies it was suggested that stock breeding was the basis of subsistence, within an open environment dominated by pasture, and with agriculture and fishing as supplementary activities depending on the location of settlements. It is to be hoped that some of the very extensive settlement excavations in the future will result in a much more detailed picture of settlement types and structures. The problems of bronze age settlements were already presented by Jensen in 1967, but only a few studies exceeding a purely empirical presentation have been published (e.g. Thrane 1971; Strømberg 1975; Hyenstrand 1968; Stjernquist 1969).

Finally, with respect to ritual and religion, the rich evidence from both rock carvings and bronzes offers an extraordinary opportunity to analyse the functioning of ritual and symbolic communication within a tribal society. A reorientation in the studies of rock carvings based on such perspectives has manifested itself in recent years (for a summary of research traditions and presentation of new approaches, see Nordbladh, 1974, 1978; also Kjellén and Hyenstrand 1977; Mandt-Larsen 1972).

The evidence suggests that symbolic and ritual complexity conforms with systems of rank and political-economic control, with regard to both prestige objects and rock carvings. In the case of rock carvings this is reflected in declining symbolic complexity with distance from settlement centres, just as regional centres of rock carvings coincide with settlement clusters and rich burials and hoards. When considering the whole range of ritual expression, including the extraordinarily valuable ritual eqipment such as lurs, bronze helmets, bronze shields, gold vessels etc., it can hardly be doubted that the bronze age societies of northern Europe are a classic example of a a theocratic chiefdom.

With this as minimal background information I shall now proceed with an analysis of the consumption of wealth with special reference to Denmark.

3.1 The consumption of wealth

Consumption, production and distribution are part of the economic reproduction of any society. In the following we shall deal more specifically with the consumption of wealth, which in bronze age Scandinavia was closely linked to the reproduction of rank and political control through the depostion of ornaments and weapons in graves and hoards according to sex, age and rank. This had two effects — one internal and one external. By removing scarce and prestigious goods from circulation their value could be regulated and controlled, just as the ritual framework of such consumption sustained religious order and ultimately political control.

As consumption necessitated replacement this would stimulate both local production and exchange. The reproduction of wealth was dependent on external supplies of raw materials from central Europe, whose procurement required the accumulation of a surplus over and above the necessary costs of reproduction, including such goods as wives and probably slaves.

Thus, the consumption of wealth — and we are here only dealing with one type of wealth, bronze and gold, and not such important wealth items as textiles which are normally not preserved, or land, stored in ten thousands of hectares of good surface soil in burial mounds — is embedded in the political control of production and exchange. As such the rate of wealth consumption would seem to be an important indicator of the economic dynamics of social systems in bronze age Denmark.

But as consumption is not necessarily a stable phenomenon, the concept of circulation time, reflecting the period of use, enters as a dynamic link between production and the time of consumption. In the following we shall deal with wealth consumption as reflected in numbers of prestige items deposited in graves and hoards and as reflected in the circulation time of prestige objects.

To obtain this information an examination of traces of wear was undertaken. The examination was restricted to full-hilted swords and decorated ornaments, and only pieces with their original surface intact were studied. This reduced the sample to a few hundred graves and hoards. From the Early Bronze Age both graves and hoards were included, from the Late Bronze Age only hoards — due to a change in burial customs.

The next step was the definition of a scale making it possible to compare the degree of wear on different ornaments and swords. The definition was composed of several associated elements, especially the relationship between horizontal and vertical intensity of wear. Only to a limited degree was this caused by polishing. Most of the wear on the ornaments was generated by the use of a covering garment of some kind (Kristiansen 1974, Fig. 16). A consistent scale, reflecting the period of use, could therefore be defined, ranging from " no wear", through " moderate wear" to " heavy wear". (Kristiansen 1977, Figs. 1-3). As for the swords, only the wear on the hilt was considered. This was caused by the clothes and the gown (Broholm and Hald 1940, Fig. 188), as well as by regular use, and a similar scale to that used for the ornaments was defined (Kristiansen 1977, Figs. 4-7).

In order to trace geographical variation in circulation time, Denmark was subdivided into five zones according to the number and the distribution of graves and hoards (Fig. 18.5). This was aimed at obtaining a fairly equal number of observations from every zone, together with a uniformity in the record. Bornholm was omitted because of too few observations, and the same goes for periods I and VI. Thus we may now proceed to analyse variations in circulation time with respect to time (periods II-V) and space (zones 1-5).

On Figs. 18.6-7 the distribution of wear on swords and daggers from periods II and III respectively has been recorded and quantified. (The analysis of the ornaments has not yet been completed). Several interesting observations can be made concerning regional development. In period II zones 1 and 5 stand out from the other zones, being dominated by unused bronzes, a feature that remains stable throughout period III, while a slight decline occurs in zone 5. Zones 3 and 4 have rather few unused bronzes in period II, while zone 2 mediates the difference between the southern and northern zones. In period III, however, the northern zones reveal a strange development. A remarkable increase of heavily worn bronzes occurs in zone 4, while an opposite development takes place in zone 3 (here the number of observations are very few, just as in zone 2, and the figures should be considered with caution). In general circulation time increases from period II to period III, which in all zones is marked by a statistically significant increase of heavily worn bronzes, a feature that is independent of the number of unused bronzes. And it should be added that among this group of heavily worn swords there occur pieces that are worn to a degree unknown in period II — the edges of the hilt being worn through (Kristiansen 1977, Figs. 9-10). This development reaches its peak in zone 4, thus defining it as a focus of divergence, which is confirmed by chi-square tests of zonal variations.

The marked regional and chronological differences in circulation time may indicate both fluctuations in external supplies, as well as regional differences in access to them. These variations also seriously affected the ability to conform to religious burial customs, which prescribed the deposition of personal wealth objects with the deceased. Thus the extremely worn swords of period III probably circulated for several generations by inheritance, and this may even apply to the whole group of heavily worn bronzes. These deviations from traditional practices reflect periods where the actual demand for keeping the weapons in circulation was stronger than burial customs — a fact that is illustrated by several examples, the best known being the young man's grave from Borum Eshøj, where a small dagger replaced the long sword in the wooden sheath (Boye 1896, Pl. 10). Such a situation could be a result of local imbalances in the exchange system, but it could also derive from a general supply crisis. As the increased number of heavily worn swords in period III is a phenomenon which characterizes all zones, it probably reflects a decrease in the supplies of bronze from central Europe. During period III, male graves with two double studs, indicating the presence of sword accesories (sheath and strap), but without the sword, are rather numerous, and thus support the evidence. If this interpretation is true we should expect an increased circulation time in period IV, reflecting the general reduction in bronze for consumption.

The general tendency of period IV, is, as predicted, a statistically significant decrease in the number of new bronzes (Fig. 18.8). This further supports the suggestion of a relation between the period of use and quantities of available bronze for consumption. The lower figures for heavily worn objects most probably reflect a stabilization in the supplies at a lower level than in the Early Bronze Age. The most remarkable feature on this figure, however, is the almost complete lack of bronze in zones 4 and 5, in spite of large numbers of graves (Fig. 18.1). We do find some sword graves, and a few graves and hoards with ornaments, but not enough to make up a reliable sample. And in period V those bronzes nearly disappear. Thus the increased circulation time of period III is seen to be followed by a general and increasing scarcity of bronze in these two zones.

In period V, (Fig. 18.9) the number of unused bronzes increases in zone 1. This development is connected to a decrease in heavily worn bronzes, but the latter is not statistically significant. An opposite development, however, takes place in zone 3, as the number of new bronzes is heavily reduced, indicating an increasing scarcity of bronze. Here chi-square tests of zonal variations indicate that zone 3 differs significantly from both zone 1 and zone 2. The general impression of bronze scarcity in the northern zones is further stressed by the use of bone as raw material for smaller implements throughout the Late Bronze Age (Fig. 18.10).

To sum up: it appears that there might exist an inverse relationship between circulation time and quantities of available bronze for consumption. According to this a sudden and marked decrease in the supplies of bronze took place during period III. This is also stressed by the fact mentioned earlier, that in all zones some of the heavily worn swords are extremely worn, reflecting a period of unexpected length when supplies of bronze were small — too small to replace the big, bronze-demanding swords. In the Late Bronze Age supplies of bronze were in general smaller, but they increased again towards the very end of the period (Late HaB and HaC), before finally ceasing during the HaD/Early La Tene phase, when nearly all known ornaments (neck rings) are extremely heavily worn.

More indirectly the high level of consumption in periods II and V is reflected in the fact that local and regional groups or workshops can be easily established by series of rather similar objects, whereas the evidence for such workshops is more scattered and less homogeneous in the intervening periods.

These general variations in consumption and circulation time were further connected to a geographical shift in consumption from western to eastern Denmark. In order to throw more light on this geographical development we will now focus our attention on the distribution of foreign imports from periods II-V, as it is assumed that this reflects the channels through which bronze flowed into Denmark, just as it points to its origin.

3.2 Trade and exchange networks

I shall not in the following deal with the organization — or the mode — of exchange, but rather give a descriptive account of the distribution of foreign imports in northern Europe. In Scandinavia, we are met with the problem that no complete analysis of foreign imports in the Early Bronze Age exists, where as the imports of the Late Bronze Age have been given a full treatment by Thrane (Thrane 1975). Thus it is not possible at present to do a statistical analysis of the relation between imports and consumption. Instead we will have to rely on impressionistic interpretations.

Throughout the Bronze Age southern Scandinavia maintained exchange, to various degrees, with both western and eastern Europe. In the following, however, we are dealing with the dominant exchange systems. Only during period I was Scandinavia supplied through both west European and south-east European exchange networks (Fig. 18.11-12). This situation changed at the transition to the fully developed Nordic Bronze Age with the collapse of the south-east European supply system and the extension of the south German Tumulus Culture.

The distribution of imports in period II reveals a western concentration, although some items, such as octagonal swords, were also distributed in eastern Denmark (Sprockhoff 1941:59); other objects have an exclusively western distribution (Randsborg 1968, Figs. 12, 14-15, 20). The majority of the imports are of west European origin, coming from the south German Tumulus Culture. From the distribution of octagonal swords (Fig. 18.13) it is seen that the first area of consumption was the mouth of the Elbe and Schleswig-Holstein, the area south of zone 5, which formed the southernmost part of the south Scandinavian exchange system. This distribution may indicate that Schleswig-Holstein now controlled bronze distribution to the rest of Scandinavia—to the western part in close co-operation with zone 5 and to the eastern part together with zone 1. Gold, which shows a predominantly western distribution, was probably also of west European origin according to Hartmann (Hartmann 1970:32ff.). This observation would further support the idea of a trade system between south-west Europe and Schleswig-Holstein along the Weser river system (Fig. 18.14), with Lüneburg as an important mediator (Sprockhoff 1940, Figs. 1-3; Kersten 1952: 20 ff., Figs. 9-10; Piesker 1958, Tables 67-72; Sprockhoff 1961, Fig. 2; Laux 1971). The position of western Denmark as a prime area of influence is also stressed by the distribution of locally produced flange-hilted swords of central-European —"Aegean" origin, especially Sprockhoff's type Ib, (Sprockhoff 1931, Tables 26-27; Randsborg 1967: 24; also Schauer 1971: 111 ff., 129 ff., Tables 117B, 118).

In period III western Denmark was still strongly connected to supplies of gold and bronze from south-west Europe (Broholm 1944, Fig. 65; Randsborg 1968: 6-62; 1972 Map 2). But an exchange network, closely connected to the Scandinavian system, seems gradually to have developed along the Oder-Elbe river systems (Fig. 18.15). This network broke the monopoly of Lüneburg and Schleswig-Holstein, and had Mecklenburg as a new recipient area of foreign imports (Sprockhoff 1931, Table 28; Aner 1958; Ottenjahn 1969, Map 2; Schubart 1972). This new situation is reflected in the distribution, for example, of beaten cups (Thrane 1962, Fig. 30) and Peschiera daggers (Randsborg 1970). Although a certain geographical development in the trade routes can be observed from period II to period III, western Denmark remained the prime area of influence, a development which is also reflected in stylistic innovations (Randsborg 1968). The distribution of imports thus seems to support the proposition that variations in consumption and circulation time are related to control over foreign trade. The more precise nature of this relationship is left to be explored by future studies of the internal exchange system — a task that exceeds the scope of this paper.

In period IV zones 1 and 2 established new contacts with eastern Europe. A primary contact area seems to have existed between the mouth of the Oder and zone 1 (Fig. 18.16) (Thrane 1975, Figs. 46 and 49)—and, as can be seen from the distribution of east Scandinavian types in the Oder Area, contacts were commercially reciprocal (Fig. 18.17) (Sprockhoff 1937, Map 7, 1956 Map 24; Baudou 1960, Maps 17 and 47). From here a chain of exchange networks extending beyond the Carpathians brought hammered bronze vessels back north (Fig. 18.18). The presence of gold, which now shows a predominantly east Danish distribution, also seems to have been a result of these new exchange networks, as its origin most probably was in south-east Europe, according to Hartmann (1970: 38ff., Fig. 3). Western Denmark continued its contacts with south-west Europe, through nodal points of exchange at the middle Elbe, the lower Elbe and Mecklenburg. From here exchange was established with zones 2 (the western part) and 3, while zones 4 and 5 were in a more neglected position. This pattern of exchange is indicated by the distribution of, for example, winged axes (Fig. 18.19) And beaten cups (Thrane 1975, Figs. 55 and 81), and by the adoption of west Danish brooches along the Elbe and in Mecklenburg (Sprockhoff 1937, Maps 15, 16, 35). Thus a western and an eastern exchange network seems to have existed at the same time in period IV, probably reflecting a dual development (Baudou 1960, Map 56). South-eastern Europe supplied hammered bronzes and gold, whereas south-western Europe supplied raw material, e.g. winged axes.

Period V reveals a changed picture. By now west European imports had become totally dominant, but the primary market was east Denmark and Sweden, as can be seen from the distribution of, for example, spearheads, swords and horse gear (Figs. 18.20-21)(Thrane 1975, Figs. 30, 74 and 119-120). The Middle Elbe was still an important transit area while Mecklenburg and the area east of the river Oder were in a position to control the distribution to the rest of Scandinavia. From here there was only a short distance to Zealand and Fyn, zones 1 and 2, where most imports accumulated (Thrane 1975, Fig. 132), and which also displayed the highest consumption and the lowest circulation time. Hammered bronze vessels from the Carpathians still found their way to Scandinavia in small numbers (Thrane 1979).

Also in the Late Bronze Age a close relationship between the distribution of foreign imports, local consumption and circulation time can be demonstrated. A dual situation existed during period IV, reflecting the growing regional contradictions between east and west Denmark which had already begun in period III. The final result of this can be seen in period V with the absolute dominance of zones 1 and 2. This shift is very clearly demonstrated by the distribution of gold in periods III and IV-V respectively (Broholm 1944, Fig. 65; Jensen 1966, Map 4). In order to see if this is reflected by a parallel shift in the consumption of bronze, the relationship between gold and bronze — represented by swords — was analyzed (Fig. 18.22). This demonstrates a close connection between consumption of bronze and gold and it further demonstrates that with respect to consumption there existed an even balance between eastern and western zones during the Early Bronze Age. This balance, however, is disturbed in the Late Bronze Age, as the eastern zones become absolutely dominant, and the difference between the zones increases correspondingly.

The question now arises whether this regional development can be explained exclusively in terms of a shift in foreign trade relations or whether local economic changes played a decisive role. Thus in order to evaluate the relationship between external and internal factors it is necessary first to analyse variations in local economic conditions of reproduction.

3.3 Economic conditions of reproduction

We will start by considering subsistence strategies, as these are thought ro reflect important aspects of the economy.

Strategy implies choice — in our case, choice between a range of soil qualities. Thus it is necessary to consider not only the settled areas, but also the unsettled areas. What is the relationship? In order to determine this the range of soil quality was calculated for each zone, using the average of the ten best and the ten poorest districts (area about 10-15 times larger than a parish). The result is seen on Fig. 18. 23 as squares of different sizes. Within each square the average soil quality of the whole zone is indicated by a cross on the middle line, showing the gradual decline in productive potential (PP) from zone 1 to zone 5. It is seen that in most cases soil of average or of less than average PP was preferred. This is the case in zones 2 and 3, where the more productive areas remained unsettled. Zone 1 lies very close to the average but zone 4 differs radically from this pattern. Here the very best soil was exploited on an extended scale from the Early to the Late Bronze Age. Zone 5 also differs from the general pattern, as it reveals a significant change in strategy from light (low PP) to more heavy soil of higher PP. In all zones period III is characterized by a preference for better soil quality. We are left, however, with a general impression of remarkable consistency in subsistence strategy characterized by small oscillations, probably reflecting local shiftings. Settlement clusters typically occur where several ecological zones/soil types could be reached from the same locality, e.g. hilly moraine and flat sandy soils.

It is not possible at present to relate this evidence to regional variations in subsistence, based on settlements, in any significant way. Our knowledge is of a most general kind, only indicating that people of the Bronze Age practised farming, including stock breeding and grain cultivation (Helbaek 1954; Jensen 1967). But it is known that areas in western Jutland (zone 5) were dominated by hard grass open commons, indicating stock breeding (Iversen 1973: 99). This would also be in good accordance with the preference for light soil in most zones, which was less densely forested and easier to transform into grassland — a process that, according to pollen analyses, accelerated in Jutland from the first appearance of the Single Grave Culture (around 2,800 B. C. in calibrated C14 years) and in eastern Denmark and southern Sweden from the beginning of the Late Neolithic or the "Dagger Period", (around 2,400 BC in calibrated C14 years). Thus it is obvious that zone 5, the poorest area in terms of PP (— in the Early Bronze Age the richest in terms of consumption —) did not owe this richness exclusively to agriculture. Stock breeding, perhaps combined with textile manufacturing, is the more probable economic basis. Apparently another economy, dependent on a more intensive soil cultivation, was practised in zone 4. It remains a remarkable feature how intensively this zone was exploited. Also the sudden change in zone 5 towards a more intensified agricultural practice should be noticed.

The general preference for light soils accords well with the proposition that stock breeding was a dominant feature in the subsistence economy (in general Higham 1967 and Fleming 1972). This promoted a preference for the open forest vegetation on the light soils, which could easily be transformed into grassland. But how do we explain the general trend in subsistence and the deviations from this pattern?

With respect to zone 4 it has been demonstrated that the settlement pattern changes significantly from period II to period III (Fig. 18.24), a shift that coincides with a remarkable increase of wealth. This wealth, however, was never fully replaced, which is indicated by the extremely prolonged circulation time of the bronzes. And from period IV to V consumption decreases to a minimum — while at the same time the exploitation of the very best soil increases, apparently as a response to an economic crisis triggered off by over-population and settlement concentration.

In zone 5 the change in subsistence strategy can be linked to a retreat from the more sandy soils of northern and western Jutland. These areas had been "colonized" by the Beaker, or the Single Grave Culture. We have ample evidence showing that already during this period a transformation from productive grassland to less productive heathland took place — a development that accelerated during the Early Bronze Age, when a recolonization of heath was undertaken in some cases (Iversen 1939). Thus over-exploitation was followed by ecological degradation, which on the sandy soils in Jutland had far more serious consequences than on the heavier soils of eastern Denmark, with its higher PP.

The local migrations from the sandy areas to the more heavy glacial soils are demonstrated on the distribution maps (Figs. 18.25-26). But they further demonstrate that settlement concentration now took place in all parts of Jutland from the Early to the Late Bronze Age. These settlement concentrations, which originally might have been triggered off by fights over land or by fights for bronze, due to the reduced supplies, seriously affected the ecology (e.g. Averdiéck and Münnich 1957: 154), placing greater strain on the soil, just as it lowered the output per head. And as the PP of the settled areas in Jutland generally was low, the consequences were disastrous in the long run.

At the same time, however, eastern Scandinavia witnesses a conspicuous settlement expansion (Steenberger 1964, Figs. 80 and 93), often into marginal areas as on Bornholm (Fig. 18.27) and in Southern Sweden (Welinder 1978).

Thus the retreat from marginal soils followed by settlement concentration in western Scandinavia occurs simultaneously with a settlement expansion into marginal lands in eastern Scandinavia. If we link this to the evidence of the previous sections a coherent picture emerges, which I shall try to summarize and explain briefly.

3.4 Economic dynamics: regressions and expansions

In the Early Bronze Age zones 4 and 5 experienced a remarkable — short-lived — economic growth, resulting in ecological over exploitation and displayed in extensive and impressive consumption. This development seems to have been accompanied by political and commercial expansion, linking South western Norway and Northwestern Germany into an extensive system of exchange. Indeed, the emergence of a centralised system may have been imminent. However, this development was blocked, first of all by the constraints imposed by ecology, but perhaps also by political and military counteraction from the other zones. As this is paralleled in decreasing consumption of bronze and increasing isolation I am inclined to believe that local economic development was crucial for establishing those exchange networks through which bronze flowed. When expansion and economic growth was blocked by the constraints of the system the exchange network fell apart and the flow of bronze declined proportionally. This again triggered off settlement concentration, imposing new constraints on the system and creating a chain of negative feed-back effects.

Against this background the economic development in zones 1 and 2 in the Late Bronze Age becomes easier to understand. Their leading position was apparently not a result of political and economic competition — not in the first place anyway. But the economic decline of zones 4 and 5 put them in an advantageous position. Due to their higher PP these zones were able to maintain a stable economy without any significant changes throughout the Late Bronze Age. In general the Late Bronze Age was a period of economic expansion and consumption in Sweden and the Baltic (Figs. 18. 4a-d), especially period V, and exchange networks were established connecting middle and eastern Sweden with northern Germany and zones 1 and 2. This expansion is reflected in extensive forest clearings and intensified agricultural activities, as demonstrated in pollen diagrams (Figs. 18. 28 and 18. 29 and Berglund 1969 with references). Again the close connection between expanded local production and commercial expansion, linking the local area to a bigger system of exchange and channeling the flow of goods and people, is demonstrated.

Thus the economic decline in western Scandinavia was counterbalanced by an economic expansion in eastern Scandinavia. Only zones 1 and 2, and southern Sweden, were able to maintain their position throughout the period, partly due to their central position, but especially due to their high productive potential. The economic development of the Nordic Bronze Age was thus centered around a western axis in the Early Bronze Age and an eastern axis in the Late Bronze Age. When viewed in this perspective we may regard the local economic declines and rises as part of the reproduction of the larger Scandinavian system. The productivity of the total system probably remained stable throughout the whole period in question, but differing areas were exploited and exhausted during the reproductive process responsible for the regional expansions and regressions. Thus the well-known distribution maps (Figs. 18. 4a-d), showing a gradual eastward expansion of "die nordische Kreis" from Period II to V, are not simply cultural or ethnic phenomana, but the outcome of specific economic processes which I have briefly tried to outline.

4. Conclusion and perspectives: towards an integrated approach

It appears that there exists an inverse relationship between circulation time and quantities of bronze for consumption. Short circulation time and abundant supplies of bronze occur with political and commercial expansion, whereas increasing circulation time and decreasing supplies of bronze occur with political and commercial contraction. These processes seem to be heavily influenced by variations in local economic conditions of reproduction, a characteristic feature of what Rowlands has termed "subsistence-based exchange" (Rowlands 1973). This implies that although both the subsistence economy and the overall settlement pattern of the Nordic Bronze Age remained stable, consumption and exchange correlated with and depended on the potential for expanded reproduction on a local and regional level. It is further suggested that these processes were operating within the framework of a tribal structure that generated local and regional expansions and regressions as an inherent feature of its social and political reproduction. Thus economic conditions determined processes of political/commercial expansion and increased accumulation only to the extent that they imposed a hierarchy of constraints on the functioning of the social system, which is essentially a negative determination, as it defines limits or barriers to development. Consequently if we want to explain the economic dynamics of the Nordic Bronze Age it is necessary to focus attention on the functioning of the political systems, that is the mode of exchange and the possible ways it was imbedded in and correlated with systems of rank and political control. This is beyond the scope of this paper, but a few points for future research will be suggested.

4.1 Expansion and exchange.

It is of crucial importance to distinguish between different types of expansion and their relation to exchange systems, both internal and external. (For a good general discussion of traditional concepts of trade, see Stjernqvist 1967).

There appears to have existed a cultural/political frontier or buffer zone between the Nordic culture and other culture groups (Fig. 18.30) throughout the Bronze Age. Explanations of how this buffer zone was crossed and how it was gradually extended is crucial for understanding both the nature of long-distance exchange networks and the nature of political expansion during the Bronze Age. (Also von Brunn 1954, Maps 1-4). As an heuristic device three different, but overlapping types of "exchange" or "expansion" may be suggested:

A. Exchange of people as part of political alliances. Wives, possibly slaves.

B. Exchange of goods either as part of social/political alliances (gifts) or through barter (metal trade).

C. Actual settlement expansion.

A. I would argue that the exchange of people is evidenced throughout the Bronze Age when a foreign outfit of clothing occurs isolated in a local context. This is clearly the case of the Lüneburger woman buried on Zealand in the Early Bronze Age with her complete outfit worn according to Lüneburger tradition (Aner and Kersten 1971-9, no. 1269A) or Nordic female outfits or ornaments in burials in Northern Germany e.g. in Pomerania (Kersten 1958, Eggers 1936) or south of the Elbe (von Brunn 1954). The same is true of many hoards with Nordic ornaments whose distribution extends beyond the Nordic area during the Late Bronze Age (Fig. 18.31). Very often, however, the evidence is less clear and requires careful examination of the objects. Thus it is a regular phenomenon that a single or a few Nordic ornaments occur in a local context in northern Europe, where an examination of wear, however, reveals that the Nordic ornament is often an old worn piece. Apparently the original outfit has been gradually replaced with new local types.

Thus, it is a characteristic feature of the Late Bronze Age that Nordic ornaments are found in local neighbouring cultural groups in northern Europe, often in contexts indicating an exchange of people rather than goods alone (most clearly in burials, but also in hoards when the ornaments show characteristic wear patterns from traditional use). The reverse situation, the occurrence of north European female outfits in Scandinavia, is more rare, with the above mentioned Lüneburger burial as a clear-cut, but rather exceptional case, just as the Mandemark hoard is in the Late Bronze Age (Aner and Kersten 1971-9, no. 1338). This is much more common in the border areas in northern Germany. In general it seems that the distribution of Nordic female ornaments extends further south of the Nordic culture than does male equipment, which is more closely linked to the core areas, but which also reveals a clear expansion during the Late Bronze Age, especially to the east. With respect to male equipment foreign objects in Scandinavia are less rare. It should be remembered, however, that good weapons are an object of trade or gift exchange and thus would tend to be more widely spread (e.g. octagonal swords during the Early Bronze Age or Möringen swords during the Late Bronze Age, see below). Thus the contact zone in northern Germany between Nordic and European elements offers an extraordinary opportunity to analyse in great detail the movements of goods and people during the Bronze Age, making possible an estimation of the balance of exchange — who gives and who receives, what is given and what is received.

B. The analysis and interpretation of exchange of goods is a complicated matter with many overlapping variations from gifts to trade in metal, (Rowlands 1971). Trade in metal supplies is testified by a rather small group of hoards, hardly representative, as most such hoards naturally were removed again (contrary to religious hoarding of personal objects). But when viewed against the composition of local religious hoards, burials and single finds one may be able to reconstruct the complicated processes of metal trade and distribution. A few hoards in Scandinavia comprise assemblages whose composition resembles that which is prevalent in their area of origin — indicating perhaps that they constitute "fresh supplies", unchanged by local redistribution. This is sometimes the case for hammered cups from south-east Europe and winged axes, showing that supplies of objects and metal were sometimes traded without much change in assemblage composition from several areas in central Europe to northern Germany. From here they were often added with local types and shipped to Scandinavia, where they were either remelted or locally distributed in smaller portions — now often mixed up with local Scandinavian types. But North German types were also directly traded to southern Scandinavia, especially during the Late Bronze Age (Thrane 1975, Figs. 131-132) when this area benefited much more directly than in the Early Bronze Age from its position as a middleman between central Europe and Scandinavia, reflected in an increased accumulation of central European imports (e.g. Sprockhoff 1950-51).

The evidence thus suggests that long-distance exchange for supplying metal was channeled through interlocking local exchange networks in a combination of barter and political alliances, organized as trading expeditions along rivers and from here to southern Scandinavia. This is reflected in the changing composition of hoards within different regions — in central Europe, e.g. as analysed by Kytlicova (1967) and von Brunn (1968) and in northern Europe by Thrane (1975). From central to northern Europe a gradual reduction of objects and metal weight in the hoards can be demonstrated. Such trading expeditions were organized from both southern Scandinavia and northern Germany, and as a result selected local types of more personal character (not for remelting) were exchanged and circulated at home. That is clearly the case when, for instance, a single knife of Oder type occurs in several graves on Zealand (Fig. 18.16) and when knives of a Zealand type likewise occur in the Oder area (Fig. 18.17). Between these two areas trading expeditions and political alliances were established during period IV, and a comparison between Fig. 18.16 and 18 gives an idea of the local networks through which beaten cups passed from the Carpathians to Scandinavia.

Along important communication lines, and in central places, chiefdoms arose, basing their wealth on trade. This is very neatly demonstrated in Fig. 18.32, where the Scandinavian chiefly symbols reflect such centres situated at regular intervals along the Elbe, most of them known for extraordinary burials of "paramount chiefs" during period V.

Thus renewed quantitative and qualitative studies of type distributions and find compositions based on the published evidence hold considerable explanatory potential when related to theories about exchange networks and political influence areas which focus on both intra- and interregional dynamics and constraints (cf. recent approaches in Green, Haselgrove, and Spriggs 1978; Burnham and Kingsbury 1979; Hodder 1978).

C. With respect to actual settlement expansion we should distinguish between primary expansion into formerly unsettled or very scarcely settled areas, and secondary expansion into settled areas. The first type is documented in Sweden, according to both pollen diagrams (Fig. 18.29) and distribution maps (Figs. 18.4a–d). In northern Europe the question about an actual Nordic settlement expansion is very difficult to answer in our present state of knowledge, as we have to deal with the second type of expansion. Thus in order to distinguish actual expansion from exchange of people and goods (A and B above) it is necessary to carry out a complete analysis of burials, hoards and settlements in order to define the socially and culturally diagnostic features, as was done by Eggers in Fig. 18.30 or von Brunn 1954).

This remains to be done in most areas (see Horst 1978 for a recent review). In the area around the mouth of the Oder it seems that we have evidence of an actual Nordic settlement, as the basic cultural features in burial rites etc. are present, just as are both male and female burials (e.g. Schulz 1972). In most other areas east or south of the Oder it seems that Nordic elements are mixed with local elements to various degrees. Also, south of the Elbe, Nordic expansion should rather be explained in terms of A and B, at least in some areas. Thus it should be stressed that only very detailed typological studies will make it possible to establish the provenance of both Nordic and other objects, as a wide range of local imitations occur. Such studies are necessary if we want to distinguish between the various types of exchange (A-C) and various degrees of acculturation.

When trying to evaluate the relationship between our three types of exchange/expansion (A-C) and explain their functioning within the political structure of the Nordic Bronze Age, the following model may be suggested: The political system of the Nordic Bronze Age was extremely competitive and expansive in nature. Thus competition for rank was dependent on success in creating alliances and partnerships. Such alliance systems could comprise rather large areas linking local chiefs together in a chain of obligations and making sure that supplies of bronze from successful expeditions were distributed according to their place within the alliance system. The basis of succesful participation in these networks was the ability to produce a surplus of exchange goods and this position was then sustained by the display of prestige goods of bronze. Central to the creation of alliances was, apparently, ritual and feasting, as evidenced by ritual gear, rock carvings, imported bronze vessels, golden drinking cups etc. What circulated within such alliance systems was basically women and bronze.

Thus the expansion of the Nordic Bronze Age to a large extent reflects the creation of political alliances, through intermarriage, as a basis for exchange of bronze and probably also other, now vanished, commodities (e.g. textiles, amber). As an extension of such alliances certain areas would gradually become overtaken by Nordic influence, through repeated influxes of Nordic women, regular contacts with trading partners, kinship obligations and other means of acculturation, which then might be followed by an actual migration of Nordic settlers. The extremely competitive nature of the system is reflected in the changing exchange networks and, more concretely, by the dominant role played by weapons in male equipment. Most of these, especially flange hilted swords, have heavy traces of actual use in fighting and resharpening. A society with too few women might tend to create groups of young unmarried warriors seeking prestige and wealth for later marriage through fighting expeditions.

Such social and economic dynamics would tend to stimulate subsistence production and local expansion, eventually beyond its ecological barriers, as suggested in the previous sections. In this way the economy is determining the social system, but the latter dominates systems of production and exchange, and thus explains the dynamics of the system.

4.2 The supply of metal: Scandinavia — Central Europe — the Mediterranean

Another, perhaps equally important factor, was the quantity of bronze supplied northwards, and the maintenance of stable exchange networks —that is, stable political systems — through which the bronze could flow from central Europe to Scandinavia. Changes in either the production of copper and tin in central Europe, or a temporary rupture of the lines of exchange, could seriously affect the balance of the Scandinavian system by raising the exchange value of bronze and creating a situation of supply scarcity. This would in turn place a harder pressure on local subsistence production and, if this did not suffice in the long run, bronze would probably kept in circulation for longer periods, i. e. consumption would be slowed down. This could threaten the stability of alliance networks, with increased warfare as a result. In such a situation adventurous chiefs would seek new trading partners, especially if the European exchange networks were unstable as well, and new lines of exchange might develop.

But in general one would expect that short local crises in the exchange networks would come and go, and not make themselves significantly felt in the archaeological record. However, a chain reaction of local crises, or a general supply crisis whatever its origin, would surely have an impact. I shall therefore in the following very briefly consider consumption and circulation time in Scandinavia from a European perspective to see how this fits the evidence, and to see if it eventually might add to a fuller explanation of the observed fluctuations (Figs. 18.6-9).

But first a short note about the absolute quantities of bronze supplied northwards.

It can be estimated with some certainty (Kristiansen forthcoming) that the minimal annual supply of bronze needed for reproducing burial and hoard consumption was rather small. On Zealand the figure is 40-50 kg, corresponding to a circulating stock of bronze of approximately 1200-1500 kg. For Denmark as a whole we may multiply these figures four or five times. Compared to the weight of hoards containing either scrap bronze or imports, normally amounting to one or a few kg during the Late Bronze Age, these figures seem realistic, and they accord well with the model of exchange presented above. They point up the difference between central and northern Europe, not to mention the Aegean/Mediterranean area (the most impressive and heaviest hoards in Scandinavia are found during periods I and II). They further indicate that the critical stage in the application of bronze technology to areas without copper and tin was in the building up of a stock of bronze. When a balance had been reached between production and consumption it could be maintained by rather small annual supplies.

During period I bronze reached southern Scandinavia in quantities large enough to create a basis for local production on a small scale, mostly primitive local imitations of imports. During this period a stock of bronze was built up, though not yet enough for burial consumption. The main influx came from south-eastern Europe — the Siebenburgen area (Fig. 18.11) and in Jutland from the south German Tumulus Culture (Fig. 18.12) A comibination of these influences was the background for the development of the original Nordic style at the transition between periods I and II (Lomborg 1969), probably around 1500 B. C. The stock of bronze now reached a level that allowed burial consumption and the production of a wide range of objects, including female ornaments. Bronze was now so common that a local tradition of metalwork on a high technical level could be developed and maintained.

During period II the influx of bronze reached a climax, passing through the exchange networks of the Late Tumulus Culture (Figs. 18.13-14). It seems clear that the transition from period I to period II marks a significant change, both in the supply of bronze and in European exchange networks. This change corresponds to the florescence of the Tumulus Culture and a temporary decline of Mycenean influences in south-eastern Europe (Vladar 1973). At this time the Tumulus Culture reached its maximum expansion, linking wide areas in central and western Europe and channeling influences between the Aegean/Mediterranean area and northern Europe. Now, too, was the florescence of the Late Mycenean Culture, and although the cultural interrelations between this area and western Europe are still badly understood, it seems clear that a prosperous time of stable political systems in both these areas was a main factor behind the development of the Nordic period II with its strange and strong signs of Mycenaean/Mediterranean influences (e.g. Randsborg 1967 with references, also Bouzek 1978, Harding 1975, Snodgrass 1975) — influences which extended even to Anatolia (Bouzek 1972). Thus the time 1500 to 1200 B. C. represents a period of acculturation and integration in European prehistory. In its final stage, corresponding to the early Montelius III/Br. D, the relations between central Europe and the Aegean area reach a climax. This is reflected, for instance, in the occurrence of central European swords in the Aegean, and the earliest body armour in central European chiefly burials (Snodgrass 1971, Sandars 1971). Immediately afterwards follows the disintegration of the Mycenaean Culture and the expansion of the Urnfield Cultures in Europe (HaA onwards).

It can hardly be doubted that the development of the Urnfield Cultures reflects significant changes both in settlement structure and in the political systems of bronze age Europe (in general Ginbutas 1965, Coles and Harding 1979), although the interpretation of the evidence is as much disputed today as 50 years ago. It seems clear, however, that a stronger social differentation develops and certain areas become very densely setted (Bouzek et al., 1966). During the early part of period III bronze is still flowing into Scandinavia from southern Germany/Bohemia, now following the Elbe route with Mecklenburg in a central position (Fig. 18.15). But from Ha A1 onwards the European exchange systems seem to change more drastically, and the flow of imports to northern Europe ceases. This also corresponds with the expansion of the Lausitz Cultures and a rising hoard frequency throughout Europe (in general von Brunn 1960 and 1968), often interpreted as reflecting an increased bronze production, most significant in south-eastern Europe (e.g. Rusu 1976). In the Lausitz Culture hoards with scrap bronze are common, perhaps indicating remelting due to bronze scarcity.

Thus it seems in good accordance with the European evidence that at sometime during period III the importation of bronze to northern Europe ceased, due to the changes in settlement structure, political systems and exchange systems that followed the expansion of the Urnfield and the Lausitz Cultures (Br. D/Ha A1).

From HaB1 onwards more stable relations between central and northern Europe developed, corresponding to a new climax of bronze production in south-eastern Europe (Fig. 18.18) and the Danube region (Kytlicova 1967, Rusu 1963). From HaB2 onwards, however, relations between Italy, south-western Europe and northern Europe intensified significantly, (in general Müller-Karpe 1959, 1961) while the eastern connections ceased. This is reflected in the spread of Pfahlbau bronzes to northern Europe, just as western Europe experiences a flourishing of bronze production and consumption — the so-called Carps-tongue Complex — which extends further in time into HaC (Savory 1949; Briard 1965; Jacob-Friesen 1968). This abundance of bronze in western Europe is paralleled in eastern Europe by a marked decline in bronze production, due to the spread of iron technology (Furmanek 1973) and perhaps also to the expansion of pre-Scythian elements (Gallus and Horvarth 1939; Podborský 1970).

Thus it appears that the expansion of bronze production and consumption in northern Europe during late period V and period VI accords well with the overflow of bronze in western Europe during that same period. (It should be noted that the decrease in circulation time and the expansion of bronze production in Scandinavia is most significantly related to the late classical period V, which in my opinion extends into Ha C).

When viewed against the European background the evidence presented in the previous sections gains a further perspective. It is seen that the two peak periods with respect to metalwork and consumption in Scandinavia — period II and late V/early VI — correspond to periods of stable political systems and long-distance exchange networks in Europe. These are also periods when relations with the Mediterranean/Mycenean area were strong, suggesting that the interaction between the Mediterranean and Europe stimulated the maintenance of stable far-reaching exchange networks. The explanation of the nature of these interregional dynamics is an important task for future research (e.g. Rowlands in press).

At present it cannot be determined whether the changes accompanying the Urnfield/Lausitz Cultures were mainly due to a chain reaction of local changes in settlement structure, economy and climate (e.g. Jäger and Lozek 1978; Bouzek, Jäger and Lozek 1976) or should also be related to the events in the Mediterranean (a recent summary in Sandars 1978; cf. Crossland and Birchall 1973; 169ff.). The evidence seems to some extent contradictory; at a time when areas in central Europe apparently reach a climax in both settlement density and metal production (1200-750 B.C.), the importation of bronze to northern Europe generally ceases. Several explanations can be suggested, and a few of them will be discussed.

A. It could be suggested that the increased hoard frequency in Europe, with many hoards containing hundreds of kg of bronze, reflects the destruction or storage of bronze in order to prevent devaluation due to overproduction. Such hoarding sequences consequently reflect crises in long-distance exchange networks and marketing conditions, resulting in an overflow of bronze (rather than an increased production of bronze). Despite good economic conditions of agricultural production the interregional circulation of bronze had ceased, resulting in periods of overproduction in certain areas and subsequent lack of bronze in others, e.g. Scandinavia.

B. It could also be suggested, however, that the main factors should rather be localized in Scandinavia. This implies that the economy in general could not meet the demands of alliance and exchange partners.

Such a temporary stagnation in the economic dynamics of southern Scandinavia could also explain why consumption does not expand geographically from period III to period IV (Fig. 18 4).

C. Finally it could be suggested that an expansion of agricultural production in central Europe increased the demands for agricultural tools so heavily that metal production was directed more towards meeting these increasing internal demands, than to exchange northwards. This is reflected in the increasing dominance of agricultural implements in hoards. Many of these, e.g. hoards of sickles, may reflect central storing during wintertime. This would imply a kind of centrally organized agricultural production, as suggested by von Bruun (1958).

It is beyond the scope of this paper to test any of these hypotheses, which eventually may be combined in several ways. The outcomes of alternatives A and B are the same, as A implies that the exchange value of bronze rose during periods III-IV, placing harder demands on the economy. This could also be the case with alternative C. Both A and C imply that interregional exchange ceased or became unstable, either due to increased political tension and warfare, (e.g. reflected in fortifications) or due to a lesser emphasis on the functioning of bronze as a prestige indicator and in creating far-reaching alliance systems (C).

At present I prefer a combination of alternatives A and C. I would argue that the general preference for better soil in period III reflects increased subsistence production in order to maintain a certain level of importation and consumption, but that from period IV onwards both the economy and the ritual-political system had adapted to the situation, thus reducing the number of bronze objects used as burial equipment (or stimulating the use of miniatures) and encouraging ritual hoarding on rare and special occasions, often including the equipment of several persons (Kristiansen 1974; Levy 1979).

Thus the European evidence adds to a fuller understanding of some of the general changes in circulation time and consumption observed in the previous sections (the conspicuous consumption in period II and V, and the decrease of consumption in periods III-IV), just as it raises several new questions concerning the interplay between local, regional and interregional exchange networks. It does not, however, challenge the conclusion that in Scandinavia local economic conditions were decisive for maintaining those exchange networks through which bronze flowed, reflected in local expansions and regressions and in a general shift of consumption from western to eastern Scandinavia from the Early to the Late Bronze Age.

With these somewhat speculative concluding remarks I hope to have directed the attention of the reader towards the scientific possibilities offered by the rich and well-published evidence of the Nordic Bronze Age. Analyses of the extremely complicated interaction between Nordic and European bronze age cultures are to-day also possible, due to the high level of published evidence for adjacent cultures in Poland, DDR, and central Europe, often too little known beyond a small group of specialists. Although many problems can only be solved in a satisfactory way by personal inspection of the finds, rewarding results can still be obtained from the literature, when approached with relevant theories and analytical techniques.

The Nordic Bronze Age covers every possible ecological variation within a temperate habitat and spans a period of more than 1000 years. Archaeologically representative and well published, it represents a laboratory for testing a wide range of hypotheses on a still badly understood epoch in European prehistory.

Note

The present article is mainly based on two earlier unpublished papers, one given at the Prehistoric Society conference in London in April 1978 on " The Context and Implications of Metalworking in European Prehistory" , the other given at a conference held in Cambridge in January 1979 on " Economic Archaeology — Towards an Integrated Approach" . I want to thank Alison Sheridan for her efforts to bring the papers of this Cambridge conference together in print, and for her extraordinary patience with the present paper.

Due to the rather broad scope of this article, and its very short form, references to literature have had to be selective, especially the sections on economic theory, history of research, and conclusion and perspectives. It is hoped that the interested reader will find his or her way to supplementary literature from the selected title.

Very extensive parts of the source material from graves and hoards are published in excellent catalogues — for the Early Bronze Age most prominently Aner and Kersten (1971-79), including Denmark and Northern Germany. The Swedish material is published by Oldeberg (1974), Mecklenburg by Schubart (1972), Pomerania by Kersten (1958). For the Late Bronze Age we have for Denmark the earlier catalogue of Broholm (1943-49) and for Schleswig-Holstein that of Menke (1973). A catalogue of the Bronze Age in Finland was published by Meinander (1954). Finally the hoards of northern Germany were published by Sprockhoff (1937 and 1956).

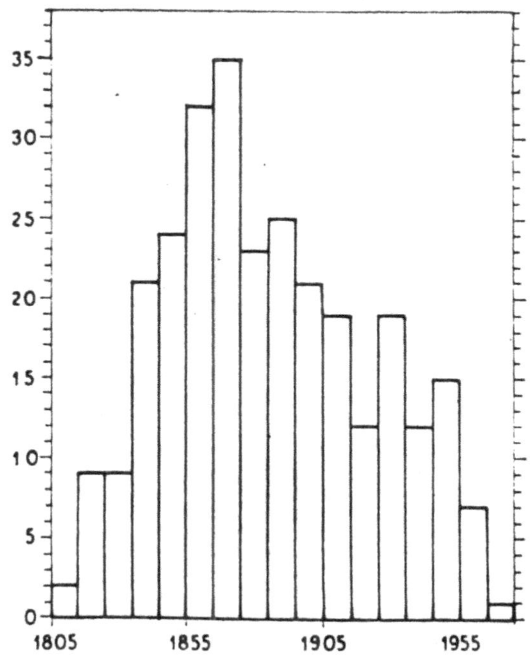

Fig. 18. 1 Frequency of late bronze age hoards in Denmark plotted against years of registration (after Kristiansen 1974).

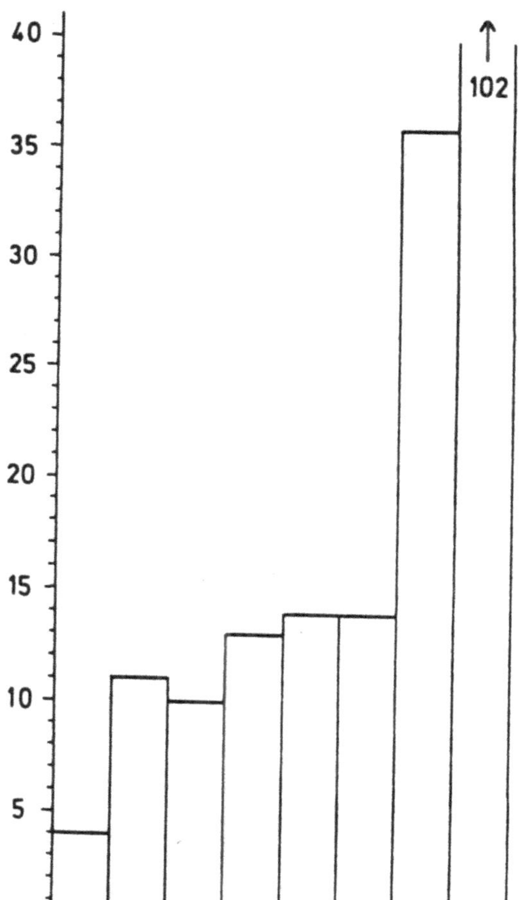

Fig. 18. 2 Frequency of late bronze age settlements plotted against years of registration (kindly placed at my disposal by Henrik Thrane).

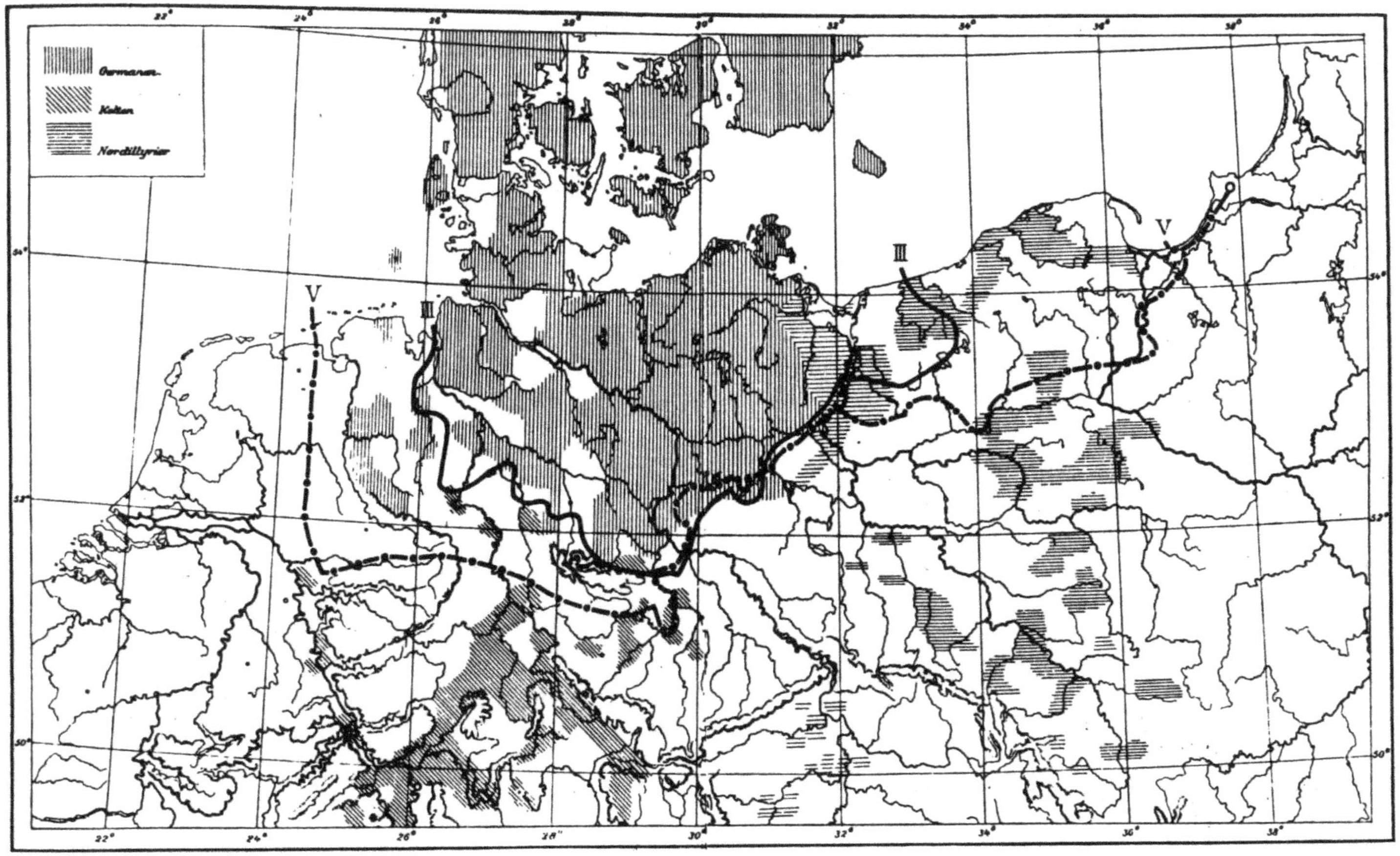

Fig. 18.3 Kossina' s map of the distribution of the Nordic Bronze Age Culture in Northern Europe (after Kossina 1928).

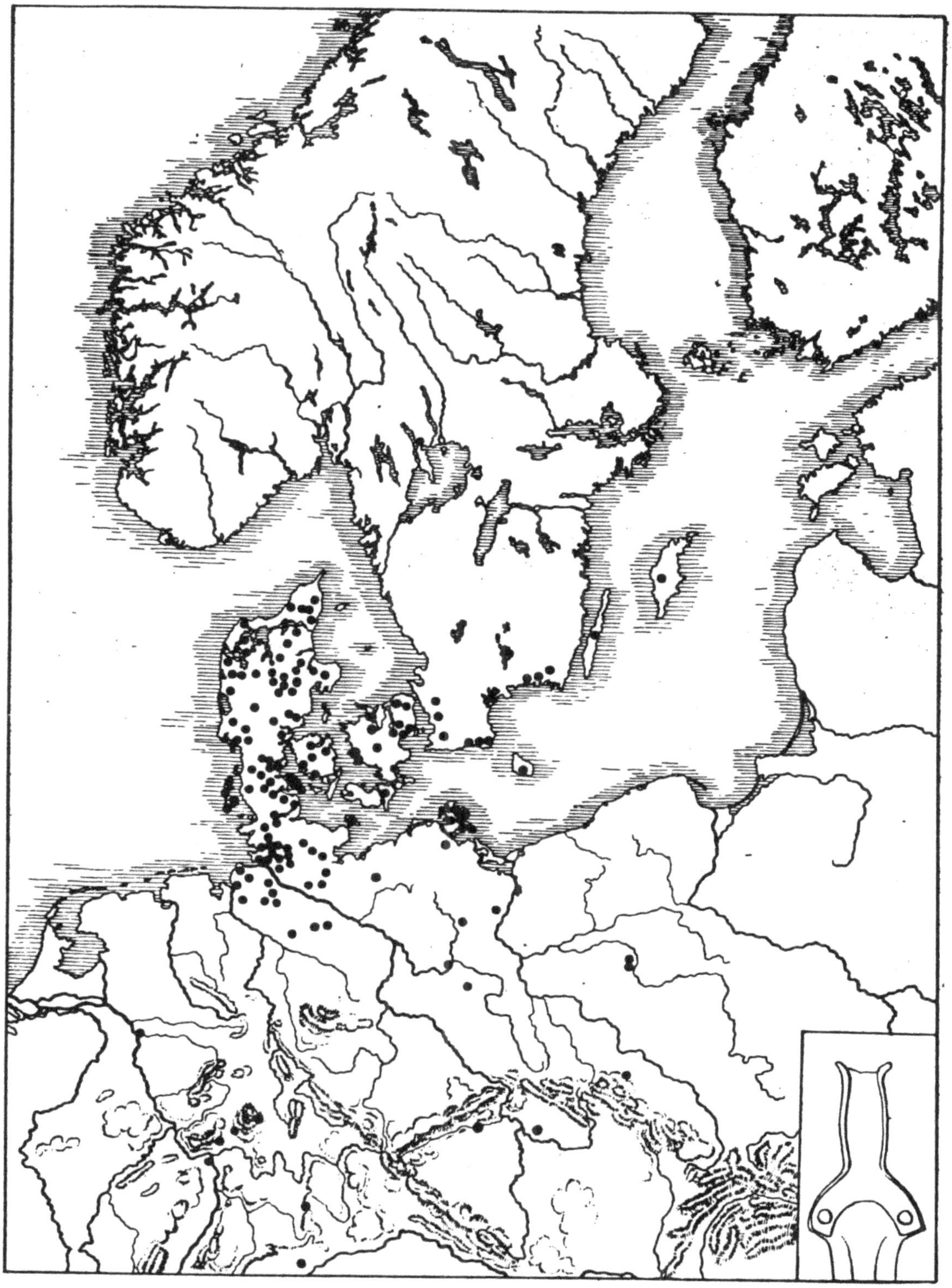

Fig. 18.4 Sprockhoff's distribution maps of the Nordic Bronze Age Culture from period II to V, based on flange hilted swords (early bronze age) and " germanic" hoards (late bronze age) after Sprockhoff 1931 and 1937.

Fig. 18. 4a

Fig. 18. 4b

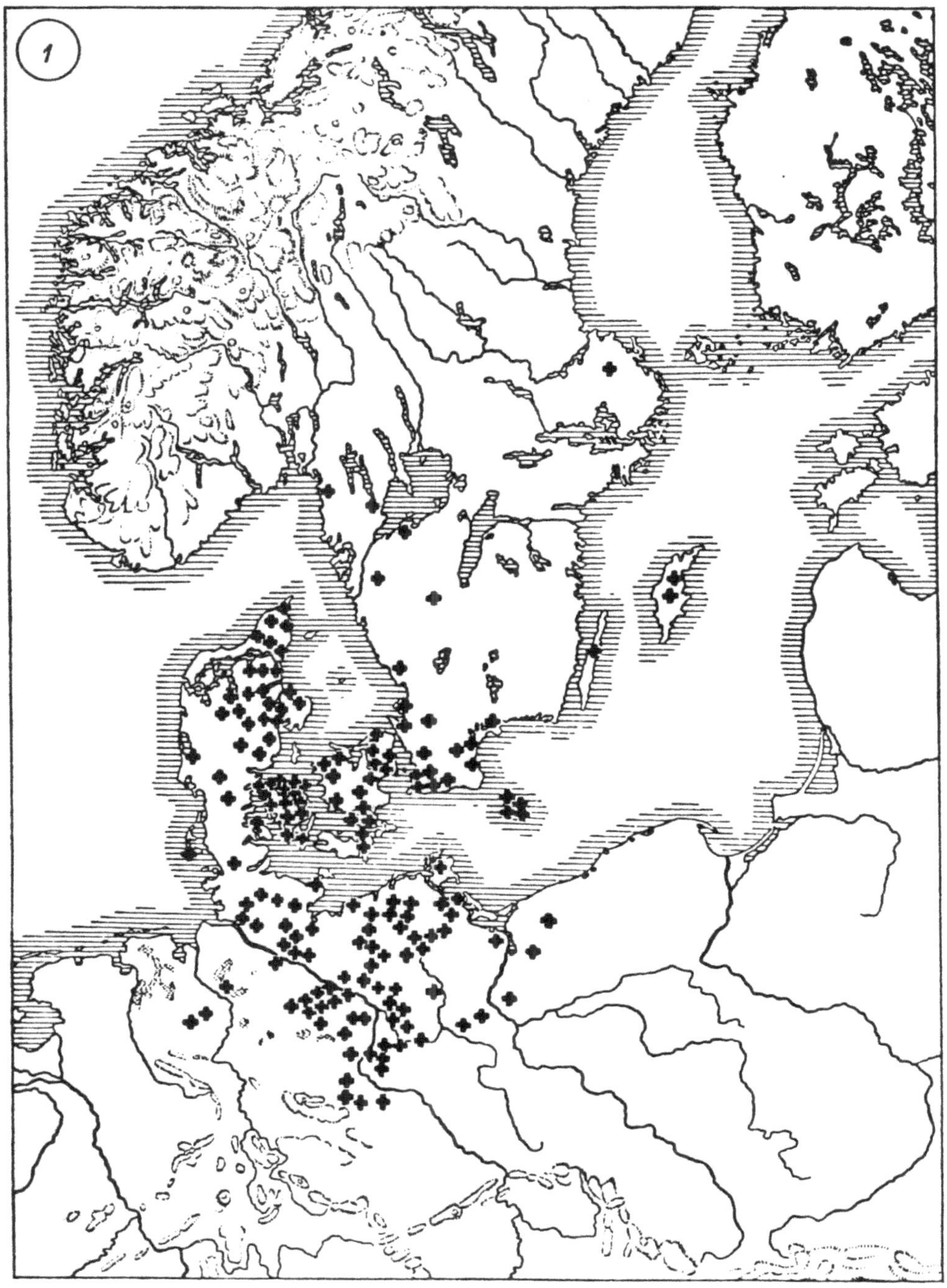

Fig. 18. 4c

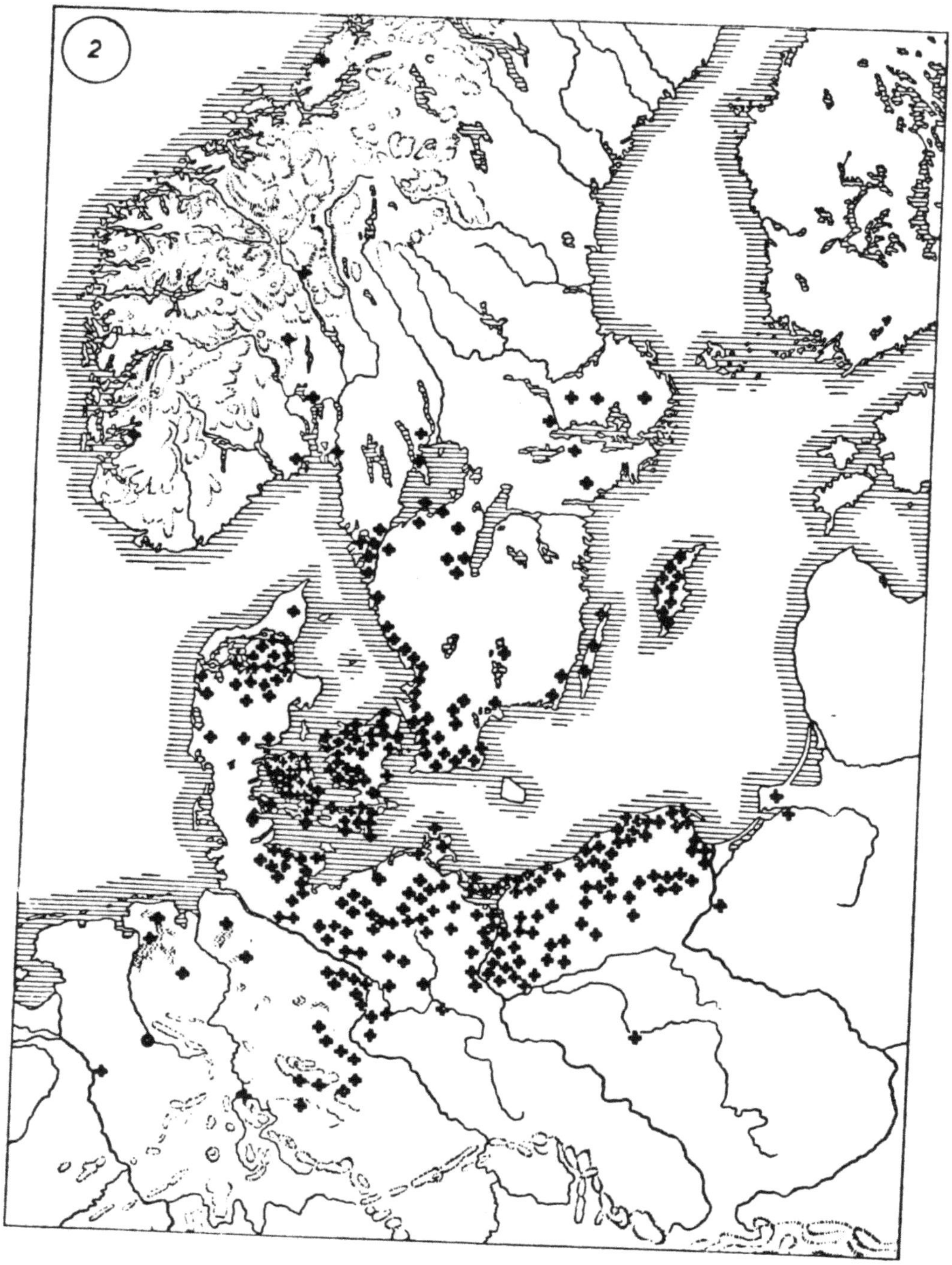

Fig. 18. 4d

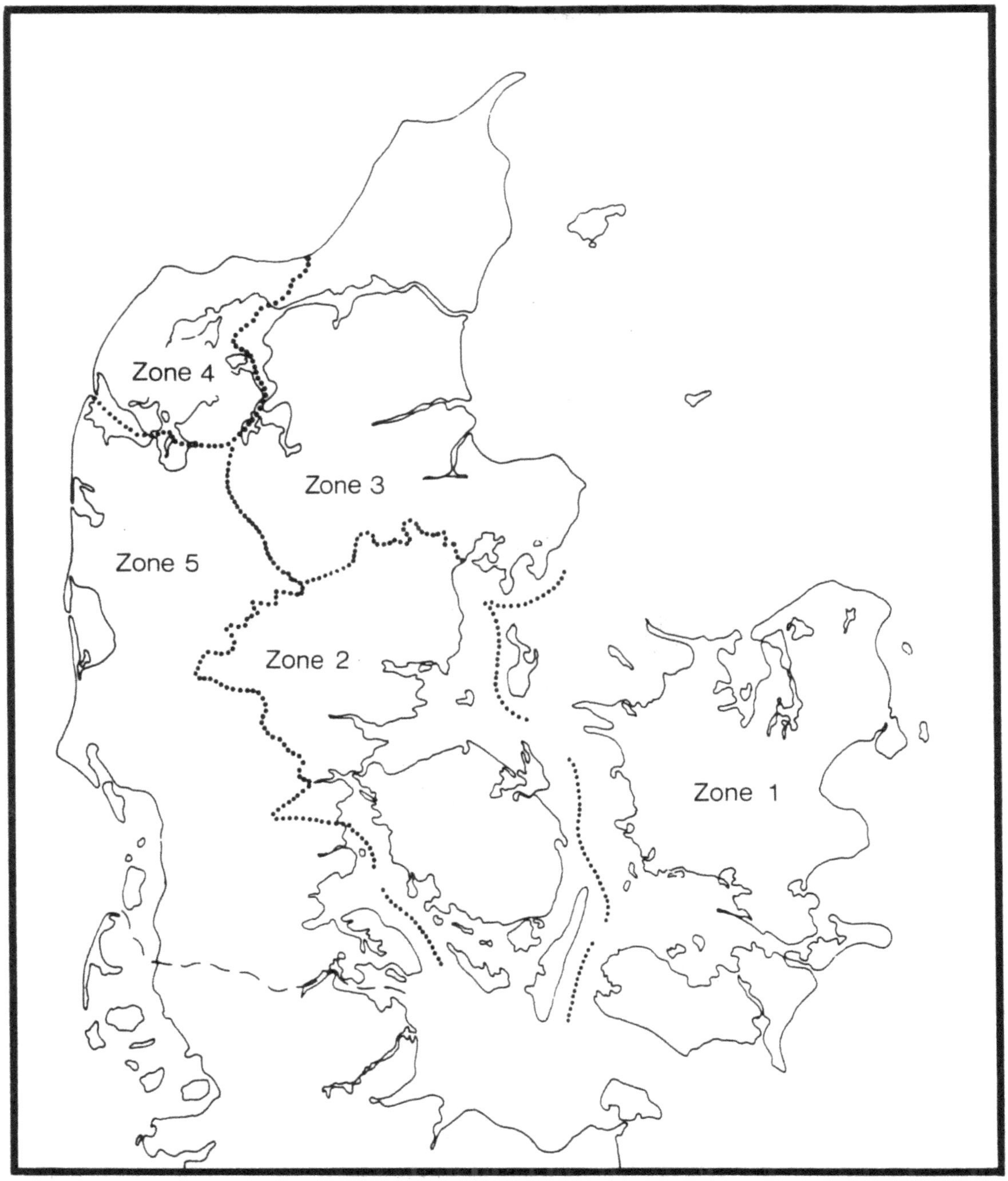

Fig. 18.5 Zonal division of Denmark (after Kristiansen 1978b).

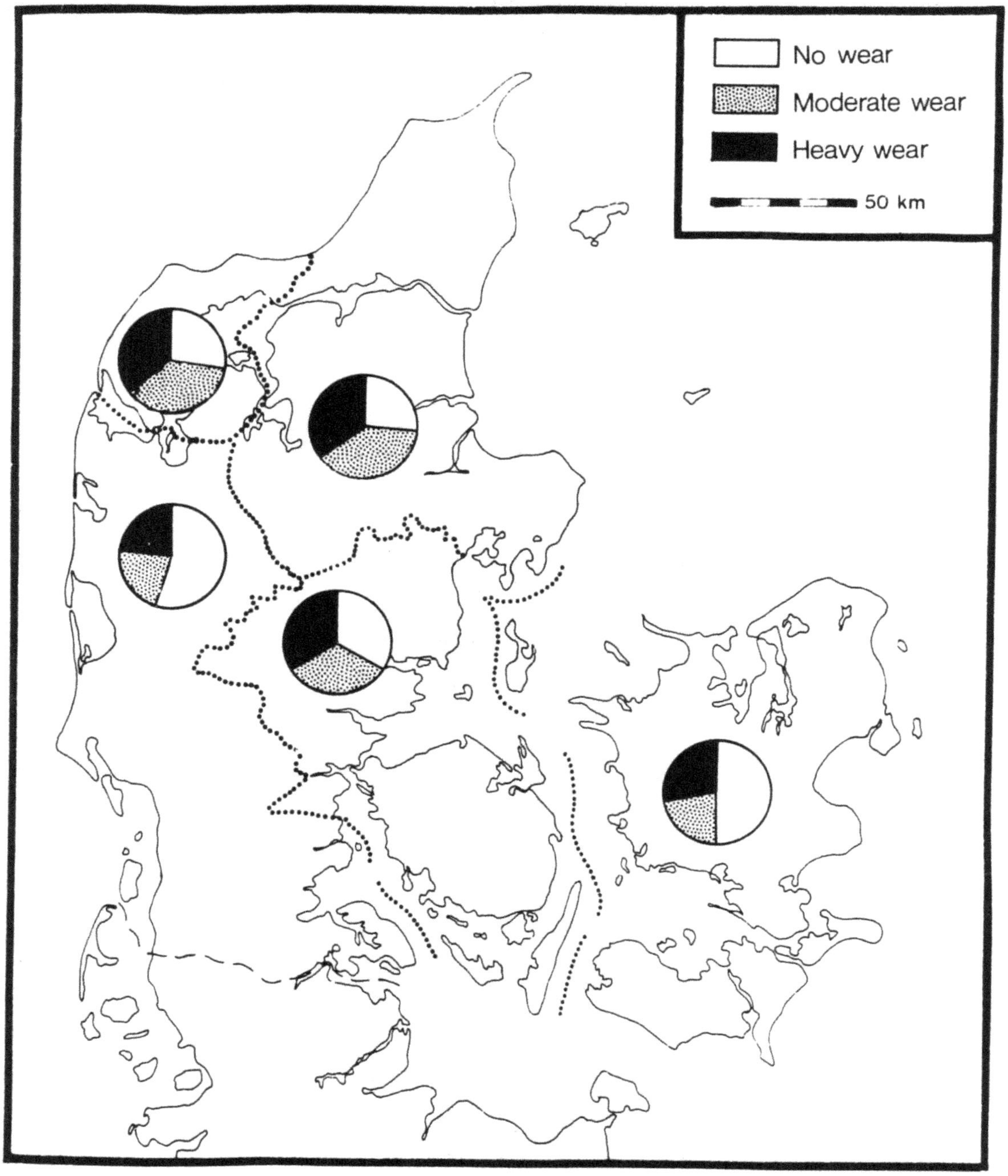

Fig. 18.6 Period II. Variations in the circulation time of full hilted swords. Sample: 174 observations (after Kristiansen 1978b).

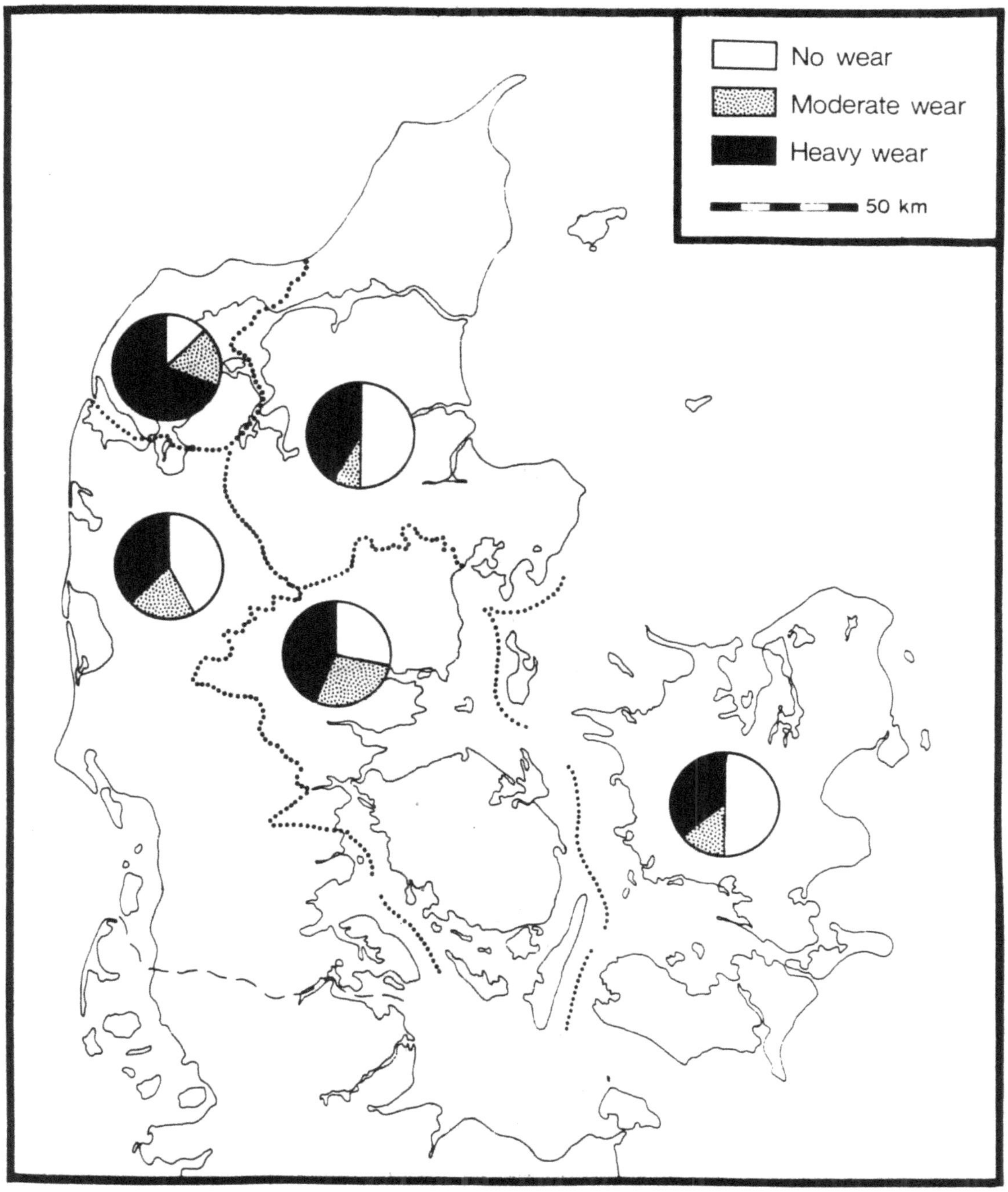

Fig. 18.7 Period III. Variations in the circulation time of full hilted swords. Sample: 104 observations (after Kristiansen 1978b).

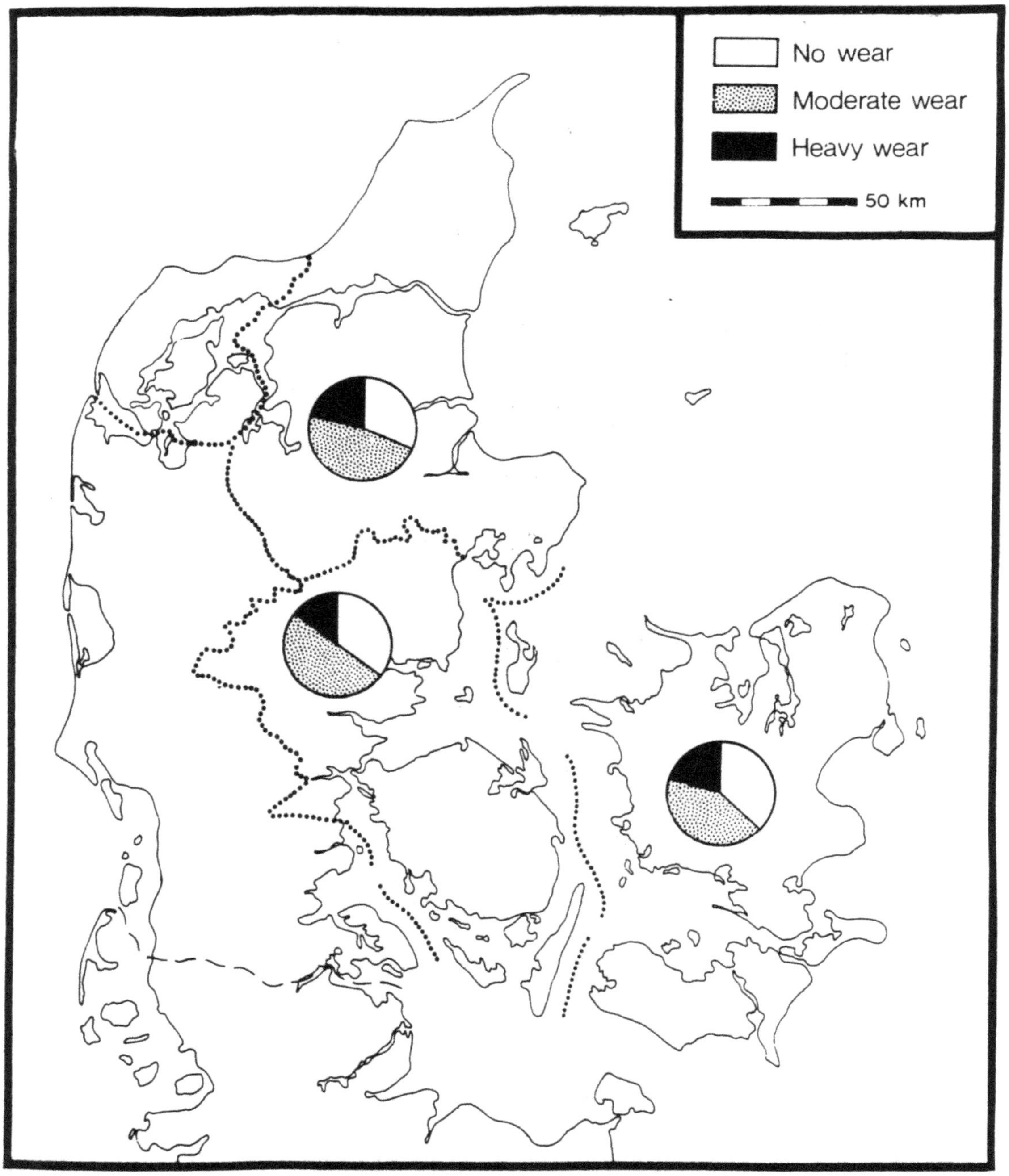

Fig. 18.8 Period IV. Variations in the circulation time of decorated ornaments. Sample: 117 observations (after Kristiansen 1978b).

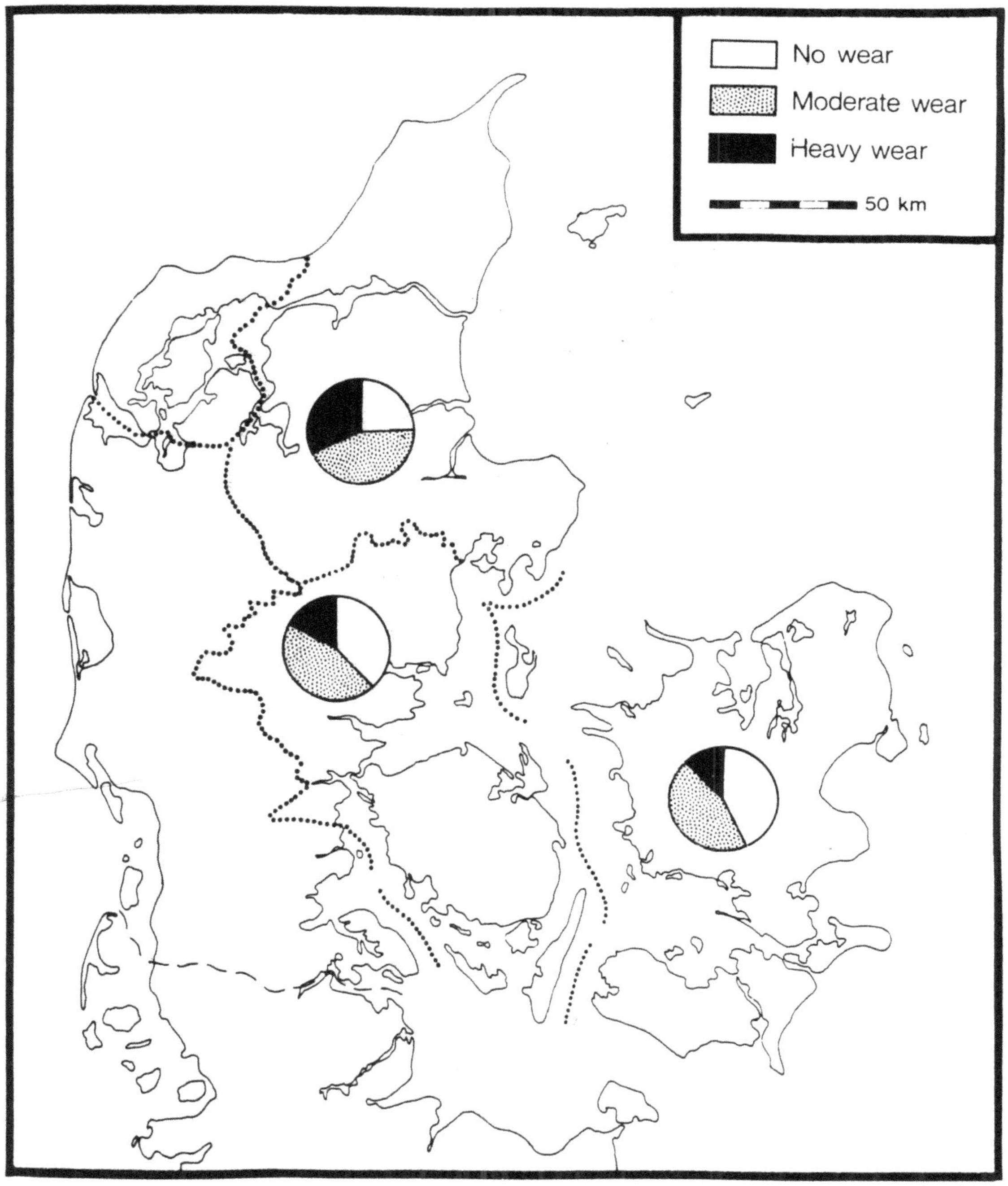

Fig. 18.9 Period V. Variations in the circulation time of decorated ornaments. Sample: 174 observations (after Kristiansen 1978b).

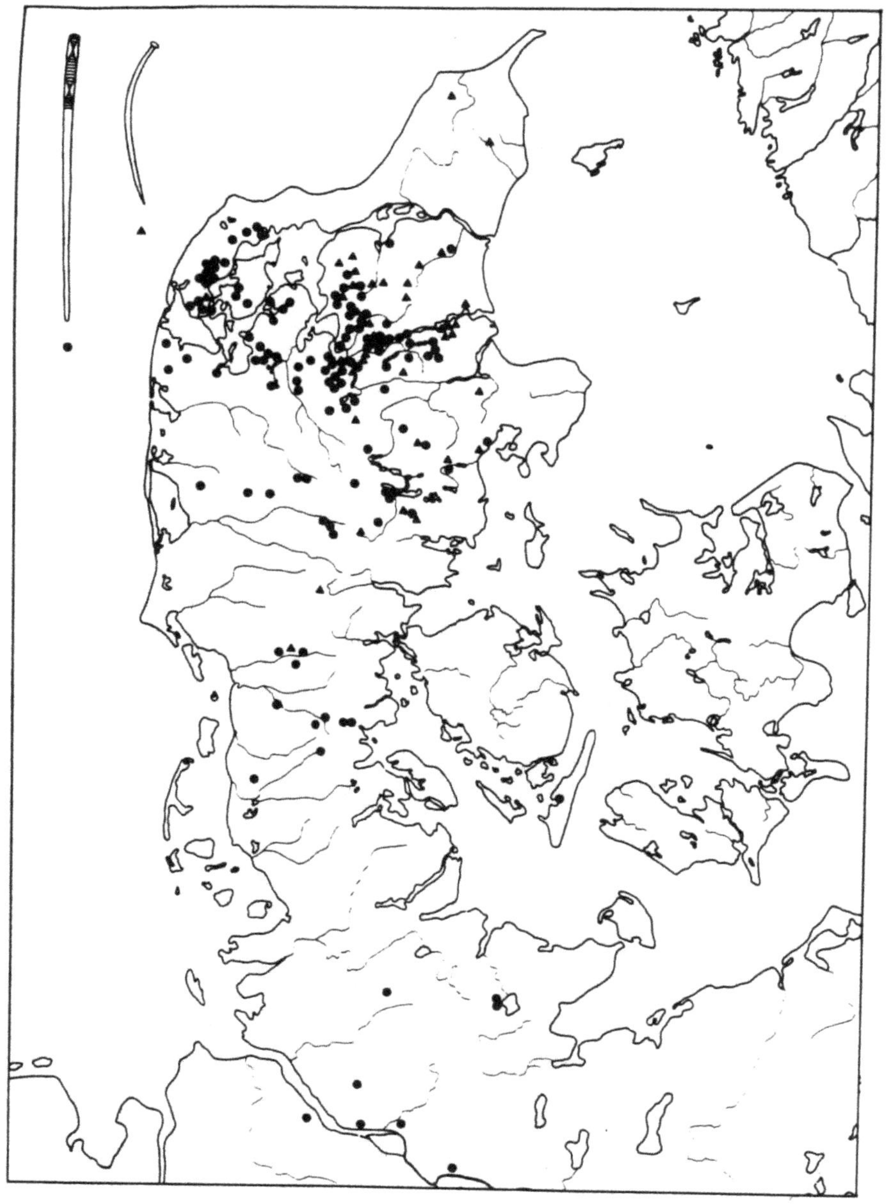

Fig. 18.10 The distribution of pins made of bone during the Late Bronze Age (after Baudou 1960, Maps 45 and 51).

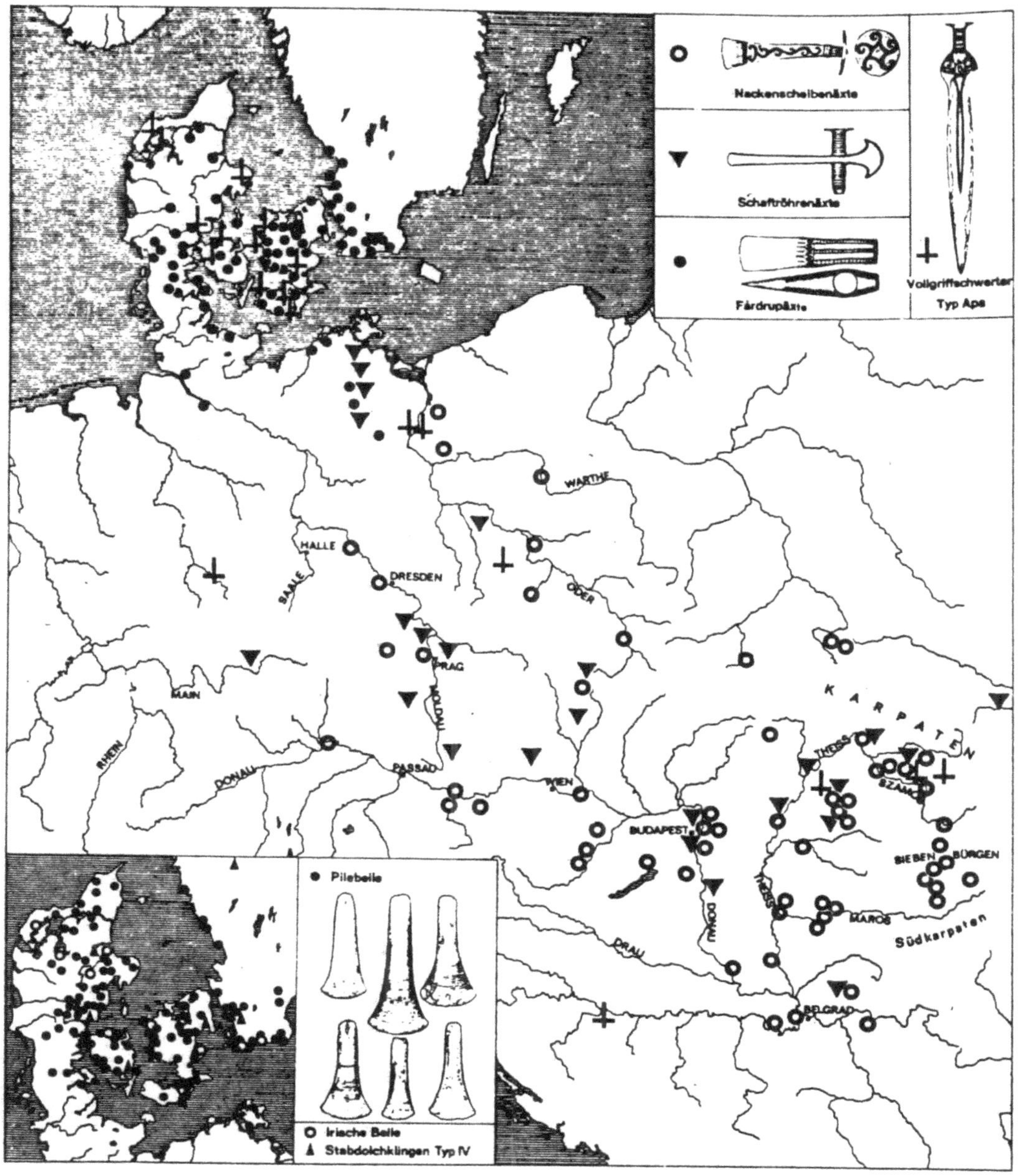

Fig. 18.11 The distribution of South East European bronzes and local Nordic bronzes in period I (after Struwe 1971, Table 2).

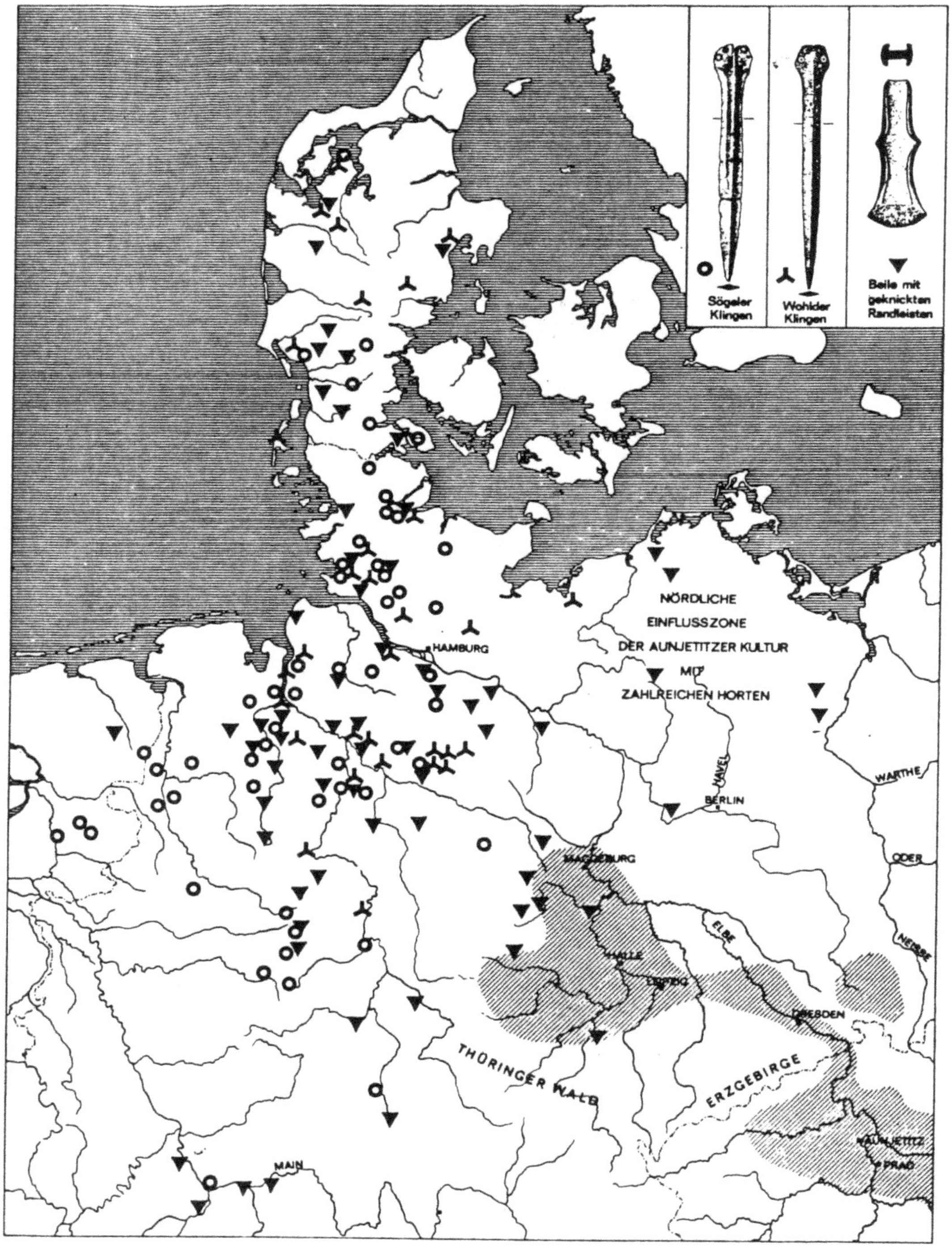

Fig. 18.12 The distribution of North West European bronzes in period I (after Struwe 1971, Table 5).

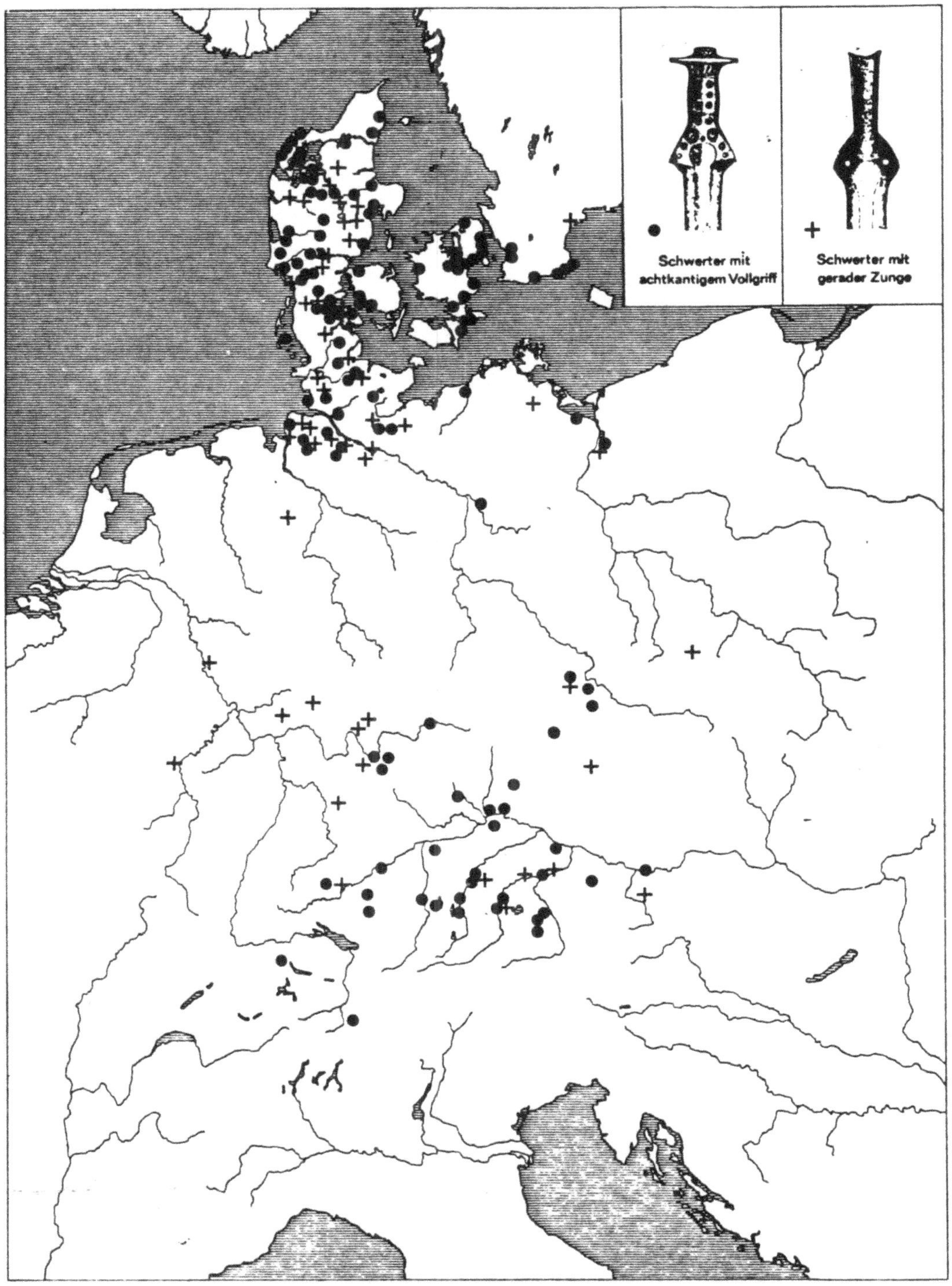

Fig. 18.13 The distribution of octagonal swords and flange hilted swords of south german influence (after Struwe 1971, Table 26).

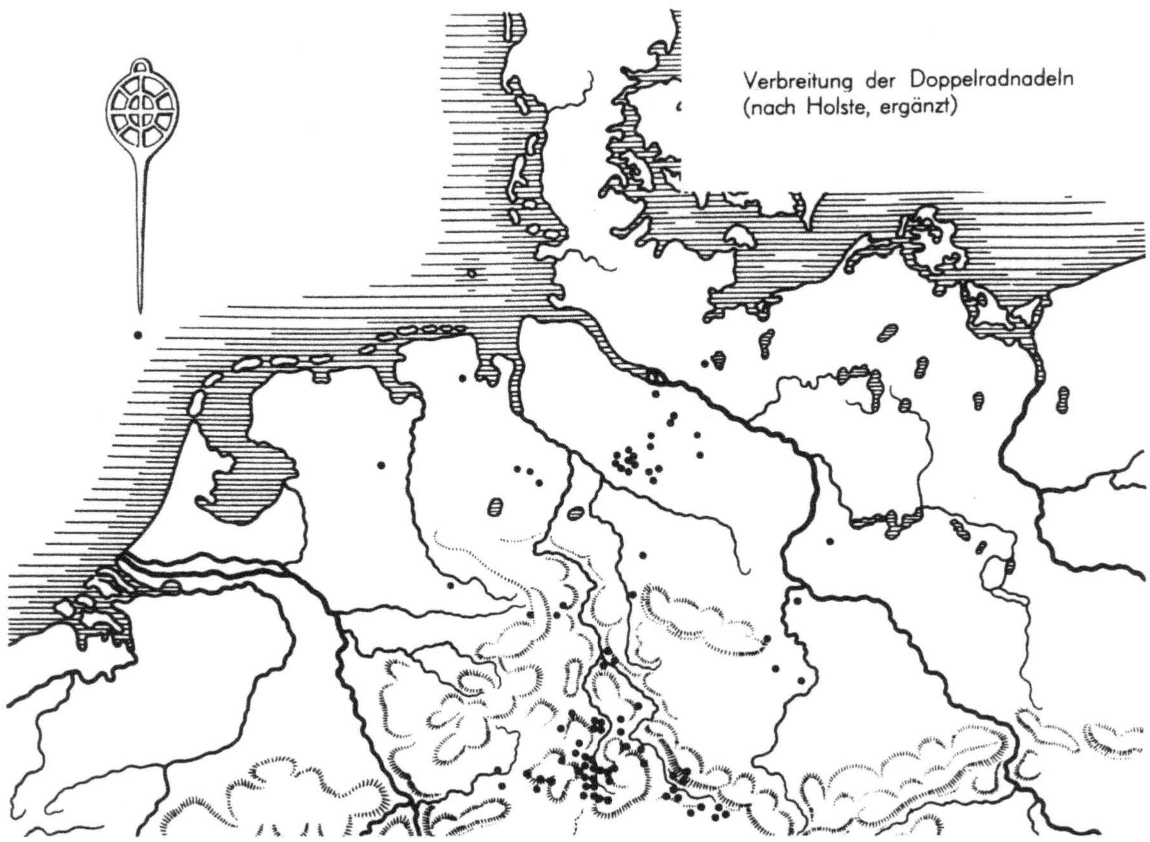

Fig. 18.14 The distribution of wheel pins of the Tumulus Culture, showing a complementary distribution to Fig. 18.11 (after Piesker 1958, Table 72).

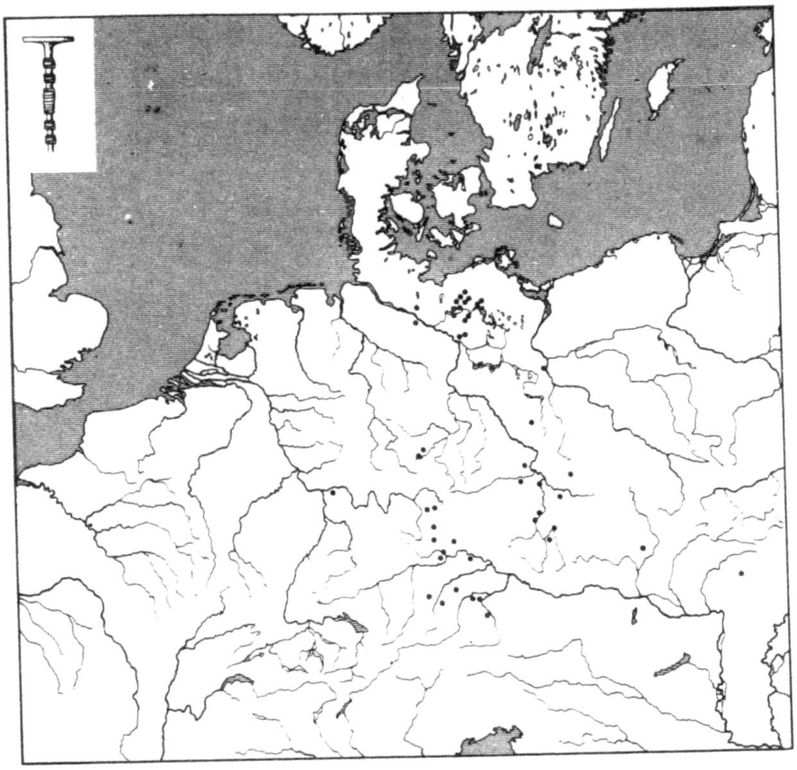

Fig. 18.15 The distribution of Urnfield D pins of Weitgendorf type (after Hundt 1978, Fig. 43).

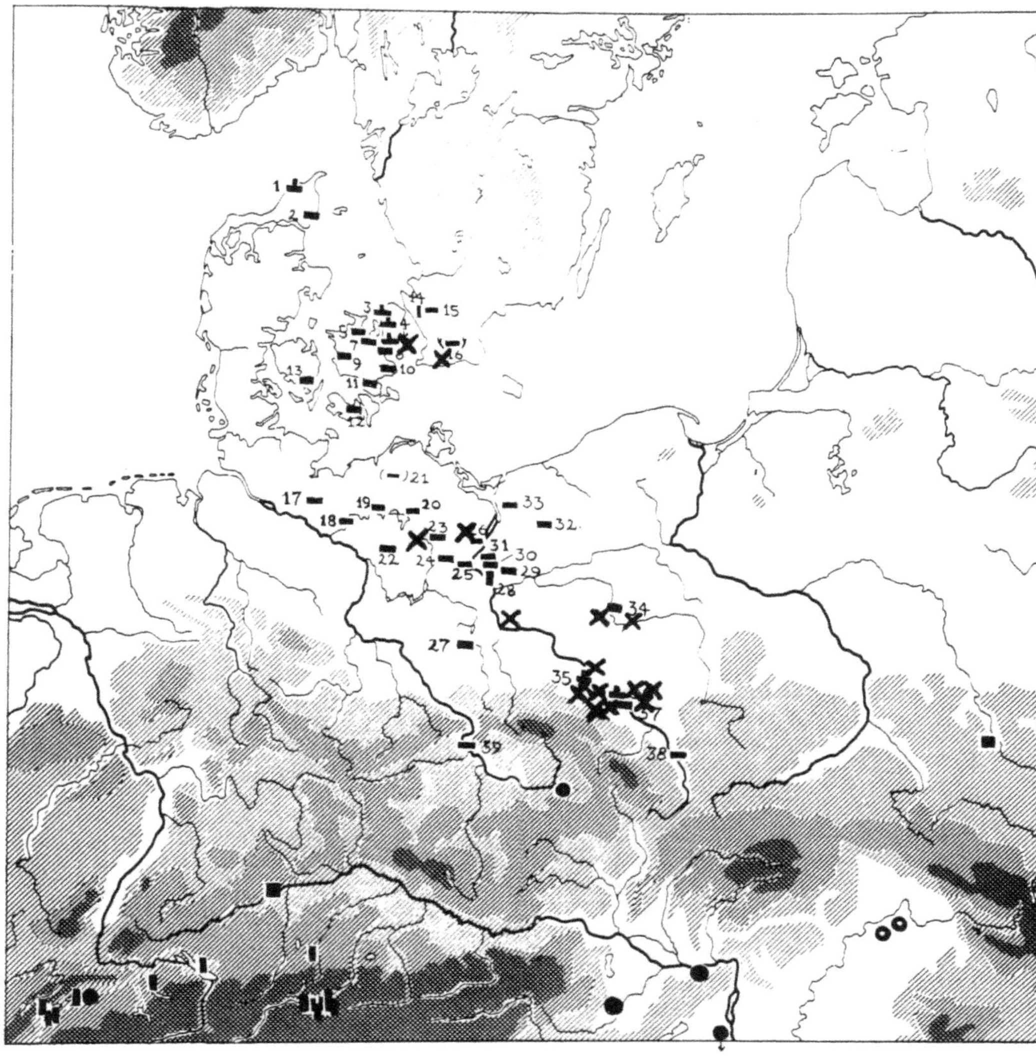

Fig. 18.16 The distribution of "Pfatten"-knives and variants. ● Danubian type, ▮ Tirolian variant, ▬ Oder variant, ▲ copies of Oder variant, ○ other variants (after Thrane 1975, Fig. 49). X Schlesian knives added after Thrane 1975, Fig. 46).

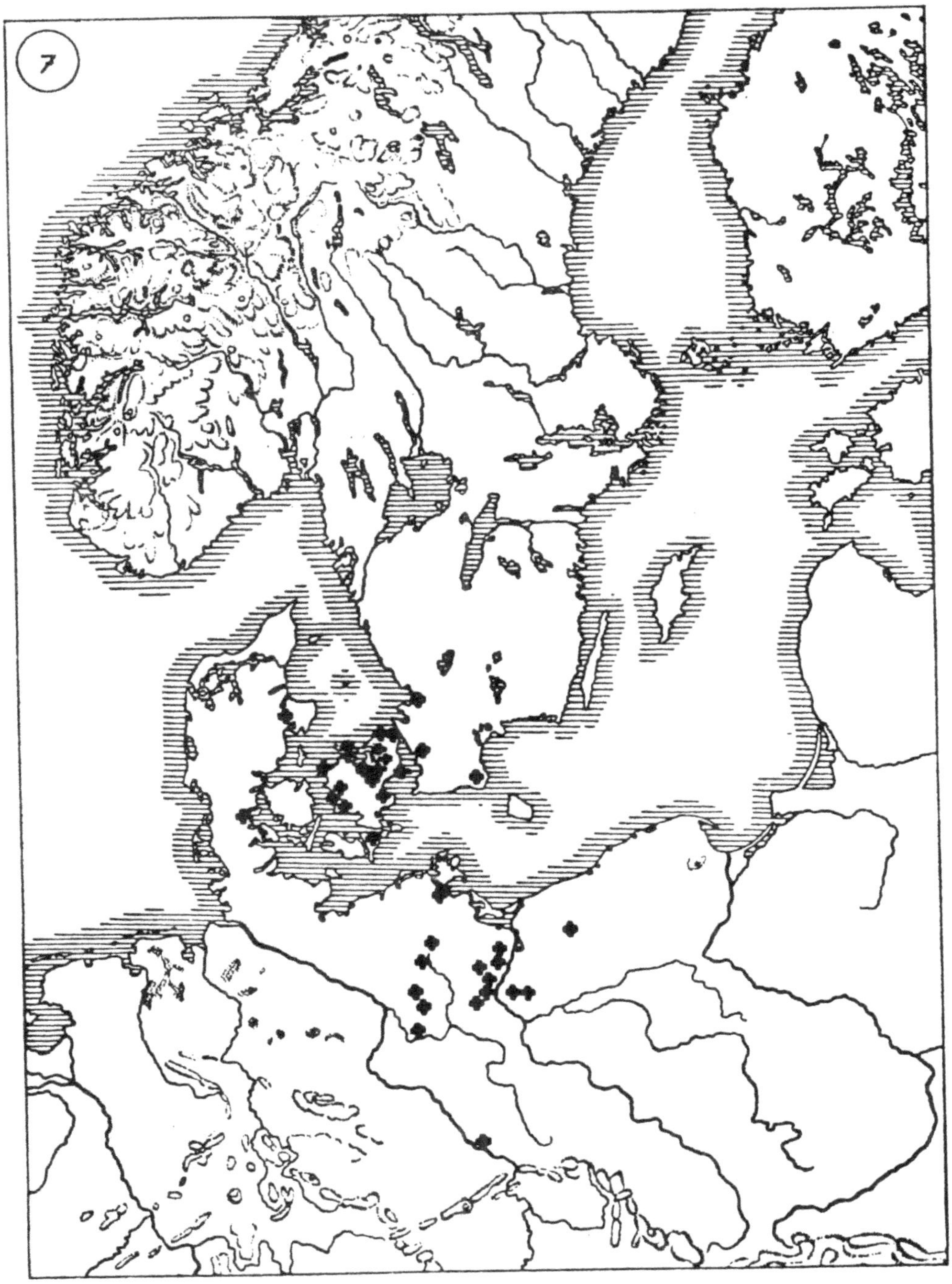

Fig. 18.17 The distribution of Nordic "Hörnerknaufmesser" (after Sprockhoff 1937, Map 7).

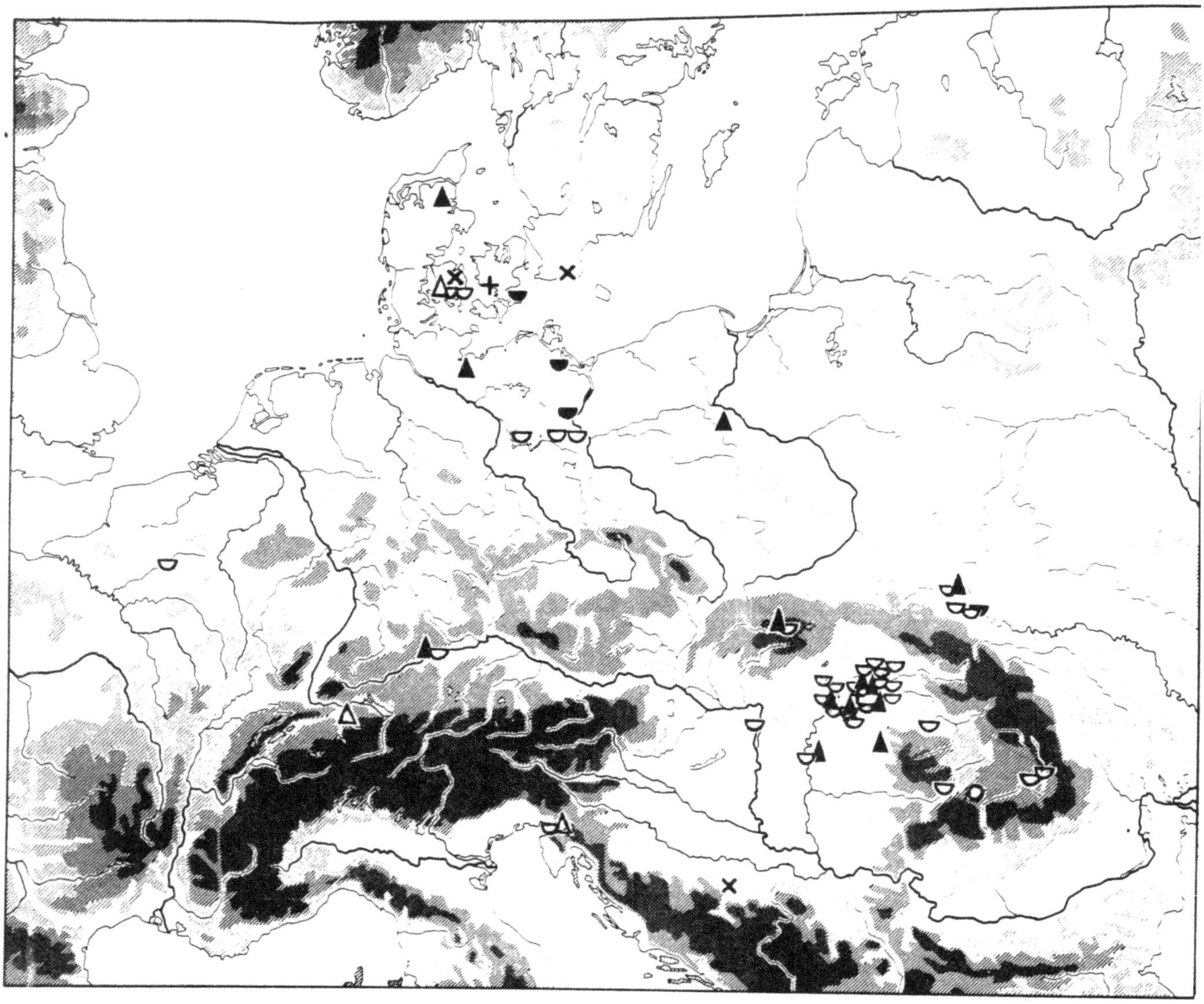

Fig. 18.18 The distribution of Ha B1 vessels and buckets. ᗜ B1 buckets ▾ Ha B2 buckets, ▲ Hajdu Böszörmeny buckets (fragments have open symbols) + sieves, × amphorae (after Thrane 1975, Fig. 89).

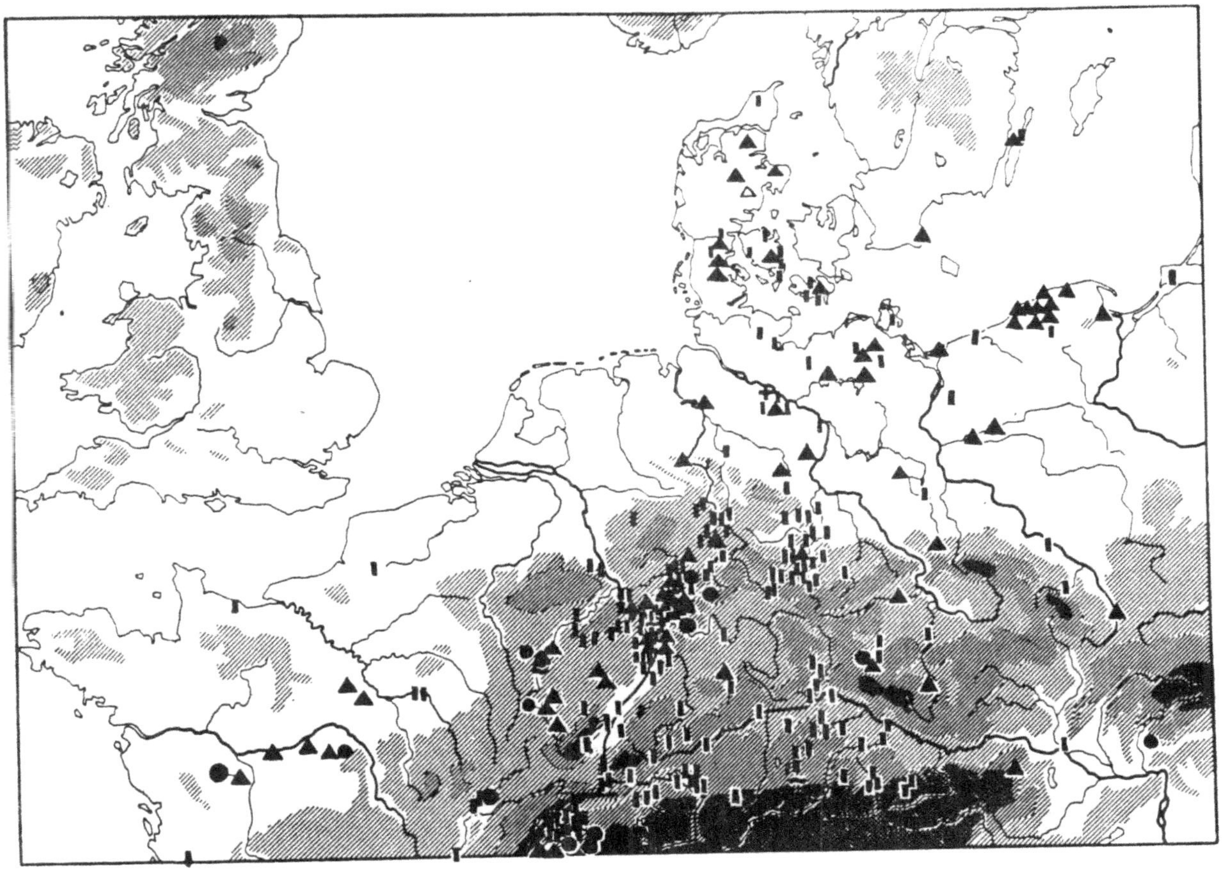

Fig. 18.19 The distribution of western Ha B winged axes. ▲ Hoards, ● moulds, ▮ single finds (after Thrane 1975, Fig. 55).

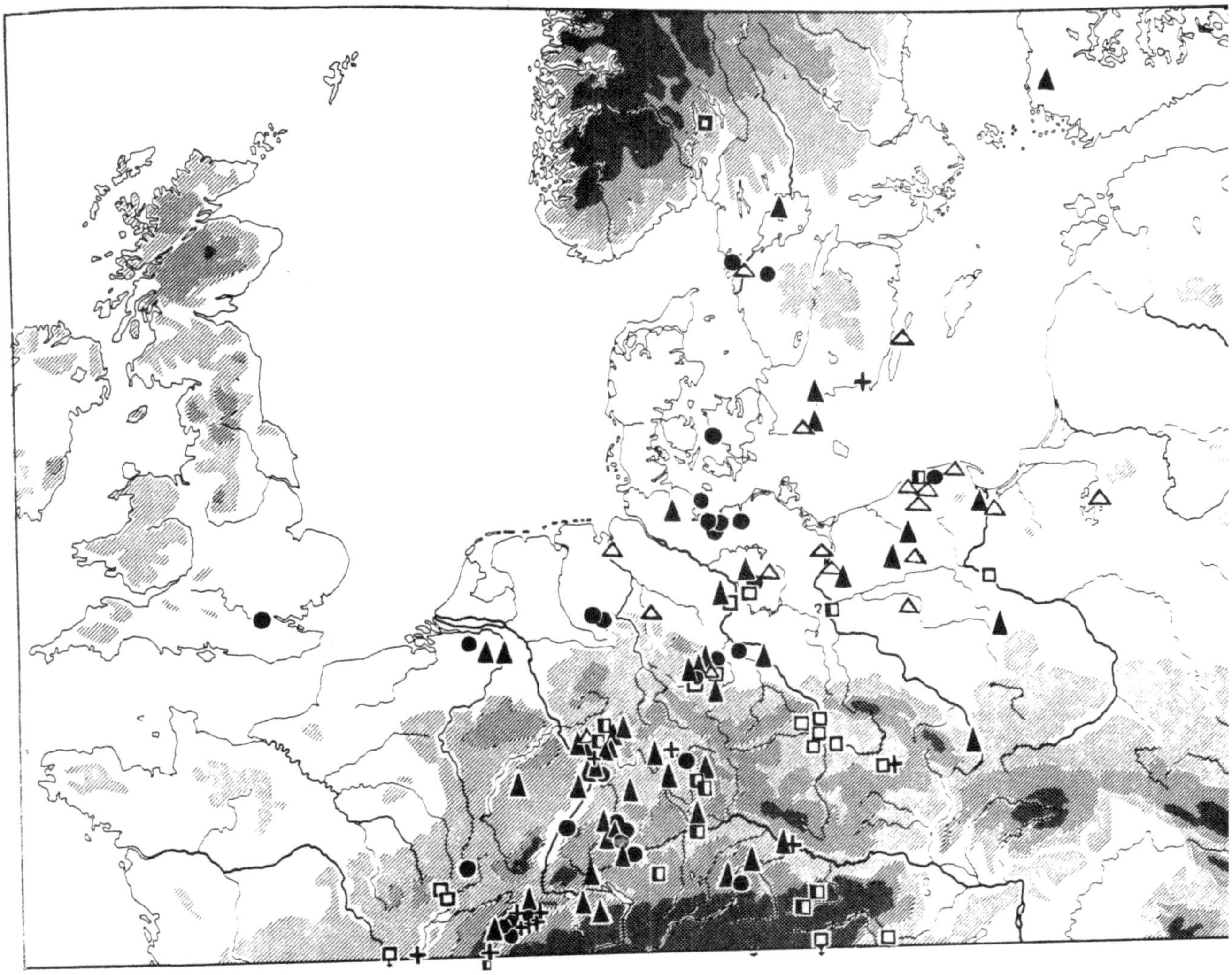

Fig. 18.20 The distribution of Möringen swords from Ha B3. ▲ Möringen I, △ north german copies, □ Tachlovice, + Möringen II, ◧ Möringen III, ● Auvernier (after Thrane 1975, Fig. 120).

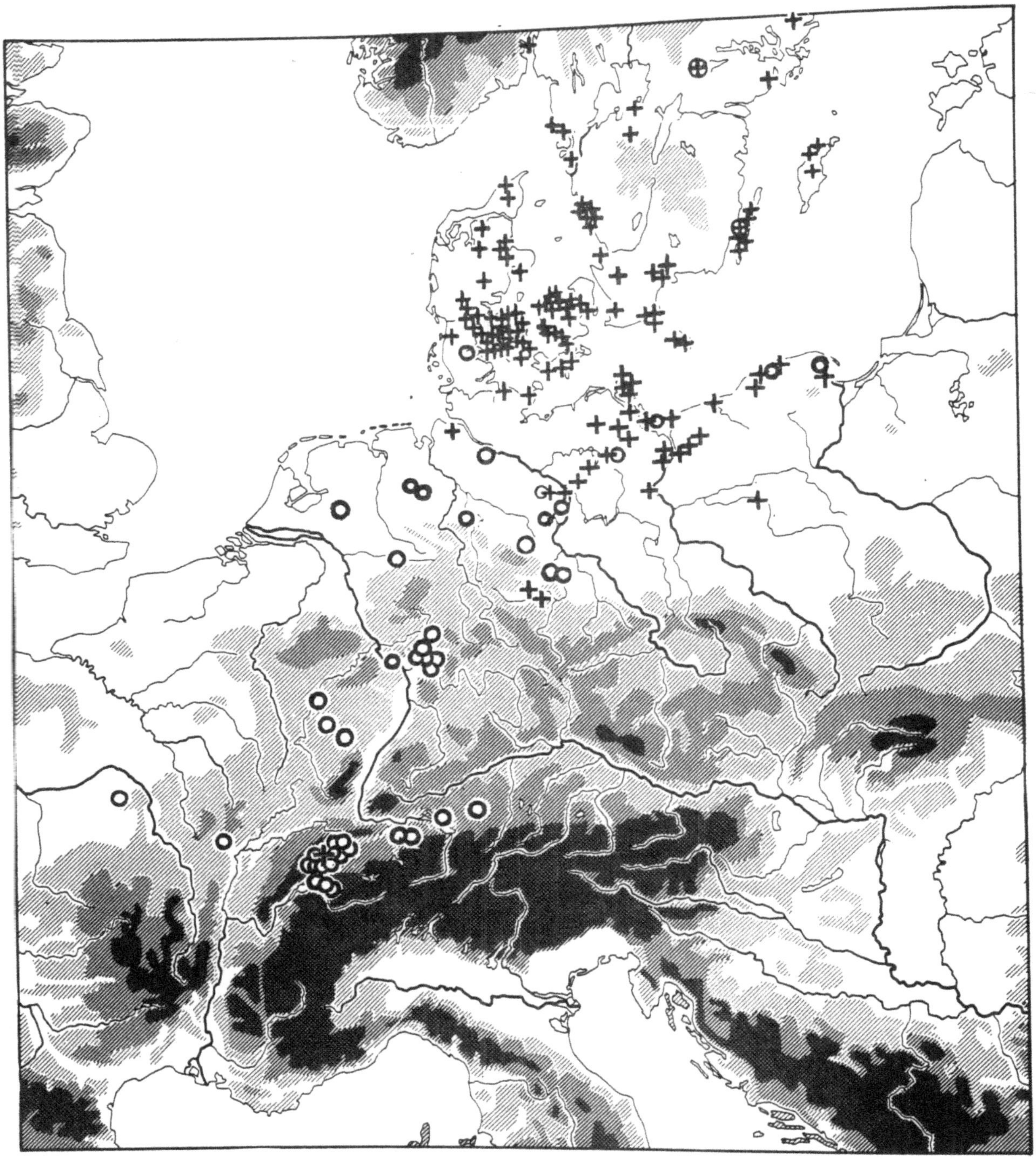

Fig. 18.21 The distribution of West Baltic spearheads + and "Pfahlbau" spearheads ○ (after Thrane 1975, Fig. 30).

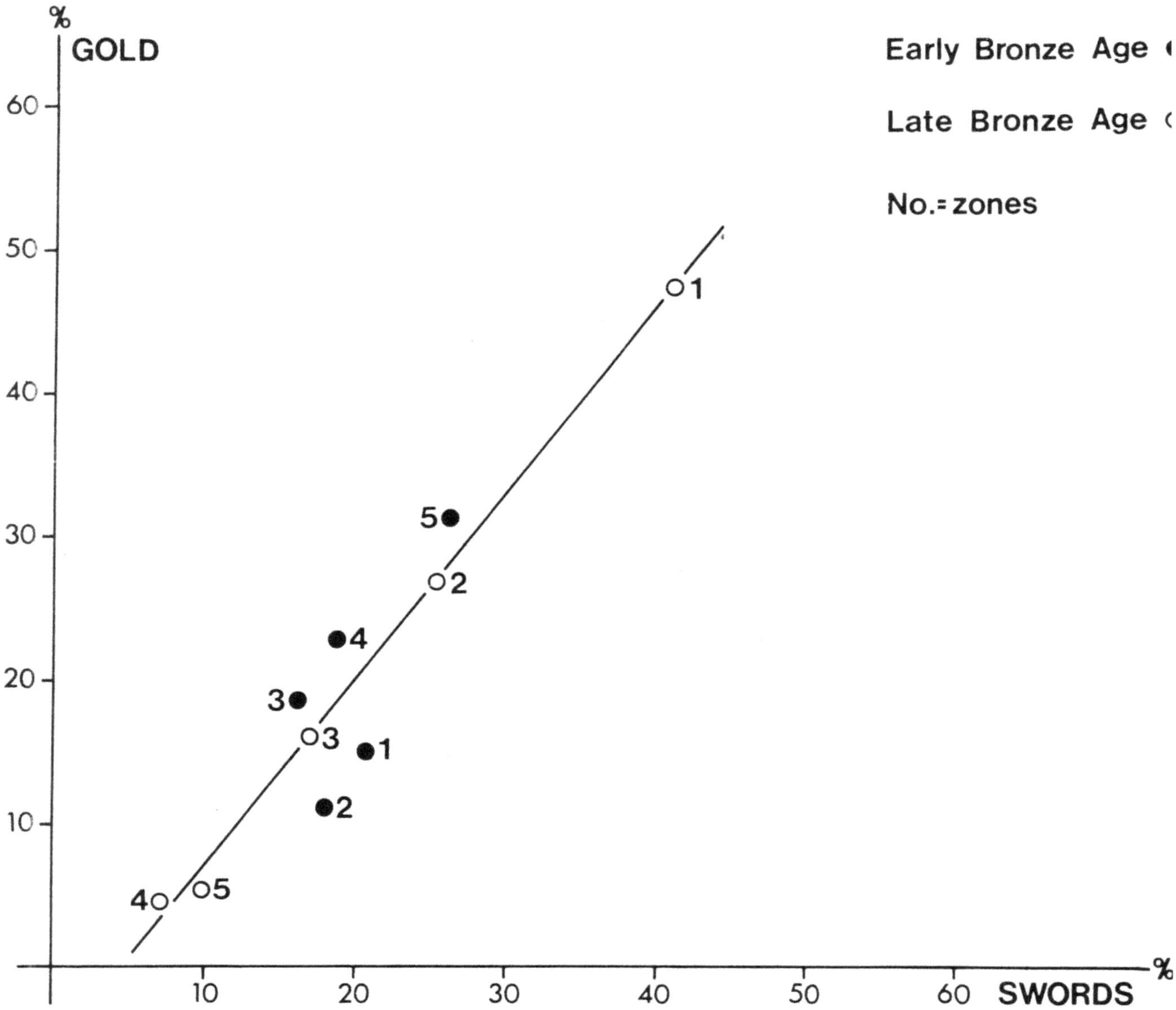

Fig. 18.22 Relationship between the consumption of gold and swords during the Bronze Age in Denmark (after Kristiansen 1978b, Fig. 6).

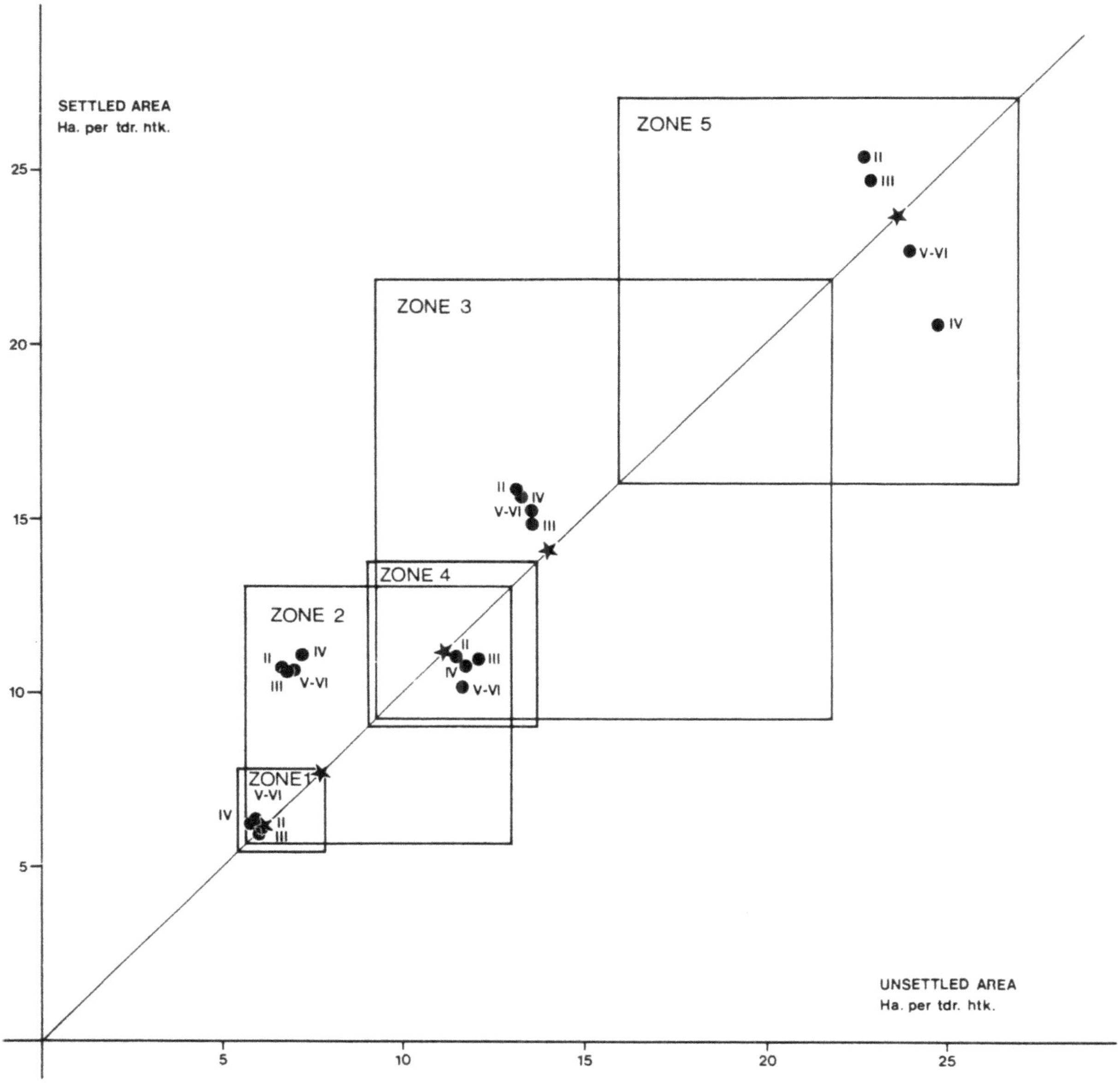

Fig. 18.23 Relationship between ha per tdr. htk (tønder hartkorn) of settled and unsettled areas, indicating subsistence strategy. No. = periods. The squares represent average of ten best and ten poorest districts. The crosses on the diagonal indicate average of each zone (after Kristiansen 1978b).

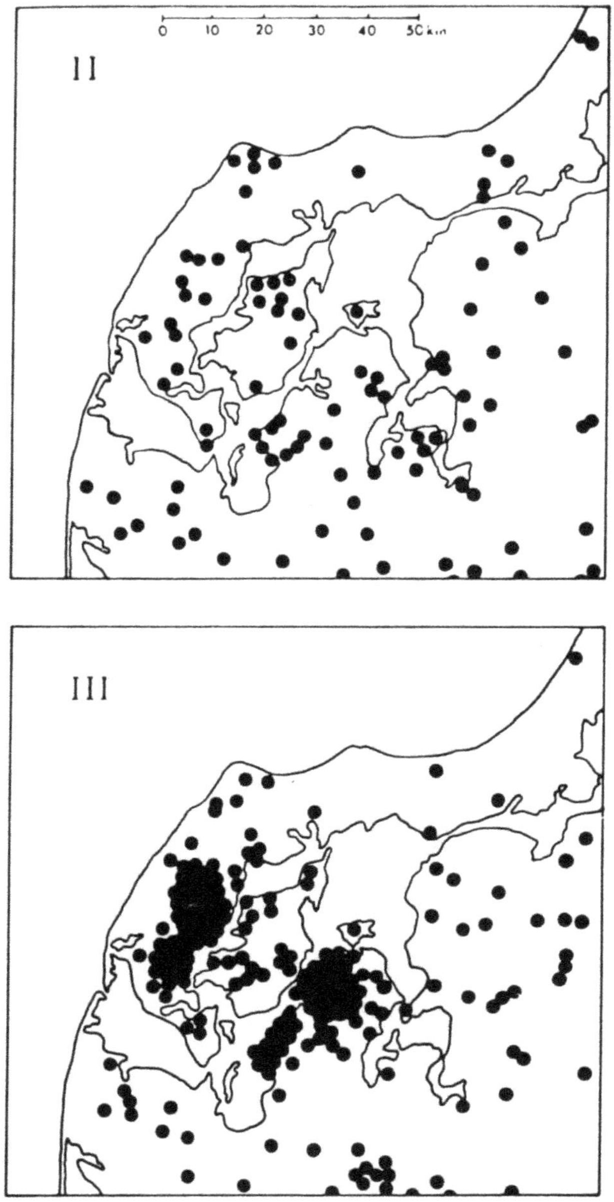

Fig. 18.24 The distribution of burials in zone 4 in period II and III (redrawn after Randsborg 1973-1974, Figs. 1 and 2).

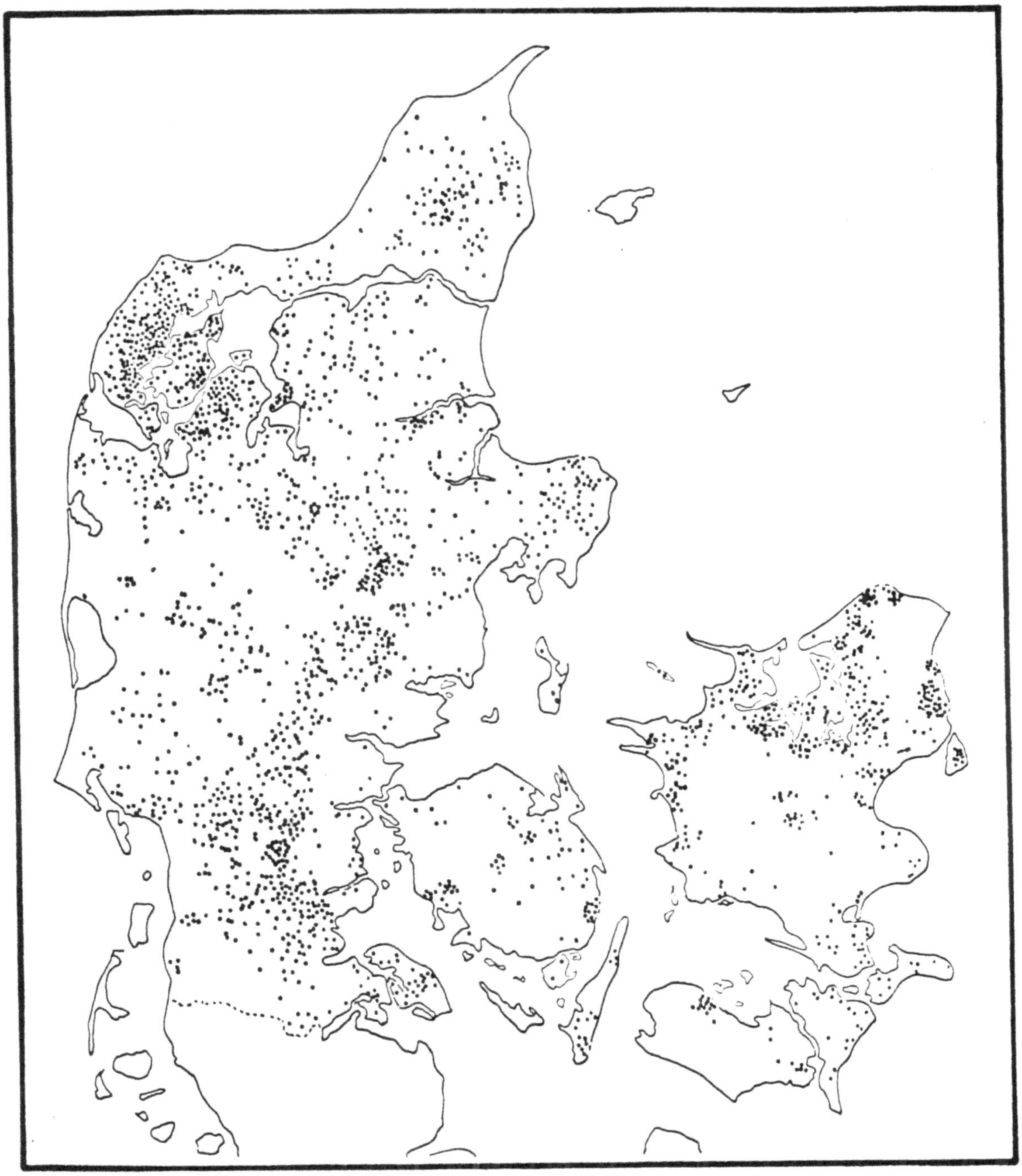

Fig. 18.25 The distribution of early bronze age graves in Denmark (redrawn after Broholm 1944, Figs. 81 and 82).

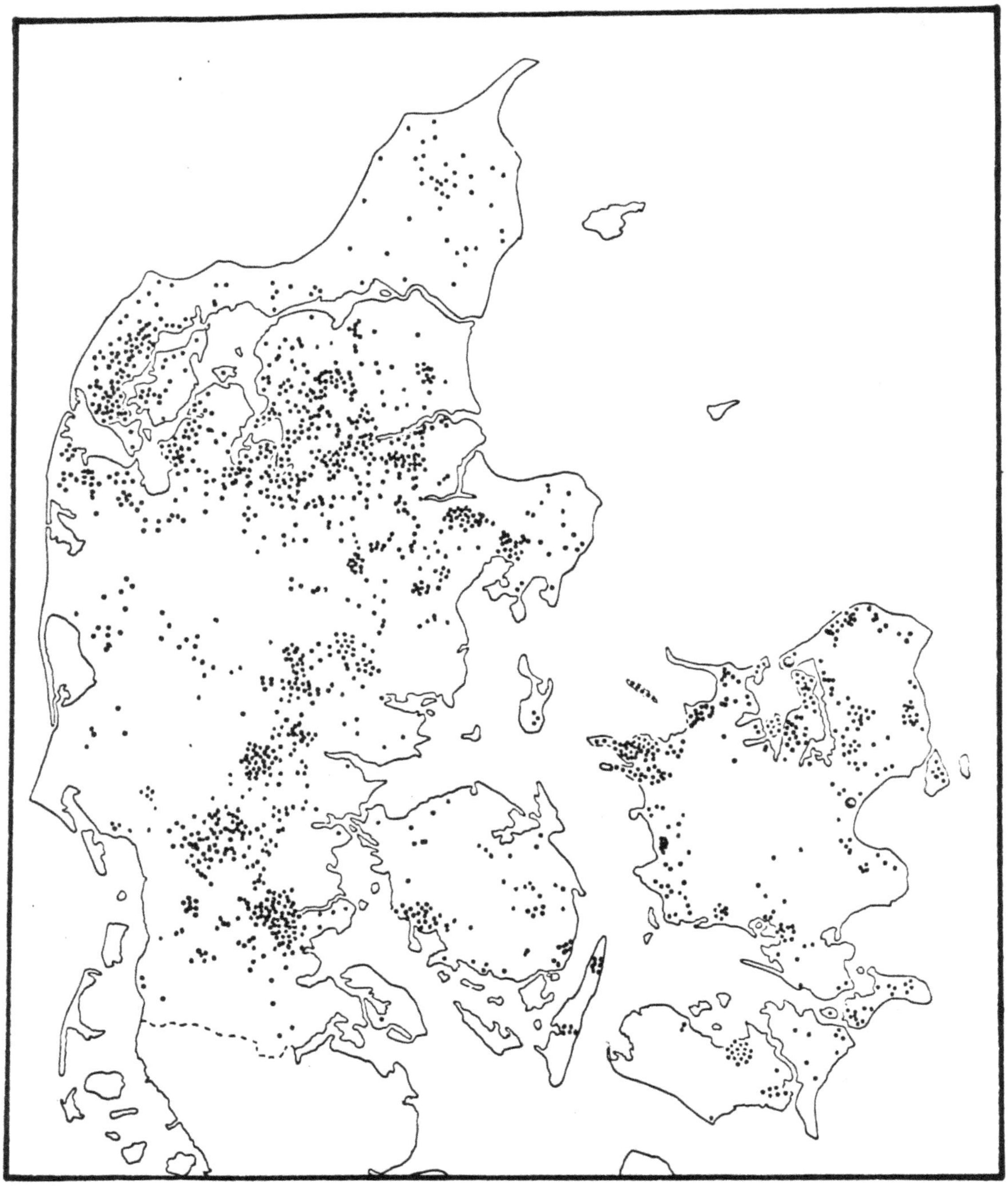

Fig. 18.26 The distribution of late bronze age graves in Denmark (redrawn after Broholm 1949, Figs. 106, 108 and 110).

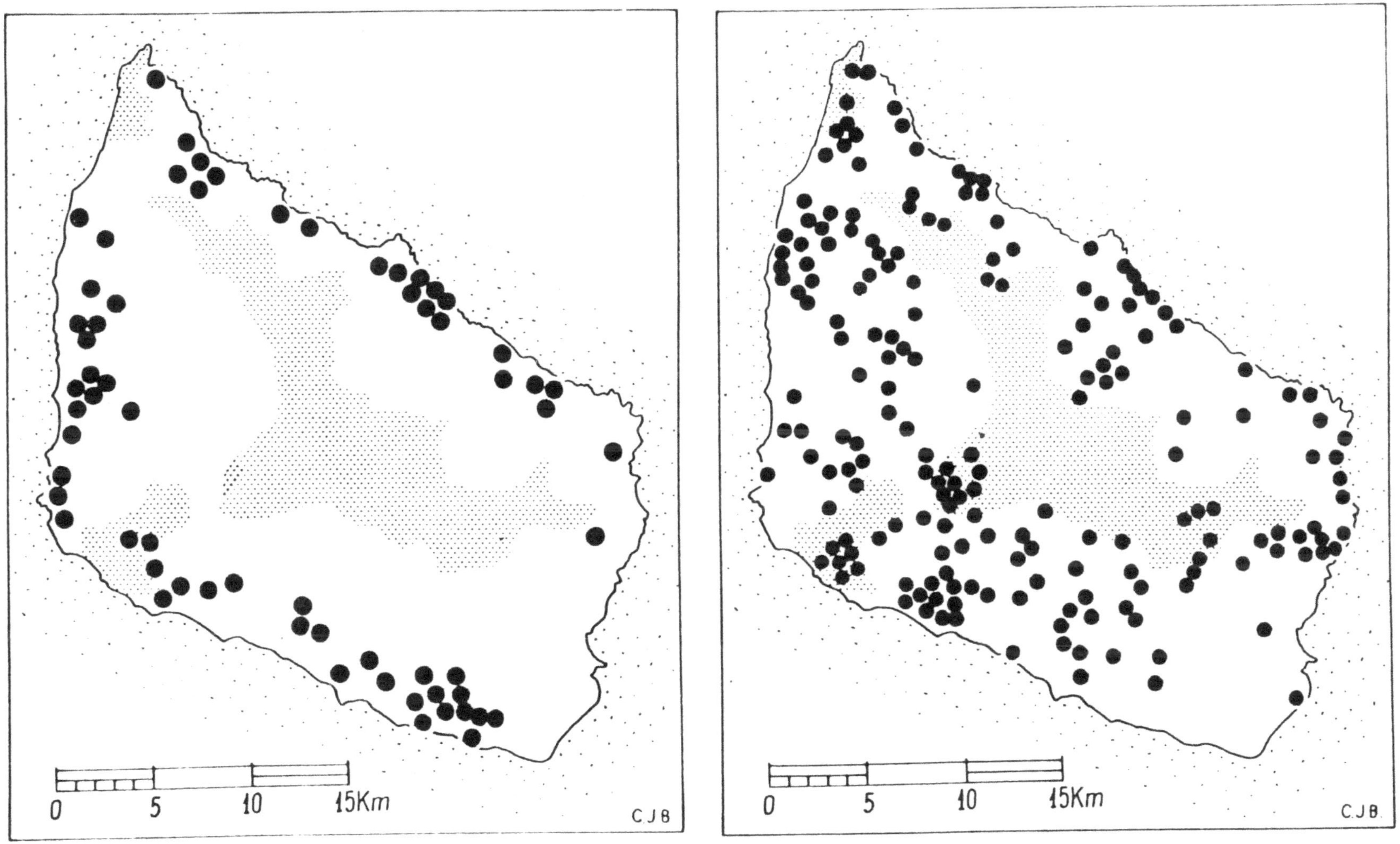

Fig. 18.27 The distribution of early and late bronze age graves on Bornholm (after Becker 1975, Figs. 5 and 6).

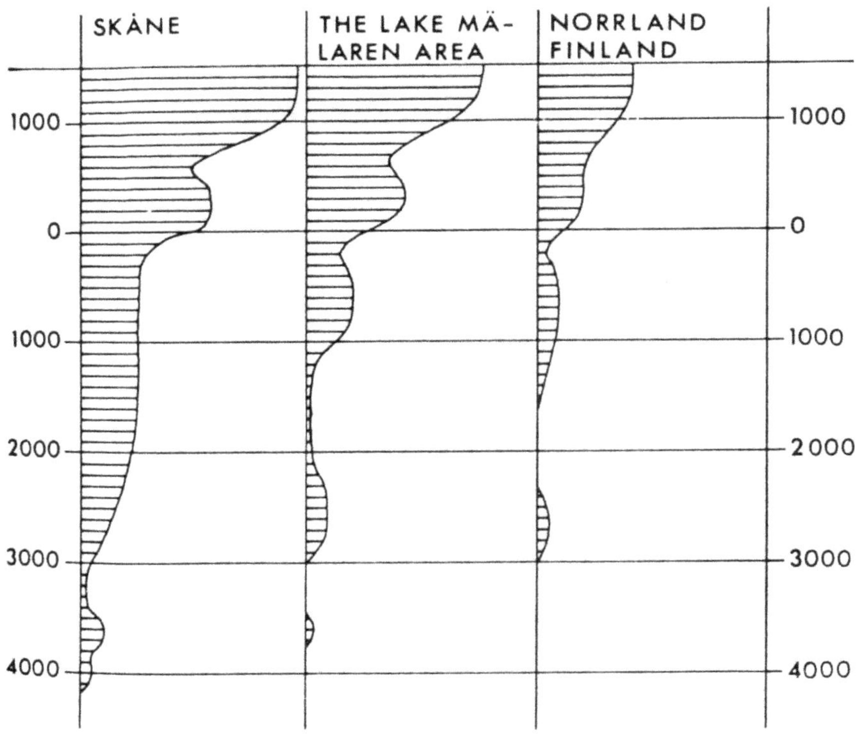

Fig. 18.28 Influence diagrams, based on pollen diagrams, showing expansion of agricultural intensification from the central area of South West Scandinavia to the marginal area of North Sweden/Finland (after Welinder 1977, Fig. 3).

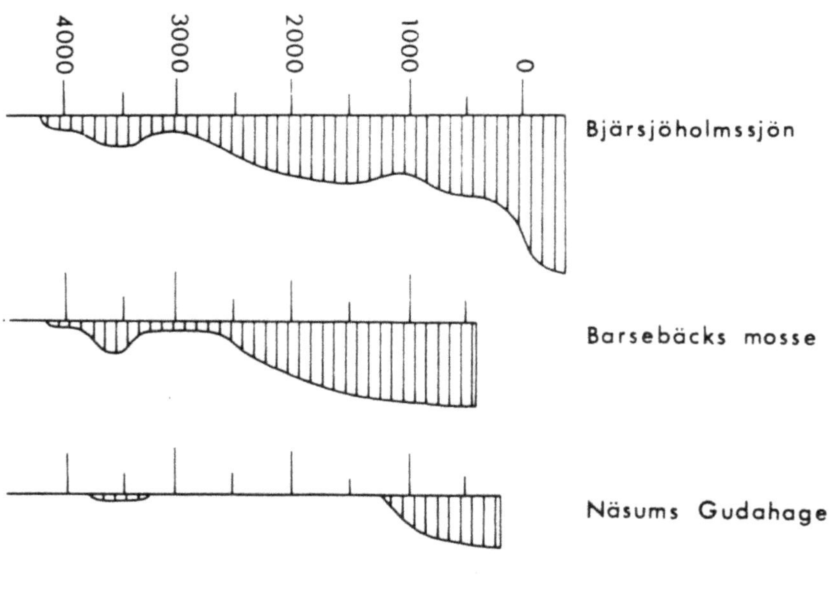

Fig. 18.29 Influence diagrams from the central area (Bjärsjö-holmssjön, Barseö bäck mosse) and the marginal area of Scania, southern Sweden (Nässum Gudahhage) (after Welinder 1977, Fig. 7).

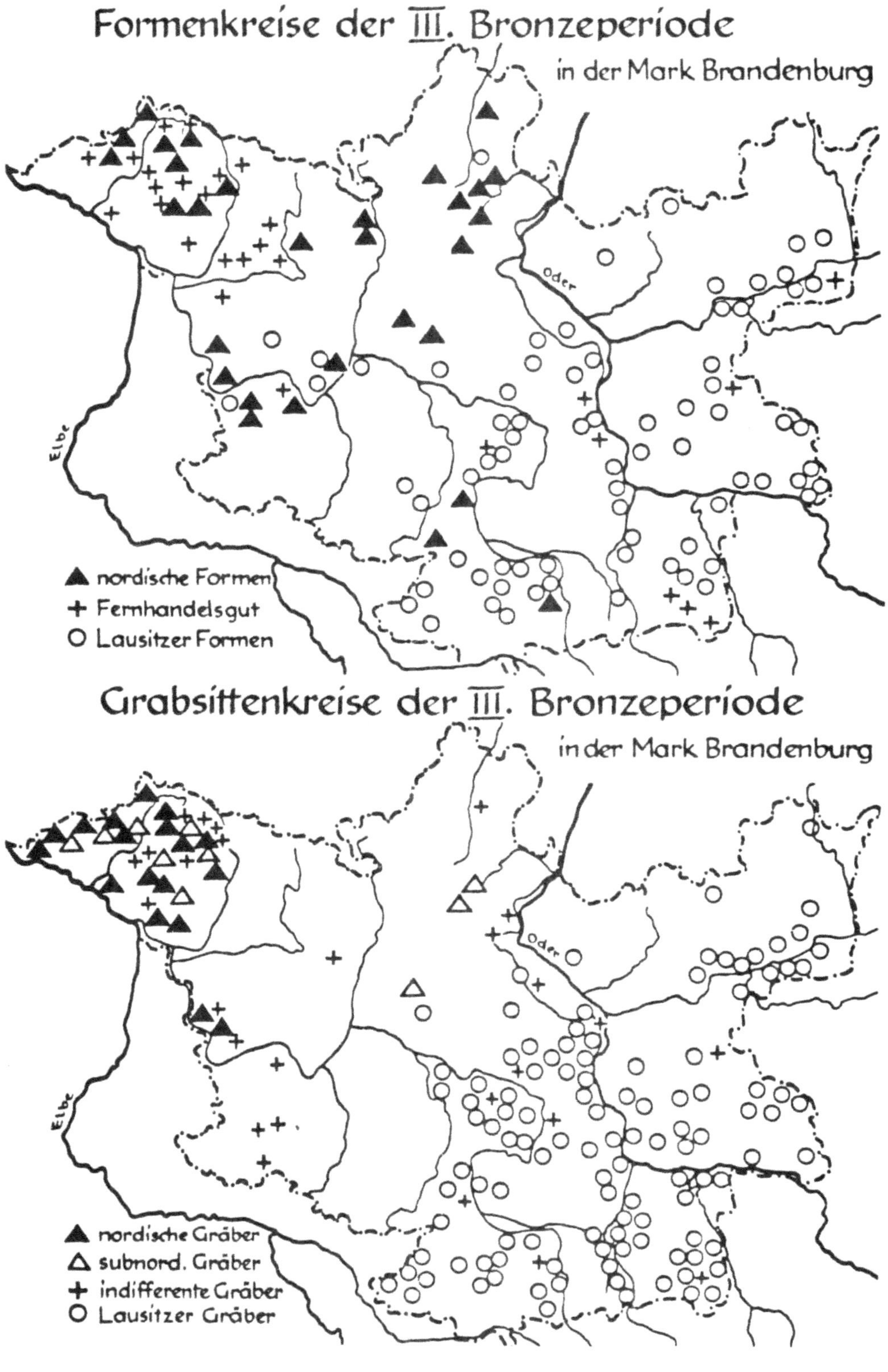

Fig. 18.30 The distribution of Nordic and Lausitz cultural elements and burial types in period III between the river Elbe and the river Oder (after Eggers 1959, Fig. 30).

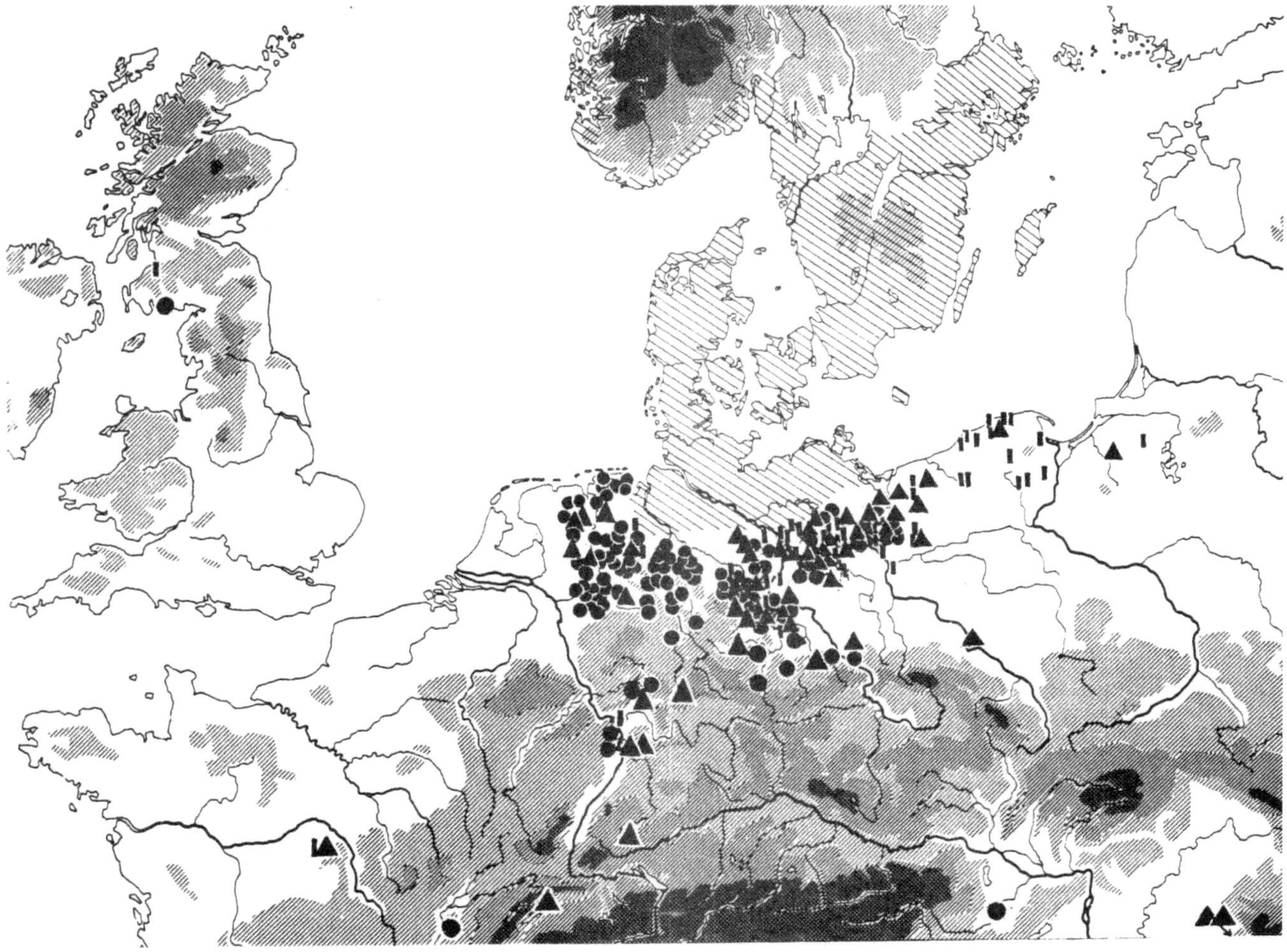

Fig. 18.31 Distribution of Scandinavian bronzes in period IV-V, extending beyond the core area of the Nordic Culture. ▮ Swords, ▲ female ornaments (fibulae, hanging vessels and belt buckles), ● other types (after Thrane 1975, Fig. 128).

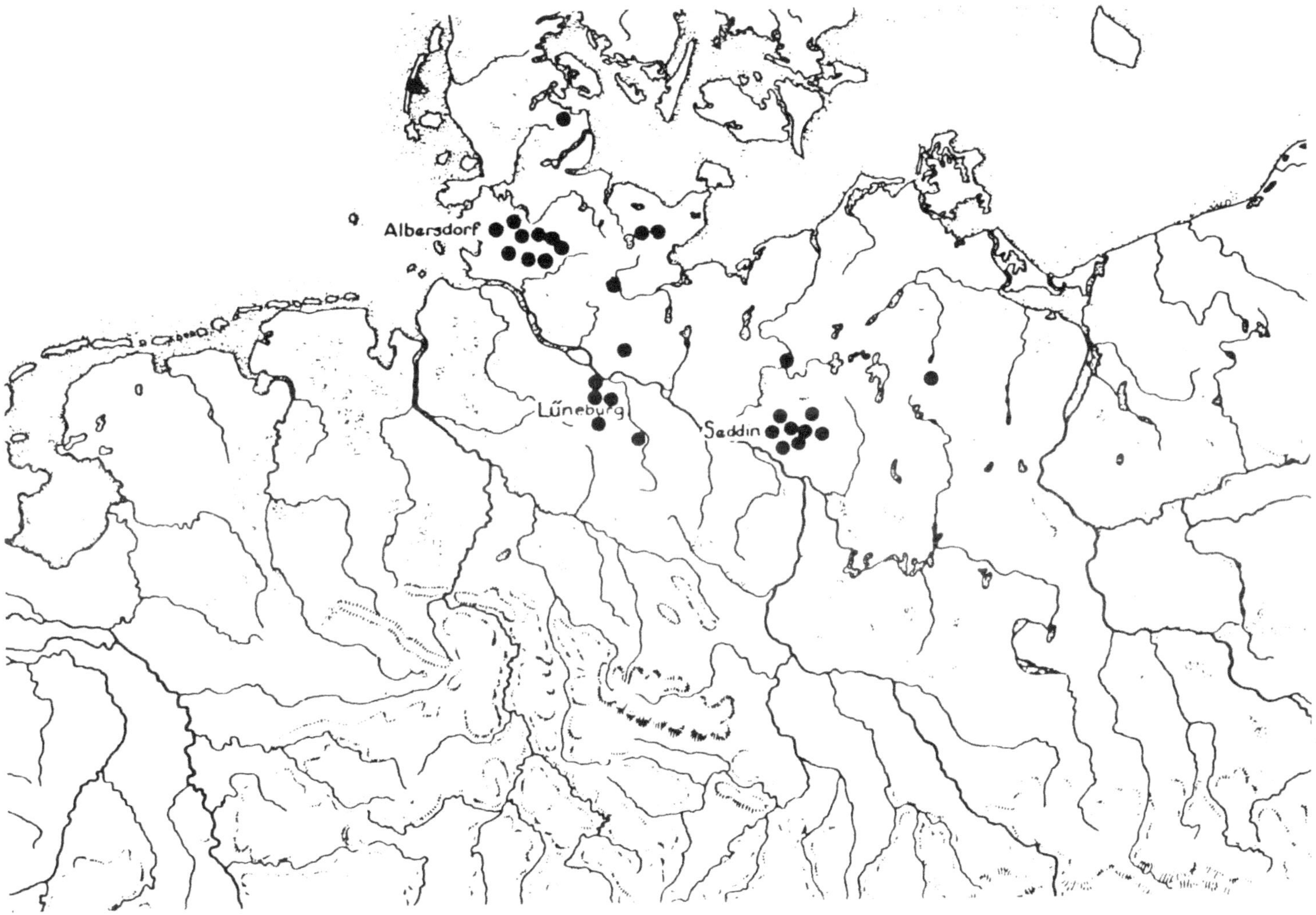

Fig. 18.32 Richly ornamented Nordic tweezers from period V (after Sprockhoff 1955, Fig. 21b).

References

Aner, E., 1958. " Zur Bedeutung der Wende von Periode II zu Periode III" in Bericht über der V. Internationalen Kongress für Vor- und Frühgeschichte. Hamburg.

Aner, E. and Kersten, K., 1971-9. Die Funde der Alteren Bronzezeit des Nordischen Kreises in Dänemark, Schleswig-Holstein und Niedersachsen. Band 1-5. Neümunster: Karl Wachholtz.

Averdiéck, F. R. and Münnich, K. O., 1957. " Palynologische Betrachtungen zur Siedlungsgeschichte im Norden Hamburgs unter Zuhilfenahme neuerer Datierungsmethoden." Hammaburg 11.

Baudou, E., 1960. Die Regionale und Chronologische Einteilung der Jüngeren Bronzezeit im Nordischen Kreis. Studies in North European Archaeology 1. Stockholm: Almqvist and Wiksell.

Becker, C. J., 1975. " Hovedlinier i Bornholm oldtidshistorie." Bornholmske Samlinger.

Berglund, B., 1969. " Vegetation and human influence in South Scandinavia during Prehistoric Time." Oikos supplementum 12.

Bergmann, J., 1968. " Ethnosoziologische Untersuchungen an Grab- und Hortfundgruppen der älteren Bronzezeit in Nordwestdeutschland." Germania 46: 224-240.

Bouzek, J., 1972. " Syrian and Anatolian bronze age figurines in Europe." P.P.S. 38: 156-164.

Bouzek, J., 1978. " Ostlicher Mittelmeerraum und Mitteleuropa. Die bronzezeitlichen Beziehungen auf Grund der archäologischen Quellen" in Mitteleuropäische Bronzezeit, eds. W. Coblenz and F. Herst. Berlin.

Bouzek, J., Jäger, K.-D. and Lozek, V., 1976. " Climatic and settlement changes in the Central European Bronze Age" in Resumé des Communications, IXième Congrès International de la Préhistoire. Nice.

Bouzek, J., Koutecký, D. and Neustupný, E., 1966. The Knovíz Settlement of North-West Bohemia. Fontes Archaeologici Pragenses 10. Prague: National Museum.

Boye, V., 1896. Fund af Egekister fra Bronzealderen i Danmark. Copenhagen.

Briard, J., 1965. Les Depôts Bretons et l' Age du Bronze Atlantique. Rennes: Université de Rennes.

Broholm, H. C., 1943-9. Danmarks Bronzealder. Bind 1-4. Copenhagen: Nyt Nordisk Forlag.

Broholm, H. C. and Hald, M., 1940. Costumes of the Bronze Age in Denmark. Copenhagen.

Brunn, W. A. von, 1954. Steinpackungsgräber von Kothen. Ein Beitrag zur Kultur der Bronzezeit Mitteldeutschlands. Berlin: Akademie Verlag.

Brunn, W. A. von, 1958. " Der Schatz vom Frankleben und die mitteldeutschen Sichelfunde." Prähistorische Zeitschrift 36: 1-70.

Brunn, W. A. von, 1960. " Zur Nordwestgrenze der Lausitzerkultur." Prähistorische Zeitschrift 38: 72-89.

Brunn, W. A. von, 1968. Mitteldeutsche Hortfunde. Römisch-Germanische Forschungen 29. Berlin: de Gruyter.

Burnham, B. C. and Kingsbury, J. (eds.), 1979. Space, Hierarchy and Society. Oxford: B.A.R. Suppl. Ser. 59.

Coles, J. and Harding, A., 1979. The Bronze Age in Europe. London: Methuen.

Crossland, R. A. and Birchall, A. (eds.), 1973. Bronze Age Migrations in the Aegean. London: Duckworth.

Dalton, G. (ed.), 1971. Primitive, Archaic and Modern Economies. Boston, Mass.: Beacon Press.

Eggers, H. J., 1936. " Das Fürstengrab von Bahn und die germanische Landnahme in Pommern." Baltische Studien N. F. 38.

Eggers, H. J., 1959. Einführung in die Vorgeschichte. Munich.

Ekholm, K., 1975. " System av sociala System och determinanterna i den sociala evolutionen." Antropologiske Studier 1976.

Fleming, A., 1972. " The genesis of pastoralism in European prehistory." World Arch. 4: 179-191.

Friedman, J., 1975. " Tribes, states and transformations" in Marxist Analyses and Social Anthropology, ed. M. Bloch. A.S.A. Monograph 2. London: Malaby; 161-202.

Friedman, J., 1976. " Marxist theory and systems of total reproduction. Part I: Negative." Critique of Anthropology 7: 3-16.

Friedman, J. and Rowlands, M., 1977. " Notes towards an epigenetic model of ' Civilisation' " in The Evolution of Social Systems, eds. J. Friedman and M. Rowlands. London: Duckworth; 201-276.

Furmanek, V., 1973. " Zu einigen social-ökonomischen Problemen der Bronzezeit." Slovenska Arch. 21: 407-408.

Gallus, S. and Horvarth, T., 1939. Un Peuple Cavalier Préscythique en Hongrie. Budapest: Université Pierre Pázmány.

Gimbutas, M., 1965. Bronze Age Cultures in Central and Eastern Europe. The Hague: Mouton.

Godelier, M., 1967. " System, structure and contradiction in Capital" in The Socialist Register, eds. R. Miliband and J. Saville. London: Merlin.

Godelier, M., 1971. " Qu' est-ce que definir une ' formation économique et sociale' ?: l' exemple des Incas." La Pensée 159: 99-106.

Godelier, M., 1973. Horizon, Trajets Marxistes en Anthropologie. Paris: F. Maspero.

Godelier, M., 1978. " Infrastructures, societies and history." Curr. Anth. 19: 763-771.

Gräslund, B., 1974. " Relativ datering. Om kronologisk metod i nordisk arkeologi." TOR 16.

Gräslund, B., 1976. " Relative chronology. Dating methods in Scandinavian archaeology." Norwegian Arch. Rev. 9: 69-82.

Green, D., Haselgrove, C. and Spriggs, M. (eds.), 1978. Social Organisation and Settlement. Oxford: B.A.R., Suppl. Ser. 47.

Harding, A., 1975. " Mycenaean Greece and Europe: the evidence of bronze tools and implements." P.P.S. 41: 183-202.

Hartmann, A., 1970. Prähistorische Goldfunde aus Europa. Studien zu den Anfangen der Metallurgie (SAM) 3. Berlin: Gebr. Mann.

Helbaek, H., 1954. " Prehistoric food plants and weeds in Denmark" in Studies in Vegetational History in Honour of Knud Jessen. Geological Survey of Denmark II, Series 80. Copenhagen: Geological Survey of Denmark.

Higham, C. F. W., 1967. " Stock rearing as a cultural factor in prehistoric Europe." P.P.S. 33: 84-106.

Hodder, I., (ed.), 1978. The Spatial Organisation of Culture. London: Duckworth.

Horst, F., 1978. " Die jungbronzezeitlichen Stämme im nördlichen Teil der DDR" in Mitteleuropäische Bronzezeit, eds. W. Coblenz and F. Horst. Berl

Hundt, H. J., 1955. " Versuch zur Deutung der Depotfunden der nordischen jüngeren Bronzezeit." Jahrbuch der Römisch-Germanischen Zentralmuseums Mainz 2: 95-140.

Hundt, H. J., 1978. " Die Rohstoffquellen des europäischen Nordens und ihr Einfluss auf der Entwicklung des nordischen Stils." Bonner Jahrbücher 178: 125-162.

Hyenstrand, Å., 1968. " Skärvstenshögar och bronzaldersmiljøer." TOR 10.

Iversen, J., 1939. " Planterester fremdraget i tre høje i Haderslev Amt" in Skrydstrupfundet, eds. H. C. Broholm and M. Hald. Nordiske Fortidsminder 3(2). Copenhagen: Nordisk Forlag.

Iversen, J., 1973. The Development of Denmark's Nature since the Last Glacial. Geological Survey of Denmark V, Series 7-8. Copenhagen: Geological Survey of Denmark.

Jacob-Friesen, G., 1967. Bronzezeitliche Lanzenspitzen Norddeutschlands und Skandinaviens. Hildesheim: August Lax.

Jacob-Friesen, G., 1968. " Ein Depotfund des Formenkreises um die ' Karpfenzungenschwerter' aus der Normandie." Germania 46: 248-274.

Jacob-Friesen, K. H., 1928. Grundfragen der Urgeschichtsforschung. Rassen, Völker und Kulturen. Hildesheim: August Lax.

Jäger, K.-D. and Lozek, V., 1978. " Umweltbedingungen und Landesausnahm während der Urnenfelderbronzezeit in Mitteleuropa" in Mitteleuropäische Bronzezeit, eds. W. Coblenz and F. Horst. Berlin.

Jensen, J., 1965. " Bernsteinfunde und Bernsteinhandel der jüngeren Bronzezeit Dänemarks." Acta Arch. 36: 43-86.

Jensen, J., 1966. " Griffzungenschwerter der späten nordischen Bronzezeit." Acta Arch. 37: 25-51.

Jensen, J., 1967. " Voldtofte-fundet. Bopladsproblemer i yngre bronzealder i Danmark." Aarbøger for nordisk Oldkyndighed og Historie 1967: 91-154.

Kersten, K., 1952. " Einige Funde der Ilmenaukultur in Schleswig-Holstein." Offa 11: 10-24.

Kersten, K., 1958. Die Funde der Älteren Bronzezeit in Pommern. 7. Beiheft zum Atlas der Urgeschichte. Hamburg: Hamburgisches Museum für Völkerkunde und Vorgeschichte.

Klejn, L. S., 1977. " A panorama of theoretical archaeology." Curr. Anth. 18: 1-42.

Kjellén, E. and Hyenstrand, Å., 1977. " Rock carvings and bronze age society in southwestern Uppland" (summary). Upplands Fornminnesförenings Tidsskrift 49.

Klindt-Jensen, O., 1975. A History of Scandinavian Archaeology. London: Thames and Hudson.

Kossinna, G., 1928. Ursprung und Verbreitung der Germanen. Mannus-Bücherei 6. Leipzig.

Kristiansen, K., 1974. " Glerupfundet. Et depotfund med kvindesmykker fra bronzealderens femte periode." Hikuin 1: 7-38.

Kristiansen, K., 1976. " A source-critical analysis of hoards from the Late Danish Bronze Age (Periods IV-V)" (summary). Aarbøger for nordisk Oldkyndighed og Historie 1974: 152-160.

Kristiansen, K., 1977. " The circulation of ornaments and weapons in bronze age Denmark." Arch. Baltica 2.

Kristiansen, K., 1978a. " Period transitions in the Nordic Bronze Age. An essay concerning the methodological foundations and the scientific function of chronological studies" (summary). Hikuin 4: 157-158.

Kristiansen, K., 1978b. " The consumption of wealth in bronze age Denmark. A study in the dynamics of economic processes in tribal societies" in New Directions in Scandinavian Archaeology, eds. K. Kristiansen and C. Paludan-Müller. Studies in Scandinavian Prehistory and Early History 1. Copenhagen: National Museum ; 158-190.

Kristiansen, K., 1980. "Besiedlung, Wirtschaftsstrategie und Bodennutzung in der Bronzezeit Dänemarks." Prähistorische Zeitschrift 55.

Kristiansen, K., (forthcoming). "The representativity of early bronze age burials in Denmark" in Studies in Scandinavian Prehistory and Early History 2. Copenhagen: National Museum.

Kytlicova, O., 1967. "Die Beziehungen der jung- und spätbronzezeitlichen Hortfunde südwärts und nordwärts des Erzgebirges." Arbeits- und Forschungsberichte 16/17: 139-177.

Laux, F., 1971. Die Bronzezeit in der Lüneburger Heide. Hildesheim: Landesmuseum zu Hannover.

LeClair, E. E. and Schneider, H. K. (eds.), 1968. Economic Anthropology. New York: Holt, Rinehart and Winston.

Levy, J., 1979. "Evidence of social stratification in bronze age Denmark." J. Field Arch. 6: 49-56.

Lomborg, E., 1969. "The chronology of the Northern Early Bronze Age" (summary). Aarbøger for nordisk Oldkyndighed og Historie 1968: 140-152.

Mandt-Larsen, G., 1972. "Rock-pictures in Hordaland. An analysis of the compostion of the pictures and their ecological and cultural background" (summary). Acta Universitatis Bergensis. Series Humaniorum Litterarum 2 (1970).

Meinander, C. F., 1954. "Die Bronzezeit in Finnland." Finska Fornminnesföreningens Tidsskrift 54.

Menke, M., 1973. Die Jüngere Bronzezeit in Holstein. Offa Bücher 25. Neumünster: Karl Wachholtz.

Montelius, O., 1885. "Om tidsbestämning inom bronsålderen med särskilt hänsyn till Skandinavien." Kongl. Vitterhets Historie och Antiqvitets Akademiens Handlingar 30.

Montelius, O., 1903. Die Typologische Methode. Die Ältere Kulturperioden im Orient und in Europa I. Stockholm.

Montelius, O., 1906. Kulturgeschichte Schwedens. Leipzig: E. A. Seemann.

Müller, S., 1898. Nordische Altertumskunde. Strassburg: K. J. Trübner.

Müller-Karpe, H., 1959. Beiträge zur Chronologie der Urnenfelderzeit Nördlich und Südlich der Alpen. Römisch-Germanische Forschungen 22. Berlin: de Gruyter.

Müller-Karpe, H., 1961. Die Vollgriffschwerter der Urnenfelderzeit aus Bayern. Münchener Beiträge zur Vor- und Frühgeschichte 6. Munich: Beck'sc

Nordbladh, J., 1974. "South Scandinavian petroglyphs. A short report on Nordic literature" in Val Camonica and Monte Bego, eds. J. Nordbladh and J. Rosvall. Goteborg: University of Goteborg.

Nordbladh, J., 1978. " The relation between rock art, religion and society." Acts of the Rock Art Symposium at Hankø, 1972.

Oldeberg, A., 1933. " Det nordiska bronsalderspännets historia." Kungl. Vitterhets Historie och Antiqvitets Akademiens Handlingar 38.

Oldeberg, A., 1974. " Die ältere Metallzeit in Schweden." Kungl. Vitterhets Historie och Antiqvitets Akademiens Handlingar 53.

Ottenjahn, H., 1969. Die Nordischen Vollgriffschwerter der Älteren und Mittleren Bronzezeit. Römisch-Germanische Forschungen 30. Berlin: de Gruyter.

Piesker, H., 1958. Untersuchungen zur Älteren Lüneburgischen Bronzezeit. Lüneburg: Nordland-Druck.

Podborský, V., 1970. Mähren in der Spätbronzezeit und an der Schwelle der Eisenzeit. Brno: University J. E. Purkyně.

Polanyi, K., 1971. " The economy as instituted process" in Primitive, Archaic and Modern Economies, ed. G. Dalton. Boston, Mass.: Beacon Press.

Randsborg, K., 1967. " 'Aegean' bronzes in a grave in Jutland." Acta Arch. 38: 1-27.

Randsborg, K., 1968. " Von Periode II zu III. Chronologische Studien über die ältere Bronzezeit Südskandinaviens und Norddeutschlands." Acta Arch. 39: 1-142.

Randsborg, K., 1970. " Zwei Peschiera-Dolche aus Südskandinavien." Acta Arch. 41: 191-195.

Randsborg, K., 1972. From Period III to Period IV. Chronological Studies of the Bronze Age in Southern Scandinavia and Northern Germany. Publications of the National Museum, Archaeological-Historical Series 1. Copenhagen: National Museum.

Randsborg, K., 1973-4. " Befolkning og social variation i aeldre bronzealders Danmark." Kuml 1973-4: 197-208.

Randsborg, K., 1974. " Social stratification in early bronze age Denmark: a study in the regulation of cultural systems." Prähistorische Zeitschrift 49: 38-61.

Rowlands, M., 1971. " The archaeological interpretation of prehistoric metalworking. " World Arch. 3: 210-224.

Rowlands, M., 1973. " Modes of exchange and the incentives for trade with reference to later European prehistory" in The Explanation of Culture Change, ed. A. C. Renfrew. London: Duckworth; 589-600.

Rowlands, M., (in press). " Kinship alliance and exchange in the European Bronze Age" in Settlement and Society in the British Later Bronze Age, eds. J. Barrett and R. Bradley. Oxford: B.A.R.

Rusu, M., 1963. " Die Verbreitung der Bronzehorte in Transsilvanien vom Ende der Bronzezeit in die mittlere Hallstattzeit." Dacia N.S. 7: 177-210.

Rusu, M., 1976. " Les relations économiques et culturelles entre le centre metallurgique Transsylvanien et d' autres centres européens aux XIIe-XIe siècles avant notre ère." Resumé des Communications, IXième Congrès International de la Préhistoire. Nice.

Sandars, N. K., 1971. " From Bronze to Iron Age: a sequel to a sequel" in The European Community in Later Prehistory, eds. J. Boardman, M. A. Brown and T. G. E. Powell. London: Routledge and Kegan Paul; 1-29.

Sandars, N. K., 1978. The Sea Peoples: Warriors of the Ancient Mediterranean. London: Thames and Hudson.

Savory, H. N., 1949. " The Atlantic Bronze Age in South-West Europe."" P.P.S. 15: 128-155.

Schauer, P., 1971. Die Schwerter in Süddeutschland, Osterreich und der Schweiz. Prähistorische Bronzefunde 4 (2). Munich: Beck' sche.

Schubart, H., 1972. Die Funde der Älteren Bronzezeit in Mecklenburg. Offa Bücher 26. Neumünster: Karl Wachholz.

Schulz, R., 1972. " Zur jüngeren Bronzezeit westlich der unteren Oder." Zeitschrift für Archäologie 6: 175-189.

Seddon, D. (ed.), 1978. Relations of Production: Marxist Approaches to Economic Anthropology. London: Frank Cass.

Shennan, S., 1975. " The social organization at Branč." Antiquity 49: 279-288.

Snodgrass, A., 1971. " The first European body-armour" in The European Community in Later Prehistory, eds. J. Boardman, M. A. Brown and T. G. E. Powell. London: Routledge and Kegan Paul; 31-50.

Snodgrass, A., 1975. " Mycenae, Northern Europe and radiocarbon dates." Arch. Atlantica 1: 33-48.

Sprockhoff, E., 1931. Die Germanischen Griffzungenschwerter. Römisch-Germanische Forschungen 5. Berlin: de Gruyter.

Sprockhoff, E., 1937. Jungbronzezeitliche Hortfunde Norddeutschlands (Periode IV). Römisch-Germanischen Zentralmuseum zu Mainz, Katalog 12.

Sprockhoff, E., 1940. " Altbronzezeitliches aus Niedersachsen" in Studien zur Vor- und Frühgeschichte Carl Schuchhardt zum Achtzigsten Geburtstag Dargebracht. Berlin: de Gruyter; 24-47.

Sprockhoff, E., 1941. Niedersachsens Bedeutung für die Bronzezeit Westeuropas. 31. Bericht der Römisch-Germanischer Kommission II.

Sprockhoff, E., 1950/51. " Pfahlbaubronzen in der Südzone des nordischen Kreises." Acta Geographica 1.

Sprockhoff, E., 1956. Jungbronzezeitliche Hortfunde der Südzone des Nordischen Kreises (Periode V). Römisch-Germanisches Zentralmuseum zu Mainz, Katalog 16.

Sprockhoff, E., 1961. " Eine mykenische Bronzetasse von Dohnsen, Kreis Celle." Germania 39: 11-22.

Stenberger, M., 1964. Det Forntida Sverige. Stockholm.

Stjernquist, B., 1962-3. " Präliminarien zu einer Untersuchung von Opferfunden." Meddelanden från Lunds Universitets Historiska Museum 1962-3.

Stjernquist, B., 1965-6. " Models of commercial diffusion in prehistoric times." Scripta Minora 1965-6, 2.

Stjernquist, B., 1969. Beiträge zum Studien von Bronzezeitlichen Siedlungen. Acta Arch. Lundensia Series in 8°, Minora 8. Lund.

Strömberg, M., 1974. "Soziale Schichtungen in der älteren Bronzezeit Südschwedens." Die Kunde N. F. 25: 89-101.

Strömberg, M., 1975. " Untersuchungen zur Bronzezeit in Südostschonen. Probleme um die Besiedlung." Meddelanden från Lunds Universitets Historiska Museum 1973-4: 101-168.

Struwe, K. W., 1971. Die Bronzezeit. Periode I-III. Neümunster: Karl Wachholtz.

Thrane, H., 1962. " The earliest bronze vessels in Denmark' s Bronze Age." Acta Arch. 33: 109-163.

Thrane, H., 1971. " En broncealderboplads ved Jyderup Skov i Odsherred." Nationalmuseets Arbejdsmark 1971: 141-164.

Thrane, H., 1975. Europaeiske Forbindelser. Nationalmuseets Skrifter, Arkaeologist — historisk raekke 16. Copenhagen: National Museum.

Thrane, H., 1979. " Odense: Fremde bronzegefässe in südskandinavischen Funden aus der jüngeren Bronzezeit (Periode V)." Acta Arch. 49: 1-35.

Thrane, H., (forthcoming). " The representativity of bronze age settlements in Denmark." in Studies in Scandinavian Prehistory and Early History 2. Copenhagen: National Museum.

Vladar, J., 1973. " Osteuropäische und mediterrane Einflüsse im Gebiet der Slowakei während der Bronzezeit. Slovenska Arch. 21: 253-357.

Welinder, S., 1977. Ekonomiska Processer i Forhistorisk Expansion. Acta Arch. Lundensia Series in 8°, Minora 7. Lund.

Wüstemann, H., 1978. " Zur sozialentwicklung während der Bronzezeit im Norden der DDR" in Mitteleuropäische Bronzezeit, eds. W. Coblenz and F. Horst. Berlin.

www.ingramcontent.com/pod-product-compliance
Ingram Content Group UK Ltd.
Pitfield, Milton Keynes, MK11 3LW, UK
UKHW061845041026
15591UKWH00015B/920